# *Math for Web Design*

PRECISION LAYOUT AND ANIMATION

PAUL MCFEDRIES

MANNING
SHELTER ISLAND

For online information and ordering of this and other Manning books, please visit www.manning.com. The publisher offers discounts on this book when ordered in quantity.

For more information, please contact

Special Sales Department
Manning Publications Co.
20 Baldwin Road
PO Box 761
Shelter Island, NY 11964
Email: orders@manning.com



Manning Publications Co.
20 Baldwin Road
PO Box 761
Shelter Island, NY 11964

Development editor: Dustin Archibald
Technical editor: Matteo Piccini
Review editor: Kishor Rit
Production editor: Andy Marinkovich
Copy editor: Lana Todorovic-Arndt
Proofreader: Mike Beady
Technical proofreader: Matt Thornfield
Typesetter: Tamara Švelić Sabljić
Cover designer: Marija Tudor

ISBN 9781633434820
Printed in the United States of America

*To all my math teachers*

# brief contents


1 ■ Web dev math fundamentals 1
2 ■ Math basics for JavaScript 22
3 ■ Math basics for CSS 55
4 ■ CSS Grid math 93
5 ■ Flexbox math 123
6 ■ The mathematics of responsive design 146
7 ■ The mathematics of color 171
8 ■ Text and typography math 206
9 ■ Trigonometry for web developers 228
10 ■ Vectors and geometry in UI design 251
11 ■ Using Bézier curves for smooth animation 277
12 ■ Physics-based animations 302
13 ■ Interactivity and gesture-based UI math 324
14 ■ Canvas-based math and drawing 345

# contents

*preface* xiii
*acknowledgments* xiv
*about this book* xvi
*about the author* xx
*about the cover illustration* xxi

**1 *Web dev math fundamentals* 1**

1.1 Why bother learning about frontend math? 2

1.2 Why math matters in frontend development 3
*The connection between mathematics and web design 4*
*Real-world examples of math in UI/UX 5 ▪ How developers use math in animations, layouts, and interactions 6*

1.3 The role of mathematics in CSS and JavaScript 6
*How CSS uses math 6 ▪ JavaScript's built-in mathematical capabilities 7 ▪ Comparing CSS and JavaScript math approaches 8*

1.4 The minimum math you need to know 9
*Arithmetic and arithmetic expressions 9 ▪ Algebra 10*
*Ratios 11 ▪ Exponents and nth roots 12 ▪ Linear equations 13 ▪ Inequalities and comparison expressions 14*
*Geometry 15 ▪ Trigonometry 17 ▪ Coordinate systems 19*

## 2 *Math basics for JavaScript* 22

2.1 Building JavaScript expressions 23

*JavaScript arithmetic operators 23 ▪ JavaScript arithmetic assignment operators 24 ▪ JavaScript comparison operators 24 JavaScript logical expressions 26 ▪ Falsy values, default values, and nullish coalescing 27 ▪ Operator precedence 27 Using parentheses to avoid ambiguity 28*

2.2 Number types in JavaScript 29

*Integer and floating-point numbers 30 ▪ Exponential notation 32 ▪ Binary, octal, and hexadecimal representations 32 ▪ NaN and Infinity in JavaScript 33 NaN 33 ▪ Infinity and –Infinity 33 ▪ Number coercion 34*

2.3 Precision issues and floating-point arithmetic 35

*Why 0.1 + 0.2 !== 0.3 35 ▪ When to be concerned about precision 36*

2.4 Working with BigInt values 37

*BigInt to the rescue 37 ▪ Mathematical operations with BigInt 38 ▪ Limitations of BigInt in JavaScript 39 When to avoid BigInt in web development 39*

2.5 Modulo logic and wrapping values 40

*JavaScript's remainder operator (%) and modulo 40 Wrapping logic in carousels, sliders, and cyclic UI 42*

2.6 Rounding numbers 43

*Rounding to whole numbers 43 ▪ Rounding to a specific number of decimal places 44 ▪ Implementing bankers' rounding 45 Use cases for rounding in frontend development 46*

2.7 Generating random numbers 47

*Generating random integers and floats 47 ▪ Seeding and repeatable randomness 48 ▪ Use cases in animations and UI behavior 50*

2.8 Solutions to exercises 51

## 3 *Math basics for CSS* 55

3.1 The math of CSS measurement units 56

*Unit conversion math 56 ▪ The cascading calculations of em units 56 ▪ Percentage computation rules 58 ▪ Viewport units and their responsive calculations 60 ▪ Mixing units with calc() 60 ▪ Combining units requires attention to scale 61*

3.2 CSS math functions 61

*CSS arithmetic operators 62 ▪ Evaluating expressions with calc() 63 ▪ Setting limits with min(), max(), and clamp() 65 More CSS math functions 68*

3.3 CSS variables in math operations 77

*Basic usage 77 ▪ Mixing units with variables 78 Fallbacks and missing variables 79*

3.4 The math of CSS inheritance 79

*The inheritance cascade formula 79 ▪ Which properties inherit mathematically? 79 ▪ Percentage values and the inheritance math 80 ▪ The em unit inheritance multiplier 80 ▪ Solving the heading size puzzle 81 ▪ Computed values vs. inherited values 82*

3.5 Box model math 85

*The default box model formulas 86 ▪ How the box-sizing property affects the box model formulas 87 ▪ Margin math and collapsing 88 ▪ Percentages and the box model 88 ▪ Using calc() for precise box model math 89*

3.6 Solutions to Exercises 91

4 ***CSS Grid math 93***

4.1 The mathematical foundations of CSS Grid 94

*Foundations of the grid formatting context 94 ▪ The coordinate system approach 94 ▪ The algebraic model 95 ▪ Mathematical differences from other layout systems 95*

4.2 The Grid coordinate system 96

*The grid model 96 ▪ Span notation and its mathematical meaning 99 ▪ Working smarter with negative indexing 99*

4.3 The grid track sizing algorithm 102

*The algebra of grid line placement 103 ▪ How fr units distribute available space 103 ▪ Taking the box model into account 104 The algorithm for calculating fr unit values 105 Troubleshooting: When <flex> resolves to 0px 106*

4.4 The math of Grid's track-sizing functions and keywords 108

*Controlling track sizes with minmax() 108 ▪ Understanding auto in grid tracks 111 ▪ The math of fit-content() 113 The repeat() function and its mathematical distribution 115*

4.5 Solutions to exercises 120

5 ***Flexbox math 123***

5.1 The flex base size calculation 124
*The base size algorithm 124*

5.2 Understanding the flex factors 127
*The flex-grow calculation 127 ▪ The flex-shrink calculation 131 The flex shorthand 135 ▪ Dealing with flex-grow values between 0 and 1 135*

5.3 Taking min/max constraints into account 139
*Using min-width to limit shrinking 140 ▪ Using max-width to limit growing 142*

5.4 Solutions to Exercises 144

6 ***The mathematics of responsive design 146***

6.1 The concept of responsiveness in web design 147
*Fixed vs. fluid: A visual thought experiment 147 The mathematical mindset 148*

6.2 Media query logic 149
*Grid and Flexbox as your first responsive tools 149 ▪ Why you might still need media queries 149 ▪ The math behind media queries 150 ▪ Using range syntax for cleaner media queries 150 Media query tips 151*

6.3 Proportional layouts 152
*How percentage-based layouts work 152 ▪ Nesting percentages 153 ▪ When to mix percentages with fixed units 153 Creating a liquid layout 154*

6.4 Viewport-based units 157
*The classic viewport units 157 ▪ Logical viewport units 158 The scrollbar problem 158 ▪ New viewport units: the sv*, lv*, and dv* families 160 ▪ Deciding which viewport unit to use 162*

6.5 Layout fluidity with CSS functions 163
*Why fluid layouts matter 163 ▪ Using clamp() for fluid container widths 163 ▪ The math behind custom fluid widths 164 ▪ Calculating preferred clamp() values 164 Fluid padding and gaps 165 ▪ How to think about CSS math for layouts 166 ▪ When to bring in JavaScript 166*

6.6 Solutions to exercises 168

7 *The mathematics of color* **171**

7.1 Color models and color spaces 172

*The RGB color model 172 ▪ The HSL color model 174 The LAB color space 176 ▪ The OKLCH color space 177*

7.2 Converting between color models 181

*Converting RGB to grayscale 181 ▪ Converting RGB to HSL 181 ▪ Converting HSL to RGB 183*

7.3 Creating harmonious color schemes with math 185

*Complementary colors 185 ▪ Analogous colors 186 Triadic colors 186 ▪ Split-complementary colors 187*

7.4 Specifying accessible colors with math 188

*The WCAG contrast requirements (AA vs. AAA) 188 The contrast ratio formula 188 ▪ Calculating relative luminance from color 189 ▪ Calculating contrast ratios with JavaScript 190*

7.5 Light mode and dark mode mathematics 193

*Why basic inversion doesn't work 193 ▪ A better approach: Inverting perceptual lightness 194 ▪ Hue and saturation adjustments for aesthetic consistency 194 ▪ Generating a paired light/dark palette 195 ▪ CSS implementation with media queries 196*

7.6 The math behind blend modes and opacity 196

*How blending works 196 ▪ Alpha compositing 197 Blending in CSS 198 ▪ The separable blend modes 199 The nonseparable blend modes 202*

7.7 Solutions to exercises 203

8 *Text and typography math* **206**

8.1 The math behind the typographic trinity 207

*General readability considerations 207 ▪ When you know the font size you want to use 208 ▪ When you know the line height you want to use 210 ▪ When you know the line length you want to use 211 ▪ Putting the formulas to work 213*

8.2 Fluid typography with CSS math functions 216

*Using vw and vh for scalable text sizes 216 ▪ Setting constraints on dynamic font scaling 217 ▪ Calculating the preferred clamp() formula for font sizes 218 ▪ Example: Hero text for a landing page 218*

8.3 Applying a modular scale to text 220
*Creating a modular scale from a scaling factor 221 ▪ Choosing a modular scale ratio 223 ▪ Implementing typographic scales with CSS variables 223*

8.4 Solutions to exercises 225

9 ***Trigonometry for web developers 228***

9.1 The basics of trigonometry for web design 228
*Sine, cosine, and tangent 229 ▪ Trigonometric units 232 Converting between degrees and radians 232 ▪ The inverse trig functions 233 ▪ Trig functions in CSS and JavaScript 233*

9.2 Circular layouts and animations 234
*Creating a circular menu 234 ▪ Animating circular motion 238 Creating an animated spinner 240*

9.3 Wave effects 241
*Arranging elements along a wave path 241 ▪ Animating elements with a wave effect 243 ▪ Animating an element with a pendulum effect 244*

9.4 Directional calculations 245

9.5 Solutions to exercises 248

10 ***Vectors and geometry in UI design 251***

10.1 Mathematical foundations: Points, vectors, and bounding boxes 251

10.2 DOM geometry: Measuring and aligning elements with JavaScript 253
*Calculating the center point of an element 254 ▪ Aligning one element relative to another 255 ▪ Geometric hover effects 257 Parallax scrolling with geometric precision 260*

10.3 Manipulating vectors in JavaScript 262
*Essential vector operations for DOM developers 263 ▪ Using vectors to have an element follow the mouse 263 ▪ Animating an element to a mouse-click position using vectors 264 ▪ Dragging with geometric constraints 266*

10.4 Geometric clipping and motion paths 270
*Clipping elements 270 ▪ Motion paths 272*

10.5 Solutions to exercises 274

11 *Using Bézier curves for smooth animation* *277*

11.1 Introduction to Bézier curves 277

*What is a Bézier curve? 278 ▪ The mathematical construction of Bézier curves 278 ▪ Quadratic vs. cubic Bézier curves 279 The role of cubic Bézier curves in animations 280*

11.2 Cubic Bézier curves in CSS 281

*The cubic-bezier() function 281 ▪ Understanding the four control point values 283 ▪ Built-in CSS easing keywords 286*

11.3 Customizing animations with Bézier curves 292

*Entrance animations 292 ▪ Exit animations 294 Interactive feedback animations 297*

11.4 Answers to exercises 299

12 *Physics-based animations* *302*

12.1 Understanding motion in UI design 303

*How real-world physics improves user experience 303 Why animations feel natural when physics is applied 305 JavaScript easing functions for natural motion 305*

12.2 Velocity and acceleration in JavaScript 308

*Applying the velocity equation in animations 309 Handling acceleration 311*

12.3 Simulating gravity and bouncing effects 313

*How to create a bouncing-ball animation 313 ▪ Using Math.sin() for pendulum-like motion 314 ▪ Simulating weight and elasticity 316*

12.4 Spring- and friction-based animations 318

*Using Hooke's law for spring motion 318 ▪ Simulating inertia with damping and friction 320*

12.5 Answers to exercises 322

13 *Interactivity and gesture-based UI math* *324*

13.1 Mouse and touch event calculations 324

*Capturing the cursor position 325 ▪ Detecting touch gestures 327 ▪ Converting screen coordinates to local element coordinates 328*

13.2 Custom slider controls 330

*Building a custom linear slider 330 ▪ Building a custom rotary control 334*

13.3 Scroll-based animations 338

*Detecting scroll position 338 ▪ Creating dynamic UI changes with intersection observers 341*

13.4 Solutions to exercises 343

## 14 *Canvas-based math and drawing 345*

14.1 Data-driven geometry and hit detection 346

*Drawing a pie chart from data 346 ▪ Creating an interactive bar chart 348 ▪ Advanced hit detection on a donut chart 353*

14.2 Dynamic motion and simulation 357

*Simulating a simple particle system 357 ▪ Creating a generative star field effect 360 ▪ Creating celebration and feedback effects 364*

14.3 Solutions to exercises 368

*index 370*

# *preface*

*Math*—that single word can trigger a slight sense of panic for many of us in the creative and visual world of web development, perhaps even a pit-of-the-stomach-deep feeling of dread. Why the foreboding? Because just reading that four-letter word often brings back memories of being bored out of our skulls as a chalk-dusted teacher droned out about abstract equations and endless proofs that felt disconnected from the tangible things of the world. True, your web dev work isn't a tangible thing either, but you're still trying to make things that look good and work well. If you've ever thought, "Dammit, Jim, I'm a designer/developer, not a mathematician," then that word math might strike fear in you to this day.

But that is *precisely* why I wrote this book: the truth is, you're already using math every day. It's the silent partner behind every fluid animation, every perfectly balanced layout, and every responsive grid. That satisfying snap of an element locking into place or the organic feel of a physics-based transition isn't magic—it's *logic*. This book isn't about turning you into a mathematician but about translating that logic into a practical and creative tool you can use with confidence.

My goal is not to revisit the dry theory you may remember from school but to connect these powerful concepts directly to the UI challenges you face daily. I want to show you how a little bit of trigonometry can create a beautiful circular menu, or how a simple physics equation can make an animation feel alive. Think of this as pulling back the curtain, giving you the power not just to use the tools of frontend development, but to truly understand them.

Welcome to the logic behind the magic.

# acknowledgments

The English priest and writer Charles Caleb Colton once wrote that "there are three difficulties in authorship: to write something worth publishing, to find honest people to publish it, and to get sensible people to read it." Only time and the Amazon review process will tell whether this book was worth publishing. And since you're here, I have to assume that you're one of the sensible people who's going to read it. In between these two, however, I needed to find honest people to publish my manuscript, and that turned out to be the good folks at Manning, who are honest, for sure, but also hard-working, dedicated, and competent.

I'm sure the editors of novels and memoirs have their hands full whipping their manuscripts into shape but spare a moment for the poor editors of computer books. Not only do they have to make sure that a computer book reads well and isn't festooned with spelling errors and grammatical gaffes, but they also must ensure that the book is technically accurate. Why? Because even the teensiest authorial (or editorial) lapse could result in a book that sows confusion and consternation rather than certainty and delight.

The good folks at Manning Publications ensure that each book reads well and is accurate by subjecting each manuscript to a barrage of reviews, not only by editorial professionals but also by a team of dedicated outsiders. Instead of a process in which single-digit numbers of eyeballs look at the manuscript, a Manning book is scrutinized by dozens. The result? The book you're reading contains accurate and relevant information that has passed muster with some of the sharpest eyes and ears in the business. Yes, my name may be the only one on the cover, but tons of people had a big role in creating what appears between the covers (be they physical or virtual). I'd like to extend warm thanks to publisher Marjan Bace, acquisitions editors Brian Sawyer and Jonathan

Gennick, development editor Dustin Archibald, technical editor Mattea Piccini, and all the rest of the production staff at Manning who helped bring this book to fruition.

To all the reviewers—Adam Wendell, Alba MÁLAGA, Ale Muñoz, Alexander Gusev, Alexandr Mirankov, América Fabiola Sánchez León, Amit Lamba, Ben Tran, Benjamin Jones, Bernard Fuentes, Christopher Kardell, Dariusz Kazik, David Cabrero Souto, David Crowley, Denis Saripov, Giorgio Vilardo, Isabel Rapando, Jason Overholt, John Mikos, Joe Chaplin, Johannes Ball, Majeed Siddiqui, Mario Arias, Martine Dowden, Pedro Seromenho, Philip Weiss, Ramani Natarajan, Rashed Hoque, Seth MacPherson, Sidharth Masaldaan, Stephan Max, Thomas Desmedt, Tom Kirby-Green, Victor Jones, Vlad Korobov, and Yves Dorfsman—your suggestions helped make this a better book.

I'd also like to thank all the people who took the time to review the early drafts of the book and offered comments and suggestions. Your couple of cents' worth was very much appreciated.

# about this book

In this book, you'll learn about the math that underlies huge chunks of modern web development, as well as how to wield mathematical tools to make your web pages more robust, better looking, and more flexible. No math degree is even close to being required to read this book! Everything you need to know is provided as you need it, and you won't find any long-winded technical discussions or philosophical arguments in these pages. That said, though, I do assume that you're familiar with HTML and CSS and know at least the basics of frontend coding with JavaScript.

I'm assuming that you have a life away from your computer screen, so this book is structured to allow nonlinear reading, letting you move directly to the sections you need. If you're just getting started, read chapter 1 to get an overview, then tackle chapters 2 and 3 for some solid mathematical foundations in JavaScript and CSS. From there, you can try out any of the other chapters in any order. To make things easier to find, the roadmap section that follows gives a summary of the book's 14 chapters.

## Who should read this book?

This book is aimed, first and foremost, at anyone who does frontend web development, whether they do it professionally, as a hobby, or out of necessity by virtue of being the most technical person in the office. Specifically, this book was written with the following readers in mind:

- Frontend developers who want to sharpen their understanding of the math behind CSS, JavaScript, and UI animations
- Web designers who work with layouts, typography, and color theory and want to better understand the math behind their design choices

- UI/UX designers who want to leverage mathematical principles for responsive design and interactive experiences
- Self-taught developers who may not have a strong math background but want to level up their frontend development skills
- JavaScript enthusiasts interested in building interactive elements, animations, and data visualizations

## *How this book is organized: A roadmap*

You don't need to read this book cover-to-cover (although feel free to do just that). If you prefer to dip in and out, then you'll need a map that shows you what is covered where. To that end, here's a chapter-by-chapter summary of what's coming up on the road ahead:

- Chapter 1 discusses the importance of math in frontend development, showing how mathematical concepts are already a part of the CSS and JavaScript you use daily. It provides a high-level overview of the essential math topics you need to know, from algebra to trigonometry.
- Chapter 2 takes you through the fundamentals of working with numbers and expressions in JavaScript. It explores arithmetic and comparison operators, different number types, and how to handle common problems such as floating-point precision errors. The chapter also covers practical skills such as rounding numbers, using modulo logic for wrapping values, and generating random numbers.
- Chapter 3 focuses on the math that powers CSS styling and layouts. You'll learn how the browser calculates different measurement units, how to use built-in math functions such as `calc()`, and how the underlying formulas shape the CSS box model and property inheritance.
- Chapter 4 delves into the mathematical foundations of the CSS Grid layout system. You'll learn to think of the grid as a coordinate system and understand the algorithm that CSS employs to calculate the size of tracks, especially when using fractional `fr` units.
- Chapter 5 explores the calculations that determine how Flexbox layouts work. The chapter breaks down the algorithms for the `flex-grow` and `flex-shrink` properties, showing exactly how Flexbox distributes available space among items in a container.
- Chapter 6 explores the math required to build fluid and responsive websites that adapt to any screen size. You'll learn to work with proportional layouts using percentages, viewport-based units, and dynamic CSS functions such as `clamp()`.
- Chapter 7 examines the deep connection between math and digital color. You'll learn about different color models such as RGB and HSL, how to use mathematical relationships to create harmonious and accessible color schemes, and how CSS blend modes are calculated.

- Chapter 8 provides the mathematical foundations you need to craft beautiful and readable text on the web. You'll learn about fluid typography that scales with the viewport, how to build a modular type scale using mathematical ratios, and the calculations needed to maintain a consistent vertical rhythm with a baseline grid.
- Chapter 9 illustrates how to apply trigonometry to solve common UI challenges. The chapter covers the basics of sine, cosine, and tangent, showing how to use them to create circular layouts, implement wave effects, and calculate angles for dynamic animations.
- Chapter 10 introduces the use of vectors and geometry to build complex and interactive user interfaces. You'll learn how to measure and align elements with precision, manipulate vectors in JavaScript to control movement, and use geometric shapes for clipping and motion paths.
- Chapter 11 uncovers the math that makes animations feel smooth and natural. You'll learn what Bézier curves are, how they're constructed mathematically, and how to use them in CSS to create custom easing functions that go beyond the standard keywords.
- Chapter 12 shows how to make your animations more realistic by applying principles from real-world physics. You'll explore how to simulate velocity, acceleration, gravity, and spring forces in JavaScript to create UI motion that feels intuitive and satisfying to users.
- Chapter 13 focuses on the math needed to respond to user input. You'll learn how to work with mouse and touch event coordinates, convert between different coordinate systems, and use that knowledge to build interactive features such as drag-and-drop interfaces and scroll-based animations.
- Chapter 14 takes your math skills to the HTML `canvas` element, where you have pixel-level control. You'll learn to use the canvas coordinate system to draw data-driven shapes, detect hits, and create complex animations such as particle systems using physics.

## About the code

Not surprisingly, a book about frontend web dev coding contains quite a bit of code! To help differentiate the web page code from the rest of the text, throughout this book the code is formatted in a `fixed-width font`. The book also has many separate code listings. In these listings, I've tried as much as possible to make each line fit into the available page width. However, there are some cases where a line is too long to fit the page width, so the line carries over to a second line and that second line is preceded with a line-continuation marker.

You might be tempted to describe some of the code in this book as a *dismaying* amount of code if you're operating under the assumption that you're going to need to type all that code by hand. Not so! You can get executable snippets of code from the liveBook (online) version of this book at https://livebook.manning.com/book/math-for-web-design. All the book's web page code is available to view, download, and copy as you see fit from the Manning website at www.manning.com/books/math-for-web-design and the book's GitHub repository at https://github.com/paulmcfe/web-dev-math. To download everything, click the green Code button, and then click Download ZIP. Otherwise, click a chapter and then select the file you want to view.

## liveBook discussion forum

Purchase of *Math for Web Design* includes free access to liveBook, Manning's online reading platform. Using liveBook's exclusive discussion features, you can attach comments to the book globally or to specific sections or paragraphs. It's a snap to make notes for yourself, ask and answer technical questions, and receive help from the author and other users. To access the forum, go to https://livebook.manning.com/book/math-for-web-design/discussion.

Manning's commitment to our readers is to provide a venue where a meaningful dialogue between individual readers and between readers and the author can take place. It is not a commitment to any specific amount of participation on the part of the author, whose contribution to the forum remains voluntary (and unpaid). We suggest you try asking the author some challenging questions lest his interest stray! The forum and the archives of previous discussions will be accessible from the publisher's website for as long as the book is in print.

# *about the author*

**Paul McFedries** has been a professional technical writer for more than 30 years. He has authored more than 110 books to his credit, with global sales topping 4 million copies. His other Manning titles include *Web Design Playground, 2nd Edition* and *Building Websites with ChatGPT.* When he's not writing books, Paul is either coding solutions to Project Euler (https://projecteuler.net/) math problems or building web pages, which he's been doing since 1996. Paul has hand-coded many sites, including his web home (https://paulmcfedries.com); Word Spy (https://wordspy.com); WebDev Workshop (https://webdevworkshop.io); and Web Design Playground (https://webdesignplayground.io/2).

# *about the cover illustration*

The figure on the cover of *Math for Web Design*, captioned "Il Conciategami," is taken from a collection originally published in 1853 by Stabilimento tipografico di G. Nobile, Napoli, and is provided by the George Peabody Library, Johns Hopkins University. Each illustration is finely drawn and colored by hand.

In those days, it was easy to identify where people lived and what their trade or station in life was just by their dress. Manning celebrates the inventiveness and initiative of the computer business with book covers based on the rich diversity of regional culture centuries ago, brought back to life by pictures from collections such as this one.

# 1 Web dev math fundamentals

**This chapter covers**

- Improving web dev precision with math
- The benefits of learning web dev math
- How math is used in CSS and JavaScript
- The math basics for coding motion and animation, layouts, and user interactions

When you design or code a website, you might not think of yourself as doing math, but there's likely at least a little mathematics behind most of what you do. Are you using relative units such as `em` or `rem`? There's math behind those units. Are you applying an easing function such as `ease-in-out` to an animation? There's math behind that function. Does your JavaScript code call the `getBoundingClientRect()` method on an element to determine its size and position? There's math behind that method.

Certainly, it's possible to design and develop websites without giving math more than a cursory thought. Whatever math lies underneath a unit such as `em` or an easing function such as `ease-in-out` might not matter to you as long as the job gets done.

However, the whole point of this book is that if you take a bit of time to understand that math, you'll find it makes a big difference in the precision and robustness of your web layouts and interfaces. The good news is that you don't need a graduate degree to build better websites. You only need to understand a small set of concepts, and none of it is as complex as the CSS and JavaScript you already know.

This chapter lays the foundation for understanding the math that powers frontend development. But don't fret, this isn't about complex equations or abstract theory. Instead, my focus here is on practical math that helps you solve real design and development problems. By the end of this chapter, you'll understand how just a bit of math can go a long way in making your designs more precise, your animations smoother, and your layouts more responsive.

## 1.1 Why bother learning about frontend math?

Okay, I get it: your job as a frontend designer or developer has a full plate as it is, so you might be wondering whether you really need to add "learn frontend math" to your already too-long to-do list. And what about AI, the web development elephant in the room? Wouldn't it be easier and faster to let your favorite AI coding agent handle all the math for you?

I wrote this book precisely because I believe every designer and developer would benefit from a bit of math background, and those benefits won't come your way if you use AI instead. Now, let me try to persuade you:

- *You'll build more precise, reliable layouts.* When you understand the math behind spacing, alignment, and sizing, you can create layouts that are cleaner, more consistent, and easier to maintain. You'll know exactly *why* a layout breaks or goes wonky, rather than just guessing and tweaking values until it looks right. Math turns guesswork into great work.
- *You'll master responsive design faster.* Responsive design is all about scaling, proportions, and constraints. Understanding how percentages, viewport units, and CSS functions such as `clamp()` work gives you the power to create fluid designs that adapt beautifully to any screen. Without math, you're just crossing your fingers and hoping things work; with math, you're in control.
- *You'll write smarter, faster code.* Animations, scroll effects, and dynamic layouts often rely on calculations under the hood. Knowing a bit of math lets you write your own logic instead of relying on a heavy library. That means smaller, faster, and more flexible code, which is always the goal, of course, but it is especially useful for performance-sensitive projects.
- *You'll debug layout and animation problems more easily.* Have you ever had two elements *almost* line up, or an animation *almost* look smooth? These almosts often come down to a missing unit, a misunderstood percentage, or a miscalculated transition. When you understand the math, you can spot the problem faster and fix it with precision.

- *You'll unlock creative design possibilities.* Math isn't just about solving problems but also about creating possibilities. Circular layouts, spiral animations, rhythmic typography, responsive grids that follow the golden ratio—these all depend on math. Once you understand the logic, you can invent your own visual systems and interactions instead of merely copying patterns.
- *You'll level up your professional value.* Let's be honest: developers and designers who can bridge the gap between visual creativity and technical logic are rare and in demand. Being able to say, "Yes, I know how to make this animation fluid *and* why it works" sets you apart. Math adds an extra layer of professionalism to your toolkit.

Convinced? I knew it! Now I want to show you why math matters so much in web development.

## 1.2 Why math matters in frontend development

If you're a web developer or designer, math might not be the first thing that comes to mind when thinking about your everyday work. After all, you're probably more familiar with pixels, colors, and typefaces than with equations or formulas. But here's the secret: math is quietly at work in almost everything you build on the web, and it's often extremely important to understand how. For an example that illustrates this importance, refer to the following listing, which illustrates a common CSS conundrum.

**Listing 1.1 A heading size conundrum**

CSS:

```
main {
    font-size: 1.25em;
}
article {
    font-size: 1.75em;
}
h2 {
    font-size: 2em;
}
```

HTML:

```
<main>
    <h2>Main Heading</h2>
    <article>
        <section>
            <h2>Section Heading</h2>
        </section>
    </article>
</main>
```

**NOTE** All the code for this chapter's listings is available in the book's GitHub repository: https://github.com/paulmcfe/web-dev-math.

Since the `h2` element is declared with `font-size: 2em`, it's understandable that you'd expect both headings on the page to appear at that size when the page is rendered in the browser. But as figure 1.1 shows, the section heading is noticeably larger than the main heading. Can you figure out why?

This is one of those apparently nonsensical CSS behaviors that drives web designers crazy. Fortunately, there's a logical explanation for such behavior, and it's all about the math. Cruelly, perhaps, I'm going to hold off on the solution to this problem until I talk about the math of CSS inheritance in chapter 3.

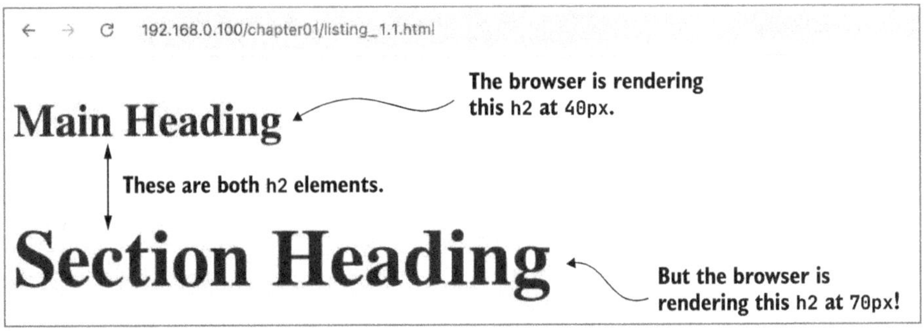


**Figure 1.1 Why is the section heading so much bigger than the main heading? Math!**

Once you start to recognize the mathematical patterns and principles behind your work, a whole new world opens up, and you begin to code with more confidence and creativity. This section is all about making that connection visible. You'll explore how math underpins many of the choices and techniques you already use, from spacing and proportions in layouts to animations, interactivity, and responsive design. You'll also look at some real-world examples that show how math helps shape the user experience. My goal here is to show you that math is already a part of your work and that understanding it just a little better can help you make smarter, more elegant, and more adaptable websites.

### 1.2.1 The connection between mathematics and web design

Web design might seem like a purely creative process that involves choosing colors, arranging elements, and adjusting typography, but beneath that shiny surface lies a solid foundation built on mathematics. Whether it's aligning items on a grid, calculating spacing, or choosing responsive breakpoints, math plays a pivotal role in how things fit together and behave on screen.

At its core, design is about balance, proportion, and structure, all of which have mathematical roots. Consider the rule of thirds in visual composition, the golden ratio in layout design, or the use of modular scales in typography. These ideas might come from the world of art and aesthetics, but they're all based on mathematical patterns that help you create harmony and clarity in your designs.

Even when you're simply setting a `max-width` for a container or centering an element horizontally, you're making a mathematical decision, even if it's happening intuitively.

### 1.2.2 Real-world examples of math in UI/UX

Math doesn't just shape the structure of a webpage. It also influences how users interact with it. In user interface (UI) and user experience (UX) design, math shows up in all sorts of practical ways:

- *Responsive layouts*—Using percentages, viewport units, and `calc()` functions to scale content based on screen size.
- *Typography*—Building a type scale using consistent ratios (e.g., 1.2 or 1.618) to maintain visual rhythm (refer to figure 1.2).
- *Color theory*—Adjusting brightness, contrast, and blending modes often involves numerical manipulation of color values.
- *Spacing and alignment*—Grid systems use consistent spacing units, gutters, and columns, essentially applying basic algebra to structure content.
- *Motion and animation*—From smooth fades to bouncy transitions, animations are powered by timing functions, easing curves, and velocity equations.

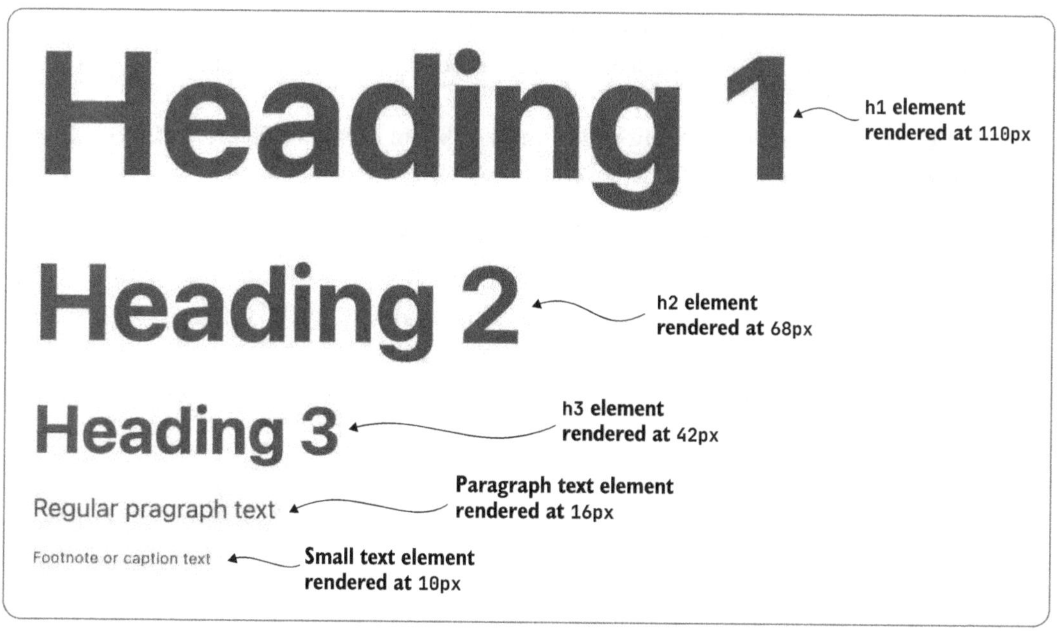


**Figure 1.2 A type scale based on the golden ratio (approximately 1.618).**

Even scroll position or cursor movement can serve as mathematical inputs that dynamically shape the UI. These are real, working examples of math directly improving UX, making interfaces more readable, accessible, and enjoyable to use.

### 1.2.3 How developers use math in animations, layouts, and interactions

As a frontend developer, you're already using math, even if you don't think of it that way. Every time you center an element horizontally with `left: 50%` and `transform: translateX(-50%)`, or calculate spacing using `margin: calc(2rem + 1vw)`, you're applying math in a creative context.

Here are a few common ways math shows up in your everyday coding:

- *Animations*—JavaScript animations often calculate positions over time using methods such as `requestAnimationFrame()`, which involves multiplying speed by time or using easing functions based on curves.
- *Layouts*—CSS Grid and Flexbox both rely heavily on concepts such as ratios, fractions, and proportional scaling. Figuring out how many columns fit into a container or how to balance widths requires basic math.
- *User interactions*—Mouse tracking, measuring drag distances, or determining when to trigger scroll effects all involve mathematical logic. Whether you're calculating distance with the Pythagorean theorem or finding the angle between two points, these UI features are built on math.

Understanding the math behind these tasks does more than help you debug or refine your code—it also helps you make better decisions about structure, flow, and behavior. The goal isn't to memorize formulas but to recognize patterns and use them to your advantage.

The next section explores how CSS and JavaScript each handle math differently and how you can use their respective strengths to build better interfaces.

## 1.3 The role of mathematics in CSS and JavaScript

When I talk about math in web development, I'm not referring to a single, monolithic object you need to learn. There's no one-ring-to-rule-them-all approach to frontend math. Instead, both CSS and JavaScript offer their own approaches to handling math, and knowing the difference, as well as when to pick one over the other, is crucial so that you can use the right mathematical tool for the right job.

### 1.3.1 How CSS uses math

At first glance, CSS might not look like a math-heavy language, but math plays a key role in how styles are calculated, layouts are structured, and elements respond to different screen sizes. Every time you set a margin, calculate a width using a CSS function such as `calc()`, or define a responsive font size, you're relying on mathematical logic, even if it's happening behind the scenes.

CSS uses math to

- *Position elements*—Whether you're using CSS declarations such as `left: 50%`, `top: 50%`, and `transform: translate(-50%, -50%)` to center an item (refer to figure 1.3) or centering with Flexbox or Grid, CSS is doing calculations based on the box model and parent-child relationships.
- *Scale layouts*—Units such as `%`, `vw`, and `em` require real-time math to compute the correct size based on the current context, including screen size, font size, and container dimensions.
- *Create responsive designs*—CSS functions such as `calc()`, `clamp()`, `min()`, and `max()` let you build layouts and type scales that adjust fluidly as conditions change.
- *Style text*—Line height, letter spacing, and font scaling rely on ratios and consistent spacing units to maintain readability and design rhythm.
- *Animate transitions*—Although animation timing is usually associated with JavaScript, CSS transitions use math-driven easing curves (such as `ease-in-out` or `cubic-bezier()`) to define how an animation progresses over time.

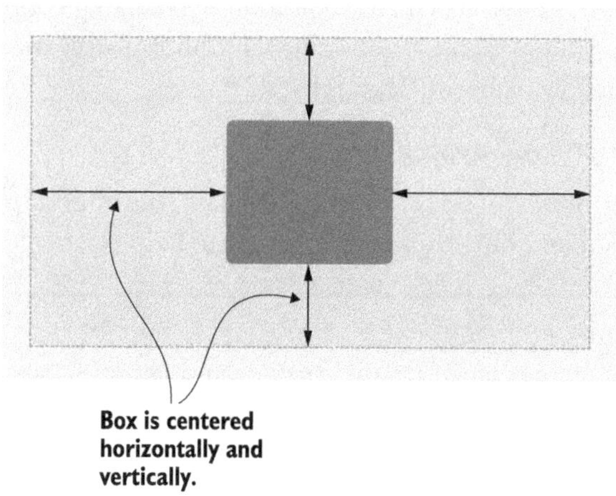


**Figure 1.3 Centering an element within its containing block requires just a few CSS declarations, but behind the scenes, the browser is jumping through many mathematical hoops to get the job done.**

Understanding the math behind CSS doesn't mean you need to solve equations. It just means learning how the browser interprets your styles mathematically. With that knowledge, you can design more flexible, precise, and scalable interfaces.

### 1.3.2 JavaScript's built-in mathematical capabilities

JavaScript includes a rich set of built-in tools for working with numbers and performing mathematical operations, many of which you're likely already using without thinking much about the math involved.

At the heart of JavaScript's math toolkit is the `Math` object, which provides functions for common operations, such as

- `Math.round()`, `Math.floor()`, and `Math.ceil()` for rounding numbers
- `Math.random()` for generating random numbers, which is useful for everything from UI effects to game logic
- `Math.max()` and `Math.min()` to determine the extremes in an array or other set of values
- `Math.abs()` to find absolute values, which is helpful in measuring distance or change
- `Math.pow()` and `Math.sqrt()` for exponentiation and square roots, such as calculating distance using the Pythagorean theorem
- Trigonometric functions such as `Math.sin()`, `Math.cos()`, and `Math.atan2()` for handling angles, curves, and circular motion

Beyond the `Math` object, JavaScript supports arithmetic operators (`+`, `-`, `*`, `/`, `%`, `**`) and enables you to build dynamic expressions that power everything from animations and physics effects to responsive layouts and charting tools. These capabilities are essential when you're calculating motion paths, handling user interactions, adjusting element positions on the fly, or creating data visualizations. Because JavaScript runs in real time in the browser, you can use math to make your UI adapt instantly to changing conditions.

With just a bit of practice, you can start combining these tools to create smarter, more interactive, and more flexible frontend experiences.

### 1.3.3 Comparing CSS and JavaScript math approaches

Both CSS and JavaScript offer powerful ways to work with math, but they approach it from different angles, and understanding those differences can help you decide which tool is best for the job.

#### CSS: Built-in, declarative math

CSS provides math functions such as `calc()`, `min()`, `max()`, and `clamp()` that you can use to perform basic arithmetic right in your style declarations. These are especially useful for layout and typography, where you want values to adjust automatically based on container size, viewport width, or other units. For example,

```
width: calc(100% - 2rem);
font-size: clamp(1rem, 2vw, 2rem);
```

CSS math is *declarative*, which means that you describe *what* you want mathematically, and the browser takes care of the rest. It's great for responsive design and clean, maintainable stylesheets. However, it's limited because you can't use loops, conditionals, or complex logic.

#### JavaScript: Dynamic, procedural math

JavaScript gives you full control with dynamic, real-time math using the `Math` object and custom logic. You can perform advanced calculations, respond to user input, and update values on the fly. For example,

```
const containerWidth = window.innerWidth;
const padding = 32;
const contentWidth = containerWidth - padding * 2;
```

JavaScript is *procedural*, which means that you define *how* you want math to modify your page elements on the fly. It's ideal when you need interactivity, animations, or custom logic that goes beyond what CSS can handle.

**WHEN TO USE EACH**

So, which math approach should you use? It depends on the context:

- *CSS*—Use CSS math for layout, sizing, spacing, and typography when the values can be determined by the browser at render time.
- *JavaScript*—Use JavaScript math when you need interaction, complex animation, or real-time adjustments based on user behavior or complex conditions.

In many cases, you'll end up using both: CSS for design and JavaScript for behavior. Learning how they complement each other is one of the keys to mastering modern frontend development.

## 1.4 The minimum math you need to know

You don't need to be a math expert to be a great frontend developer, but there are a handful of key concepts that show up repeatedly in layout, animation, interaction, and design logic. This section outlines the essential math you'll encounter in frontend development, along with examples of where and how each concept is used. Think of this as your frontend developer's math survival kit—just enough to understand what's happening, solve problems with confidence, and build smarter interfaces.

### 1.4.1 Arithmetic and arithmetic expressions

Most frontend math requires nothing more serious than the most familiar arithmetic operations: addition, subtraction, multiplication, and division. You use these operations to manipulate numeric values to some end within an *expression*, which is a collection of values and symbols that performs a calculation and produces a result. In CSS and JavaScript, an arithmetic expression takes one or more inputs and combines them in some way using one or more arithmetic operations. The inputs are called *operands*, and they're combined using special symbols called *operators*:

- *operand*—An input value for an expression. It could be a number, a string, a variable, a function result, or an object property.
- *operator*—A symbol that represents a particular action performed on one or more operands. For example, the * operator represents multiplication, and the + operator represents addition.

Table 1.1 presents a few examples.

**Table 1.1 Some frontend arithmetic examples**

| Task | Code | Operation |
|---|---|---|
| Set an element's width in CSS. | `.card { width: calc(100px + 50px + 20px); }` | Addition (+) |
| Calculate the discounted price in a JavaScript statement. | `const discountedPrice = 21.55 - 5;` | Subtraction (-) |
| Determine a fixed font size for an element in CSS. | `h1 { font-size: calc(16px * 2.5); }` | Multiplication (*) |
| Calculate the pre-tax price in JavaScript. | `const originalPrice = 21.55 / 0.08;` | Division (/) |

Refer to chapter 3 for more about performing calculations in CSS using the `calc()` function.

These examples are a bit contrived because you won't use known quantities in your CSS and JavaScript code often. You're far more likely to use variable or unknown quantities, as described in the next section.

### 1.4.2 Algebra

*Algebra* is a branch of mathematics that deals with general statements about the relationships among numbers, using letters (such as $x$ and $y$) and other symbols to represent them. Algebra makes it possible to create formulas, solve equations, and describe patterns or real-world situations abstractly.

Much of the math you do in frontend development is algebraic in nature, even if it doesn't look like it, so it will help you to get a basic understanding of algebraic principles. Here are the key elements of algebra you need to know:

- *Variable value*—A letter or other symbol that stands for an unknown value
- *Constant*—A fixed value (also called a *numeric literal*), such as `2`, `0.5`, or `3rem`
- *Operation*—The standard arithmetic operations (i.e., addition, subtraction, multiplication, and division) represented, respectively, by the operators `+`, `-`, `*`, and `/`
- *Expression*—A combination of one or more variable values, constants, and operators (e.g., `3x + 2`)
- *Equation*—Two expressions set equal to each other (e.g., `3x + 2 = 11`)
- *Inequality*—An expression that compares two values to determine if they're not equal (refer to section 1.4.6 for more)
- *Function*—A relationship between inputs and outputs, for example, `f(x) = 2x + 1`

In frontend development, algebra involves expressions with one or more variable values. That variable may be a JavaScript or CSS variable defined elsewhere in your code, the result of a CSS or JavaScript function, or a value determined by something external, such as the browser environment (e.g., the width of the user's viewport) or the current date or time.

For example, imagine you're building a product detail page for an online store. The page header height varies depending on whether a promotional banner is displayed. You need to calculate the height of the remaining space to position the product gallery below the header:

```
const remainingHeight = window.innerHeight - headerHeight;
```

This is algebra at work: you're solving for a value using variable quantities from the browser environment. Table 1.2 offers a few more examples.

**Table 1.2 Some frontend algebra examples**

| Task | Code | Algebraic explanation |
|---|---|---|
| Set a responsive width in CSS. | `.container { width: calc(100% - 2rem); }` | The variable value in this example is `100%`, which in this context represents the full width of the container's parent element. It's variable because the parent width could change (e.g., if the browser window is resized or content is added or removed dynamically). |
| Adjust an opacity value in JavaScript. | `const opacity = 1- window.scrollY / maxScroll;` | The two variable values here are the vertical scroll position (given by the `Window` object's `scrollY` property) and the variable `maxScroll` (the maximum amount the user can scroll, usually given by `document.body.scrollHeight - window .innerHeight`). |
| Calculate the current position of something moving in JavaScript. | `let position = 100 + speed * time;` | The two variable values here are the JavaScript variables named `speed` and `time`. |
| Determine a grid item's width in CSS. | `.grid-item { width: calc(100% / 3 - var(--gutter)); }` | The two variable values here are `100%` and a CSS variable named `gutter`. |

Most of your frontend math will involve algebraic expressions such as these. Check out chapter 2 to learn all about operators and expressions in JavaScript, and refer to chapter 3 to read about operators and expressions in CSS.

### 1.4.3 Ratios

A *ratio* is a mathematical comparison between two or more quantities, showing how many times one value contains or is contained in another. A ratio is typically written as a:b or a/b, but it can also be represented as a decimal or a percentage.

For example, a frequently used ratio in web design is the *aspect ratio,* which is the ratio of width to height. To say that an element (such as a video or an image) has a 16:9 aspect ratio means that for every 16 units of width, there are 9 units of height. Imagine you're designing a video gallery for a media company. The video thumbnails must all keep a 16:9 aspect ratio so that they don't appear distorted. You can use the `aspect-ratio` property in CSS (or a custom calculation in JavaScript) to ensure consistent dimensions:

```
.video-thumbnail {
    aspect-ratio: 16 / 9;
}
```

Table 1.3 presents a few more examples of ratios in CSS and JavaScript.

**Table 1.3 Some example ratios**

| Task | Code | Explanation |
|---|---|---|
| Define a typographic scale based on a ratio in CSS. | `:root {   --base-font-size: 1rem;   --ratio: 1.618;   }  h2 {   font-size: calc(var(--base-font-size) * var(--ratio));   }` | Such scales typically use powers of the ratio value to scale the font sizes: positive powers increase the base font size, and negative powers decrease the base font size. |
| Calculate an aspect ratio dynamically in JavaScript. | `const width = 1920;  const height = 1080;   const aspectRatio = width / height;` | Dynamic aspect ratios are useful for image/video rendering or canvas drawing to maintain proportions. |
| Set up a grid layout with fractional ratios in CSS. | `.container {  display: grid; grid-template-columns: 3fr 2fr 1fr;   }` | Ratios can involve more than two quantities. This example creates a 3:2:1 ratio of column widths. |
| Scale a UI element based on a ratio in JavaScript. | `const baseSize = 100;  const scaleRatio = 1.5;   const newSize = baseSize * scaleRatio;` | This sort of ratio-based calculation can be used for zoom effects, responsive scaling, or animations. |

Here are some other ways ratios are used in web development:

- Calculating proportions in Flexbox layouts (covered in chapter 5)
- Applying the golden ratio (1:1.618) for visual harmony (check out chapter 8 for more about the golden ratio)
- Using percentages to scale child elements along with their parents (covered in chapter 6)
- Creating a typographic scale: `1rem`, `1.25rem`, `1.563rem`, and so on (refer to chapter 8 to learn more about modular typography scales)

Frontend math gets real interesting once you start working with exponents and roots, a topic covered in the next section.

### 1.4.4 Exponents and nth roots

An *exponent* is the number of times a value (called the *base*) is multiplied by itself. For example, in $r^2$, the exponent is 2 and the base $r$ is multiplied by itself twice; in $x^3$, the exponent is 3 and the base $x$ is multiplied by itself three times. When the highest exponent in a mathematical expression is 2, the expression is said to be *quadratic*.

The *nth root* of a value is the number that, when raised to the $n$th power, produces the value. For example, 2 is the 4th root of 16 (that is, $2^4 = 16$), and 3 is the 5th root of 243 ($3^5 = 243$). Two special cases are the *square root*, where $n$ equals 2, and the *cube root*, where $n$ equals 3.

For example, suppose you're working on a simulation where you need to know the distance between two points (x1, y1) and (x2, y2):

```
const dx = x2 - x1;
const dy = y2 - y1;
const distance = Math.sqrt(dx * dx + dy * dy);
```

The final statement takes the square root of the sum of the squares of the two sides that form a right triangle between the two points. This is the famous Pythagorean theorem in action. Refer to chapter 2 to learn about the `Math.sqrt()` method. Table 1.4 takes you through another couple of examples.

**Table 1.4 Exponent and *n*th root examples**

| Task | Code | Explanation |
|---|---|---|
| Set up an animation with a deceleration effect in CSS. | `.box { animation: moveLeft 2s ease -out; }` | The `ease-out` timing function uses exponential math to animate something fast at first, then slower over the duration of the animation. |
| Calculate an opacity that fades out quadratically over time in JavaScript. | `const opacity = 1 - Math.pow(time / duration, 2);` | Raises `time / duration` to the power of 2. The opacity fades slowly at the beginning, then speeds up as time progresses. Refer to chapter 2 to learn about the `Math.pow()` method. |

Be sure to peruse chapter 11 to learn all about the math behind easing functions and use that know-how to create custom easings.

### 1.4.5 Linear equations

A *linear equation* is a type of equation that forms a straight line when you graph it. In terms of exponents, when the highest exponent in a mathematical expression is 1, the expression is said to be *linear*. Such an expression represents a relationship between variables in which the rate of change is constant.

The standard form of a linear equation looks like this:

```
y = mx + b
```

where

- `y` is the output and is called the *dependent variable.*
- `x` is the input and is called the *independent variable.*
- `m` is the slope of the line, which tells you the rate of change.
- `b` is the *y*-intercept and is often called the *starting value* because it's the value of the equation when `x` is 0. In that sense, `b` represents a vertical translation.

Linear equations help frontend developers model relationships between quantities, including size, time, position, and speed.

For example, suppose you're building a documentation site, and you want a progress bar at the top that fills as the user scrolls down. To calculate how far they've scrolled, you use a linear formula:

```
const scrollY = window.scrollY;                          ← Current vertical scroll position
const totalHeight = document.body.scrollHeight -
                                    window.innerHeight;  ← Total scrollable height of page
const progress = scrollY / totalHeight;                  ← Scroll progress
```

The final statement is a linear equation:

- *y*: `progress`
- *m*: `1 / totalHeight`
- *x*: `scrollY`
- *b*: `0`

Table 1.5 offers a couple of other ways that linear equations are used in CSS and JavaScript.

**Table 1.5 Examples of linear equations**

| Task | Code | Explanation (`y = mx + b`) |
|---|---|---|
| Define a responsive width in CSS. | `width: calc(50vw + 20px);` | m is 0.5, x is the viewport `width`, and b is `20px` (a fixed offset). |
| Calculate consistent motion in JavaScript. | `const position = initial + speed * time;` | m is the variable `speed`, x is the variable `time`, and b is the variable `initial` (the position when `time` is `0`). |

Linear equations are the math that enables smooth interactions, scalable layouts, and dynamic designs.

### 1.4.6 Inequalities and comparison expressions

A mathematical *inequality* is a statement that compares two values to check whether they're not equal. An inequality is an example of a *comparison expression* in which the operator is a symbol such as the following:

- > (greater than)—The comparison expression `x > 100` is true whenever the value of `x` is larger than `100`.
- < (less than)—The comparison expression `x < 100` is true whenever the value of `x` is smaller than `100`.
- `!==` (not equal)—In JavaScript, the comparison expression `x !== 100` is true whenever the value of `x` is any value other than `100`. Note that CSS doesn't offer an equivalent of the not equal operator.

Other comparison expressions use operators that take the possibility of equality into account:

- `>=` (greater than or equal)—The comparison expression `x >= 100` is true whenever the value of `x` is equal to or larger than `100`.
- `<=` (less than or equal)—The comparison expression `x <= 100` is true whenever the value of `x` is equal to or smaller than `100`.
- `===` (equal)—In JavaScript, the comparison expression `x === 100` is true whenever the value of `x` is equal to `100`. CSS supports the `=` operator for equality tests.

For example, suppose you're coding a responsive layout that switches to a two-column view when the screen width is `768px` or more. You need a simple condition to check the viewport width and apply the right layout:

```
if (window.innerWidth >= 768) {
    // Your layout code goes here
}
```

This lets you create dynamic breakpoints using JavaScript instead of media queries. Table 1.6 takes you through a few more examples.

**Table 1.6 Examples of inequalities and comparison expressions**

| Task | Code | Explanation |
|---|---|---|
| Define a breakpoint in CSS. | `@media (min-width: 50rem)` | The at-rule applies when the viewport width is greater than or equal to (>=) `50rem`. |
| Set lower and upper bounds on an element's font size in CSS. | `.title { font-size: clamp(1rem, 2vw, 2rem); }` | The font size must be greater than or equal to (>=) `1rem` and less than or equal to (<=) `2rem`. |
| Apply a style to a particular input type. | `input[type="number"] { border: 2px solid green; }` | The border style only gets applied to `input` elements where the `type` attribute is equal to (=) `number`. |
| Check for a too-short password in JavaScript. | `if (password.length < 8) { alert("Password must be at least 8 characters long."); }` | An alert is displayed if the length of the password is less than (<) 8 characters. |

Note that CSS comparison expressions use implicit comparison operators (for example, `min-width` implies `>=`), while JavaScript comparison expressions use explicit comparison operators.

### 1.4.7 Geometry

*Geometry* is the branch of mathematics that studies the properties, relationships, and measurements of objects in 2D or 3D space. Geometry is a massive subject, so, luckily for you, this book is about web development, which means you only need to know a few geometry concepts to level up your design and development chops:

- *Point*—A location in space, often described using x (horizontal) and y (vertical) coordinates. In CSS, layout positions are based on the box model and flow, but pixel-level precision can still depend on (x, y) coordinates, especially with transforms or when positioning elements absolutely.

- *Line*—A straight, one-dimensional figure that extends infinitely in both directions. A *line segment* is a portion of a line that connects two points. A *ray* is a portion of a line that starts at a point and extends infinitely in one direction. When working with the canvas (see chapter 14), you often create lines explicitly.
- *Vector*—A way to represent movement or direction (think of it as an arrow from one point to another). You work with vectors in JavaScript (as described in chapter 10) to move an element in a specific direction, apply physics-like forces (see chapter 12), and calculate swipe directions.
- *Angle*—A figure formed when two rays (or line segments) meet at a common point, called the *vertex*. The angle measures the amount of rotation from one ray to the other. Angles are measured in *degrees*, where there are 360 degrees in a circle, or *radians*, where 180 degrees equals π (pi) radians. Angles play a big part in web development, including animating or rotating elements, creating circular layouts or radial menus, drawing arcs in canvas or SVG, and tracking movement and direction.

Figure 1.4 illustrates these geometric concepts.

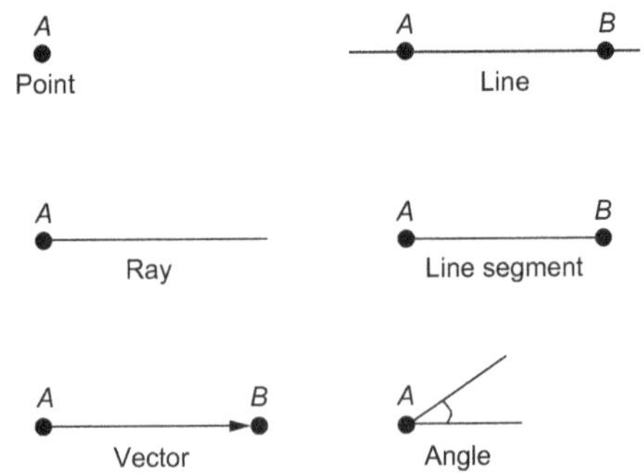


**Figure 1.4 Some basic geometric figures**

In web development, you also use geometric shapes such as triangles, circles, and polygons to lay out page elements; geometric paths such as arcs and other curves; and geometric transformations such as rotations and scaling.

For example, suppose you're creating a drawing app that lets users sketch directly on a canvas. Every time the user moves the mouse, you record the x and y coordinates of their cursor to draw a line:

```
ctx.lineTo(e.clientX, e.clientY);
```

You're working with points, lines, and distances, all classic geometry in action. Table 1.7 provides more examples of using geometry in a web dev context.

**Table 1.7 Some geometric examples**

| Task | Code | Explanation |
|---|---|---|
| Find the x and y coordinates of the point that represents the current mouse position in JavaScript. | `element.addEventListener ('mousemove', (e) => {  const x = e.clientX;  const y = e.clientY; });` | The `MouseEvent` properties `clientX` and `clientY` return the horizontal and vertical positions of the mouse pointer relative to the top-left corner (0, 0) of the browser viewport. |

**Table 1.7 Some geometric examples (*continued*)**

| Task | Code | Explanation |
|---|---|---|
| Draw a line on a canvas element with JavaScript. | `ctx.beginPath();` `ctx.moveTo(50, 50);    // Start point` `ctx.lineTo(250, 100); // End point` `ctx.stroke();` | Given a canvas context `ctx`, this code draws a line from the point (50, 50) to (250, 100). |
| Rotate an element 45 degrees in CSS. | `.box {   transform: rotate(45deg);   }` | The `rotate()` CSS function rotates an element. A positive angle rotates the element clockwise; a negative angle rotates it counterclockwise. |
| Create a shape in CSS. | `.shape {   clip-path: polygon(    25% 0%, 75% 0%,    100% 50%, 75% 100%, 25% 100%, 0% 50%    );   }` | The `clip-path` property sets an element's clipping region to a custom shape—a hexagon, in this case—as defined by the `polygon` function. |

As mentioned in chapter 10, you'll use geometry constantly in web dev, especially when dealing with the CSS box model, calculating element positions, determining if a point is within a box or shape, and much more.

### 1.4.8 *Trigonometry*

*Trigonometry* (often shortened to *trig*) is the branch of mathematics that studies the relationships between the sides and angles of triangles, especially *right triangles* where two sides meet at a 90-degree angle. For such a triangle (refer to figure 1.5), the following three main trigonometric functions are defined:

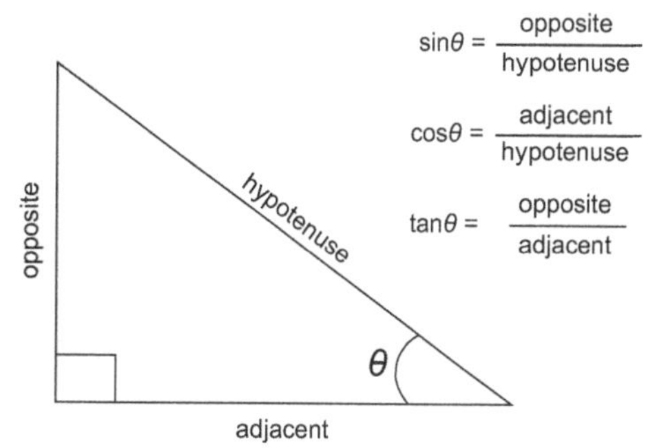


**Figure 1.5 A right triangle and its sides relative to the angle theta (θ)**

- *Sine (sin)*—The length of the side opposite the angle divided by the length of the hypotenuse
- *Cosine (cos)*—The length of the side adjacent to the angle divided by the length of the hypotenuse
- *Tangent (tan)*—The length of the side opposite the angle divided by the length of the side adjacent to the angle

For example, imagine you're designing a radial menu that fans out when a user clicks a button. You use trigonometric functions to calculate where each menu item should go along the circle:

```
const items = document.querySelectorAll('.menu-item');
items.forEach((item, i) => {
    const angle = (2 * Math.PI / totalItems) * i;
```

**Get all the menu items**

**Loop through the menu items**

**Calculate the angle, in radians**

```
    const x = centerX + radius * Math.cos(angle) - 20;
    const y = centerY + radius * Math.sin(angle) - 20;
    item.style.left = `${x}px`;
    item.style.top = `${y}px`;
});
```

**Calculate the x coordinate using cos()**
**Calculate the y coordinate using sin()**
**Set the item's left**
**Set the item's top**

Given a circle centered at (centerX, centerY) with a specified radius, the trigonometric functions cos() and sin() are used to calculate the (x, y) coordinates of points evenly spaced around a circle, as demonstrated in figure 1.6.

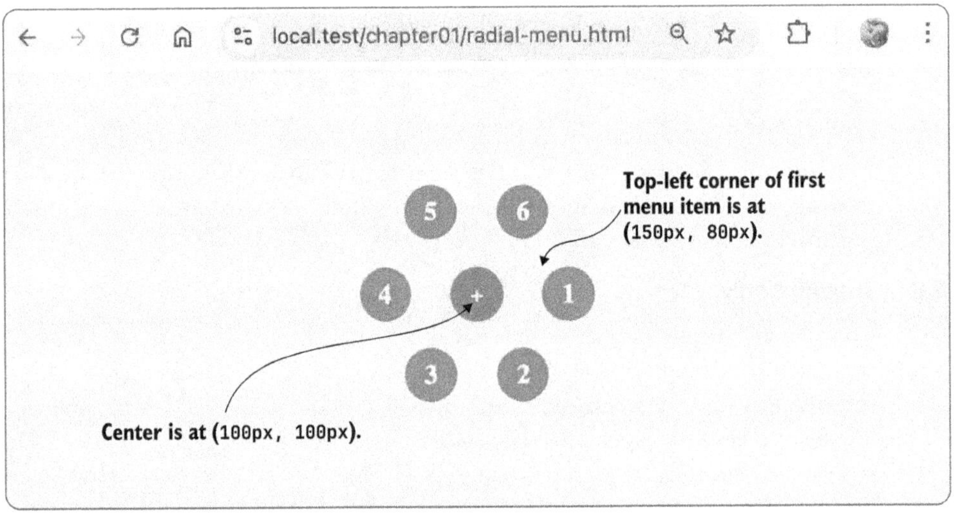


**Figure 1.6 Using trigonometry to arrange menu items in a circle**

Here's how the first menu item's position is calculated:

- Assume the center of the menu is at (100px, 100px), its radius is 70px. Each menu item has a width and height of 40px, and there are six menu items.
- For the first item, `i = 0`, so `angle = (2 * Math.PI / 6) * i = 0`.
- `x = centerX + radius * Math.cos(0) - 20 = 100 + 70 * 1 - 20 = 150.`
- `y = centerY + radius * Math.sin(angle) - 20 = 100 + 70 * 0 - 20 = 80.`

Table 1.8 presents a few more examples of using trig functions in web development.

**Table 1.8 Some examples of using trig in web dev**

| Task | Code | Explanation |
|---|---|---|
| Create a wave or bounce effect in JavaScript. | `const y = 20 * Math.sin(time * 0.05);` `element.style.transform = `translateY(${y}px)`;` | A trigonometric sine wave is used to create a floating or bouncing animation. |

**Table 1.8 Some examples of using trig in web dev (*continued*)**

| Task | Code | Explanation |
|---|---|---|
| Make an element move in a circle in CSS. | `.element {`<br>`offset-path: path("M100,100 A50,50 0 1,1 150,150");`<br>`animation: move 5s linear infinite;`<br>`}` | Arc-based paths in `offset-path` mimic circular or curved motion, which is governed by trigonometric curves under the hood. |
| Rotate an element along a circle in CSS. | `.item:nth-child(1) {`<br>`transform: rotate(60deg) translate(100px) rotate(-60deg);`<br>`}` | The browser uses sine and cosine calculations to determine each position of the element. |

You'll also use trig when you're rotating elements, creating circular animations or spiral patterns, calculating direction of movement, and setting up oscillating UI effects using sine waves. See chapter 9 for all things trigonometric.

### 1.4.9 Coordinate systems

A *coordinate system* is a mathematical framework used to locate and describe points in space using numbers called *coordinates*. It provides a standardized way to represent positions in two-dimensional (2D), three-dimensional (3D), or even higher-dimensional spaces.

For web development, there are three main concepts you need to understand about coordinate systems:

- *Axes*—The coordinate system's reference lines. For a 2D coordinate system, these lines are usually the x-axis (the horizontal axis) and the y-axis (the vertical axis), which are perpendicular to each other.
- *Origin*—The point where the axes intersect, which is typically the coordinate (0, 0) in a 2D coordinate system.
- *Coordinates*—A set of numbers that define a point's position relative to the origin. In a 2D coordinate system, each coordinate uses the general format (x, y), where x is the point's position on the x-axis and y is the point's position on the y-axis.

In web development, you use the *viewport coordinate system*—a 2D coordinate system where positions are measured relative to the visible area of the browser window, known in the trade as the *viewport*. The viewport coordinate system is used all over the place, including CSS positioning, DOM measurements, mouse events, and `getBoundingClientRect()` in JavaScript.

The viewport coordinate system has the following characteristics:

- *Origin (0, 0)*—Located at the top-left corner of the viewport.
- *Positive x-axis*—Extends rightward across the screen.
- *Positive y-axis*—Extends downward along the screen.
- *Unit of measurement*—Pixels (`px`) by default.

- *Negative values are allowed*—You can use negative values of *x* and *y* to position elements entirely or partially outside the viewport to the left or above the top-left corner.
- *Values can exceed the viewport width or height*—You can use values of *x* and *y* that are larger than the dimensions of the viewport to position elements entirely or partially outside the viewport to the right or below the bottom-right corner.

For example, imagine you're working on a hero section where an image should cover the full screen regardless of device. You can use viewport units to scale the image to fit exactly:

```
.hero {
    height: 100vh;
    width: 100vw;
}
```

The `vh` unit represents 1/100th of the viewport height, while the `vw` unit represents 1/100th of the viewport width. This ties your layout directly to the coordinate system of the viewport. Table 1.9 offers a few more examples.

**Table 1.9 Some uses of coordinate systems in CSS and JavaScript**

| Task | Code | Explanation |
|---|---|---|
| Get an element's current viewport position in JavaScript. | `const rect = element .getBoundingClientRect();` | The `getBoundingClientRect()` method returns the positions of an element's top, right, bottom, and left sides relative to the viewport origin. |
| Return the mouse pointer's current viewport position in JavaScript. | `window.addEventListener("mousemove", (e) => { console.log(e.clientX, e.clientY); });` | For a `mousemove` event `e`, the properties `e.clientX` and `e.clientY` represent the pointer's current position relative to the viewport's origin. |
| Scale a heading based on the viewport width in CSS. | `h1 { font-size: 5vw; }` | As the viewport widens or narrows, the font size of each `h1` heading will grow or shrink proportionately. |

Other web development uses for coordinate systems include positioning elements; working within a canvas; drawing shapes, arcs, and paths; working with movement, collision detection, rotations, and transformations; drag-and-drop interactions; and parallax effects based on scroll position.

## Summary

- Learning about frontend math will help you build more precise and reliable layouts, write more performant code, and debug layout problems faster.
- Mathematics in UI and UX design has practical use cases for responsive layouts, typography, color, spacing, and alignment.
- Developers use math when coding motion and animation, layouts, and user interactions.
- In CSS, you use math to position and transform elements, scale layouts, build responsive elements, style text, and animate transitions.
- CSS provides math functions that can be used to perform basic arithmetic right in your style declarations.
- JavaScript gives you full control with dynamic, real-time math using the `Math` object and custom logic.
- Use CSS math for layout, sizing, spacing, simple animation, and typography when the values can be determined by the browser at render time.
- Use JavaScript math when you need interaction, advanced animation, or real-time adjustments based on user behavior or complex conditions.

# 2 Math basics for JavaScript

**This chapter covers**

- JavaScript's arithmetic and comparison operators
- JavaScript number types and precision issues
- Working with really large integers
- Rounding numbers in JavaScript
- Generating random numbers

JavaScript is chock full of numbers. Whether your code calculates element dimensions, animates transitions, works with dates or financial data, or just loops through an array, the numbers are there, sometimes right out in the open, other times lurking in the shadows. When it comes to doing math with JavaScript, the good news is that JavaScript makes it easy to work with numbers; the bad news is that those numbers don't always behave the way you might expect. The goal of this chapter is to meet you at those expectations and show you how to adjust them so that when you do math with JavaScript you don't end up pulling out all your hair in frustration.

To that end, this chapter helps you build a rock-solid understanding of how JavaScript handles numbers behind the scenes, so you can write code that's more accurate, reliable, and bug-free.

## 2.1 Building JavaScript expressions

Most of your JavaScript math career will involve building *expressions*, which are combinations of *operands* (expression input values such as numbers, variables, object property values, or method or function results) and *operators* (symbols that specify the action you want JavaScript to perform on one or more of the operands) that return a value.

### 2.1.1 JavaScript arithmetic operators

Arithmetic is everywhere in frontend development, from positioning elements on a page to calculating animation frames or dynamically adjusting font sizes. JavaScript gives you all the standard arithmetic operators you'd expect, plus a few non-standard operators, as shown in Table 2.1.

**Table 2.1 JavaScript arithmetic operators**

| Operator | Name | Example (*n* = 5) | Result |
|---|---|---|---|
| + | Addition | n + 2 | 7 |
| ++ | Increment | n++ | 6 |
| + | Unary plus | +'5' | 5 |
| - | Subtraction | n - 2 | 3 |
| - | Unary negation | -n | -5 |
| -- | Decrement | n-- | 4 |
| * | Multiplication | n * 2 | 10 |
| / | Division | n / 2 | 2.5 |
| ** | Exponentiation | n ** 2 | 25 |
| % | Remainder | n % 2 | 1 |

You want to be a little careful when using the increment (++) and decrement (--) operators. For example, consider the following code:

```
let x = 5;
let y = x++;
```

What is the value of y? If you look too quickly, you might think that y is 6, but that's not right. When ++ follows a value in an assignment statement, it's known as the *post-increment* operator because JavaScript performs the assignment first, *then* it performs the increment. So, in the above code, after the second statement is executed, the value of y is 5 and the value of x is 6. If you want the increment to happen before the assignment, you need to place ++ before the value to make it the *pre-increment* operator:

```
let x = 5;
let y = ++x;
```

After these statements, the values of both y and x is 6.

All of this can be confusing, so now many JavaScript style guides recommend that you avoid ++ and -- altogether or use them only as loop counters:

```
for (let i = 0; i < 10; i++) {
    console.log(i);
}
```

### 2.1.2 JavaScript arithmetic assignment operators

JavaScript also offers a few so-called *arithmetic assignment operators* that combine some of the arithmetic operators and the assignment operator (=) for more concise expressions. Table 2.2 lists the arithmetic assignment operators.

**Table 2.2 JavaScript arithmetic assignment operators**

| Operator | Example | Equivalent |
|---|---|---|
| `+=` | `x += y` | `x = x + y` |
| `-=` | `x -= y` | `x = x - y` |
| `*=` | `x *= y` | `x = x * y` |
| `/=` | `x /= y` | `x = x / y` |
| `**=` | `x **= y` | `x = x ** y` |
| `%=` | `x %= y` | `x = x % y` |

Instead of using ++ or -- in your expressions, it's generally safer and clearer to use the += or -= operators, respectively (for example, `x += 1` instead of `x++`).

### 2.1.3 JavaScript comparison operators

Whether you're checking if a layout fits within a container or comparing two values during an animation loop, comparison operators are essential tools in JavaScript. They help you evaluate conditions and make decisions in your code. But JavaScript can be tricky when it comes to comparisons, especially when you try to compare different data types. This section will help you understand how comparisons work and avoid common pitfalls.

Table 2.3 lists the most commonly used comparison operators.

**Table 2.3 JavaScript comparison operators**

| Operator | Name | Example | Result |
|---|---|---|---|
| `==` | Equal (loose) | `"5" == 5` | `true` |
| `===` | Equal (strict) | `"5" === 5` | `false` |
| `!=` | Not equal (loose) | `"5" != 5` | `false` |
| `!==` | Not equal (strict) | `"5" !== 5` | `true` |
| `<` | Less than | `3 < 5` | `true` |
| `>` | Greater than | `4 > 5` | `false` |
| `<=` | Less than or equal | `4 <= 4` | `true` |
| `>=` | Greater than or equal | `5 >= 6` | `false` |

The main thing to understand here is the difference between loose (`==` or `!=`) and strict (`===` or `!==`) comparisons. Loose equality (`==`) allows type coercion (discussed a bit later in section 2.2.7), meaning it will try to convert one value to match the other before comparing:

```
console.log("10" == 10);      // true
console.log(false == 0);      // true
```

Strict equality (`===`) doesn't allow coercion. Both the type and value must be the same to return a result of `true`:

```
console.log("10" === 10);     // false
console.log(false === 0);     // false
```

In almost all cases, you should use `===` and `!==`. They're more predictable than `==` and `!=` and help prevent bugs caused by automatic type conversions, especially when you're dealing with values from the DOM, user input, or layout calculations.

Because `+` can either add or concatenate, and `==` can convert types, you may run into bugs when comparing values that come from different sources, such as user input (which is often a string) or the server:

```
let input = "100";
let width = 100;

console.log(input == width);     // true (yikes!)
console.log(input === width);    // false (nice!)
```

If you expect numeric input, convert the value first:

```
let numericInput = Number(input);
console.log(numericInput === width);    ← true
```

This is especially important when comparing values used for positioning, dimensions, or animation timing. (Refer to section 2.2.7 to learn about the `Number()` function.)

Comparison operators are at the heart of your app's logic, whether you're checking element sizes, setting breakpoints, or triggering animations. Use strict equality and type-safe comparisons to keep your code predictable and easier to debug.

### 2.1.4 JavaScript logical expressions

You use *logical expressions* to combine or manipulate Boolean values, particularly comparison expressions. For example, if your code needs to test whether two different comparison expressions are both `true` before proceeding, you can do that with a logical expression.

Table 2.4 lists JavaScript's logical operators.

**Table 2.4 JavaScript logical operators**

| Operator | Name | General Syntax | Returned Value |
|---|---|---|---|
| && | AND | *expr1 && expr2* | `true` if both *expr1* and *expr2* are truthy; `false` otherwise (refer to the next section to learn about truthy and falsy in JavaScript) |
| \|\| | OR | *expr1 \|\| expr2* | `true` if one or both of *expr1* and *expr2* are truthy; `false` otherwise |
| ! | NOT | *!expr* | `true` if *expr* is `falsy`; `false` if *expr* is truthy |
| ?? | Nullish coalescing | *expr1 ?? expr2* | *expr2* if *expr1* is `null` or `undefined`; `expr1` otherwise |

Boolean values are the simplest of all JavaScript's literal data types because they can assume only one of two values: `true` or `false`. Booleans are extremely useful because being able to test whether a particular variable or condition is `true` or `false` is invaluable in JavaScript programming.

You can assign Boolean literals directly to a variable, like this:

```
taskCompleted = true;
```

Alternatively, you can work with Boolean values implicitly using expressions:

```
currentMonth === "August"
```

### 2.1.5 Falsy values, default values, and nullish coalescing

In JavaScript, a *falsy* value is any value that's treated the same as `false` in a Boolean context. The following values are falsy:

- `false` (the Boolean value)
- `0` (the number zero)
- `-0` (negative zero)
- `0n` (BigInt zero)
- `""` or `''` (the empty string)
- `null` (the absence of any object value)
- `undefined` (for example, the "value" of an uninitialized variable)
- `NaN` ("Not a Number")
- `document.all` (all of the current document's elements [deprecated])

Everything else in JavaScript is treated as *truthy*, which refers to any value that's treated the same as `true` in a Boolean context.

These falsy values come in handy when you need to assign a default value. Given some value—which might come directly from a user or from data fetched from the server—you want to use that value if it's not falsy; otherwise, you want to assign a default value.

The standard way to accomplish this is to use the `||` (Or) operator:

```
const userName = inputName || 'Anonymous';
```

This statement says: "If `inputName` is falsy, use the default name `Anonymous`, instead; if `inputName` is not falsy, use the value of `inputName`. For example, if your page has a text box for the user to enter a name and the user leaves the text box blank, the value of the input will be `""` (the empty string), which is falsy, so your code will assign the default name `Anonymous`.

That works fine in many cases, but what if in your app the empty string is a legit value? Or what if `0` or `false` are valid values for you? For these kinds of situations, you need to replace `||` with `??`, the nullish coalescing operator. The `??` operator returns the value to its right only if the value to its left is `null` or `undefined`. That is, it ignores falsy values such as `false`, `0`, and `""`:

```
const userName = inputName ?? 'Anonymous';
```

In this case, if the user leaves the text box blank so that the value of the input is `""`, the value of username is set to `""` since the empty string is not `null` or `undefined`.

### 2.1.6 Operator precedence

As in regular math, JavaScript follows operator precedence rules when evaluating expressions. Some operators are evaluated before others, unless you explicitly group them using parentheses.

Table 2.5 lists the order of operations for every JavaScript operator (including a few not covered in this book). In the Precedence column, the higher the value, the greater the precedence.

**Table 2.5 JavaScript operator order of precedence**

| Precedence | Operator(s) | Description | Order of evaluation |
|---|---|---|---|
| 21 | `( )` | Grouping (parentheses) | n/a |
| 20 | `new` | Object instantiation | right-to-left |
| 19 | `., [], (), ?.` | Member access, computed member, call, optional chaining | left-to-right |
| 18 | `new` (without arguments) | Object instantiation | right-to-left |
| 17 | `++, --` | Post-increment, post-decrement | left-to-right |
| 16 | `+, -, ~, !, delete, void, typeof` | Unary operators | right-to-left |
| 15 | `**` | Exponentiation | right-to-left |
| 14 | `*, /, %` | Multiplication, division, remainder | left-to-right |
| 13 | `+, -` | Addition, subtraction | left-to-right |
| 12 | `<<, >>, >>>` | Bitwise shifts | left-to-right |
| 11 | `<, <=, >, >=, in, instanceof` | Comparisons | left-to-right |
| 10 | `==, !=, ===, !==` | Equality | left-to-right |
| 9 | `&` | Bitwise AND | left-to-right |
| 8 | `^` | Bitwise XOR | left-to-right |
| 7 | `\|` | Bitwise OR | left-to-right |
| 6 | `&&` | Logical AND | left-to-right |
| 5 | `\|\|` | Logical OR | left-to-right |
| 4 | `??` | Nullish coalescing | left-to-right |
| 3 | `?:` | Ternary conditional | right-to-left |
| 2 | `=, +=, -=, *=, /=, etc.` | Assignment | right-to-left |
| 1 | `,` | Comma (sequence) | left-to-right |

### 2.1.7 *Using parentheses to avoid ambiguity*

In Table 2.5, notice that parentheses appear right at the top, meaning they have the highest precedence in any JavaScript expression. That's awesome because even when the math is simple, parentheses help clarify your intent and prevent subtle bugs when refactoring or combining expressions.

Compare these two expressions:

```
let resultA = 100 / 2 + 10;
let resultB = 100 / (2 + 10);
```

**60**

**8.333...**

Adding parentheses makes your logic easier to read and avoids surprises, especially in style-related calculations such as spacing, scaling, or breakpoints:

```
let sidebarWidth = (containerWidth - gutter * 2) / 3;
```

Without parentheses, this kind of math can easily go wrong, especially when chaining multiple operators or mixing strings and numbers (for example, `+` can mean addition or it can mean string concatenation).

**EXERCISES**

**Exercise 2.1:** What value is stored in the `result` variable in the following JavaScript statement?

```
let result = 10 + 4 * 2 ** 2;
```

1. 64
2. 26
3. 36
4. 18

**Exercise 2.2:** Consider the following code:

```
let a = 1;
let b = 2;
a += b * 3;
console.log(a)
```

What value of `a` is written to the console?

## 2.2 Number types in JavaScript

In all programming languages, a variable's *data type* specifies what kind of data is stored in that variable. Common data types include strings (such as `"Hello, World!"`), booleans (`true` or `false`), objects, and, of course, numbers. In most programming languages, a numeric variable can assume one of a handful of different types: integers, floats, doubles, decimals, and so on. But JavaScript takes a simpler (and sometimes more confusing) approach.

To see what I mean, first know that in JavaScript you can use the `typeof` operator to return the data type of a variable or literal. Here are some examples that you can type into a console (such as the Console pane of your favorite browser's devtools or, if you have Node.js installed, at the Node REPL (type `node` and press Enter or Return):

```
typeof 'Hello, World!'
typeof true
typeof Math
typeof 42
typeof 3.14159
typeof 7.6543e+21
typeof NaN
typeof Infinity
```

**Returns 'string'**
**Returns 'boolean'**
**Returns 'object'**
**Returns 'number'**
**Returns 'number'**
**Returns 'number'**
**Returns 'number'**
**Returns 'number'**

Well, look at that: whether the numeric literal is an integer, floating-point number, uses exponential notation, or is the global property `NaN` or `Infinity` (more on these shortly; refer to section 2.2.4), the data type is the same: `number`. In fact, almost *all* numbers in JavaScript are of the data type `number`. (The other numeric data type in JavaScript is called `BigInt` and I talk about it a bit later in this chapter; refer to section 2.4.) That one type covers both whole numbers (integers) and decimal numbers (floating-point values). Understanding how this unified system works is crucial to avoiding surprises in your code, especially when you're doing layout calculations, animations, or any sort of precision math in the browser.

> **NOTE** If you run `typeof null` in the Node REPL, the result is `'object'`. Wait, what!? This is one of JavaScript's most famous quirks and it's a bug that dates to the very first implementation way back in 1995. Why hasn't it been fixed? Because there are just too many websites that would break! So, if your code needs to know whether something is an honest-to-goodness object, then you need to check for `null`, just to be safe: `if (value !== null && typeof value === "object") {...}`.

### 2.2.1 Integer and floating-point numbers

JavaScript treats all numbers the same, true, but what that really means is that JavaScript treats all numbers as floating-point values. Specifically, JavaScript uses 64-bit floating numbers based on the IEEE 754 standard. In practice, this means that your JavaScript code can use the same operators to perform calculations on both integers and floating-point values:

```
2 + 3
2.2 + 3.7
```

**5**
**5.9**

However, it does put a limit on the maximum and minimum integer values that your code can work with while still maintaining precision. Anything beyond these limits is considered *unsafe* in the sense that the calculation results are no longer guaranteed to be correct. These limits are defined in JavaScript's `Number` object as the `MAX_SAFE_INTEGER` and `MIN_SAFE_INTEGER` properties:

```
Number.MAX_SAFE_INTEGER         ◄── 9007199254740991
Number.MIN_SAFE_INTEGER         ◄── -9007199254740991
```

(Where do these seemingly arbitrary values come from? JavaScript uses 64-bit floating-point numbers, but several of those bits are used for the sign and exponent, leaving 53 bits left over. With 53 bits, you can exactly represent every integer from $-(2^{53} - 1)$ to $2^{53} - 1$, which is –9007199254740991 to 9007199254740991.)

If you try to use a number outside this safe range, the number can be represented, but not reliably distinguished from nearby values thanks to JavaScript's precision limits. The following listing provides a code snippet to prove it:

**Listing 2.1 Working with unsafe integers**

```
console.log(`The maximum safe integer is ${Number.MAX_SAFE_INTEGER}`);
const unsafeNum1 = Number.MAX_SAFE_INTEGER + 1;
const unsafeNum2 = Number.MAX_SAFE_INTEGER + 2;
console.log(`The maximum safe integer plus 1 is ${unsafeNum1}`);
console.log(`The maximum safe integer plus 2 is ${unsafeNum2}`);
```

Here's the output:

```
The maximum safe integer is 9007199254740991
The maximum safe integer plus 1 is 9007199254740992
The maximum safe integer plus 2 is 9007199254740992
```

> **NOTE** All the code for this chapter's listings is available in this book's GitHub repository: https://github.com/paulmcfe/web-dev-math.

As shown in the final two lines, JavaScript is happy to work with unsafe numbers, but the result will often not be what you expect!

> **TIP** To check whether a value is within the safe range, you can use the `Number` object's `isSafeInteger(value)` method, which returns `true` if *`value`* is a safe integer:

```
Number.isSafeInteger(42)                              ◄── true
Number.isSafeInteger(Number.MAX_SAFE_INTEGER + 1)     ◄── false
```

JavaScript's use of 64-bit floating-point numbers means that even seemingly simple whole numbers are stored in a way that allows for fractions and very large or very small values. But this flexibility comes with a tradeoff: JavaScript can't represent every decimal number precisely. You'll see how that plays out in practice later in this chapter when I discuss floating-point precision issues (refer to section 2.3).

### 2.2.2 Exponential notation

In your JavaScript code, you can use exponential notation, an efficient way to represent very large or very small floating-point numbers. Exponential notation uses a number—known as the *mantissa* or *fraction*—then an `e` (or `E`) followed by the *exponent*, which is a number preceded by a plus sign (`+`) or a minus sign (`-`).

You multiply the mantissa by 10 to the power of the exponent. Here's an example:

```
1.23456e+5
```

The exponent is 5, and 10 to the power of 5 is 100,000. So, multiplying 1.23456 by 100,000 results in the value 123,456.

Here's another example:

```
9.8765e-4;
```

The exponent is –4, and 10 to the power of –4 is 0.0001. So, multiplying 9.8765 by 0.0001 results in the value .00098765.

### 2.2.3 Binary, octal, and hexadecimal representations

Besides the familiar base-10 (decimal) numbers, JavaScript also supports numbers in binary (base-2), octal (base-8), and hexadecimal (base-16) formats. These aren't used often in frontend work, but they're good to know, especially when dealing with color values, bitwise operations, or low-level animation math.

Binary numbers start with `0b`, octal numbers start with `0o`, and hexadecimal numbers start with `0x`:

```
let bin = 0b1010;
let oct = 0o17;
let hex = 0xFF;
```

**10 in decimal**

**15 in decimal**

**255 in decimal**

Whether your code uses binary, octal, or hexadecimal, the number gets converted to a base-10 number behind the scenes, so you can use these different representations in any math operation. For example, you can add `0b1010 + 0xFF + 5` and the result will be `270`.

### 2.2.4 *NaN and Infinity in JavaScript*

JavaScript includes two special numeric values that will come up occasionally whenever you deal with numbers in your code: `NaN` and `Infinity`.

### 2.2.5 *NaN*

`NaN` stands for "Not a Number," and it shows up when a mathematical operation fails in a way that doesn't throw an error but also doesn't produce a valid result:

```
let whoops = 0 / 0;
let fail = Math.sqrt(-1);
let doh = parseInt("Three");
let oy = Number("123abc");
let uhoh = 0 * Infinity;
```

**All these expressions return NaN**

What makes `NaN` a head-scratcher is that it's the only value in JavaScript that's not equal to itself:

```
console.log(NaN === NaN);      // false!
```

**TIP** To check whether a value is NaN, you can use `Number.isNaN(value)`:

```
console.log(Number.isNaN(NaN));        // true
console.log(Number.isNaN(0 / 0));      // true
console.log(Number.isNaN("hello"));    // false
```

The `Number.isNaN()` method is helpful when you're dealing with user input, form values, or dynamically calculated dimensions that could blow up in unexpected ways.

### 2.2.6 *Infinity and –Infinity*

Although `MAX_SAFE_INTEGER` and `MIN_SAFE_INTEGER` represent the largest and smallest integer values that are safe to use, JavaScript can actually represent much larger values, given by the `Number` object's `MAX_VALUE` property:

```
Number.MAX_VALUE       // 1.7976931348623157e+308
-Number.MAX_VALUE      // –1.7976931348623157e+308
```

`Infinity` and `-Infinity` represent values that go beyond these numeric limits:

```
let wait = 1 / 0;                     // Infinity
let what = -1 / 0;                    // –Infinity
let tooMuch = Number.MAX_VALUE * 2;   // Infinity
let yikes = Math.pow(10, 1000)        // Infinity
```

These values don't crash your program, but they often indicate something's gone wrong (or at least unexpected) in your math.

**TIP** To check for values that are within JavaScript's limits, you can use `Number.isFinite(value)`, which checks whether *`value`* is a finite number (that is, not `Infinity` or `-Infinity`):

```
console.log(Number.isFinite(100));
console.log(Number.isFinite(1 / 0));
console.log(Number.isFinite(Infinity));
```

**true**
**false**
**false**

### 2.2.7 Number coercion

JavaScript is a loosely typed language, which means it often tries to convert one type of value into another automatically. This is known as *type coercion*, and it frequently happens when numbers are involved.

Here are a few examples of number coercion in action:

```
console.log("5" * 2);
console.log("5" + 2);
console.log(true + 1);
```

**10 (string is coerced to number)**
**"52" (string concatenation, not addition)**
**2 (true is coerced to 1)**

This behavior can be helpful or dangerous depending on your expectations! When dealing with layout math or animation timing, it's often best to explicitly convert values using `+` (the unary operator), `Number()`, `parseInt()`, or `parseFloat()` to avoid bugs caused by unexpected coercion:

```
let meaning = +"42";
let toggle = Number(true);
let width = parseInt("20em");
let typeSize = parseFloat("32.5px");
```

**42**
**1**
**20**
**32.5**

With a clear understanding of how JavaScript treats numbers, you'll be in a better position to write reliable, bug-resistant code, especially when working on visual or interactive features that depend on precise math.

#### EXERCISES

**Exercise 2.3:** What is the result of the following?

```
typeof NaN
```

1. number
2. NaN
3. undefined

**Exercise 2.4:** What will the following log to the console?

```
console.log(Number.MAX_SAFE_INTEGER + 1 === Number.MAX_SAFE_INTEGER + 2)
```

**Exercise 2.5:** The following code prompts for a restaurant bill total, calculates a 15 percent tip, then calculates and displays the total of the bill:

```
let input = prompt("Enter the restaurant bill amount:");
let tip = input * 1.15;
let billTotal = input + tip;
console.log(billTotal);
```

If the user enters `20`, here's the total that's displayed in the console:

```
2023
```

Can you spot the problem?

## 2.3 Precision issues and floating-point arithmetic

In a browser devtools console or a Node.js REPL, type the following and press Enter or Return:

```
0.1 + 0.2 === 0.3
```

Here's the output:

```
false
```

Wait! What? How can that be? It looks like some kind of mistake. Have you discovered a bug in JavaScript? Nope. That perplexing result would hold true in most programming languages, not just JavaScript, because that's just how floating-point numbers work. Once you understand why this happens, you'll be much better prepared to handle it in your own code.

### 2.3.1 Why 0.1 + 0.2 !== 0.3

JavaScript stores all its regular numbers as 64-bit floating-point values, following the IEEE 754 standard. This format can only approximate most decimal fractions. In particular, some numbers—including 0.1 and 0.2—can't be represented exactly in binary.

Consider, once again, the following expression:

```
0.1 + 0.2
```

JavaScript does the math in binary, where `0.1` and `0.2` don't have exact binary equivalents. They're actually repeating fractions in base 2, much like 1/3 = 0.333... in base 10. `0.1` in binary looks like this:

```
0.00011001100110011001100110011001100110011001100110011...
```

This repeats forever, so it must be cut off and rounded, and the stored decimal approximation is:

```
0.1000000000000000055511151231257827021181583404541015625
```

Similarly, `0.2` in binary looks like this:

```
0.0011001100110011001100110011001100110011001100110011...
```

This also repeats forever, so the rounded approximation in decimal is:

```
0.200000000000000011102230246251565404236316680908203125
```

To get `0.1 + 0.2`, JavaScript adds the approximations:

```
0.1000000000000000055... +
0.2000000000000000111...
```

Here's the result:

```
0.3000000000000000444089209850062616169452667236328125
```

Therefore, `0.1 + 0.2 === 0.3` returns `false`.

What can you do about this? If you come across this sort of situation, you can take advantage of the `Number` object's `EPSILON` property, which represents the smallest gap between 1 and the next representable number. `Number.EPSILON` is equal to $2^{-52}$, or about `2.220446049250313080847263336181 6e-16`. Using this value, you can test whether two numbers are "close enough":

```
Math.abs((0.1 + 0.2) - 0.3) < Number.EPSILON    ◄── true
```

This issue isn't just academic because it can cause real problems when comparing values, setting dimensions, or triggering UI changes based on calculations.

### 2.3.2 When to be concerned about precision

Precision issues won't bite you in every project, but when they do, it's usually in one of these areas:

- Animation timing or easing functions
- Layout spacing and element alignment

- Visual snapping and rounding
- Financial calculations or pricing interfaces
- Any place where decimals are compared directly

When in doubt, round your values (refer to section 2.6), compare them using an `EPSILON` "close enough" margin, or format them for display using a specified number of decimal places (check out section 2.6.2).

With a solid understanding of how floating-point numbers work, and how to tame them, you'll avoid a ton of subtle bugs that can be really hard to track down, especially in UI code where things "almost" line up but don't quite. (We've all been there!)

**EXERCISE**

**Exercise 2.6:** Write a function `isRoughlyEqual(a, b)` that returns `true` if the difference between `a` and `b` is less than `Number.EPSILON`.

## 2.4 Working with BigInt values

JavaScript's maximum safe integer value is around nine *quadrillion*. That's nine thousand trillion or nine million billion. It is, in short, a more-or-less unfathomably large number. It's so large, in fact, that you might be tempted to think that you'll never come close to it in your web development work. You're probably right, but what if you need to work with numbers from scientific APIs, financial data, cryptography, timestamps, or even numeric IDs from the backend? You can't be sure that any of the numbers you work with from these and similar sources won't be larger than `MAX_SAFE_INTEGER` (or smaller than `MIN_SAFE_INTEGER`), which means you can't be sure if your code is producing precise results. Not good!

### 2.4.1 BigInt to the rescue

If there's even a small chance that your code will need to handle "unsafe" integer values, then you need to go beyond the standard `number` data type and work with BigInt values, instead. The `bigint` data type is designed to handle arbitrarily large integers and, in particular, to handle integers that are larger than `MAX_SAFE_INTEGER` or smaller than `MIN_SAFE_INTEGER`.

You create a BigInt by adding an `n` to the end of an integer, or by using the `BigInt()` constructor:

```
const regular = 9007199254740991;      // Maximum safe integer (2 ^ 53 – 1)
const tooBig = 9007199254740992;       // Not safe
const safeBig = 9007199254740992n;     // Safe as a BigInt

const fromString = BigInt("123456789012345678901234567890");
```

The key benefit of BigInt is that it can safely store very large integers that `number` can't handle accurately. For example, check out the code in the following listing:

**Listing 2.2 Working with BigInt values**

```
const previousMax = BigInt(Number.MAX_SAFE_INTEGER);
const noLongerUnsafe1 = previousMax + 1n;
const noLongerUnsafe2 = previousMax + 2n;
console.log(`The old maximum safe integer: ${previousMax}`);
console.log(`The old maximum plus 1 equals ${noLongerUnsafe1}`);
console.log(`The old maximum plus 2 equals ${noLongerUnsafe2}`);
```

Here's the output:

```
The old maximum safe integer: 9007199254740991
The old maximum plus 1 equals 9007199254740992
The old maximum plus 2 equals 9007199254740993
```

With BigInt values, your large-integer calculations are precise because BigInt doesn't suffer from the limitations of the `number` data type.

### 2.4.2 Mathematical operations with BigInt

You can use BigInts with most basic arithmetic operators (the main exception is the unary (+) operator, which can't be used with BigInt values). The key rule for arithmetic operation is that you can't mix regular numbers with BigInt values in an expression. For example, the following raises a `TypeError`:

```
console.log(5n + 1);
Uncaught TypeError: Cannot mix BigInt and other types,
use explicit conversions
```

"Explicit conversions" in the error message means using either the `BigInt()` constructor or tacking `n` onto the end of an integer literal. The following listing shows a few example operations with BigInt values.

**Listing 2.3 Mathematical operations with BigInt values**

```
const a = 20000000000000000n;
const b = 30000000000000000n;

console.log(a + b);
console.log(b - a);
console.log(b * 2n);
console.log(b / a);
console.log(b % a);
console.log(a ** 2n)
```

- `console.log(a + b);` → **50000000000000000n**
- `console.log(b - a);` → **10000000000000000n**
- `console.log(b * 2n);` → **60000000000000000n**
- `console.log(b / a);` → **1n (truncated because integer!)**
- `console.log(b % a);` → **10000000000000000n**
- `console.log(a ** 2n)` → **400000000000000000000000000000000n**

For the expression `b / a` in listing 2.3, you might expect the result to be `1.5n`, but there are no floating-point values allowed in BigInt world, which is an integers-only place.

When BigInt comes across a floating-point value, it truncates the fractional part of the value.

> **REMEMBER** Although you can't mix `number` and `bigint` types in arithmetic operations, it's totally fine to mix these types in comparison expressions.

### 2.4.3 Limitations of BigInt in JavaScript

BigInt is powerful, but it doesn't work everywhere. Some built-in JavaScript features don't support it:

- You can't use BigInt in `Math` methods:

```
Math.sqrt(25n);        ◄— TypeError
```

- It doesn't play well with `JSON.stringify()`:

```
JSON.stringify({ value: 5n });     ◄— TypeError: BigInt value can't be serialized
```

- It doesn't automatically work with DOM APIs or CSS, which expect regular numbers.

That's why you'll mostly use BigInt for calculations behind the scenes, not for anything involving visual rendering.

### 2.4.4 When to avoid BigInt in web development

While BigInt solves the precision problem for large integers, it's not a drop-in replacement for `number`. You should avoid BigInt if

- You need to use the value in animations, styles, or layout (for example, `element.style.width = "500npx"` won't work).
- You plan to serialize the value as JSON or store it in `localStorage`.
- You don't need to go beyond the safe integer limits.

In most cases, regular numbers are more than good enough for UI work. But if you ever need to deal with really big integers, BigInt gives you peace of mind that your math won't silently fail.

**EXERCISES**

**Exercise 2.7:** Create a function `isSafeInt()` that accepts either a `number` or a `bigint` data type and returns `true` if the value is within the safe integer range.

**Exercise 2.8:** Why does the following throw a `TypeError`:

```
console.log(9007199254740991n + 10);
```

## 2.5 Modulo logic and wrapping values

Have you ever needed to cycle through a list of items, loop back to the start of a slider, or keep animation values within a certain range? That's where modulo logic comes in. The remainder operator (`%`) is often used for these kinds of wrapping behaviors, but it doesn't always behave the way you expect in JavaScript, especially with negative numbers.

This section shows you how to use remainder safely and effectively, so you can build reliable, looping interfaces and animations.

### 2.5.1 JavaScript's remainder operator (%) and modulo

The *mathematical modulo* operation gives you the remainder after dividing one number—the *dividend*—by another number—the *divisor*. In number theory, the remainder is always positive, but programming languages usually diverge from theory by specifying that the remainder have the same sign as either the dividend or the divisor. JavaScript's remainder operator (`%`) returns a negative value if the dividend is negative, but let's see how that can produce unintuitive behavior for cyclical use cases.

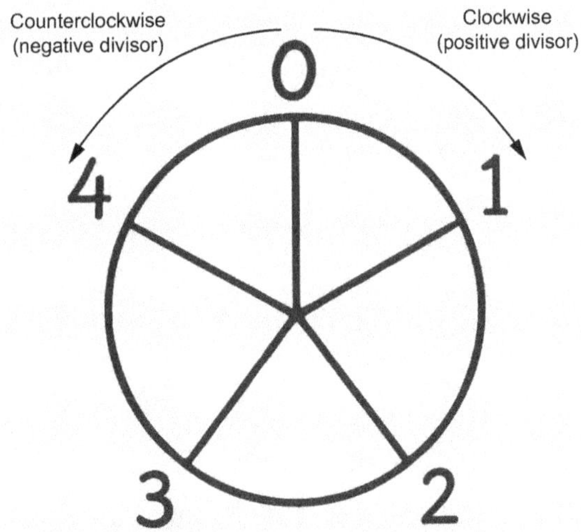


**Figure 2.1 Modulo logic is like moving around a circle.**

Begin by assuming that the remainder has the same sign as the divisor. Think of it as wrapping around a circle like the one shown in figure 2.1, which contains 5 items (0 through 4).

First, imagine that the default order to move around the circle is clockwise, which implies a positive divisor. In that case, you get results such as the following:

- If you start at position 0 and move clockwise 5 items, you end up back at item 0: `5 mod 5 = 0` (where `mod` is short for mathematical modulo).
- If you start at position 0 and move clockwise 6 items, you circle around and end up at item 1: `6 mod 5 = 1`.
- If you start at position 0 and move counterclockwise 1 item, you end up at item 4: `-1 mod 5 = 4`.

Now imagine that the default order to move around the circle is counterclockwise, which implies a negative divisor. In that case, you get results such as the following:

- If you start at position 0 and move clockwise 2 items, you end up at item 2, which in the counterclockwise order is represented as –3: `2 mod -5 = -3`.
- If you start at position 0 and move clockwise 6 items, you circle around and end up at item 1, which in the counterclockwise order is represented as –4: `6 mod -5 = -4`.
- If you start at position 0 and move counterclockwise 1 item, you end up at item 4, which in the counterclockwise order is represented as –1: `-1 mod -5 = -1`.

That's all intuitively reasonable when you think of modulo as wrapping around a circle. But look what happens when you use JavaScript's remainder operator (`%`) for each of the above movements around the circle:

```
console.log(5 % 5)      ← 0 (so far, so good)
console.log(6 % 5)      ← 1 (smooth sailing)
console.log(-1 % 5)     ← −1 (wait, what?)
```

As that last example demonstrates, the remainder operator doesn't return an intuitively reasonable result when you have a cyclical use case. And that can be a real problem if, say, you're implementing an image carousel and you're using the remainder operation results as the index for an array of image file names. A negative result is going to play havoc with your code.

To get a modulo that returns a result that has the same sign as the divisor, you can use this utility function:

```
function mod(dividend, divisor) {
    return ((dividend % divisor) + divisor) % divisor;
}
```

This function works because adding `divisor` to the result of `dividend % divisor` always returns a value with the same sign as `divisor`; applying `% divisor` to that value returns a final result with the same sign as that value.

Here are some example outputs:

```
console.log(mod(5, 5));      ← 0
console.log(mod(6, 5));      ← 1
console.log(mod(-1, 5));     ← 4
console.log(mod(2, -5));     ← −3
console.log(mod(6, -5));     ← −4
console.log(mod(-1, -5));    ← −1
```

This is the function you should use instead of the remainder operator (`%`) when building any of the following:

- Carousel images
- Tab panels
- Color palettes
- Pagination controls
- Looping animation frames

This kind of logic shows up a lot in UI development, and once you start using true mathematical modulo, you'll wonder how you ever lived without it.

### 2.5.2 Wrapping logic in carousels, sliders, and cyclic UI

The following listing presents an example that implements a simple image carousel using true modulo operations.

**Listing 2.4 Using a true modulo to wrap an image carousel**

```
<body>
    <h1>Listing 2.4-Using a true modulo to wrap an image carousel</h1>
    <img id="imageDisplay"
         src="../images/one.png"
         alt="Image Viewer">
    <br>
    <button id="backButton">Back</button>
    <button id="forwardButton">Forward</button>
    <script>
        const images = ["one.png", "two.png", "three.png",
                        "four.png", "five.png"];
        let currentIndex = 0;

        function mod(current, length) {
            return ((current % length) + length) % length;
        }

        const imageDisplay = document.getElementById("imageDisplay");

        document.getElementById("backButton")
                .addEventListener("click", function () {
            currentIndex = mod(currentIndex - 1,
➥ images.length);
            imageDisplay.src = '../images/' + images[currentIndex];
        });

        document.getElementById("forwardButton")
                .addEventListener("click", function () {
            currentIndex = mod(currentIndex + 1,
➥ images.length);
            imageDisplay.src = '../images/' + images[currentIndex];
        });
    </script>
</body>
```

img element

Back and Forward buttons

Array of image filenames

Utility function to return a true modulo

Click event handler for the Back button

Click event handler for the Forward button

Move forward: increment index, wrap if needed

Move backward: decrement index, wrap if needed

The code adds an `img` element and two `button` elements: one for cycling backward through the images, and one for cycling forward. The JavaScript stores the image filenames in an array named `images`, sets the initial index value (`currentIndex`), and then includes the `mod()` utility function for returning a true modulo. Finally, the code sets up two event listeners to handle clicks on the Back and Forward buttons, with both handlers using the `mod()` function to ensure that the array index value wraps correctly.

**EXERCISES**

**Exercise 2.9:** What does `-1 % 5` return in JavaScript?

1. 4
2. –4
3. 1
4. –1

**Exercise 2.10:** Why would a carousel loop crash on certain back-button clicks if the loop included the following index update code?

```
index = (index - 1) % items.length;
```

## 2.6 Rounding numbers

When working with layouts, animations, or any kind of user-facing number formatting, it's common to run into situations where you need to round a number. JavaScript gives you several built-in ways to round values, each with slightly different behavior.

In this section, you learn how to round numbers up, down, or to the nearest whole number; how to control decimal precision, how to handle special cases like bankers' rounding; and when you'll use rounding most often in your web development work.

### 2.6.1 Rounding to whole numbers

JavaScript offers three main methods for rounding numbers, plus a fourth method for removing the fractional part of a number. These functions are listed in Table 2.6.

**Table 2.6 JavaScript rounding methods**

| Function | Behavior | Examples | Results |
|---|---|---|---|
| `Math.round(n)` | Rounds *n* to the nearest whole number | `Math.round(2.5)` | 3 |
| | | `Math.round(2.4)` | 2 |
| | | `Math.round(-2.6)` | -3 |
| | | `Math.round(-2.5)` | -2 |
| | | `Math.round(-2.4)` | -2 |

**Table 2.6 JavaScript rounding methods (*continued*)**

| Function | Behavior | Examples | Results |
|---|---|---|---|
| `Math.floor(n)` | Rounds *n* down (toward $-\infty$) | `Math.floor(2.9)` | 2 |
| | | `Math.floor(-2.9)` | -3 |
| `Math.ceil(n)` | Rounds *n* up (toward $+\infty$) | `Math.ceil(2.1)` | 3 |
| | | `Math.ceil(-2.1)` | -2 |
| `Math.trunc(n)` | Removes the fractional part of *n* | `Math.trunc(2.4)` | 2 |

These methods are useful for layout calculations where you're working in pixel units and need to avoid fractional values:

```
let width = Math.floor(containerWidth / 3);
```

When you're working with any of the rounding methods, you need to pay attention to the *direction* of the rounding because it's not always obvious. For example, the rounding direction of `Math.round()` depends on the value of the fractional part:

- *If the fractional part is exactly .5*—`Math.round(n)` rounds up toward $+\infty$. (This is true even if *n* is negative, which is why `Math.round(-2.5)` rounds to `-2`.)
- *If the fractional part is less than .5*—`Math.round(n)` rounds toward 0.
- *If the fractional part is greater than .5*—`Math.round(n)` rounds away from 0 (that is greater if *n* is positive, more negative if *n* is negative).

Note, too, that the behavior of `Math.floor()` and `Math.ceil()` is perhaps a tad unintuitive for negative numbers:

```
Math.floor(-2.3);     ← −3
Math.ceil(-2.3);      ← −2
```

You'll mostly use whole-number rounding in your web dev work, but there are plenty of use cases for rounding to specific decimals, and I cover that topic next.

### 2.6.2 Rounding to a specific number of decimal places

When you're displaying numbers in a UI, you'll often want to control the number of decimal places the user sees. To gain that control, you can use the `.toFixed()` or `.toPrecision()` method:

- `number.toFixed(digits)`: Returns a string with *number* rounded to *digits* decimal places. If you omit `digits`, the default value of `0` is used.
- `number.toPrecision(digits)`: Returns a string with *number* rounded to *digits* significant digits, which includes both sides of the decimal point.

Here are some examples:

```
let num = 123.456;
console.log(num.toFixed(2));          "123.46"
console.log(num.toPrecision(4));      "123.5"
```

Both methods return a string, not a number, so if you want to continue using the result numerically, you need to convert it back to a number:

```
let num = 123.456;
console.log(parseFloat(num.toFixed(2)));        123.46
console.log(parseFloat(num.toPrecision(4)));    123.5
```

The `.toFixed()` method is great for display purposes, like formatting currency or showing a precise measurement in a tooltip. The `.toPrecision()` method is useful when working with values that span multiple orders of magnitude, such as scientific data or logarithmic scales.

### 2.6.3 Implementing bankers' rounding

*Bankers' rounding* (also called *round half to even*) is a rounding strategy used in financial calculations to reduce bias over many roundings. Bankers' rounding is applied as follows:

- If a number is exactly halfway between two whole numbers, the number is rounded to the nearest even whole number.
- For any other number, the number is rounded to the nearest whole number.

Table 2.7 lists some examples:

**Table 2.7 A few examples of bankers' rounding**

| Number | Bankers' rounding |
|---|---|
| 1.5 | 2 |
| 3.5 | 4 |
| -1.5 | -2 |
| -3.5 | -4 |
| 1.6 | 2 |
| 1.4 | 1 |

JavaScript's `Math.round()` method doesn't use bankers' rounding. It always rounds `.5` values up toward +∞. If you're building a finance-related UI or doing statistical reporting where bias matters, you may need to implement custom rounding logic that performs bankers' rounding. The following listing presents a JavaScript function that performs bankers' rounding.

**Listing 2.5 Implementing bankers' rounding in JavaScript**

```
function bankersRound(num) {
    const integer = Math.floor(num);      Get integer part of number
```

```
    const fraction = num - integer;                  ◄── Get fractional part of number

    if (fraction === 0.5 || fraction === -0.5) {
        return (integer % 2 === 0)
            ? integer                                 If integer part is even,
            : integer + Math.sign(num);               return integer part...
    } else {
        return Math.round(num);          ◄── ...otherwise, round to
    }                                        nearest even number.
}
```

This function first gets the integer and fractional parts of the passed number. Then the code tests the fractional part to check whether it's exactly `0.5` or `-0.5`. If it is, the function checks whether the integer part of `num` is even:

- If the integer part is even, that's the closest even number to `num`, so the integer part is returned.
- If the integer part is odd, then the closest even number will be the `integer + 1` if `num` is positive, or `integer - 1` if `num` is negative. This is handled in the function using `Math.sign(num)`, which returns `1` when `num` is positive or `-1` when `num` is negative.

For all other cases (that is, all numbers where the fractional part is not `0.5` or `-0.5`), the function falls back to regular `Math.round()`.

### 2.6.4 Use cases for rounding in frontend development

Here are a few examples where rounding comes into play in real-world frontend work:

- *Pixel-perfect layouts*—Round widths to whole pixels to prevent blurry edges.

  ```
  let columnWidth = Math.round(containerWidth / 3);
  ```

- *Responsive typography*—Keep scale-based decimal font sizes from getting out of hand by rounding them to some fixed number of decimal places.

  ```
  let fontSize = parseFloat((baseSize * scale).toFixed(2));
  ```

- *Currency formatting*—For currency amounts, always show two decimals, even for whole numbers.

  ```
  let display = "$" + amount.toFixed(2);
  ```

- *Progress indicators*—It's usually best to display whole-number percentages when showing the progress of an operation.

  ```
  let percent = Math.round((current / total) * 100) + "%";
  ```

Rounding is one of those small things that can have a big visual impact. Knowing which rounding method to use and how to control the result is essential for making your UI feel polished, accurate, and consistent.

**EXERCISES**

**Exercise 2.11:** What does `Math.round(-2.5)` return in JavaScript?

1. –3
2. –2
3. 0
4. NaN

**Exercise 2.12:** The following code is meant to round a price to the nearest integer and format it with a dollar sign:

```
let price = 9.95;
let formatted = "$" + price.toFixed;
console.log(formatted);
```

However, the code doesn't work as expected. Can you spot the error?

## 2.7 Generating random numbers

A *random number* is a number selected in such a way that every value within a defined range has an equal chance of being chosen. In everyday use, such as rolling dice or picking a lottery number, randomness is genuinely unpredictable.

Randomness plays a huge role in modern frontend development. Whether you're animating stars across a sky, shuffling a deck of cards, adding variability to a particle system, or creating organic-looking layouts, being able to generate random numbers is essential.

JavaScript makes it easy to create random values, but there are some important quirks and limitations you need to know, especially if you want predictable or repeatable results.

### 2.7.1 Generating random integers and floats

JavaScript's built-in tool for randomness is `Math.random()`. This method returns a floating-point number in the range [0, 1), which is to say between 0 (inclusive) and 1 (exclusive):

```
console.log(Math.random());
```

Example output: 0.472389123

It's sometimes useful to generate random values between 0 and 1, but most of the time you'll need a different range. To simulate throws of a standard six-sided die, for example, you need to generate random numbers from 1 to 6.

JavaScript has no built-in method for generating a random floating-point number or integer between two values, but you can implement such features in your JavaScript code.

The simplest case is when your lower bound remains at `0` and you want to generate a random floating-point number or integer up to (but not including) some maximum value. In this case, multiply `Math.random()` by that maximum. For example, the following generates a random floating-point value between 0 and 100 (exclusive):

```
let randomFP = Math.random() * 100;
```

Similarly, the following generates a random (integer) index value for an array:

```
let randomIndex = Math.floor(Math.random() * array.length));
```

For a non-zero minimum, the following listing presents a function that generates a random floating-point number between a lower bound (inclusive) and a higher bound (exclusive).

**Listing 2.6 Generating a random floating-point number between two values**

```
function randomFloat(min, max) {
    return Math.random() * (max - min) + min;
}
```

For example, the following call generates a random floating-point number greater than or equal to 5 and less than 10:

```
console.log(randomFloat(5, 10));
```

The next listing offers a function that generates a random integer between a lower bound (inclusive) and a higher bound (inclusive).

**Listing 2.7 Generating a random integer between two values**

```
function randomInt(min, max) {
    return Math.floor(Math.random() * (max - min + 1)) + min;
}
```

Here's an example call:

```
console.log(randomInt(1, 6));
```

This call generates a random integer greater than or equal to 1 and less than or equal to 6, which could be used to simulate rolling a six-sided die.

### 2.7.2 Seeding and repeatable randomness

In programming, most "random" numbers are not truly random. Instead, they're pseudo-random. A *pseudo-random number* is a number that appears random but is actually generated by a deterministic algorithm. In JavaScript, `Math.random()` produces pseudo-random numbers between 0 (inclusive) and 1 (exclusive).

Each `Math.random()` call gives you a different value that appears random, but it's not because each number is generated by an algorithm in which JavaScript uses a specific formula and an internal state (called a *seed*) to produce these values. In fact, `Math.random()` would produce the same sequence of numbers if you were somehow able to run the algorithm using the same internal seed. However, that seed isn't exposed or controllable through the language.

> **WARNING** Just because pseudo-random numbers aren't truly random, it doesn't mean that they're useless. They're perfectly fine when you need random values for games, shuffling arrays, or creating simulations. However, under no circumstances should they be used for cryptography, secure token generation, or password generation.

The fact that `Math.random()` isn't seedable means that you can't control the random sequence and you can't reproduce the same random numbers if you reload or rerun the code. This can be a problem if you need deterministic behavior for testing or repeatable animations or procedural generation.

If your app needs repeatable pseudo-random numbers, then you can roll your own pseudo-random number generator. The following listing demonstrates a very simple pseudo-random generator that's seedable and therefore repeatable.

**Listing 2.8 A simple, seedable pseudo-random number generator**

```
function seedRandom(seed) {
    return function() {
        seed = (seed * 16807) % 2147483647;
        return (seed - 1) / 2147483646;
    };
}
```

This is a basic implementation of a Linear Congruential Generator (LCG), one of the oldest and simplest ways to produce a repeatable pseudo-random number sequence. Each time the inner function is called:

- It multiplies the current seed by 16807, which is a prime number that helps distribute values well.
- It takes the remainder when divided by 2147483647, which is large prime (it's $2^{31} - 1$) that's often used in LCGs.
- It then normalizes the result into the range [0, 1) by dividing by 2147483646.

Because the seed is being reassigned inside the closure, every call updates the internal state, so each result depends on the last one. Let's see how it works. First, you seed the generator:

```
const seededRandom = seedRandom(12345);
```

Now seededRandom() is a function that generates repeatable pseudo-random numbers:

```
console.log(seededRandom());    ← Always 0.09661652808693845
console.log(seededRandom());    ← Always 0.8339946273099581
console.log(seededRandom());    ← Always 0.9477024976608367
console.log(seededRandom());    ← Always 0.035878594532495915
console.log(seededRandom());    ← Always 0.011545852768743274
```

If you need a different set of repeatable, pseudo-random numbers, just change the seed value (any integer from 1 to 2147483647 will work just fine).

### 2.7.3 Use cases in animations and UI behavior

Random numbers show up all over the place in frontend work:

- *Particle animations*—Randomize particle speeds, directions, or sizes.
- *Organic layouts*—Add subtle randomness to spacing or positioning so elements don't look too mechanical.
- *Hover effects*—Trigger random visual changes when a user interacts with an element.
- *Procedural generation*—Create backgrounds, shapes, or decorative elements on the fly.
- *Randomized transitions*—Animate list items with slightly staggered delays.

The following listing presents a quick example of creating a random staggered animation.

**Listing 2.9 A random staggered animation**

```
<body>
    <div class="stagger-item"></div>
    <div class="stagger-item"></div>
    <div class="stagger-item"></div>
    <div class="stagger-item"></div>
    <div class="stagger-item"></div>
    <div class="stagger-item"></div>       Items to animate
    <div class="stagger-item"></div>
    <div class="stagger-item"></div>
    <div class="stagger-item"></div>
    <div class="stagger-item"></div>

    <script>
        function randomFloat(min, max) {
            return Math.random() * (max - min) + min;       Function to generate
        }                                                   a random float

        const items = document.querySelectorAll(            Get all items
➥ ".stagger-item");
```

```
        items.forEach(item => {
            const delay = randomFloat(0, 0.5);

            item.style.transitionDelay =
➥ delay + "s";

            setTimeout(() => {
                item.classList.add("visible");
            }, 100);
        });
    </script>
</body>
```

Get random delay between 0 and 0.5 seconds

Loop through items

Add “visible” class after a short delay

Update item’s transition-delay property

This code sets up ten `div` elements, each with the class `stagger-item` (not shown). The JavaScript includes the `randomFloat()` function for generating random floating-point values. The code then gets all the items with class `stagger-item` and uses a `forEach` loop to iterate through them. For each item, the code generates a random delay between `0` and `0.5`, uses that value to update the item’s `transition-delay` property (adding the string `"s"`, for seconds), then sets a short timeout to ensure the transition has time to apply before adding the `visible` class which makes the item visible:

```
.stagger-item.visible {
    opacity: 1;
    transform: translateY(0);
}
```

**EXERCISES**

**Exercise 2.13:** What is the range of values returned by `Math.random()`?

1 [0, 1]
2 [0, 1)
3 (0, 1]
4 (0, 1)

**Exercise 2.14:** Build a function `getRandomColor()` that returns a random RGB color string, such as `"rgb(123, 45, 67)"`.

## 2.8 Solutions to exercises

**Exercise 2.1:** According to JavaScript’s order of precedence, exponentiation is performed before multiplication, which is performed before addition. So, the correct answer is 26.

**Exercise 2.2:** You might be tempted to think the arithmetic assignment in the final statement is equivalent to this:

```
a = (a + b) * 3
```

That produces the result 9, which is incorrect. Referring to table 2.5, the multiplication operator (*) has a precedence level of 14, while the arithmetic assignment operator (+=) has a lower precedence level of 2. Therefore, JavaScript performs the multiplication first, then the arithmetic assignment:

```
a = a + (b * 3)
```

The correct result is 7.

**Exercise 2.3:** The correct answer is `number`.

**Exercise 2.4:** This will display `true`.

**Exercise 2.5:** The `prompt()` function returns a string value, so `input` stores `"20"` instead of `20`. That's not a problem for the `tip` calculation because in the expression `input * 1.15`, `input` is coerced to a number, so the `tip` variable stores the correct value of `23`. But because `input` is a string, JavaScript interprets the `+` operator in `input + tip` as concatenation: `"20" + "23"`, so `billTotal` stores `"2023"`.

**Exercise 2.6:** Use `Math.abs()` to return the absolute value of the difference between `a` and `b`, then compare that difference with `Number.EPSILON`:

```
function isRoughlyEqual(a, b) {
    return Math.abs(a - b) < Number.EPSILON;
}
```

**Exercise 2.7:** The built-in `Number.isSafeInteger()` method tells you whether a number is within the safe range, but that method only accepts `number` type values. If you're working in an environment where both `number` and `bigint` values might appear, then you need a function that accepts both data types:

```
function isSafeInt(value) {

  if (typeof value === "number") {          // Is it a number?
      return Number.isSafeInteger(value);   // If so, use isSafeInteger()
  }

  if (typeof value === "bigint") {          // Is it a BigInt?
      return value >= BigInt(Number.MIN_SAFE_INTEGER) &&
             value <= BigInt(Number.MAX_SAFE_INTEGER);   // If so, check the range...
  }

  return false;    // ...otherwise, it's not a safe integer.
}
```

**Exercise 2.8:** You can't mix regular numbers with BigInt values in an expression. You need to turn the `number` 10 into a `bigint` value by adding `n`:

```
console.log(9007199254740991n + 10n);
```

**Exercise 2.9:** The correct answer is `-1`.

**Exercise 2.10:** The carousel loop would crash on certain back-button clicks because of how the `%` (remainder) operator behaves with negative numbers in JavaScript. In particular, notice what happens when `index` is `0` and the user clicks the back button:

```
index = (0 - 1) % items.length
      = -1 % items.length
      = -1
```

Aha! The value of `index` becomes `-1` (it doesn't matter what the value of `items.length` is), which is an invalid array index, and trying to access `items[-1]` will return `undefined`, causing your carousel code to fail or behave unexpectedly. Either use the `mod()` utility function from section 2.5.1, or bake the same logic into your `index` update statement:

```
index = ((index - 1 + items.length) % items.length);
```

**Exercise 2.11:** If the fractional part is exactly .5, `Math.round()` rounds up toward $+\infty$, so the correct answer is –2.

**Exercise 2.12:** The `toFixed()`method is missing its required parentheses:

```
let formatted = "$" + price.toFixed();
```

**Exercise 2.13:** `Math.random()` returns values greater than or equal to `0` and less than `1`, so the answer is [0, 1).

**Exercise 2.14:** The color string represents the CSS `rgb(red, green, blue)` function, which could then be used to apply a color to an element. Each component of the `rgb()` function is an integer in the range [0, 255], so `Math.random() * 256` will return values within that range:

```
function getRandomColor() {
    const r = Math.floor(Math.random() * 256);
    const g = Math.floor(Math.random() * 256);
    const b = Math.floor(Math.random() * 256);
    return `rgb(${r}, ${g}, ${b})`;
}
```

## Summary

- Operators follow standard precedence rules.
- Use parentheses to make calculations clearer and avoid bugs in layout or animation math.
- Use strict equality (===) to avoid unexpected type coercion in comparisons.
- JavaScript uses a single `number` type for both integers and floating-point values.
- Decimal math is imprecise due to JavaScript's internal binary representations. That's why `0.1 + 0.2 !== 0.3`.

- The BigInt data type enables you to work with integers beyond JavaScript's safe number range.
- JavaScript's `%` operator returns a remainder with the same sign as the dividend.
- Use `Math.round()`, `Math.floor()`, and `Math.ceil()` to round values up, down, or to the nearest whole number.
- For formatted display, use `.toFixed()` to control decimal places.
- `Math.random()` returns a pseudo-random float in the range [0, 1).

# 3 Math basics for CSS

***This chapter covers***

- CSS measurement units
- Calculating values in CSS
- CSS math functions and variables
- The math of CSS inheritance
- The mathematics of the box model

CSS is, in a word, tricky. You carefully hand-code each declaration, combine them with precision into a style rule, refresh your browser, and the result is all too often an unholy mess that looks nothing like the clean, professional design you imagined in your head. Welcome to the frequently frustrating, always adventuresome world of CSS!

It's true that CSS can make even the most Zen-like designer become a puller-of-hair or a gnasher-of-teeth. But if you've come to believe that wrestling with CSS is a no-win situation, may I offer some good news? Many, perhaps even most, CSS problems are math related and eminently fixable. Surely, there must be a catch! And there is! You have to learn the basics of how CSS uses math, which is what this chapter is all about. Here you'll learn all about CSS measurement units and operators, the most useful CSS math functions, how to wield CSS variables in math operations, the ins and outs of box model math, and much more.

## 3.1 The math of CSS measurement units

CSS measurement units may seem straightforward on the surface, but there's fascinating mathematical interplay happening behind the scenes. Understanding these mathematical relationships gives you more precise control over your layouts and helps explain why certain CSS techniques work the way they do. This section digs into the numbers behind those units, so you can debug with confidence and design with mathematical precision.

### 3.1.1 Unit conversion math

At its core, CSS rendering requires converting all measurements to absolute pixel values before drawing elements on screen. This conversion follows specific mathematical rules, as demonstrated in the following listing, where all five `font-size` declarations compute to the same value.

**Listing 3.1 Converting measurements to pixel values**

```
font-size: 16px;
font-size: 1rem;
font-size: 100%;
font-size: 12pt;
font-size: 0.166667in;
```

**1rem = 16px if root font size is 16px**

**100% = 16px if the parent font size is 16px**

**12pt * (96px/72pt) = 16px**

**0.166667in × 96px/in = 16px**

**NOTE** All the code for this chapter's listings is available in this book's GitHub repository: https://github.com/paulmcfe/web-dev-math.

The browser's rendering engine uses the following conversion formulas:

- `1in` = `96px` (CSS standard, regardless of actual screen DPI)
- `1pt` = 1/72 of an inch = `96px`/72 = `1.333px`
- `1pc` (pica) = `12pt` = `16px`
- `1rem` = `root` element's `font-size` value in pixels
- `1em` = current element's computed `font-size` value in pixels

Understanding these formulas makes it easier to use different units with confidence and precision.

### 3.1.2 The cascading calculations of em units

The compounding effect of `em` units follows a mathematical progression where each level multiplies the previous result, as shown in the following listing and demonstrated in figure 3.1.

**Listing 3.2 The compounding effect of em units**

CSS:

```
html {
    font-size: 16px;
}
.parent {
    font-size: 1.5em;              ← 16 × 1.5 = 24px
}
.child {
    font-size: 1.2em;              ← 24 × 1.2 = 28.8px
}
```

HTML:

```
<body>
    <p>
        This is regular paragraph text set at 16px.
    </p>
    <article class="parent">
        <p>
            This is parent text set at 1.5em.
        </p>
        <section class="child">
            <p>
                This is child text set at 1.2em.
            </p>
        </section>
    </article>
</body>
```

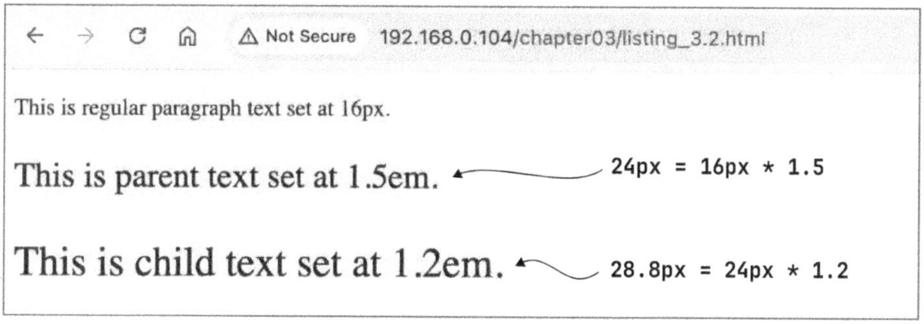


**Figure 3.1 An ostensibly smaller font size (`1.2em`) is rendered larger than an ostensibly bigger font size (`1.5em`) thanks to the compounding effects of `em` units.**

Applying `em` units from a base level down through multiple generations of child elements creates a geometric sequence where

- The first level is base × $\text{multiplier}_1$.
- The second level is base × $\text{multiplier}_1$ × $\text{multiplier}_2$.
- The third level is base × $\text{multiplier}_1$ × $\text{multiplier}_2$ × $\text{multiplier}_3$.

The relationship can be expressed as

$$\text{computed\_size} = \text{base\_size} \times \prod_{i=1}^{n} m_i$$

where $\prod m_i$ (the capital Greek letter pi) represents the product of all the parent multipliers (represented by $m_i$). For the example's `.child` class, the base size is `16px` and the two multipliers are `1.5` and `1.2`, so we have the following calculation:

```
computed_size = 16px × (1.5 * 1.2) = 16px * 1.8 = 28.8px
```

Now let's look at percentage units, which can trip up even experienced designers.

### 3.1.3 Percentage computation rules

CSS percentage values follow their own mathematical rules depending on the property:

- For the `width`, `left`, `right`, `padding`, and `margin` properties,

  ```
  value = parent_width * percentage / 100
  ```

- For the `height`, `top`, and `bottom` properties,

  ```
  value = parent_height × percentage / 100 (if parent height is defined)
  ```

- For the `border-radius` property,

  ```
  horizontal radius = element_width × percentage / 100
  ```

  and

  ```
  vertical radius = element_height × percentage / 100
  ```

- For transforms, `transform: scale(1.5)` scales by 150 percent from the transform origin.
- For the `line-height` property, percentages are calculated based on the element's font size, and not its parent's font size.

When percentages are nested, the calculation follows a multiplicative progression, as shown in the following listing and demonstrated in figure 3.2.

**Listing 3.3 The multiplicative progression of percentages**

CSS:

```
.grandparent {
    width: 800px;
}
.parent {
    width: 50%;
}
.child {
    width: 50%;
}
```

800px × 0.5 = 400px

400px × 0.5 = 200px

HTML:

```
<main class="grandparent">
    <h1>Main (.grandparent)</h1>
    <article class="parent">
        <h2>Article (.parent)</h2>
            <section class="child">
                <h3>Section (.child)</h3>
            </section>
    </article>
</main>
```

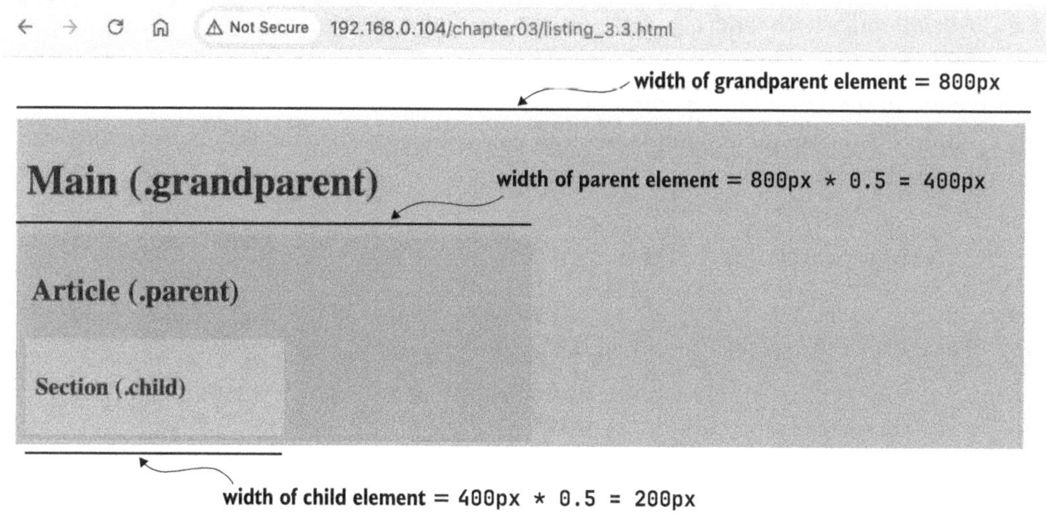


**Figure 3.2 A demonstration of the multiplicative progression of percentages**

This progression creates the formula child_width = root_width × $\text{percentage}_1$ × $\text{percentage}_2$ × ... × $\text{percentage}_n$. The relationship can be expressed as

$$\text{child\_width} = \text{root\_width} \times \prod_{i=1}^{n} p_i$$

where $\prod p_i$ represents the product of all the parent percentages.

### 3.1.4 Viewport units and their responsive calculations

Viewport units provide a direct mathematical relationship to screen dimensions:

- `1vw` = viewport_width / 100
- `1vh` = viewport_height / 100
- `1vmin` = min(viewport_width, viewport_height) / 100
- `1vmax` = max(viewport_width, viewport_height) / 100

If the viewport is `1200px` wide, then an `h1` with `font-size` set to `10vw` is rendered at `120px` (since `0.10 × 1200 = 120`):

```
h1 {
    font-size: 10vw;
}
```

That value updates as the window resizes. That's real-time math: every time the screen size changes, the browser recalculates the equation.

The newer dynamic viewport units (`dvh`, etc.) adjust based on visible viewport area, accounting for dynamic UI elements, such as mobile browser address bars.

### 3.1.5 Mixing units with calc()

When you mix different units, such as combining percentages and `rem` values, CSS needs to resolve them to a common base before doing the math. The `calc()` function, covered in more detail later in section 3.2.2, does this by converting everything into pixels. For example,

```
.card {
    width: calc(100% - 2rem);
}
```

Here's what the browser might do behind the scenes:

1. Convert `rem` to pixels based on the root font size—for example, if the root font size is `16px`, then `2rem = 2 × 16px = 32px`.
2. Convert the percentage to pixels based on the width of the element's parent—for example, if the parent element has a width of `600px`, then `100% = 600px`.
3. Perform the subtraction operation—`600px - 32px = 568px`.
4. Apply the final pixel value to the `.card` element.

The following formula is used:

```
final_value = (parent_width × percentage / 100) - (root_font_size × rem_value)
```

### 3.1.6 Combining units requires attention to scale

When you mix units in a design system—for example, using `rem` for spacing, `%` for layout, and `vh` for hero banners—it's easy to lose track of scale. You might end up subtracting values that come from very different coordinate systems.

To keep things predictable,

- Always resolve unit values to pixels in your head when doing layout math.
- Use `calc()` to keep unit math explicit and readable.
- Lean on consistent base units such as `rem` to avoid unexpected compounding.

Understanding these mathematical principles helps you create more precise, predictable layouts and explains why CSS sometimes behaves in seemingly mysterious ways. It transforms CSS from a collection of properties into a coherent mathematical system for describing visual relationships.

**EXERCISES**

**Exercise 3.1:** What is the computed pixel value of `font-size: 0.25in`?

1. 16px
2. 24px
3. 96px
4. 384px

**Exercise 3.2:** What is the computed `font-size` value, in pixels, of the `grandchild` class in the following code (assume `grandparent` is the ancestor of `parent`, which is the ancestor of `child`, which is the ancestor of `grandchild`):

```
.grandparent {
    font-size: 16px;
}
.parent {
    font-size: 1.25em;
}
.child {
    font-size: 1.25em;
}
.grandchild {
    font-size: 1.25em;
}
```

## 3.2 CSS math functions

CSS isn't a programming language, but it does offer a few built-in functions that, combined with some standard arithmetic operators, enable the building of sophisticated mathematical expressions that can be incorporated directly into style declarations.

### 3.2.1 CSS arithmetic operators

Arithmetic is a huge part of frontend design work, so CSS helps out by supporting the four standard arithmetic operators, as shown in table 3.1.

**Table 3.1 CSS arithmetic operators**

| Operator | Name | Example | Result |
|---|---|---|---|
| + | Addition | `16px + 24px` | `40px` |
| - | Subtraction | `50rem - 5rem` | `45rem` |
| * | Multiplication | `10em * 2` | `20em` |
| / | Division | `100% / 3` | `33.333%` |

However, you can't just plop an arithmetic expression anywhere it suits you. The following is invalid syntax:

```
width: 100% - 2rem;
```

Instead, you can use an arithmetic expression only as an argument passed to a CSS math function, such as `calc()`, as discussed in section 3.2.2:

```
width: calc(100% - 2rem);
```

Here are a few things to bear in mind when building your CSS arithmetic expressions:

- You must have at least one space on either side of the addition (`+`) or subtraction (`-`) operator. The multiplication (`*`) and division (`/`) operators don't require spaces around them, but it's a good idea to add them anyway for readability.
  The following line is invalid:

  ```
  height: calc(100vh-3rem);
  ```

  In this case, the expression is valid:

  ```
  height: calc(100vh - 3rem);
  ```

- Your arithmetic expressions can mix unit types, but only if those types are compatible. That is, you can mix length with length (e.g., `px` with `rem`) or angle with angle (e.g., `deg` with `rad`), but you can't mix length with angle.
  This expression is invalid:

  ```
  transform: rotate(calc(10px + 45deg));
  ```

The expression is valid in this case:

```
transform: rotate(calc(0.1rad + 45deg));
```

- In expressions involving multiplication or division, one of the operands must be a scalar (literal) value. For division, the scalar value must be on the right side of the operator.

  The following expression is invalid:

  ```
  font-size: calc(36px / 2px)
  ```

  This expression is also invalid:

  ```
  font-size: calc(36 / 2px)
  ```

  And here is the valid approach:

  ```
  font-size: calc(36px / 2);
  ```

- The order of operations is as follows: parentheses, multiplication/division, addition/subtraction.
- Since parentheses have the highest precedence, you can use them to ensure your expressions calculate using the order of operations you prefer. For example, in the declaration `width: calc((100% - 2rem) * 2);`, the browser calculates `100% - 2rem` first because it's within parentheses. Then, it multiplies that result by `2`.

You'll use `calc()` extensively when wielding CSS expressions, so I discuss this important function next.

### 3.2.2 Evaluating expressions with calc()

The `calc()` function is one of the most powerful and useful weapons in your CSS math arsenal. With `calc()`, you can perform calculations directly in your stylesheets, creating dynamic, responsive, and precise designs based on mathematical relationships rather than fixed values.

At its core, `calc()` evaluates a mathematical expression and returns the result. The browser handles unit conversions and calculations at runtime, giving you the flexibility to express relationships between elements instead of hardcoding specific measurements.

For example, suppose you're designing an account dashboard page for a user profile, with a dialog overlay appearing when the user clicks a button to edit their profile (listing 3.4). On smaller screens, you don't want the dialog touching the viewport edges. Instead, the overlay will look better if it leaves a bit of breathing room around the dialog, say `20px` on all four sides. The easiest way to do that responsively is to use viewport units and a `calc()` expression that removes `40px` from both the width and height of the dialog. Figure 3.3 shows the overlay in action.

**Listing 3.4 Using `calc()` to size a dialog overlay**

```
.dialog {
    width: calc(100vw - 40px);          ◄ Leave room left and right
    max-width: 500px;
    max-height: calc(100vh - 40px);     ◄ Leave room top and bottom
}
```

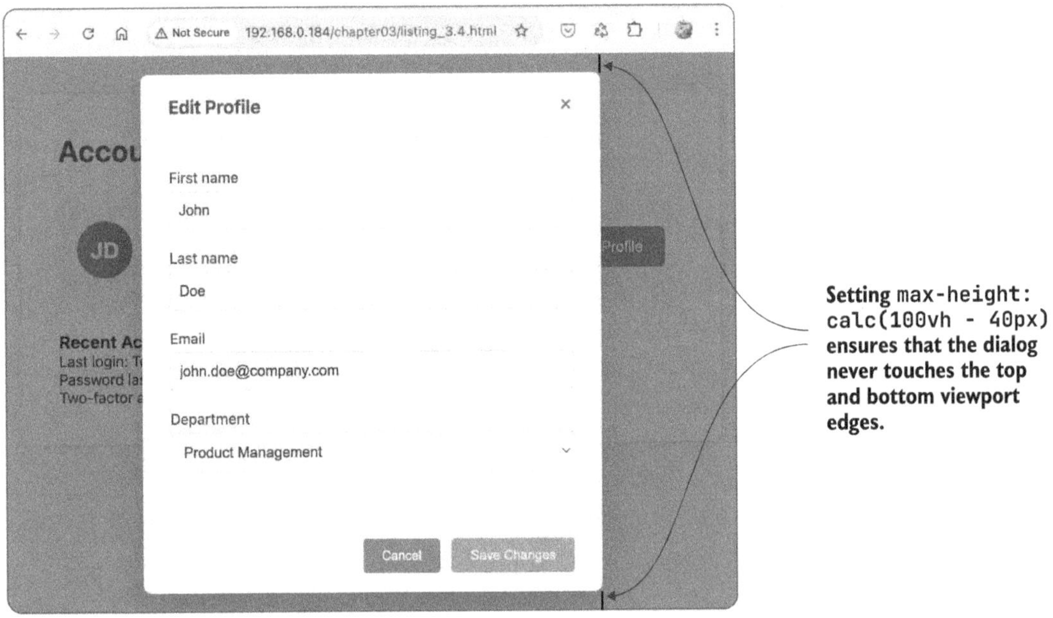


**Figure 3.3 This dialog uses `calc()` to ensure that there is always a bit of space around it, even on small screens.**

In this example, the browser goes through the following steps to determine the height of the `dialog` element:

1. Gets the viewport height (that is, `100vh`)
2. Converts to pixels (e.g., in figure 3.3, `100vh` = `585px`).
3. Performs the subtraction: `585px - 40px = 545px`.
4. Applies the final computed value to the element's property. In this example, the `dialog` element's `height` property is set to `545px`.

This process happens dynamically—whenever the viewport height (or the viewport width for the `width` calculation) changes, the calculation is re-evaluated automatically.

You can build your `calc()` expressions using any of the following CSS data types: angle, color-function (refer to chapter 7), frequency, integer, length, number, percentage, and time. (Remember that you can't mix incompatible types, such as length and time.)

Your `calc()` expression operands can also be other CSS functions, including `calc()`, `clamp()`, `env()`, `var()`, as well as all CSS mathematical functions (such as the `max()`, `min()`, `cos()`, `sin()`, `pow()`, and `sqrt()` functions). All other CSS functions are invalid within a `calc()` expression.

When your `calc()` expressions don't behave as expected, here are some troubleshooting ideas:

- Check that you've got the required whitespace around the + and - operators.
- Verify that you're only combining compatible unit types.
- If you're controlling the order of operations using parentheses, check that every left parenthesis has a corresponding right parenthesis and that the parentheses surround the correct expression.
- If you're using CSS variables within your expression, confirm that the variables have the values you expect. (In your browser's devtools, locate the declaration that uses the variable within a `calc()` expression; next, hover your mouse pointer over the variable name. The browser displays a tooltip that shows the variable's current value.)
- Use your browser devtools to inspect the computed value of the property.

What happens when the browser comes across a `calc()` syntax error or similar problem? It typically ignores the entire expression and renders the property with its default or inherited value.

### 3.2.3 *Setting limits with min(), max(), and clamp()*

While `calc()` enables you to perform arithmetic operations in CSS, it doesn't provide a way to constrain values within boundaries. This is where the `min()`, `max()`, and `clamp()` functions come in, because they act as mathematical constraints that help you create resilient layouts that stay within desired ranges.

The `min()` and `max()` functions operate exactly as their names suggest, following these mathematical rules:

- `min(a, b, c, ...)` returns the smallest value from a list of comma-separated values.
- `max(a, b, c, ...)` returns the largest value from a list of comma-separated values.

These functions shine when you need to establish either upper or lower bounds on a value, especially when dealing with responsive layouts.

#### USING MIN() FOR MAXIMUM CONSTRAINTS

The `min()` function is perfect when you need to set an upper limit that a value shouldn't exceed. This approach is particularly useful for preventing elements from becoming too large on wide screens, while remaining proportional on smaller screens.

For example, suppose your page has a hero section with `h1` and `p` text that you want to scale with the viewport width. The problem with scaling text this way is that it can end up absurdly large on very wide screens. To solve that problem, you can use `min()` to constrain the maximum size, as shown in the following listing.

**Listing 3.5 Using `min()` to constrain the maximum font size**

```
.hero {
    background: linear-gradient(135deg, #667eea 0%, #764ba2 100%);
    color: white;
    text-align: center;
    padding: 80px 20px;
}

.hero h1 {
    font-size: min(8vw, 64px);      ◀ Scales with viewport width,
}                                     but always <= 64px

.hero p {
    font-size: min(4vw, 24px);      ◀ Scales with viewport width,
}                                     but always <= 24px
```

What's happening mathematically for the hero `h1` is

- *On small screens*—If the parent is, say, `500px` wide, then `8vw = 40px`. Therefore, `min(8vw, 64px) = min(40px, 64px) = 40px`.
- *On large screens*—If the parent is, say, `1000px`, then `8vw = 80px`. Therefore, `min(8vw, 64px) = min(80px, 64px) = 64px`.

The browser automatically adjusts these values based on the viewport dimensions.

#### USING MAX() FOR MINIMUM CONSTRAINTS

Conversely, `max()` establishes a lower bound that shouldn't be undercut. For a hero section with `h1` and `p` text that scales with the viewport width, you might not mind very large text on large screens, but you don't want the text to become too tiny on small screens. To ensure the text never gets too small, you can use `max()` to set the minimum size, as demonstrated in the following listing.

**Listing 3.6 Using `max()` to constrain the minimum font size**

```
.hero {
    background: linear-gradient(135deg, #667eea 0%, #764ba2 100%);
    color: white;
    text-align: center;
    padding: 80px 20px;
}

.hero h1 {
    font-size: max(32px, 8vw);      ◀ Scales with viewport width,
}                                     but always >= 32px
```

```
.hero p {
    font-size: max(16px, 4vw);
}
```

Scales with viewport width, but always >= 16px

For the hero `p`, here's what's happening mathematically:

- *On large screens*—If the parent is, say, `1000px`, then `4vw = 40px`. Therefore, `max(16px, 4vw) = max(16px, 40px) = 40px`.
- *On small screens*—If the parent is, say, `375px` wide, then `4vw = 15px`. Therefore, `max(16px, 4vw) = max(16px, 15px) = 16px`.

What if you need both a minimum and a maximum? That's the job of the `clamp()` function.

#### Combining constraints with clamp()

The `clamp()` function combines both `min()` and `max()` into a single expression, enabling you to set both upper and lower bounds with a preferred value in between:

```
clamp(MIN, VAL, MAX)
```

where

- `MIN` is the minimum value (lower bound).
- `VAL` is the preferred value.
- `MAX` is the maximum value (upper bound).

Mathematically, this is equivalent to

```
max(MIN, min(VAL, MAX))
```

The browser returns the preferred value if it falls between the bounds; otherwise, it returns whichever bound was exceeded.

For example, you usually never want a font size to get either unreadably small or so big that it breaks the layout. For a hero section with `h1` and `p` text where the font size varies with viewport width, `clamp()` helps you constrain the font size on both ends, as shown in the following listing.

**Listing 3.7 Using `clamp()` to constrain a font size**

```
.hero {
    background: linear-gradient(135deg, #667eea 0%, #764ba2 100%);
    color: white;
    text-align: center;
    padding: 80px 20px;
}

.hero h1 {
    font-size: clamp(32px, 8vw, 64px);
}
```

Scales with viewport width, but always >= 32px and <= 64px

```
.hero p {
    font-size: clamp(16px, 4vw, 24x);      ◄── Scales with viewport width, but
}                                               always >= 16px and <=24px
```

For the hero h1, here's what's happening mathematically:

- *On large screens*—If the parent is 1200px, then 8vw = 96px. Therefore, clamp(32px, 8vw, 64px) = clamp(32px, 96px, 64px) = 64px.
- *On medium screens*—If the parent is 750px, then 8vw = 60px. Therefore, clamp(32px, 8vw, 64px) = clamp(32px, 60px, 64px) = 60px.
- *On small screens*—If the parent is 375px wide, then 8vw = 30px. Therefore, clamp(32px, 8vw, 64px) = clamp(32px, 30px, 64px) = 32px.

### 3.2.4 More CSS math functions

Most of your CSS mathematics will involve calc(), clamp(), max(), and min(), but CSS offers quite a few more math-related functions that could come in handy in certain situations. To learn about the CSS trigonometric functions, head over to chapter 9. The next few sections offer a quick overview of the remaining CSS math functions.

**NOTE** All the functions discussed in the following are relatively new to CSS, but they are all supported in evergreen browsers released since 2023 or 2024 (depending on the function). If you need to use one or more of these functions, but you also need to support older or legacy browsers, consider implementing the equivalent functionality using JavaScript, provided here for each CSS function.

#### EXPONENTIAL FUNCTION: EXP()

The exp($x$) function returns the mathematical constant $e$ raised to the power of $x$. $e$ is the base of the natural logarithm, in math terms, $\ln(x) = \log_e(x)$, and its value is approximately 2.71828. (If you're not sure what a logarithm is, check out the "Logarithm function: log()" section) Describing $e$ as the base of the natural logarithm means that it's the number used to define logarithms that grow and change in sync with certain natural processes, such as growth, radioactive decay, and compound interest. For example, the following listing shows a partial animation example that uses exp() to mimic exponential growth.

**Listing 3.8 Simulating exponential growth with exp()**

```
@keyframes exponential-growth {
    0% { transform: scale(1); }
    50% { transform: scale(exp(1)); }      ◄── Scales with e
    100% { transform: scale(exp(2)); }     ◄── Scales with e ^ 2
}
.grow {
    animation: exponential-growth 2s linear infinite;
}
```

Browser support: Chrome 120+, Firefox 118+, Safari 15.4+

JavaScript equivalent: `Math.exp()`

#### HYPOTENUSE FUNCTION: HYPOT()

The `hypot(`*x*`, `*y*`, ...)` function returns the square root of the sum of the squares of its arguments. It's called the *hypotenuse* function because its canonical use case is to calculate the length of the hypotenuse of a right-angled triangle by taking the square root of the sum of the squares of the other sides of the triangle:

```
width: hypot(3em, 4em);        ← 5em
```

But the `hypot()` function can take any number of comma-separated arguments, with or without units. (If you include units, they must all be the same.) For example, if you provide three arguments, you're effectively calculating the distance from the origin (0, 0, 0) to a point (x, y, z) in 3D space.

The following listing offers an example that uses `hypot(100vw, 100vh) / 100` to calculate a responsive `blur` strength based on the length of the viewport diagonal, which ensures that the blur feels consistent on any screen size.

**Listing 3.9 Responsive blur strength using `hypot()`**

```
.overlay {
    position: absolute;
    inset: 0;
    backdrop-filter: blur(calc(hypot(100vw, 100vh) / 100);
);
    background-color: rgba(0, 0, 0, 0.3);
}
```

Browser support: Chrome 120+, Firefox 118+, Safari 15.4+

JavaScript equivalent: `Math.hypot()`

#### LOGARITHM FUNCTION: LOG()

The `log(x, `*base*`)` function returns the *logarithm* of *x*, which is the value that *base* has to be raised to in order to yield the number. It's easiest to think of a logarithm as the inverse of exponentiation. For example, $2^3 = 8$, so the logarithm of 8 base 2, written as $\log_2(8)$, equals 3. In CSS, you'd write

```
log(8, 2) = 3
```

The second argument is the base, and it's optional. If you leave it out, CSS uses *e* as the base.

One use case for the `log()` function is to create a font size scale that grows quickly and then levels off:

```
font-size: calc((log(var(--step) + 1) + 1) * 1rem);
```

Here, increasing the value of the `--step` variable increases the font size, quickly at first, then more slowly as the step value increases. The following listing presents an example of such a scale.

**Listing 3.10 Creating a font size scale with `log()`**

```
<head>
    <style>
        .log-scale {
            font-size: calc((log(var(--step) + 1) + 1) * 1rem);
        }
        .log-scale.step-0 { --step: 0; }
        .log-scale.step-2 { --step: 2; }
        .log-scale.step-4 { --step: 4; }
        .log-scale.step-6 { --step: 6; }
        .log-scale.step-8 { --step: 8; }
        .log-scale.step-10 { --step: 10; }
        .log-scale.step-12 { --step: 12; }
    </style>
</head>
<body>
    <h1 class="log-scale step-12">Step 12</h1>
    <h2 class="log-scale step-10">Step 10</h2>
    <h3 class="log-scale step-8">Step 8</h3>
    <h4 class="log-scale step-6">Step 6</h4>
    <h5 class="log-scale step-4">Step 4</h5>
    <h6 class="log-scale step-2">Step 2</h6>
    <p class="log-scale step-0">Step 0 (base size)</p>
</body>
```

Figure 3.4 shows this logarithmic font size scale in action.

Browser support: Chrome 120+, Firefox 118+, Safari 15.4+

JavaScript equivalent: `Math.log()`

#### MODULUS FUNCTION: MOD()

The `mod(`*dividend*`,` *divisor*`)` function returns the remainder when the *dividend* is divided by the *divisor*. The result always takes the sign of the divisor, so `mod()` is useful whenever you need cyclical values or values that wrap, such as those on a color wheel or the index of a slider or carousel.

For example, a good use case for `mod()` is to automatically calculate a color's complementary counterpart. The *complementary color* is defined as the color that's opposite the original on the color wheel. Since the color wheel is 360 degrees, any color's complement will be 180 degrees around the wheel. So, the complement of hue 0 will be 180, and the complement of hue 45 will be hue 225, but what will be the complement of hue 225? Adding 180 wraps around past the start of the wheel, so we're in modulus territory:

```
mod(225 + 180, 360) = mod(405, 360) = 45
```

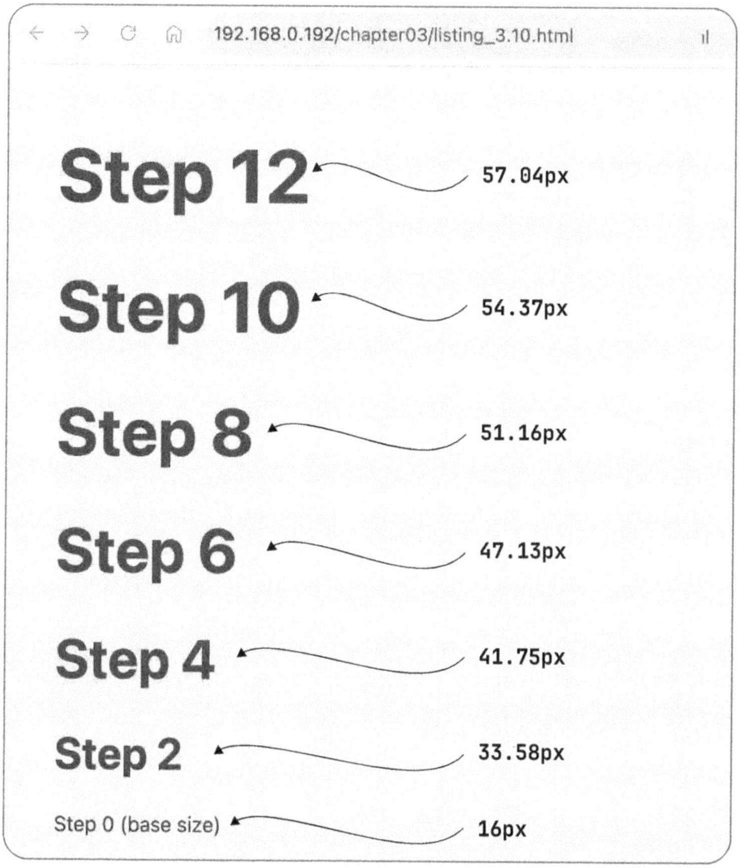


**Figure 3.4** A logarithmic font size scale built using the CSS `log()` function

The result is 45, so hue 45 is the complement of hue 225. The following listing presents some CSS code that uses `mod()` to calculate a base hue's complementary color using the CSS `hsl()` function:

**Listing 3.11 Calculating a complentary color using `mod()`**

```
:root {                                              Change this to any base hue
    --base-hue: 225deg;                          ◄──┘
    --complement-hue: mod(calc(var(--base-hue) + 180deg), 360deg);
    --saturation: 60%;
    --lightness: 50%;
}
.original {
    background-color: hsl(var(--base-hue)
                          var(--saturation)
                          var(--lightness));
}
.complement {
```

```
    background-color: hsl(var(--complement-hue)
                          var(--saturation)
                          var(--lightness));
}
```

This code defines a `--base-hue` variable, then uses it within the `mod()` function to calculate the `--complement-hue` variable. The `--saturation` and `--lightness` variables are set to default values and are used to set the background color of two elements.

Browser support: Chrome 125+, Firefox 118+, Safari 15.4+

JavaScript equivalent:

```
const mod = (a, b) => ((a % b) + b) % b;
```

#### POWER FUNCTION: POW()

The `pow(`*base*`,` *exponent*`)` function returns the result of raising one number (the *base*) to the power of another number (the *exponent*). For example, the following returns the value 8:

```
pow(2, 3)
```

A useful example where `pow()` comes in handy is creating a typographic scale where the font sizes change exponentially:

```
font-size: calc(1rem * pow(1.25, 3));
font-size: calc(1rem * pow(1.25, 2));
font-size: calc(1rem * pow(1.25, 1));
font-size: calc(1rem * pow(1.25, 0));
font-size: calc(1rem * pow(1.25, -1));
font-size: calc(1rem * pow(1.25, -2));
```

31.25px
25px
20px
16px
12.8px
10.24px

A default font size of `1rem` is multiplied by an exponential factor calculated using `pow()`, with a base of `1.25` and exponent values ranging from `3` (positive values increase the font size) to `-2` (negative values decrease the font size). You can use higher base values for more aggressive growth, as shown in the next listing.

**Listing 3.12 An exponential typographic scale using pow()**

```
<head>
    <style>
        .scale {
            font-size: calc(1rem * pow(1.25, var(--step)));
        }
        .step-3 { --step: 3; }
        .step-2 { --step: 2; }
```

```
        .step-1 { --step: 1; }
        .step-0 { --step: 0; }
        .step--1 { --step: -1; }
        .step--2 { --step: -2; }
    </style>
</head>
<body>
    <h1 class="scale step-3">Heading (Step 3)</h1>
    <h2 class="scale step-2">Subheading (Step 2)</h2>
    <h3 class="scale step-1">Section title (Step 1)</h3>
    <p class="scale step-0">Body text (Step 0)</p>
    <p class="scale step--1">Small caption (Step -1)</p>
    <p class="scale step--2">Footnote (Step -2)</p>
</body>
```

Figure 3.5 shows this exponential typographic scale at work.

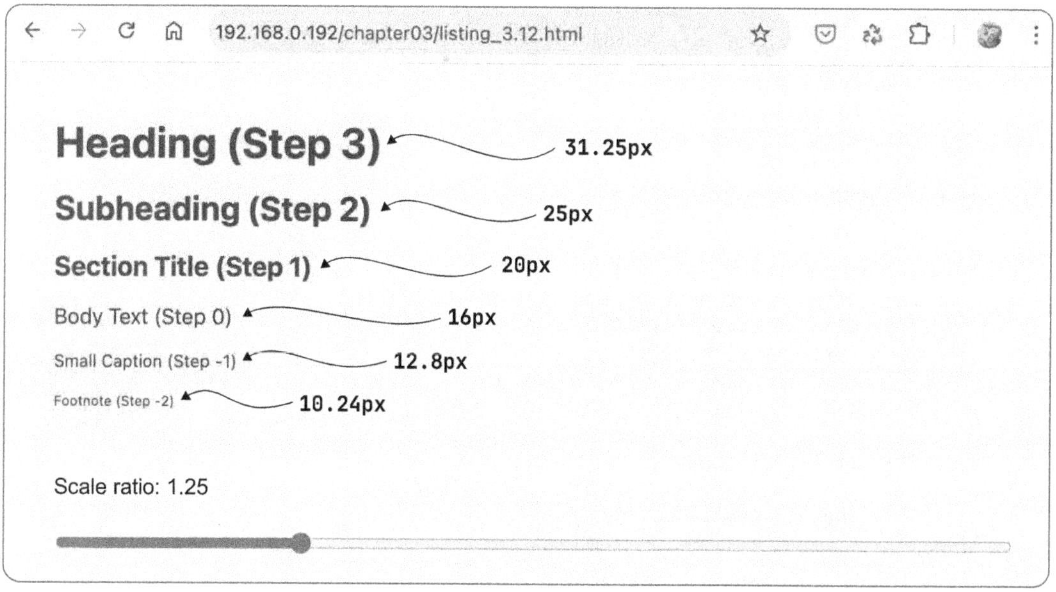


**Figure 3.5 An exponential typographic scale created with the CSS `pow()` function**

Browser support: Chrome 120+, Firefox 118+, Safari 15.4+
JavaScript equivalent: `Math.pow()`

#### REMAINDER FUNCTION: REM()

The `rem(`*dividend*`,` *divisor*`)` function returns the remainder when one number (the *dividend*) is divided by another number (the *divisor*). The result always takes the sign of the dividend (in contrast to the `mod()` function, which always takes the sign of the divisor). This means that the `rem()` function works just like JavaScript's remainder (`%`) operator.

One example where preserving the sign of the dividend comes in handy is when you want to build an interface (e.g., a timeline) where you create a zigzag offset pattern that grows outward from the center, while alternating directions:

```
.item {
    transform: translateX(calc(rem(var(--index), 2) * 30px));
}
```

When `--index` values are negative, `rem()` preserves the negativity and shifts the item to the left; when `--index` values are positive, the item shifts to the right. You can generate the index values using JavaScript, as shown in the next listing.

**Listing 3.13 Generating alternating index values**

```
const timeline = document.getElementById('timeline');
let offsetDirection = -1;

const events = [
    'Launched MVP',
    'Reached 1,000 users',
    'Raised seed round',
    'Hired first engineer',
    'Redesigned homepage',
    'Expanded internationally',
];

events.forEach((text, i) => {
    const item = document.createElement('div');
    item.classList.add('item');
    item.textContent = text;

    if(i % 2 !== 0) { offsetDirection *= -1; }

    item.style.setProperty('--index',
                          (i + 1) * offsetDirection);
    timeline.appendChild(item);
});
```

Initial offset direction (left)

A list of events for the timeline

Iterate the events

Create the item

Set the --index property for this item

Value is negative when offsetDirection = -1

For odd indexes, change the offset direction

The values assigned to the `--index` variable follow this repeating pattern: –1 (item is shifted left), 0 (item is unshifted), 1 (item is shifted left), and 0 (item is unshifted). Figure 3.6 demonstrates the effect.

Browser support: Chrome 125+, Firefox 118+, Safari 15.4+

JavaScript equivalent: `x % y`

#### ROUND FUNCTION: ROUND()

The `round(`*strategy*`,` *number*`,` *interval*`)` function returns *number* rounded to the nearest value using one of the following *rounding strategies*:

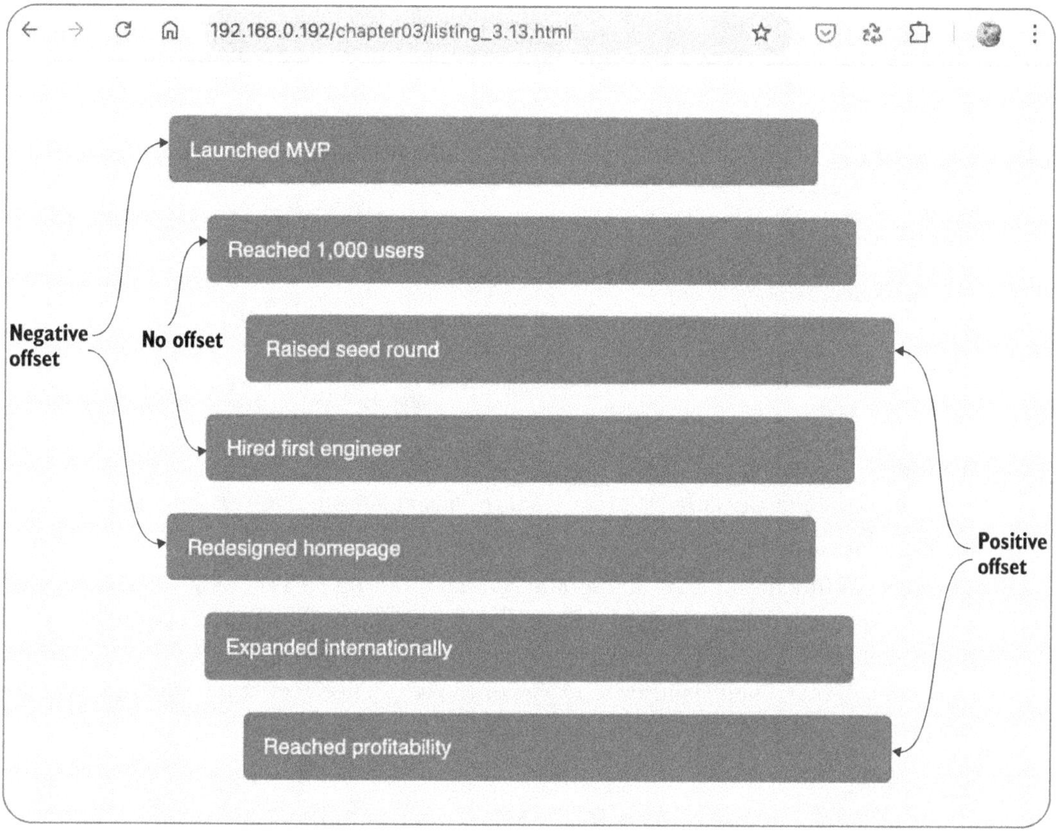


**Figure 3.6 A zigzag timeline created using the CSS `rem()` function**

- `down`—Rounds the number down to the nearest value. If the number is negative, it's rounded to the nearest lower (more negative) value. This rounding strategy is equivalent to JavaScript's `Math.floor()` method.
- `nearest`—Rounds the number to the nearest value. If the number is halfway between two possibilities, the result is rounded up. This rounding strategy is equivalent to JavaScript's `Math.round()` method. This is the default strategy that CSS uses if you omit the *strategy* argument.
- `to-zero`—Rounds the number to the nearest value closer to 0. If the number is positive, it's rounded down to the nearest lower value. If the number is negative, it's rounded up to the nearest higher (less negative) value. This rounding strategy is equivalent to to JavaScript's `Math.trunc()` method.
- `up`—Rounds the number up to the nearest value. If the number is negative, it's rounded to the nearest higher (less negative) value. This rounding strategy is equivalent to JavaScript's `Math.ceil()` method.

For each rounding strategy, you can also specify a *rounding interval*—a multiple to which the value is rounded (the default interval is 1). Here are some examples:

```
z-index: round(4.7);
width: round(down, 26px, 10px);
width: round(nearest, 26px, 10px);
margin: round(to-zero, -26px, 10px);
width: round(up, 26px, 10px);
width: round(27px, 10px);
opacity: round(0.78, 0.25);
```

Result: 5
Result: 20px
Result: 30px
Result: −20px
Result: 30px
Result: 30px
Result: 0.75

Browser support: Chrome 125+, Firefox 118+, Safari 15.4+

JavaScript equivalents: `Math.floor()`, `Math.round()`, `Math.trunc()`, `Math.ceil()`

#### SQUARE ROOT FUNCTION: SQRT()

The `sqrt(`*x*`)` function returns the square root of *x*. Listing 13.4 shows a CSS rule for the `circle` class on a page that displays several circles arranged in a radial pattern. Using linear scaling for the width and height (e.g., `width: calc(--base-size * 1.5)`) often creates elements that feel either too large or too small; however, using square root scaling produces a more natural visual hierarchy.

**Listing 3.14 Scaling a circle's width and height using `sqrt()`**

```
:root {
    --circle-size-base: 160px;
}
.circle {
    --base-size: var(--circle-size-base);
    width: calc(var(--base-size) * sqrt(var(--distance-factor)));
    height: calc(var(--base-size) * sqrt(var(--distance-factor)));
}
.circle:nth-child(2) {
    --angle: 0deg;
    --distance: calc(var(--radius) * 0.6);
    --distance-factor: 1;
}
etc.
```

Browser support: Chrome 120+, Firefox 118+, Safari 15.4+

JavaScript equivalent: `Math.sqrt()`

#### EXERCISES

**Exercise 3.3:** Which of the following is a valid declaration in CSS?

1. `width: 100% - 2rem;`
2. `width: calc(100% - 2rem);`

3. `width: calc(100% + 20deg);`
4. `width: calc(36px / 2px);`

**Exercise 3.4:** In the following rule, what expression must be entered into the `calc()` function to ensure that the `column` class divides its parent container into three columns, each separated by a `15px` gutter?

```
.column {
    width: calc(_________________);
}
```

**Exercise 3.5:** Build a headline (`h1`) with the following font-size characteristics: scales with viewport width, no smaller than `40px`, no larger than `72px`, and renders at `56px` when the viewport width is `800px`.

## 3.3 CSS variables in math operations

You define CSS variables (also known as custom properties) with a double-hyphen prefix (`--`), usually as a `:root` declaration for global use:

```
:root {
    --primary-color: #3498db;
    --base-spacing: 8px;
    --font-size-base: 16px;
}
```

You then access them anywhere in your CSS by using the `var()` function:

```
.element {
    color: var(--primary-color);
    padding: var(--base-spacing);
    font-size: var(--font-size-base);
}
```

This basic usage already makes CSS more maintainable: even if you've used a particular variable a few dozen times throughout your stylesheet, you only have to change its value once in the original `:root` declaration.

But CSS variables can do a lot more than store colors or font sizes. When used in math expressions, they become powerful tools for creating scalable, maintainable layouts because they let you abstract values, avoid duplication, and build logic into your design system.

### 3.3.1 Basic usage

To insert a variable into a math expression, you wrap it with `var()` just like you would in any other context:

```
:root {
    --gap: 1rem;
```

```
}

.card {
    padding: calc(var(--gap) * 2);
}
```

Here, `--gap` is resolved to `1rem`, so the final padding value becomes `2rem`.

Variables even work inside nested functions:

```
.subhead {
    width: min(100%, calc(60ch + var(--gap)));
}
```

### 3.3.2 Mixing units with variables

Variables can hold values in any unit (`px`, `rem`, `%`, `vw`, etc.), but the math expression has to make sense once those units are substituted. For example,

```
:root {
    --unit: 2rem;
}

.box {
    margin-left: calc(100% - var(--unit));
}
```

This example is valid CSS because `%` and `rem` are compatible units.

But you need to be careful when combining unitless and unit-bearing variables in expressions that use multiplication or division:

```
:root {
    --scale: 1.5;
}

.story {
    font-size: calc(var(--scale) * 1rem);
}
```

This example works because it multiplies the unitless `--scale` variable by a unit-bearing value (`1rem`). However, the following code would fail:

```
:root {
--size1: 1rem;
--size2: 2rem;
}

.container {
    width: calc(var(--size1) * var(--size2));
}
```

This is invalid CSS because multiplying or dividing two values that both have units is not allowed in CSS math.

### 3.3.3 Fallbacks and missing variables

You can add a second argument to your `var()` function and, if a variable is undefined or invalid, CSS will fall back to the value of that argument:

```
.sidebar-header {
    font-size: calc(var(--heading-size, 2rem) + 0.5rem);
}
```

CSS interprets the `var()` arguments to mean, "Use the value of `--heading-size` here if that variable is defined; if not, use `2rem` instead."

> **WARNING** If the variable is missing and there's no fallback, the entire property becomes invalid and is ignored by the browser.

## 3.4 The math of CSS inheritance

Inheritance is one of the most powerful yet sometimes perplexing aspects of CSS. You already know that some CSS properties inherit their values from parent elements, including `font-size`, `line-height`, and `color`. But it's often not obvious how *math* shapes those inherited values. That's because, at its core, inheritance is really a mathematical concept that determines how property values flow from parent elements to their children. Understanding the math behind CSS inheritance will help you predict how styles cascade down the DOM and solve common styling head-scratchers.

### 3.4.1 The inheritance cascade formula

When the browser renders a page, it computes the value of each CSS property for every element using a complex but deterministic formula. For inherited properties, the computation follows this general pattern:

1. If the property is set explicitly on the element, use that value.
2. If not, check if the property inherits by default and the parent has a computed value.
3. If both conditions are true, mathematically transform the parent's value as needed.
4. If not, apply the default value for that property.

This process creates a mathematical chain of value calculations that flows through your document tree.

### 3.4.2 Which properties inherit mathematically?

Not all CSS properties participate in this mathematical inheritance. From an inheritance perspective, properties generally fall into two categories:

- *Inherited properties*—Properties such as `color`, `font-family`, and `line-height` that pass their values down to descendant elements
- *Non-inherited properties*—Properties such as `border`, `margin`, and `padding` that don't cascade to children

The logic behind which properties inherit is largely based on whether the property logically applies to content (these typically inherit) or to boxes (these typically don't inherit).

### 3.4.3 Percentage values and the inheritance math

Percentage values in CSS introduce an interesting mathematical relationship during inheritance. When a percentage is used, its computed value depends on some reference value from the parent element. The specific reference value varies by property, as shown in the following example:

```
.parent {
    width: 400px;
}
.child {
    width: 50%;
    margin-top: 10%;
    line-height: 150%;
}
```

**200px based on parent's width** (width: 50%)

**40px based on parent's width(!)** (margin-top: 10%)

**1.5 * font-size** (line-height: 150%)

The key mathematical insight here is that percentages are always relative to some other value and that reference value differs by property:

- For `width`, `margin`, and `padding`, percentages are calculated against the parent's `width`.
- For `height`, percentages are calculated against the parent's `height`.
- For `top`/`bottom`, percentages are calculated against the containing block's `height`.
- For `left`/`right`, percentages are calculated against the containing block's `width`.
- For `line-height`, percentages are calculated against the element's own `font-size`.

These reference values make sense for the most part, but note that it's easy to forget that when you use percentage values for vertical properties, such as `margin-top` and `padding-bottom`, CSS calculates those values based on a horizontal property (the parent's `width`).

### 3.4.4 The em unit inheritance multiplier

The `em` unit introduces an interesting mathematical behavior in CSS inheritance. One `em` equals the current font size of the element. But when used on properties that affect font size itself, it creates a compound multiplier effect:

```
body {
    font-size: 16px;
```

```
}
.parent {
    font-size: 1.5em;        ◄── 16px × 1.5 = 24px
}
.child {
    font-size: 1.5em;        ◄── 24px × 1.5 = 36px
}
```

This creates a mathematical progression where each level multiplies the previous result:

- *Level 1*—base-value × $\text{multiplier}_1$
- *Level 2*—base-value × $\text{multiplier}_1$ × $\text{multiplier}_2$
- *Level 3*—base-value × $\text{multiplier}_1$ × $\text{multiplier}_2$ × $\text{multiplier}_3$

This geometric sequence can lead to unexpected results in deeply nested structures, which is why many developers prefer `rem` units for font sizing, which always reference the root element's font size.

### 3.4.5 *Solving the heading size puzzle*

Using the following listing, you can solve the puzzle I presented in chapter 1, where nested headings unexpectedly grew in size (refer to figure 3.7):

**Listing 3.15 The heading-size conundrum**

CSS:

```
main {
    font-size: 1.25em;       ◄── 1.25em = 20px (assuming
}                                root font size is 16px)
article {
    font-size: 1.75em;       ◄── 1.75em = 20px * 1.75 = 35px
}
h2 {
    font-size: 2em;
}
```

HTML:

```
<main>
    <h2>Main Heading</h2>         ◄── 2em = 20px * 2 = 40px
    <article>
        <section>
            <h2>Section Heading</h2>     ◄── 2em = 35px * 2 = 70px
        </section>
    </article>
</main>
```

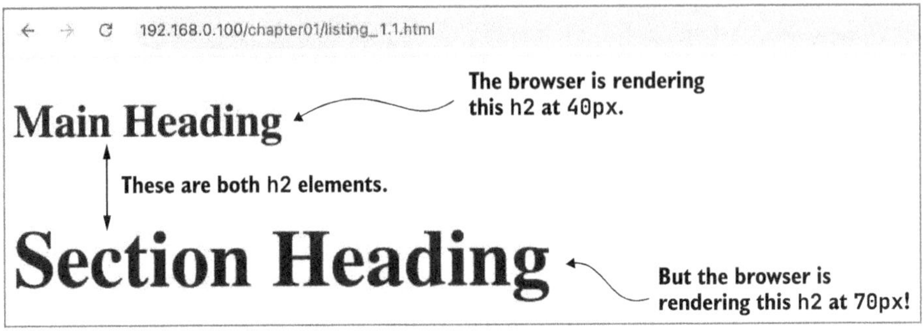


**Figure 3.7 The em unit inheritance multiplier explains why one h2 is rendered much bigger than the other.**

The mathematical explanation is that each em-based font size compounds through inheritance:

1. Assuming a root font size of 16px, the main element font size (A) is 16px * 1.25 = 20px.
2. For the first h2 directly inside main (C), the font size is 20px * 2 = 40px.
3. For the article element, the font size (B) is 20px * 1.75 = 35px.
4. For the second h2 inside article (D), the font size is 35px * 2 = 70px.

So, the "Main Heading" h2 renders at 40px, while the "Section Heading" h2 renders at 70px, all because em-based font sizes compound through the inheritance chain.

The solution, shown in the next listing, is to use rem units for the headings to avoid this compounding effect.

**Listing 3.16 Solving the heading-size conundrum**

```
h2 {
    font-size: 2rem;
}
```

Since rem units are always calculated relative to the root, not to the parent, this declaration means all your h2 headings will render at 32px (assuming a root font size of 16px).

### 3.4.6 Computed values vs. inherited values

A critical mathematical aspect of inheritance is that elements generally inherit the *computed value* of their parent, not the parent's specified value. This means the browser first calculates the absolute, pixel-based value for the parent, and then that absolute value is what gets inherited. For example, consider the following:

CSS:

```
.article {
    font-size: 2vw;
}
```

HTML:

```
<article>
    <section>
        <p>Hello world</p>
    </section>
</article>
```

What is the `font-size` value of the `section` element if the current viewport width is `1000px`? Inheritance passes computed values, not specified ones, so the final value of `font-size` for the `section` element is `20px` (`1000px * 0.02`).

That's why inherited values often resolve to pixels, even when the parent used a relative unit. Here's another example:

```
.parent {
    font-size: 20px;
    line-height: 150%;        ◄── Computed as 30px
}
.child {
    font-size: 16px;          ◄── Changed from parent
}
```

What's the `line-height` of the child element? At first glance, you might think that the child inherits a `line-height` value of `150%` from the parent element, so the child's computed `line-height` would be `24px` (`16px * 150%`). Not so! What the child actually inherits is the parent's computed `line-height` value of `30px`.

However, when `line-height` is specified as a unitless number, it creates a special mathematical relationship in which the computed value remains a multiplier:

```
.parent {
    font-size: 20px;
    line-height: 1.5;         ◄── Still computed as 30px
}
.child {
    font-size: 16px;
}
```

In this case, because the parent uses a unitless value for `line-height`, the child inherits that unitless value, so its `line-height` computes to `24px` (`16px × 1.5`).

This distinction explains why unitless values for `line-height` are generally recommended, since they maintain the intended proportional relationship through the inheritance chain.

At the beginning of this section, I said that elements *generally* inherit their parent's computed value rather than its specified value. One important exception to this rule occurs when the parent element uses percentage values for properties whose percentage value depends on the dimensions of their containing block. In these cases—most notably with `margin` and `padding`, but also with `text-indent`, `height`, and `top`—the percentage relationship must be preserved until layout can determine the final value.

For example, consider the following listing.

**Listing 3.17 Inheritance and percentages**

CSS:

```
article {
    width: 600px;
    padding: 10%;
}
section {
    padding: inherit;
}
```

HTML:

```
<article>
    <section>
        <p>Hello world</p>
    </section>
</article>
```

What will be the `padding` value of the `section` element? You might think it will be the computed value of the `article` element's `padding` property, but that's not the case. Because `padding` is a property whose percentages depend on the dimensions of the containing block, the final value for the `section` element's `padding` property in this case is `60px`—that is, `10%` of the `article` element's `600px` width.

#### EXERCISES

**Exercise 3.6:** What font size will the `p` element render at?

CSS:

```
html {
    font-size: 16px;
}
article {
    font-size: 1.25rem;
}
section {
    font-size: 1.2em;
}
p {
    font-size: inherit;
}
```

HTML:

```
<article>
    <section>
```

```
        <p>Hello world</p>
    </section>
</article>
```

1. `16px`
2. `19.2px`
3. `20px`
4. `24px`

**Exercise 3.7:** What is the final `margin` value for the `section` element?

CSS:

```
body {
    width: 1000px;
}
article {
    margin: 5%;
}
section {
    margin: inherit;
}
```

HTML:

```
<body>
    <article>
        <section>
            <p>Hello world</p>
        </section>
    </article>
</body>
```

## 3.5 Box model math

You might normally think of the CSS box model as a visual concept: a nested series of boxes, with the innermost content box surrounded by padding, then a border, then a margin. However, in this section, I want to make the case that you should augment that visual model with the idea that the box model is fundamentally a *mathematical* model that defines how browsers calculate the dimensions and spacing of elements on a page. Embracing the math of the box model, and thereby understanding the precise calculations involved, helps you create predictable layouts and troubleshoot common sizing problems. As you'll learn over the next few sections, the box model is essentially an arithmetic formula for determining an element's total rendered size based on several component properties.

### 3.5.1 The default box model formulas

In the default CSS box model, the total width of an element is calculated using the following formula (refer to figure 3.8):

```
width + padding-left + padding-right + border-left-width + border-right-width
```

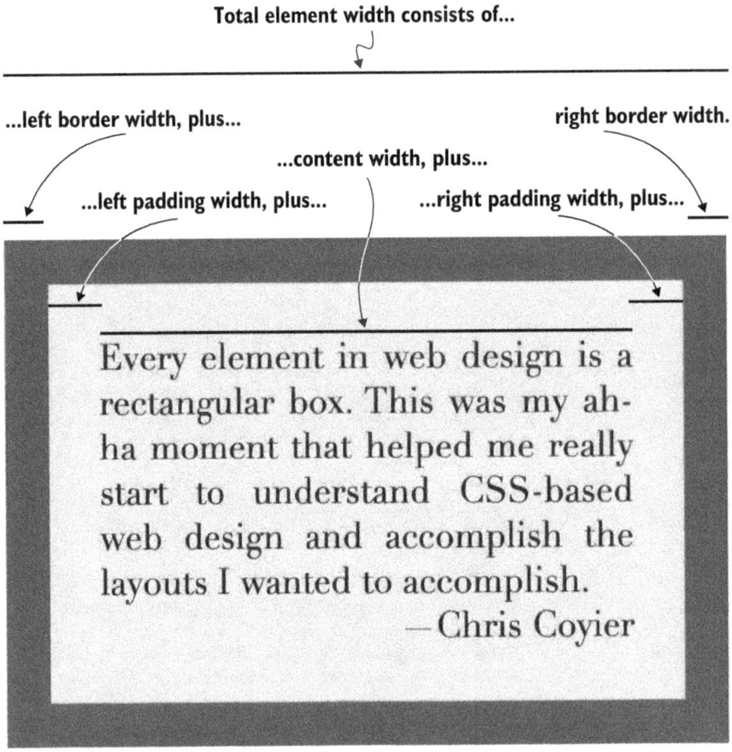


**Figure 3.8 The total width of an element is the sum of the following widths: left border and padding, content, and right padding and border.**

Similarly, by default, the total height of an element is calculated as follows:

```
height + padding-top + padding-bottom + border-top-width + border-bottom-width
```

Here, `height` is either a declared `height` property value or, more likely, the computed height of the element based on its content.

So, for example, the total width formula means that when you set `width: 300px` on an element, the actual space it occupies on the page will be wider if you add padding and/or borders:

```
.box {
    width: 300px;
    padding: 20px;
    border: 10px solid black;
}
```

The total rendered width of the element will be `360px`:

```
300px + 20px + 20px + 10px + 10px
```

This behavior often challenges design intuition because the declared width isn't the final rendered width.

### 3.5.2 How the box-sizing property affects the box model formulas

The `box-sizing` property changes how the browser calculates an element's dimensions. It has two primary values: `content-box` and `border-box`. `box-sizing: content-box` is the default and implements the box model formulas from the previous section:

```
.content-box {
    width: 300px;
    padding: 20px;
    border: 10px solid black;
}
```

Here, the total width is `360px` (`300px + 40px + 20px`), and the content area width is `300px`.

However, many developers make their lives easier by using `box-sizing: border-box` instead. Switching to `box-sizing: border-box` changes the formulas by including padding and border within the declared width or height. This alternative model simplifies layout math because the element's outer dimensions directly match the value you specify. For example,

```
* {
    box-sizing: border-box;     ← Apply border-box to all box model elements
}
.box {
    width: 300px;
    padding: 20px;
    border: 10px solid black;
}
```

Now the total width is `300px` because the padding and border are included; the content area width is `240px` (`300px - 40px - 20px`).

If you need to know the dimensions of your content, you need to subtract the padding and borders. Here's the formula for the content width:

```
width - padding-left - padding-right - border-left-width - border-right-width
```

And here's the formula for the content height:

```
height - padding-top - padding-bottom - border-top-width - border-bottom-width
```

### 3.5.3 Margin math and collapsing

Margins add another layer to box model calculations, but they don't affect the element's own dimensions; they affect the spacing between elements. When working with vertical margins between elements in particular, a mathematical phenomenon called "margin collapsing" occurs, as shown in the following listing.

**Listing 3.18 Margin collapsing**

```
.box1 {
    margin-bottom: 30px;
}

.box2 {
    margin-top: 20px;
}
```

Intuitively, you might expect the total space between these elements to be `50px` (`30px` + `20px`). However, vertical margins collapse, and only the larger of the two values takes effect.

The mathematical rule is

```
Collapsed margin height = max(margin-bottom of previous element, margin-top
of next element)
```

In this example, the space between the boxes will be `30px`, not `50px`.

> **NOTE** Margin collapse happens only between block-level boxes participating in a *block formatting context* (BFC). So, elements with `display: block` or `display: list-item` can have their vertical margins collapse. However, collapsing stops the moment you switch to a different formatting context, such as `display: inline-block`, `display: grid`, or `display: flex`.

### 3.5.4 Percentages and the box model

Percentage-based dimensions add another level of mathematical complexity to the box model. When using percentage values, the calculations depend on the parent element, as shown in the following listing.

**Listing 3.19 Percentages and the box model**

```
.parent {
    width: 500px;
}
```

```
.child {
    width: 50%;          ← 250px
    padding: 5%;         ← 25px on each side
    margin: 10%;         ← 50px on each side
}
```

Here, the total child width using `content-box` would be `300px` (`250px + 25px + 25px`), while the total width using `border-box` would be `250px`.

The critical detail is that percentage-based padding and margin values are calculated based on the parent's width, not the element's own width. This is true even for top and bottom padding and margin values, which can be more than a little counterintuitive, as shown in the following listing.

**Listing 3.20 Percentages and the box model (part 2)**

```
.parent {
    width: 400px;
    height: 100vh;
}
.child {
    padding-top: 5%;        ← 20px (5% of parent width, not height)
    margin-bottom: 10%;     ← 40px (10% of parent width, not height)
}
```

For both the `padding-top` and `margin-bottom` values in this example, the parent's declared `height` value is ignored, and the parent's declared `width` value is used to derive the padding and margin values.

### 3.5.5 Using calc() for precise box model math

As shown in the next listing, the `calc()` function is particularly valuable for box model calculations, especially when mixing units or solving layout equations.

**Listing 3.21 Precision box model math with `calc()`**

```
.container {
    width: 90vw;
}
.column {
    width: calc((100% - 40px) / 3);    ← Create three equal columns
    margin-right: 20px;                ← Use 20px gutters
}
.column:last-child {
    margin-right: 0;
}
```

Here, the calculation ensures that three columns plus two gutters exactly fit the container width. The formula is

```
column width = (container width - total gutter width) / number of columns
```

As another example, a common web dev problem is how to fit a child element inside a padded container. As shown in the following listing, the `calc()` function is your friend here.

**Listing 3.22 Fitting a child element inside a padded container**

```
.container {
    padding: 1rem;
}
.child {
    width: calc(100% - 2rem);      ◄── Subtract left + right padding
}
```

The `calc()` expression subtracts the container's padding on both sides, which ensures that the child's width fits inside the container's content area. (This calculation is needed only if you're using `box-sizing: content-box` on these elements. If you're using `box-sizing: border-box`, you can declare `width: 100%` on the child to make it fit.)

#### EXERCISES

**Exercise 3.8:** Given the following code, what is the rendered width of the `.box` element?

```
* {
    box-sizing: content-box;
}
.box {
    width: 300px;
    padding: 10px;
    border: 5px solid black;
}
```

1. `300px`
2. `320px`
3. `330px`
4. `350px`

**Exercise 3.9:** For the following CSS rules, assume in the page's HTML that a `div` with a class of `box2` appears immediately after a `div` with a class of `box1`. What is the vertical margin space between the two elements?

```
.box1 {
    margin-bottom: 25px;
}

.box2 {
    margin-top: 40px;
}
```

1. 0px
2. 15px
3. 25px
4. 40px

## 3.6 Solutions to Exercises

**Exercise 3.1:** In CSS, `1in` is equal to `96px`. Therefore,

```
0.25in = 0.25 * 96 = 24px
```

The correct answer is `24px`.

**Exercise 3.2:** The `grandparent` class sets the base font size of `16px`, so calculating the `grandchild` font size requires a multiplicative progression through the generations:

```
16px * 1.25 = 20px
20px * 1.25 = 25px
25px * 1.25 = 31.25x
```

The parent font size

The child font size

The grandchild font size

The answer is `31.25px`.

**Exercise 3.3:** 1 is invalid syntax; 3 mixes incompatible units; and 4 divides two unit-bearing values. Therefore, the correct answer is 2.

**Exercise 3.4:** Subtract `30px` (there are two gutters, so `15px * 2 = 30px`) from the total parent width, then divide by `3`:

```
.column {
    width: calc((100% - 30px) / 3);
}
```

**Exercise 3.5:** This is a job for the CSS `clamp()` function:

```
h1 {
    font-size: clamp(40px, 7vw, 72px);
}
```

**Exercise 3.6:** From the `html` rule, `1rem = 16px`. The `article` element's `font-size` value is `1.25rem = (16px * 1.25) = 20px`. The `section` element's `font-size` value is `1.2em = (20px * 1.2) = 24px`. The `p` element inherits from the `section` element, so the correct answer is `24px`.

**Exercise 3.7:** The `article` element's rendered width is `1000px - ((1000px * 5%) * 2) = 900px`. Since `margin` percentages depend on the dimensions of the containing block, the final value for the `section` element's `margin` property is `900px * 5% = 45px`.

**Exercise 3.8:** With `box-sizing: content-box`, the rendered width is the declared width plus the left and right padding and the left and right border: `300px + 20px + 10px = 330px`. Therefore, 3 is the correct answer.

**Exercise 3.9:** These margin values collapse, and the browser chooses the larger of the two, so the correct answer is `40px`.

## Summary

- Understanding how `em`, `rem`, `vw`, `vh`, and percentage values are calculated lets you create properly scaled interfaces that maintain proper proportions.
- The `calc()` function can perform arithmetic with different units, such as combining percentages with pixels.
- The `calc()` function works in combination with CSS variables for dynamic calculations.
- Constraint functions such as `min()`, `max()`, and `clamp()` establish boundaries for values.
- The `rem()` function preserves the sign of the dividend, making it suitable for certain physics calculations.
- The `mod()` function takes the sign of the divisor, making it better for cyclic behaviors such as color wheels and carousels.
- Functions such as `sqrt()` and `pow()` let you create proportional scaling effects.
- Inheritance in CSS usually involves computed values, not just specified ones.
- `box-sizing: content-box` (the CSS default) means that the true rendered dimensions of each element are the content size plus the padding and margins.
- `box-sizing: border-box` means that the declared dimensions of each element include the content size plus the padding and margins.
- When an element's bottom margin meets the next element's top margin, the margins collapse into a single value, which is the larger of the two margin values.

# 4 CSS Grid math

**This chapter covers**

- The math that underlies CSS Grid
- The Grid coordinate system
- The grid track sizing algorithm
- Putting Grid's track-sizing functions to good use

It's hard to even imagine it now, but there was a time not that long ago when a web designer's go-to layout tool was an HTML table! It actually made a bit of sense back then since a table provided structure, and what web pages desperately needed in the early days was some sort of structure. Ah, but what a rigid, unforgiving scaffolding it was!

Those primitive days are happily behind us now that we have CSS Grid as the basic layout engine of the modern web (along with Flexbox, covered in chapter 5). But the power of CSS Grid comes at the cost of increased complexity, especially as the number of page components increases. Still, that complexity is fundamentally a math problem because Grid is using math behind the scenes to divide up your page. When you understand that math, which is the goal of this chapter, it becomes much easier to create robust, creative layouts and to troubleshoot any Grid layout problems that arise.

## 4.1 The mathematical foundations of CSS Grid

CSS Grid gives you precise control over how the space within a grid container is carved up vertically and horizontally. Underneath that control is a whole lot of mathematics. Whether you define your grid columns and rows using a fixed unit such as `px`, a flexible unit such as `fr`, a function such as `minmax()`, or a keyword such as `auto` (or, often, a combination of all of these), the browser runs through a series of behind-the-page calculations to determine how much space each grid track is allotted and where the page items should be placed.

I believe that most web developers use Grid by trial and error, tinkering with Grid-related properties and keywords until they get something that works. While there's nothing wrong with such Grid hacking, understanding the mathematical foundations that power CSS Grid will help you create more precise and more intentional layouts.

CSS Grid is, at heart, a radical shift in the mathematics of web layout. Unlike the default browser layout model, which relies primarily on the linear flow of elements, and unlike the one-dimensional approach of Flexbox, Grid introduces a true two-dimensional coordinate system with its own algebraic model. This mathematical foundation is what makes Grid so powerful and lets web developers like you build complex, intricate layouts that, even a few years ago, were exceedingly difficult or even impossible to achieve.

### 4.1.1 Foundations of the grid formatting context

CSS Grid might seem like a fundamentally visual layout model, but really, it's mathematics all the way down. However, before getting into the nitty-gritty of fractional units, track calculations, and other Grid-based math, it's crucial to understand the environment in which Grid operates: the grid formatting context. This context governs how items are placed and sized within a grid container and how the grid itself is constructed in relation to the box model.

When you set `display: grid` on a container, it establishes a *grid formatting context*, which is a layout mode where the container's child elements are treated as grid items and are laid out according to the grid model rather than the browser's default flow.

Establishing a grid formatting context has three main consequences:

- Child elements are no longer part of the default block or inline flow.
- The grid container becomes responsible for computing child sizes and positions.
- Inline children don't line-wrap. Instead, they're placed in individual grid cells.

### 4.1.2 The coordinate system approach

Mathematically speaking, CSS Grid implements a discrete coordinate system. When you define a grid container, you're essentially establishing a coordinate plane where

- The horizontal axis represents columns.
- The vertical axis represents rows.
- The intersection of a column and a row forms a cell where content is placed.

This coordinate-based approach differs fundamentally from the flow-based mathematics of traditional CSS. In flow layout, positions are calculated sequentially and relatively, with each element affecting those that follow. Grid, however, establishes absolute positions within a defined space, similar to how you might plot points on a graph.

### 4.1.3 The algebraic model

The mathematics of Grid isn't just about coordinates; it's also built on algebraic relationships that determine how space is calculated and distributed. These relationships are especially evident in how Grid handles available space.

When you use values like `fr` units or functions like `minmax()`, you're creating algebraic expressions that the browser must solve. For example,

```
grid-template-columns: 1fr 2fr 1fr;
```

This declaration creates an algebraic equation where the total available width equals some value $w$, and we need to solve for $x$. Here's what's known from the declaration:

- Column 1 equals $x$.
- Column 2 equals $2x$.
- Column 3 equals $x$.

Therefore, this declaration results in the following algebraic sequence:

```
x + 2x + x = w
4x = w
x = w/4
```

With this result in hand, the browser can now parcel out the space for each column.

The browser dynamically solves this equation whenever the container width changes, recalculating the value of each track. This algebraic approach enables Grid's responsiveness, while maintaining proportional relationships between elements.

### 4.1.4 Mathematical differences from other layout systems

One way to appreciate the mathematical model that underlies Grid is to compare it with the math used by other major CSS layout systems:

- *Block flow*—Calculates heights and widths sequentially as elements flow down the page in source code order. Space distribution is indirect, often requiring percentage-based calculations that can be imprecise.
- *Float*—Uses displacement calculations where elements shift to allow floated elements to move left or right. Mathematically, it creates complex

spatial relationships that become increasingly unpredictable as floated elements interact.

- *Positioning*—Uses offset calculations from reference points but lacks the ability to establish mathematical relationships between multiple elements.
- *Table based*—Slots elements into table cells, so its calculations are limited to cell sizing within rows and columns.
- *Flexbox*—Uses a constraint-based mathematical model for one-dimensional layouts. It distributes space by solving for flex factors (I go into this in geeky detail in chapter 5) but operates along a single axis at a time.

Grid takes the best mathematical aspects of many of these models and extends them by

- Creating predictable layout mathematics (unlike, say, the complex interactions of floats)
- Providing precise coordinate-based placement (similar to positioning)
- Implementing two-dimensional constraints (beyond what tables can do)
- Offering flexible space distribution (similar to Flexbox, but in two dimensions)
- Supporting both explicit and implicit track creation (unlike any previous layout system)

This mathematical foundation enables Grid to handle complex layouts with fewer calculations and more predictable results than any previous layout method.

## 4.2 The Grid coordinate system

CSS Grid is based on a simple coordinate system, reminiscent of a sheet of graph paper or a spreadsheet. That is, a grid is best pictured as a two-dimensional Cartesian plane. When you create a grid container, you're essentially drawing invisible lines that create rows and columns. These lines form a framework that lets you place items precisely, so it's no stretch to say that grid lines are the fundamental building blocks of the CSS Grid coordinate system.

### 4.2.1 The grid model

Consider the following listing.

**Listing 4.1 A grid container**

```
.container {
    display: grid;
    grid-template-columns: 100px 200px 100px;
    grid-template-rows: 50px 150px;
}
```

**NOTE** All the code for this chapter's listings is available in this book's GitHub repository: https://github.com/paulmcfe/web-dev-math.

This rule creates a grid with four vertical lines (one for each of the three columns, plus one at the end) and three horizontal lines (one for each of the two rows, plus one at the end), as shown in figure 4.1.

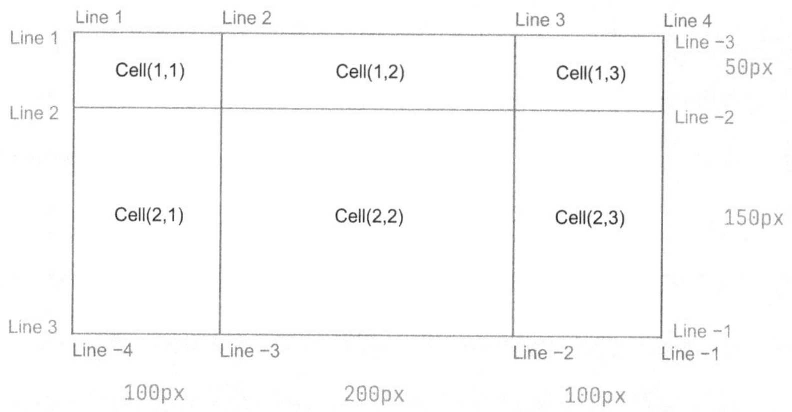


**Figure 4.1 A 3x2 grid formatting context**

Here are some points of interest to note in figure 4.1:

- Each column or row exists between two grid lines.
- Grid lines are numbered starting from 1, not 0.
- You can refer to grid lines by positive numbers, which start at 1 from the top-left corner, or by negative numbers, which start at –1 from the bottom-right corner.
- Grid items are placed into the cells between these lines, which are numbered and can also be named.

Note, too, that you can display these line numbers as annotations over your grid by opening your browser's devtools, displaying the Layout tab, enabling the grid overlay, and then setting the overlay to display line numbers, as shown in figure 4.2.

A grid cell is the space between four grid lines: two vertical and two horizontal. For example, the cell at column 3, row 2 is bound by vertical lines 3 and 4 and horizontal lines 2 and 3. This is why when you place an item at a specific grid position, you're actually specifying which grid lines it should sit between:

```
.item {
    grid-column: 3 / 4;      ◄── Between vertical lines 3 and 4
    grid-row: 2 / 3;         ◄── Between horizontal lines 2 and 3
}
```

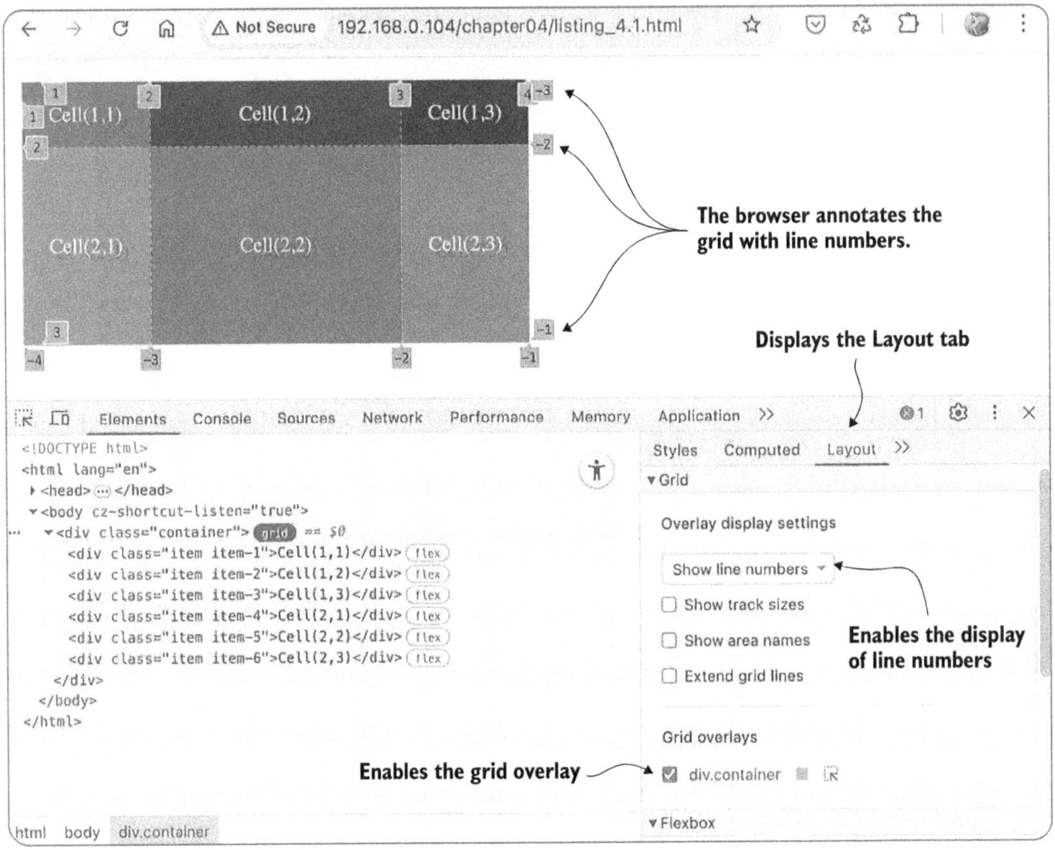


**Figure 4.2 You can enable the display of grid line numbers in your browser's devtools.**

> **NOTE** Remember that `grid-column` is a shorthand property for `grid-column-start` (the first number) and `grid-column-end` (the second number). Similarly, `grid-row` is a shorthand for `grid-row-start` and `grid-row-end`.

A grid item can occupy multiple cells:

```
.item {
    grid-column: 2 / 4;
    grid-row: 1 / 3;
}
```

**Spans columns between lines 2 and 4 (2 tracks)**

**Spans rows between lines 1 and 3 (2 tracks)**

> **NOTE** If you have a coding background, you're no doubt used to *zero-based indexing*, where things such as array indexes start at 0 instead of 1. So, note well that CSS Grid uses one-based numbering for its grid lines, which is why the first grid line is line 1, not line 0.

### 4.2.2 Span notation and its mathematical meaning

The span keyword introduces another mathematical concept in Grid's coordinate system. Instead of specifying absolute end coordinates, span defines a relative distance from the starting position.

Mathematically, if an item starts at line n and spans m tracks, its end line will be at line n + m. For example,

```
.item {
    grid-column: 2 / span 3;     ← Starts at line 2 and spans 3 columns
}
```

Since 2 + 3 = 5, the preceding rule is equivalent to the following:

```
.item {
    grid-column: 2 / 5;
}
```

The span notation is particularly useful when you don't know the exact size of the grid but want to ensure an element covers a specific number of tracks. It creates a relative mathematical relationship rather than an absolute position.

### 4.2.3 Working smarter with negative indexing

Grid's coordinate system gets more mathematically sophisticated with its support for negative indices. Negative grid lines are counted backward from the end of the grid. Line –1 refers to the last grid line, line –2 refers to the second-to-last grid line, and so on.

> **WARNING** CSS Grid only assigns negative line numbers to explicit grid tracks. If you're letting the browser auto-generate rows or columns, those implicit tracks don't get assigned negative line numbers.

Negative grid lines might seem like a quirky or esoteric addition to the Grid spec, but negative indexing can be a powerful addition to your design toolkit. Why? Because it lets you reference tracks relative to the end of the grid without knowing the grid's exact size. For dynamic or responsive layouts, this means you can ensure that an item is always placed relative to the right or bottom of the grid, regardless of how many tracks are created.

#### SPANNING AN ITEM ACROSS A CHANGING NUMBER OF COLUMNS

One common grid need is for an item to span the entire width of the table. For example, you might need to do this for a title, a caption, or a footnote. If the number of columns is fixed, then you could use a simple span:

```
.container {
    display: grid;
    grid-template-columns: 2fr 1fr 1fr;
```

```
}

.title-row {
    grid-column: 1 / span 3;     ◄── Spans across all three columns
}
```

But what if the number of columns can change? In that case, you can design a smarter grid by taking advantage of negative line numbers, as shown in the following listing:

**Listing 4.2 Placing an item as the last row of the grid container**

```
.title-row {
    grid-column: 1 / -1;     ◄── Spans every column, regardless of the number
}
```

The `grid-column` value creates a span that runs from the first line number (`1`) to the last line number (`-1`). By using `-1` to designate the last line in the grid, it doesn't matter how many columns are in the table, and it still works, even if the number of columns changes.

#### Making sure an item is always the last row

Another powerful use of negative line numbers is ensuring that an item always takes up the last row of the grid container, even in a dynamic layout where the number of rows can change. For example, if you have a web page showing a grid of products with inventory, you might want a row showing the total inventory, and it makes sense for that to be the last row of the grid, as shown in the following listing.

**Listing 4.3 Placing an item as the last row of the grid container**

```
.total-row {
    grid-column: 1 / -1;     ◄── Spans every column
    grid-row: -2 / -1;       ◄── Occupies the last row
}
```

The `grid-column` value creates a span across the entire grid, regardless of how many columns the grid contains, and still works even if the number of columns changes. Similarly, the `grid-row` value defines a track that runs from the second-last horizontal line in the grid to the last horizontal line, regardless of how many rows precede it or how many rows are inserted or removed above it. In other words, this item will always occupy the last row of the grid container. Figure 4.3 shows an example grid that includes a title row and a total row, both placed using negative line numbers.

Understanding Grid's coordinate system gives you the mathematical foundation to place elements precisely within your layouts. As you progress through this chapter, you'll see how this coordinate system interacts with Grid's sizing algorithm to create flexible yet predictable layouts that adapt to different content and container sizes.

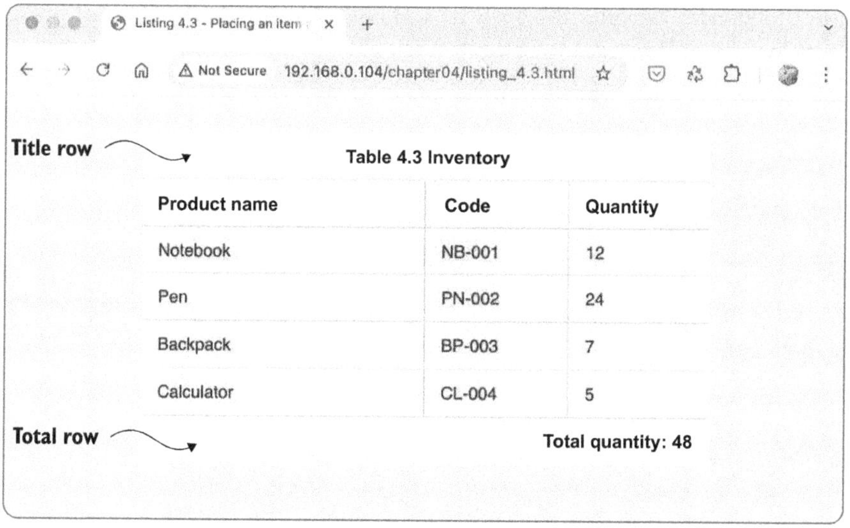


**Figure 4.3 The first row and last row are placed using negative line numbers.**

### EXERCISES

**Exercise 4.1:** In a four-column, two-row grid, which grid line numbers bound the third column?

1. 2 and 3
2. 3 and 4
3. 1 and 2
4. 4 and 5

**Exercise 4.2:** Convert the following to use the `span` keyword:

```
.item {
    grid-column: 3 / 8;
}
```

**Exercise 4.3:** Suppose you want to build a grid with a footer in the last row, so you use the following grid structure:

```
.grid {
    display: grid;
    grid-template-columns: 1fr 1fr 1fr;
    grid-auto-rows: 200px;
}
.footer {
    grid-column: 1 / -1;
    grid-row: -2 / -1;
}
```

However, when you display the page as shown in figure 4.4, the footer appears in the top row instead of the bottom. Why?

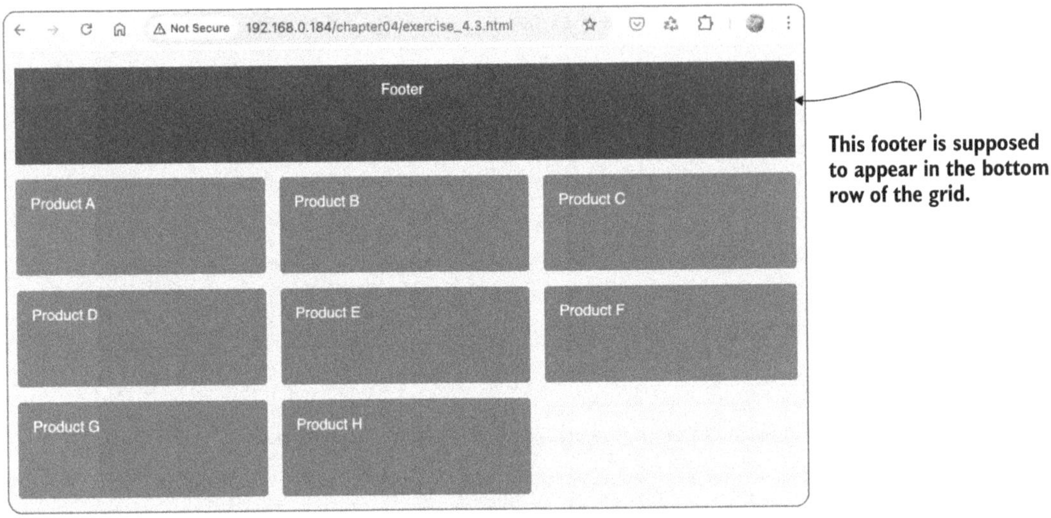


**Figure 4.4 The footer is placed in the top row instead of the bottom.**

## 4.3 The grid track sizing algorithm

One of the most powerful (and most misunderstood) features of CSS Grid is its ability to size tracks dynamically based on multiple factors, including the structure of the grid container, the contents of grid items, and flexible units like `fr`. This dynamic sizing is governed by the *grid track sizing algorithm*, a deterministic set of rules that defines exactly how wide or tall each row or column should be.

The grid track sizing algorithm consists of four main phases, executed in order. Each track (row or column) goes through the following sequence to determine its final size:

1. Determine which tracks exist. Grid looks for two track types:
   - *Explicit tracks*—Tracks defined by `grid-template-columns` and `grid-template-rows`.
   - *Implicit tracks*—Tracks that are deliberately placed outside the explicit grid (such as setting `grid-column: 5` in a three-column layout) or that Grid adds automatically when it determines that it needs extra columns or rows to place all the items.
2. Set the intrinsic size of each track. Tracks sized with keywords such as `min-content`, `max-content`, or `auto` rely on intrinsic sizing where these values are derived from the contents of the items inside the tracks. For each track, the algorithm calculates

   - *Minimum contribution*—The smallest the track can be without clipping
   - *Maximum contribution*—The space the track needs if all its content expands fully
3. Determine the content-based growth or shrinkage of each track that depends on explicit constraints, such as a `min-content` keyword or a `minmax()` function.
4. Distribute the remaining space to tracks that use `fr` units.

Each of these steps includes mathematical operations and constraints that determine the final size of each track. The next few sections delve into some of the details of this algorithm.

### 4.3.1 The algebra of grid line placement

Fundamentally, a grid container is an algebraic system. For example, consider a basic definition for grid columns:

```
grid-template-columns: 200px 2fr 1fr;
```

The value for the `grid-template-columns` property is essentially an algebraic equation where `1fr` is `x`. What the browser does is solve for `x`:

```
Container width = 200 + 2x + x
Container width - 200 = 3x
(Container width - 200) / 3 = x
```

For example, consider the following rule:

```
.container {
    display: grid;
    grid-template-columns: 200px 2fr 1fr;
    width: 800px;
}
```

The grid container width is `800px`, so you can plug that value into the equation:

```
800 = 200 + 2x + 1x
800 - 200 = 3x
600 / 3 = x
200 = x
```

Since `x` represents `1fr`, this result means that the second column (defined as `2fr`) will be `400px` wide and the third column (defined as `1fr`) will be `200px` wide.

### 4.3.2 How fr units distribute available space

The fractional (`fr`) unit, a length of which is called a *flexible length* or *<flex>*, is surely Grid's most innovative contribution to layout mathematics. It represents a fraction of the available space in the grid container after accounting for all fixed-size tracks and grid gaps.

`fr` units work as follows:

1. The browser determines the container size.
2. The browser subtracts the space occupied by the fixed-size tracks and the grid gaps from the container size.
3. The remaining space as calculated in step 2 is then distributed proportionally according to the `fr` values.

Let's express this mathematically. Let

- $C$ = container width
- $F$ = sum of all fixed track widths
- $G$ = sum of all grid gap widths
- $R$ = remaining free space = $C - F - G$
- $T$ = total of all `fr` units

Then, for any flexible track with a value of *n*`fr`, the track's actual width $W$ is given by the following formula:

```
W = (n / T) * R
```

For example,

```
.container {
    display: grid;
    width: 1000px;
    grid-template-columns: 100px 1fr 2fr 120px;
    column-gap: 20px;
}
```

Let's do the math:

- Fixed tracks are `100px + 120px = 220px`
- Grid gaps are `20px * 3 = 60px`
- Remaining free space is `1000px - 220px - 60px = 720px`
- Total `fr` units are `1fr + 2fr = 3fr`
- Width of `1fr` track is `(1/3) * 720px = 240px`
- Width of `2fr` track is `(2/3) * 720px = 480px`

Ah, but we're not done yet. There are usually a few other measures to take into account, as described in the next section.

### 4.3.3 Taking the box model into account

In the previous section, I mentioned that a grid container's available space was the total space minus the fixed-size tracks and the grid gaps. But if you have `box-sizing:`

`border-box` set on the container, there are a few other box model items to consider. With columns, for example, you also have to factor in the left and right padding and the left and right border widths.

Consider the following grid container:

```
.container {
    display: grid;
    grid-template-columns: 200px 2fr 1fr;
    gap: 30px;
    border: 6px solid black;
    padding: 15px;
    width: 800px;
}
```

What size is applied to the second and third columns? Let's work through the math:

- *C* = container width = `800px`
- *F* = sum of all fixed track widths = `200px`
- *G* = sum of all grid gap widths = `30px * 2 = 60px`
- *B* = sum of left and right border widths = `2 * 6px = 12px`
- *P* = sum of left and right padding widths = `2 * 15px = 30px`
- *R* = remaining free space = *C* – *F* – *G* – *B* – *P* = `800px - 200px - 60px - 12px - 30px = 498px`
- *T* = total of all `fr` units = `2 + 1 = 3`
- Width of `2fr` track = `(2/3) * 498px = 332px`
- Width of `1fr` track = `(1/3) * 498px = 166px`

This is finicky stuff, and forgetting to take padding and borders into account might be why your grid layout isn't behaving the way you expect.

### 4.3.4 The algorithm for calculating fr unit values

The browser's algorithm for resolving `fr` units follows a more complex mathematical process than the previous simplified explanation, especially when combined with other sizing constraints. The complete algorithm involves

1. Calculating what the CSS Grid spec calls the "hypothetical `fr` size" by distributing free space
2. Checking this size against `min-content`, `max-content`, and `minmax()` constraints (refer to section 4.4)
3. Adjusting the distribution if tracks hit their minimum or maximum constraints
4. Recalculating the distribution for the remaining tracks, if needed

This iterative mathematical process ensures that `fr` units distribute space optimally while respecting all content-based constraints.

### 4.3.5 Troubleshooting: When <flex> resolves to 0px

If your grid is overflowing or if an item is displaying with far less space than you expected, one common culprit is a flexible track with a calculated <flex> of `0px`. This can happen if the sum of fixed tracks equals or exceeds the container width. In that case, there's no available space left in the container, so all <flex> values evaluate to `0px`, as shown in the following listing.

**Listing 4.4 When a <flex> resolves to `0px`**

```
.narrow-container
    display: grid;
    width: 300px;                                  ◄ Container is just 300px wide
    grid-template-columns: 200px 100px 1fr;        ◄ Fixed tracks sum to 300px
}
```

In this case, since the sum of the fixed-size tracks (`300px`) equals the width of the container (also `300px`), the `1fr` column mathematically resolves to `0px`. However, the browser will still display the column as overflow, and the column will be given its minimum required width (based on its minimum content width or some other minimum constraint specified elsewhere). Figure 4.5 shows an example.

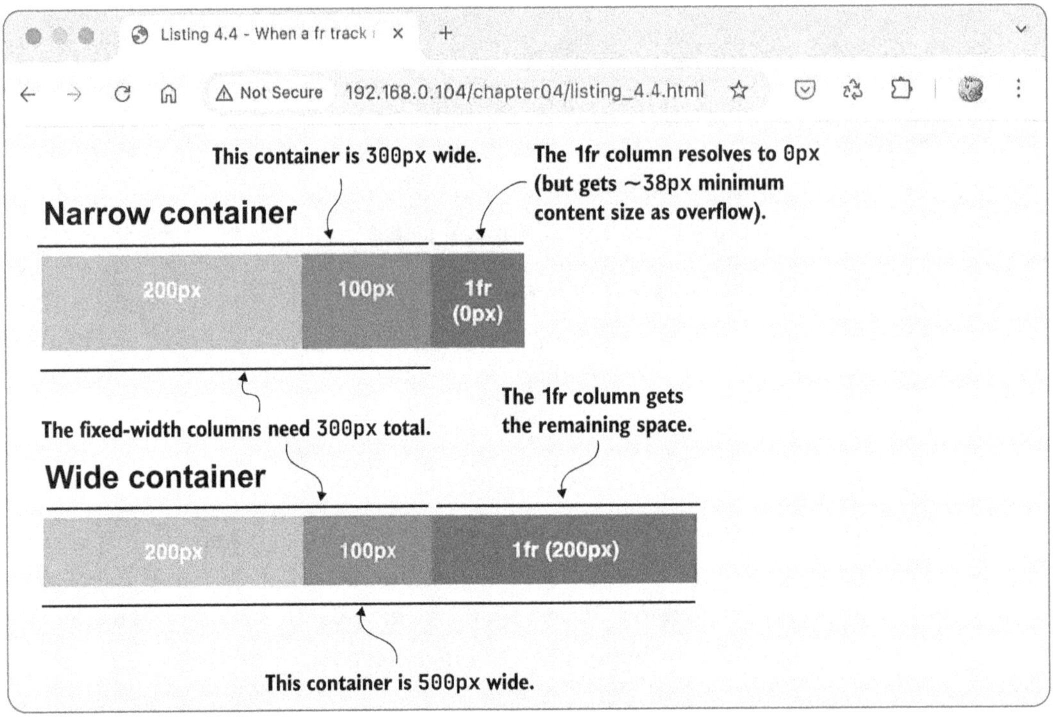


Figure 4.5 In the narrow container, the `1fr` column resolves to `0px`, but it is still displayed at its content minimum width.

`fr` units never cause a track to become smaller than its minimum content size, unless explicitly overridden (say, with a `max-width` value smaller than the item's minimum size). Mathematically, this creates the following relationship:

```
actual_track_width = max(calculated_flex_value, min_content_width)
```

In the previous example, the calculated `<flex>` value of the third column is `0px`, while the item's padding and text give it a minimum content size of approximately `38px`. Therefore,

```
actual_track_width = max(0px, 38px)
                   = 38px
```

The first two columns continue to take up the entirety of the container, so the third column is displayed as overflow.

#### Exercises

**Exercise 4.4:** Given the following grid,

```
.container {
    width: 960px;
    display: grid;
    grid-template-columns: 80px 3fr 2fr 1fr 120px;
    column-gap: 15px;
}
```

calculate the widths of the middle three columns.

**Exercise 4.5:** In a fixed-width, two-column grid, a developer expects their `fr` columns to be `200px` and `400px`, respectively, but they're getting different values. Find the error (assume `box-sizing: border-box` is set on all elements):

```
.container {
    display: grid;
    grid-template-columns: 1fr 2fr;
    width: 600px;
    border: 10px solid black;
    padding: 20px;
}
```

**Exercise 4.6:** Consider the following code to establish a three-column grid:

CSS:

```
.grid {
    display: grid;
    grid-template-columns: 300px 200px 1fr;
    gap: 1px;
    background-color: black;
    border: 1px solid black;
    width: 503px;
}
```

HTML:

```
<div class="grid">
    <div class="item final">Product A</div>
    <div class="item final">Product B</div>
    <div class="item provisional"></div>
</div>
```

Figure 4.6 shows the result. Why are only two columns shown?

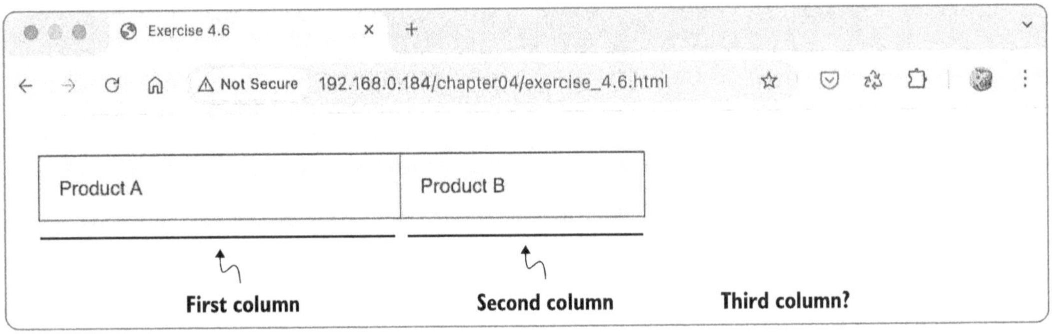


**Figure 4.6** The container is defined as a three-column grid, but only two columns are rendered.

## 4.4 The math of Grid's track-sizing functions and keywords

CSS Grid provides several specialized functions and keywords that calculate track sizes dynamically based on content, container dimensions, or repeating patterns. These functions implement sophisticated mathematical algorithms that go beyond simple fixed or fractional sizing. Understanding the math behind these functions and keywords will go a long way toward helping you predict how they'll behave in different scenarios.

### 4.4.1 Controlling track sizes with minmax()

For more control over your track sizes, you can turn to the `minmax(min, max)` function, which defines a track size that's greater than or equal to `min` and less than or equal to `max`. (If `max` happens to be less than `min`, the browser ignores `max` and just uses `min`.) `minmax()` really shines when you use a `<flex>` value as the `max` parameter (`fr` units are invalid to use as the `min` parameter). Here's an example:

```
grid-template-columns: 3fr minmax(250px, 1fr);
```

This code defines two columns:

- The first column gets three fractions of the grid container's available space.
- The second column gets one fraction of the available space, unless that fraction is less than `250px`. If it is, then the column's width is set to `250px`.

#### UNDERSTANDING MINMAX() WITH AN EXAMPLE

For example, consider the rule in the following listing.

**Listing 4.5 minmax() example**

```
.container {
    display: grid;
    grid-template-columns: 3fr minmax(250px, 1fr);
    width: 1200px;
}
```

The browser sees that this rule would like to divide the container into two columns and a maximum of four fractional units. It first calculates the value of `1fr` in that scenario:

```
1200px = 3fr + 1fr
1200px = 4fr
300px = 1fr
```

The first column width is `3fr = 900px`. The second column width is `1fr = 300px`. Since the width of the second column is greater than the minimum set by the `minmax()` function (i.e., `250px`), that column's width is set to `300px`, as shown in figure 4.7 (top).

Now consider the rule in the next listing.

**Listing 4.6 minmax() example (continued)**

```
.container {
    display: grid;
    grid-template-columns: 3fr minmax(250px, 1fr);
    width: 800px;
}
```

The container now has a width of `800px`, so the calculation of `1fr` changes accordingly:

```
800px = 3fr + 1fr
800px = 4fr
200px = 1fr
```

The first column width is `3fr = 600px`. The second column width is `1fr = 200px`. However, since the width of the second column is less than the minimum set by the `minmax()` function, that column's width is set to that minimum (i.e., `250px`) and the first column's width is reduced to `550px`. Figure 4.7 (bottom) shows the effect of these two rules.

#### PUTTING MINMAX() TO WORK: A PRODUCT CARD GRID

A great use-case for `minmax()` is a grid of product cards where you want the cards displayed at a minimum width for readability, but it's okay for the card width to expand with the viewport width, as shown in the following listing.

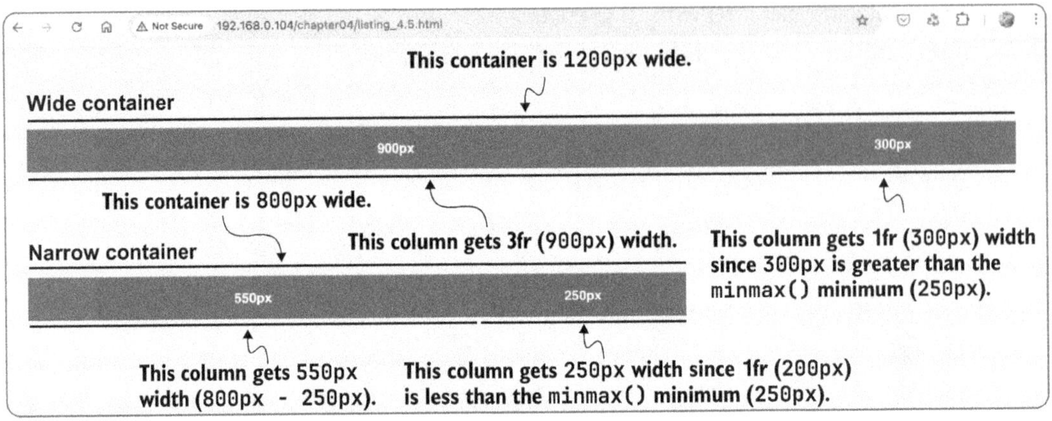


**Figure 4.7** The `minmax()` function gives you more control over your grid tracks.

**Listing 4.7 Using `minmax()` to constrain a product card grid**

```
<head>
    <style>
        .product-grid {
            display: grid;
            grid-template-columns: repeat(4, minmax(250px, 1fr));
            gap: 1.5rem;
        }
    </style>
</head>
<body>

    <h1>Featured Products</h1>

    <div class="product-grid">
        <div class="product-card">
            <img src="https://placehold.co/150" alt="Product 1">
            <h3>Notebook</h3>
            <p>Premium hardcover notebook with 200 pages.</p>
            <button>Add to Cart</button>
        </div>

        <div class="product-card">
            <img src="https://placehold.co/150" alt="Product 2">
            <h3>Wireless Mouse</h3>
            <p>Ergonomic mouse with 2.4GHz wireless connection.</p>
            <button>Add to Cart</button>
        </div>

        <div class="product-card">
            <img src="https://placehold.co/150" alt="Product 3">
            <h3>Backpack</h3>
            <p>Durable backpack with padded laptop compartment.</p>
```

```
            <button>Add to Cart</button>
        </div>

        <div class="product-card">
            <img src="https://placehold.co/150" alt="Product 4">
            <h3>USB-C Charger</h3>
            <p>Fast-charging USB-C wall adapter (60W).</p>
            <button>Add to Cart</button>
        </div>
    </div>

</body>
```

This code defines four grid columns:

```
grid-template-columns: repeat(4, minmax(250px, 1fr));
```

Each column has a minimum width of `250px` but can grow beyond that into the available space. (You'll learn about the `repeat()` function in section 4.4.4.) Figure 4.8 shows the cards at their minimum size.

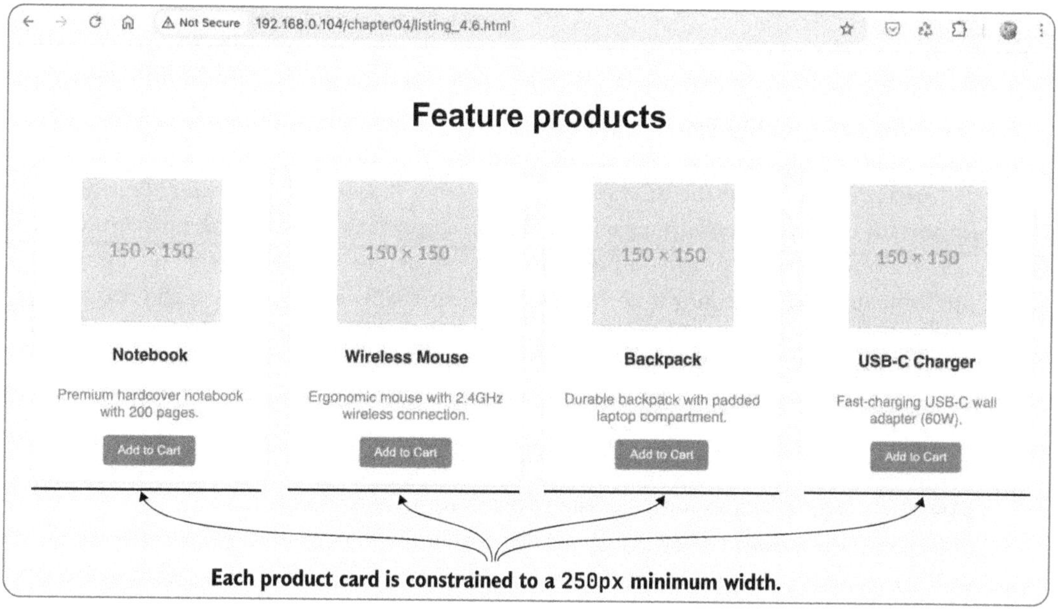


**Figure 4.8 The `minmax()` function constrains the product cards to be no narrower than shown here.**

### 4.4.2 *Understanding auto in grid tracks*

If you prefer to let the browser do more of the work of choosing grid track sizes, then the `auto` keyword is your new best friend. When you specify `auto` as a track size, you're creating a bounded, content-aware track. That is, you're effectively saying to the browser, "Okay, *you* choose the size based on the content inside the track, taking into account the content's intrinsic minimum and maximum sizes."

These intrinsic minimum and maximum sizes are given by the following keywords (respectively):

- `min-content`—The smallest possible size the track can be without overflow based on the content. For width, this means the track becomes as narrow as the widest unbreakable part of content, which is usually the longest word, but it could also be some other fixed-sized element.
- `max-content`—The greatest possible size the track can be without wrapping based on the content. For width, this means the track becomes as wide as needed to fit all its content on a single line.

For example,

```
grid-template-columns: 1fr auto;
```

This is essentially the same as

```
grid-template-columns: 1fr minmax(min-content, max-content);
```

That is, for the second column, you're telling the browser to allow that column's width to shrink down to, but not less than, its intrinsic minimum width, and to grow up to, but not more than, its intrinsic maximum width.

I said previously that the `minmax()` version is only "essentially" the same because one important extra you get with `auto` is that it also respects the values of the `min-width` and `max-width` properties (or `min-height` and `max-height`, for rows) if they're set. For width, the browser applies the larger of the `min-width` and `min-content` values, and the smaller of the `max-width` and `max-content` values. All this means that `auto` is really equivalent to the following (for columns):

```
minmax(max(min-width, min-content), min(max-width, max-content))
```

#### EXAMPLE: CONSTRAINING AN AUTO SIDEBAR WITH MIN-WIDTH AND MAX-WIDTH

One common design scenario is to require that a sidebar be responsive to viewport width but not shrink to its `min-content` width or expand to its `max-content` width, because either would make the content break in some way, usually by making it difficult to read. You solve this problem by setting `auto` on the column and then constraining the element with `min-width` and `max-width` values, as shown in the following listing.

**Listing 4.8 Combining `auto`, `min-width`, and `max-width`**

```
.layout {
    display: grid;
```

```
    grid-template-columns: auto 1fr;
}

.sidebar {
    min-width: 150px;
    max-width: 300px;
}
```

Figure 4.9 (a composite image) shows the result on a narrow viewport and a wider viewport.

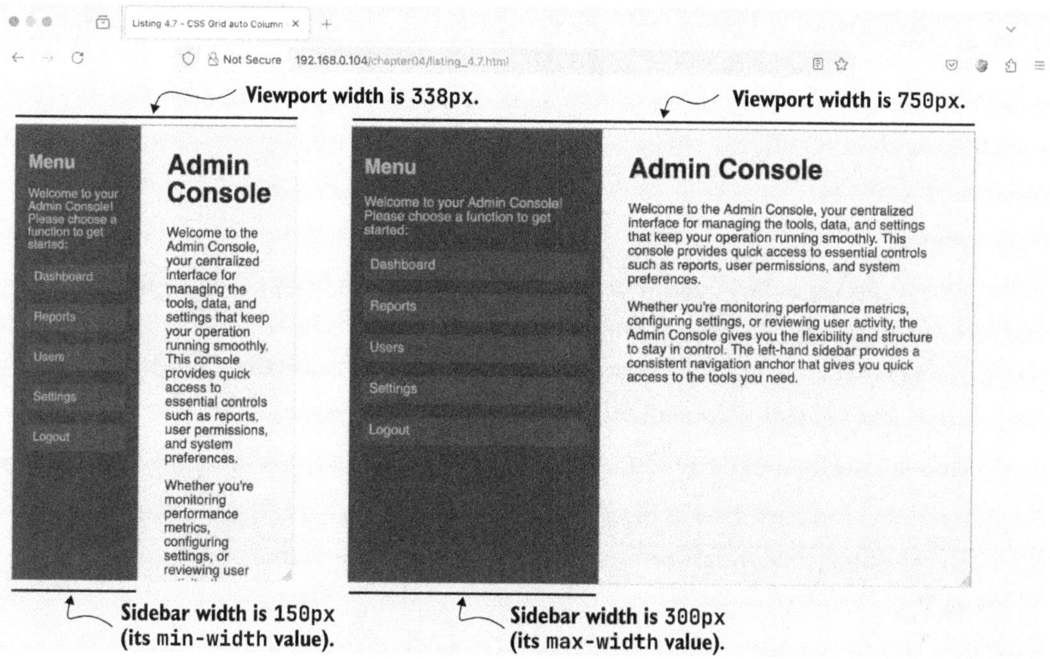


**Figure 4.9 In a narrow viewport (left), the sidebar width doesn't shrink below 150px; in a wider viewport (right), the sidebar width maxes out at 300px.**

In this example, the `min-content` value of the sidebar is `119px` and the `max-content` value is `555px`. So, the `auto` calculation boils down to

```
width = minmax(max(150px, 119px), min(350px, 555px))
      = minmax(150px, 350px)
```

That is, the sidebar's width varies responsively between `150px` and `350px`.

### 4.4.3 The math of fit-content()

The `auto` keyword is great when you want the browser to figure out a particular track size, but it's a bit of a crapshoot because any constraints on an item's size, such as `min-width` and `max-width`, live in the item's CSS, which might reside in another CSS file and not even be available to you. Therefore, you can't be certain how wide, say, a particular column might end up once the grid dust settles. If a column ends up wider than a particular width, your layout might break.

If you like the hands-off approach of `auto` but want to add a bit of discipline by setting a strict upper limit on a column's width (or a row's height), a limit that, moreover, overrides any `max-width` (or `max-height`) that might be set on the item, then your go-to grid track sizing function is `fit-content(limit)`, where *`limit`* is the maximum allowed width (or height). The `fit-content()` function works only with `grid-template-columns`, `grid-template-rows`, `grid-auto-columns`, or `grid-auto-rows`, so the maximum constraint on the track size lives within your grid definition.

The `fit-content(limit)` function implements the following expression:

```
max(minimum, min(limit, max-content)
```

where

- *`minimum`* is the larger of the content's `min-content` value or some other minimizing constraint, such as `min-width`.
- *`limit`* is the value passed as an argument to the `fit-content()` function.
- `max-content` is the content's maximum content size.

In other words, using `fit-content(limit)` gives the browser the following instructions:

- Let this track grow as big as the content needs, but never bigger than *`limit`*.
- Don't let this track shrink smaller than the content's minimum size.

Here's an example:

```
grid-template-columns: fit-content(250px) fit-content(250px);
```

This declaration tells the browser, "Size each of the two columns to be as wide as its content, but no wider than `250px`." For example,

- *If the first column's content width is `200px`*—This is less than the `250px` limit specified by `fit-content()`, so that column's width is set to `200px`.
- *If the second column's content width is `300px`*—This is more than the `250px` limit specified by `fit-content()`, so that column's width is capped at `250px`.

#### EXAMPLE: CONSTRAINING A SIDEBAR MAXIMUM WIDTH WITH FIT-CONTENT()

In listing 4.7, the code set `max-width: 300px` on a sidebar to cap the sidebar's width when its track size was defined with `auto`. To bring that constraint into the grid definition where you can see it, use `fit-content()`, as shown in the following listing.

**Listing 4.9 Constraining a sidebar's maximum width with `fit-content()`**

```
.layout {
    display: grid;
    grid-template-columns: fit-content(300px) 1fr;
}
```

The browser will allow the sidebar width to expand up to `300px`. However, if the maximum width of the sidebar's content is less than `300px`, the browser uses that maximum content width to cap the sidebar's width, as demonstrated in figure 4.10.

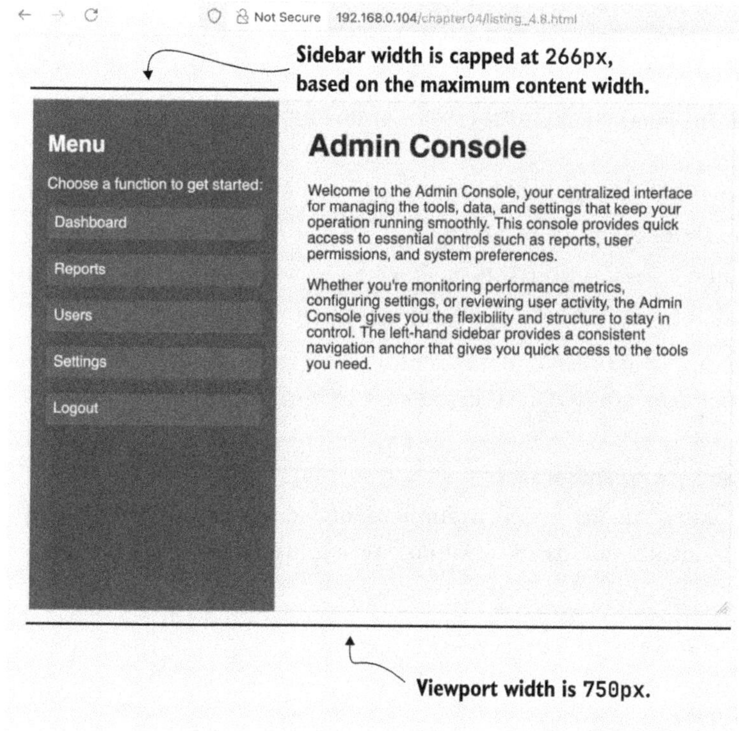


**Figure 4.10 The sidebar's maximum content width is less than the `300px` limit passed to the `fit-content()` function, so the sidebar's width grows no larger than that maximum value.**

### 4.4.4 *The repeat() function and its mathematical distribution*

The `repeat()` function creates a mathematical pattern of track sizes, letting you express repeating sequences concisely. Its mathematical implementation depends on whether you're using a fixed number of repetitions or an `auto-fill`/`auto-fit` modifier.

#### FIXED REPETITION MATHEMATICS

Given `repeat(n, size)`, the result is equivalent to writing the `size` value or pattern `n` times in sequence. For example,

```
grid-template-columns: repeat(3, 100px);
```

is equivalent to

```
grid-template-columns: 100px 100px 100px;
```

You get similar results when you use multiple values in the pattern. For example,

```
grid-template-columns: repeat(2, 100px 200px 50px);
```

is equivalent to

```
grid-template-columns: 100px 200px 50px 100px 200px 50px;
```

Here, the mathematical transformation creates a sequence where

- The pattern length is three tracks.
- The number of repetitions is two.
- The total number of tracks is `pattern_length * repetitions = 3 × 2 = 6`.

This sequence can be expressed mathematically as a function that maps a single input value (the repetition count) to a sequence of output values (the expanded track listing).

#### THE AUTO-FILL AND AUTO-FIT ALGORITHMS

The `auto-fill` and `auto-fit` keywords implement a more complex mathematical algorithm that dynamically calculates how many repetitions can fit in the available space. For example,

```
grid-template-columns: repeat(auto-fill, 100px);
```

Mathematically, this is calculated as

```
num_repetitions = floor((container_width - sum_of_gaps) / track_width)
```

where

- `container_width` is the width of the grid container.
- `sum_of_gaps` is the total width of all grid gaps.
- `track_width` is the width of each repeated track.
- `floor()` rounds down to the nearest integer.

For example, with a `450px` container, `10px` gaps, and `100px` tracks,

```
num_repetitions = floor((450px - 3 * 10px) / 100px)
                = floor(420px / 100px)
                = floor(4.2)
                = 4
```

the grid creates four columns of `100px` each (with the remaining `50px` as unused space).

This mathematical function adapts as the container width changes, automatically recalculating the optimal number of repetitions.

While `auto-fill` and `auto-fit` use the same formula to calculate the number of repetitions, they differ in how they handle empty tracks.

For example, `auto-fill`

- Always maintains the calculated number of tracks
- Retains the size of empty tracks.
- Mathematically fixes the total used with `num_repetitions * track_width`

For example, `auto-fit`

- Collapses empty tracks to `0px` width
- Redistributes their space to other tracks (particularly those with `fr` units)
- Mathematically sets the total used width to become a function of content

These differences create two distinct mathematical models for space utilization:

- `auto-fill` prioritizes a predictable filling of the container.
- `auto-fit` prioritizes efficient use of available space.

When no tracks are empty, both values produce identical results. The difference emerges only when there are more tracks than needed for the content. See the following listing for an example.

**Listing 4.10 Demonstrating the difference between `auto-fill` and `auto-fit`**

```
<head>
    <style>
        .grid-container {
            display: grid;
            gap: 1rem;
            grid-auto-rows: 100px;
            width: 850px
        }

        .auto-fill-grid {
            grid-template-columns: repeat(auto-fill, minmax(200px, 1fr));
        }

        .auto-fit-grid {
            grid-template-columns: repeat(auto-fit, minmax(200px, 1fr));
        }
    </style>
```

```
</head>
<body>
    <div class="grid-container auto-fill-grid">
        <div class="card">Item A</div>
        <div class="card">Item B</div>
    </div>

    <div class="grid-container auto-fit-grid">
        <div class="card">Item A</div>
        <div class="card">Item B</div>
    </div>
</body>
```

Let's drill down and see how the browser handles these two grid containers. First up is the `auto-fill` grid:

```
grid-template-columns: repeat(auto-fill, minmax(200px, 1fr));
```

This declaration combines the following three track-sizing concepts:

- Dynamic repetition counting based on container width
- Minimum size constraints from `minmax()`
- Flexible growth with `fr` units

The resolution algorithm follows these steps:

1. Calculates how many minimum-sized tracks (`200px`) can fit
2. Creates that many tracks
3. Applies the `fr` unit distribution to allow tracks to grow
4. Ensures no track violates its minimum or maximum constraint

The container width is `850px`. Therefore, we have

- The minimum number of tracks that can fit is `floor(850px / 200px) = 4`.
- Initial track allocation is `4 tracks * 200px each = 800px`.
- Remaining space is `850px - 800px = 50px`.
- Since each track has a maximum of `1fr`, the `50px` is distributed evenly: `50px / 4 = 12.5px`.
- The final track sizes are `200px + 12.5px = 212.5px`.

Next is the `auto-fit` grid:

```
grid-template-columns: repeat(auto-fit, minmax(200px, 1fr));
```

The resolution algorithm follows these steps:

1. Calculates how many minimum-sized tracks (`200px`) can fit
2. Creates that many tracks

3 Collapses any tracks that are empty
4 Applies the `fr` unit distribution to allow nonempty tracks to grow into the available space
5 Ensures no track violates its minimum or maximum constraint

The container width is `850px`. Therefore, we have

- The minimum number of tracks that can fit is `floor(850px / 200px) = 4`.
- Initial track allocation is `4 tracks * 200px each = 800px`.
- The number of empty tracks is 2.
- Track allocation after collapsing the empty tracks: `2 tracks * 200px each = 400px`.
- Available space is `(850px - 800px) + 400px = 450px`.
- Since each track has a maximum of `1fr`, the `450px` is distributed evenly among the two nonempty tracks: `450px / 2 = 225px`.
- The final track sizes are `200px + 225px = 425px`.

Figure 4.11 shows how these two calculation algorithms play out on the page.

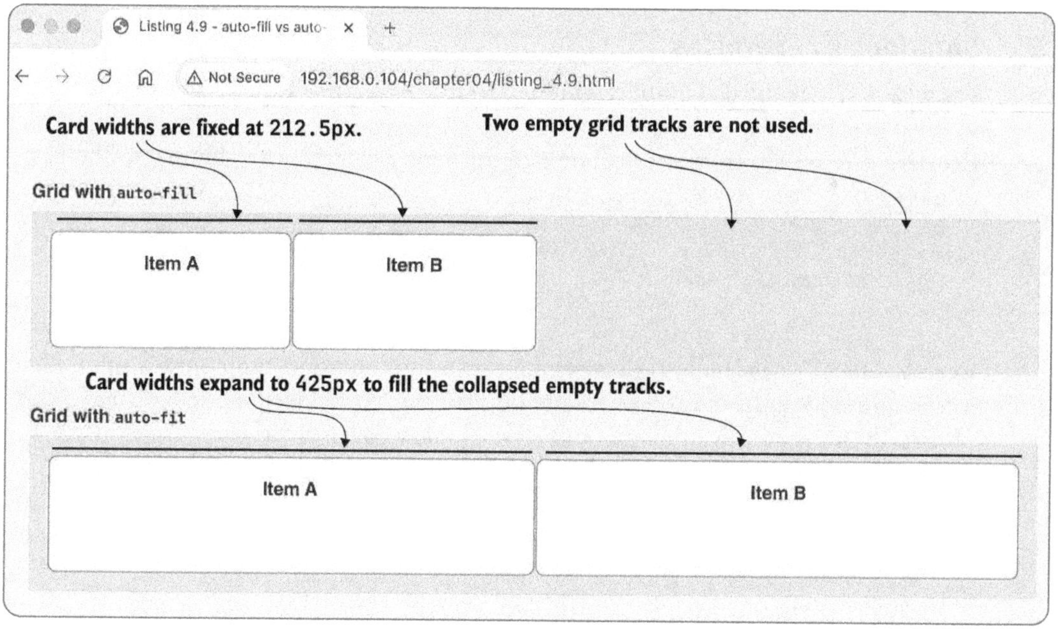


**Figure 4.11 In the `auto-fill` example (top), the card widths are fixed at `212.5px`, and the two empty columns remain in the grid container. In the `auto-fit` example (bottom), the two empty columns collapse and the card widths expand to `425px` to fill the released space.**

**EXERCISES**

**Exercise 4.7:** Complete the following grid rule in a way that ensures the second column never gets smaller than `200px` but can grow with the container:

```
.container {
    display: grid;
    grid-template-columns: 1fr __________________;
}
```

**Exercise 4.8:** What are the final widths of the three columns in the following grid definition?

```
.container {
    display: grid;
    grid-template-columns: 2fr 2fr minmax(300px, 1fr);
    width: 1000px;
}
```

**Exercise 4.9:** Suppose you need to build a responsive image grid. Create a grid rule that meets the following requirements:

- Displays items in columns that are at least `180px` wide
- Grows each column with the container
- Collapses unused columns

## 4.5 Solutions to exercises

**Exercise 4.1:** The third column is bounded by line 3 on the left and line 4 on the right, so the correct answer is 2: 3 and 4.

**Exercise 4.2:** This item crosses columns 3 through 7, which is 5 columns, so the `span` value is 5:

```
.item {
    grid-column: 3 / span 5;
}
```

**Exercise 4.3:** The problem is that negative grid line numbers only work with explicit tracks, and since `grid-auto-rows` creates implicit tracks, the declaration `grid-row: -2 / -1` fails. In this example, one fix would be to create explicit rows:

```
.grid {
    display: grid;
    grid-template-columns: 1fr 1fr 1fr;
    grid-template-rows: 200px 200px 200px 100px;
}
```

**Exercise 4.4:** Here's the calculation:

- Fixed track: `80px + 120px = 200px`
- Grid gaps: `15px * 4 = 60px`

- Remaining free space: `960px - 200px - 60px = 700px`
- Total `fr` units: `3fr + 2fr + 1fr = 6fr`
- Width of `3fr` track: `(3/6) * 700px = 350px`
- Width of `2fr` track: `(2/6) * 700px = 233.33px`
- Width of `1fr` track: `(1/6) * 700px = 116.67px`

**Exercise 4.5:** The developer forgot to account for padding and borders in their math. Here's the correct calculation:

- $C$ = container width = `600px`
- $F$ = sum of all fixed track widths = `0px`
- $G$ = sum of all grid gap width = `0px`
- $B$ = sum of left and right border widths = `2 * 10px = 20px`
- $P$ = sum of left and right padding widths = `2 * 20px = 40px`
- $R$ = remaining free space = $C - F - G - B - P$ = `600px - 0px - 0px - 20px - 40px = 540px`
- $T$ = total of all `fr` units = `1 + 2 = 3`
- Width of `1fr` track: `(1/3) * 540px = 180px`
- Width of `2fr` track: `(2/3) * 540px = 360px`

**Exercise 4.6:** The width of the fixed-size columns (`300px` and `200px`), plus the gap (`1px`), plus the left and right border widths (`2 * 1px = 2px`) equals the width of the container (`503px`). Therefore, the `1fr` track resolves to `0px`. However, because the column contains no content, the browser has no minimum content width constraint, so the browser displays it with `0px` width.

**Exercise 4.7:** To ensure the second column never gets smaller than `200px` but can grow with the container, use the following snippet:

```
.container {
    display: grid;
    grid-template-columns: 1fr minmax(200px, 1fr);
}
```

**Exercise 4.8:** The total number of flexible track units is `2fr + 2fr + 1fr = 5fr`. Given the grid container width, then `1fr = 1000px / 5 = 200px`. The final width of the third column is therefore `minmax(300px, 200px) = 300px`. The remaining space is divided equally between the first two columns: `(1000px - 300px) / 2 = 700px / 2 = 350px`. Therefore, the first column is `350px`, the second column is `350px`, and the third column is `300px`.

**Exercise 4.9:** Here's a grid rule that satisfies these conditions:

```
.gallery {
    display: grid;
    grid-template-columns: repeat(auto-fit, minmax(180px, 1fr));
}
```

## Summary

- CSS Grid uses a two-dimensional coordinate system that lets you position elements independently in horizontal and vertical directions.
- Grid lines are numbered starting from 1, not 0, which helps avoid confusion but requires careful attention if you're used to zero-based indexing.
- Negative grid line numbers let you reference positions from the end of the grid, making dynamic layouts easier and more robust. Remember, though, that negative grid line numbers only work with explicit tracks, not auto-generated implicit tracks.
- The `span` keyword simplifies layout math by letting you define how many tracks an item should cover, rather than calculating endpoint positions.
- Fractional (`fr`) units enable the web browser to distribute leftover space proportionally, depending on how many fractions you allocate to each track. The `fr` unit represents a fraction of available space after subtracting fixed tracks, gaps, padding, and borders.
- When `fr` tracks can't fit in available space, they resolve to `0px` but still display at their minimum content width.
- The `minmax()` function enforces flexible minimum and maximum sizes, giving you control over how elements grow and shrink within responsive layouts.
- The `auto` keyword makes tracks sized between `min-content` and `max-content`, respecting `min-width` and `max-width`.
- The `fit-content()` function caps a track's maximum size, while allowing it to shrink to fit content.
- The `repeat()` function with `auto-fit` collapses empty tracks and redistributes their space, enabling flexible layouts that shrink gracefully when fewer items are present. Use `repeat()` with `auto-fill` if you want to preserve empty tracks.

# 5 Flexbox math

**_This chapter covers_**

- How browsers determine the base size of each item
- The `flex-grow` algorithm
- The math of `flex-shrink`
- How to set constraints on the growth or shrinkage of flex items

When Flexbox was introduced into a world accustomed to laying out page elements using an HTML table, it seemed like nothing less than magic. Elements could now grow, shrink, and align themselves according to whatever space was available, and it was all done by using just a few lines of CSS code. What sorcery was this?

But, of course, the awesomeness of Flexbox is based on math, not magic. Pop the Flexbox hood, and the engine powering this technology is a robust and often exceedingly complex mathematical system. That system can do amazing things, but its complexity sometimes means that Flexbox can act in weird and seemingly unpredictable ways. This chapter explores the math that underlies Flexbox, which will enable you not only to build more precise and predictable layouts but will also let you solve any Flexbox-related layout problems that arise.

## 5.1 The flex base size calculation

While CSS Grid lets you control how a container's space is divided in two dimensions, vertically *and* horizontally, Flexbox gives you control over a single dimension, vertically *or* horizontally. That control is based on two properties that work together to determine how the space within a flex container is distributed: `flex-grow` and `flex-shrink`. These two properties are known in the Flexbox trade as the *flex factors.*

However, before that distribution can take place, the web browser has to figure out exactly what it's dealing with. In Flexbox World, that means determining each flex item's starting size, known as its *flex base size,* which is the size the browser assigns to the item before deciding whether the item needs to grow or shrink. Note that "size" depends on the direction of the flex container's main axis:

- If the container has `flex-direction: row`, the main axis is horizontal, so "size" refers to width.
- If the container has `flex-direction: column`, the main axis is vertical, so "size" refers to height.

For simplicity, in this chapter, I assume a horizontal main axis, so all the examples deal with width.

### 5.1.1 The base size algorithm

Here's the process the web browser runs through to determine a flex item's base size:

1. If `flex-basis` is set to a specific value (a length, a percentage, or one of the following keywords: `content`, `max-content`, `min-content`, or `fit-content`), that value is used directly as the flex base size.
2. If `flex-basis` is set to `auto`, which is the default, the browser checks two things:
   - If the item has a `width` value, that value is used.
   - If the item's `width` property isn't specified, the browser uses the item's intrinsic content size.

For example (assuming `item` is a class applied to all the items in a flex container),

```
.item {
    flex-basis: 250px;
}
```

In this case, the browser uses the `flex-basis` value of `250px` as the item's base size.

Another example,

```
.item {
    flex-basis: auto;
    width: 180px;
}
```

Since `flex-basis` is set to `auto`, the web browser looks for a `width` value. That's set here, so the browser uses the `width` value of `180px` as the item's base size.

Here is another example:

```
.item {
    flex-basis: auto;
}
```

In this case, `flex-basis` is set to `auto`, but there's no `width` value, so the browser measures how big the item needs to be to fit its content and uses that value as the item's base size.

Here is the last example:

```
.item {
    flex-basis: 100px;
    width: 200px;
}
```

In this case, `flex-basis` is assigned a specific value (that is, it's not set to `auto`), so it overrides the declared `width` value, and the browser uses the `flex-basis` value of `100px` as the item's base size. Listing 5.1 provides a more in-depth example, which is rendered in Figure 5.1.

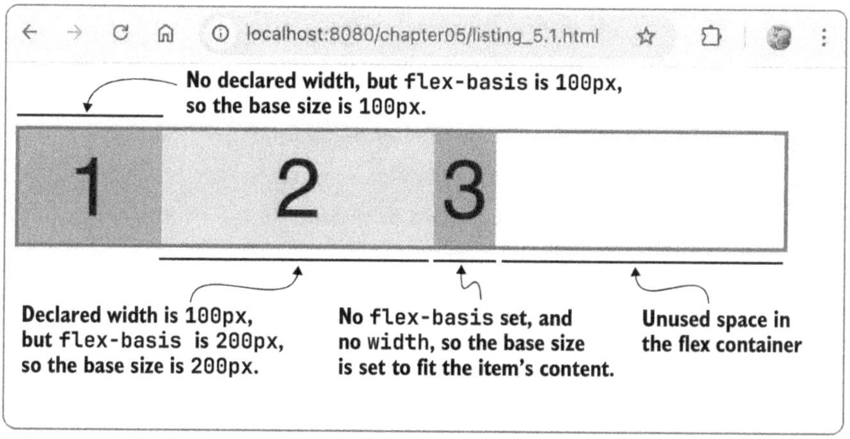


**Figure 5.1** How the browser determines the flex base size

**Listing 5.1 The flex base size calculation**

```
<head>
    <style>
        .container {
            display: flex;
            flex-direction: row;
            width: 600px;
        }
        .item-1 {
            background-color: rgb(166, 166, 166);
            flex-basis: 100px;
        }
        .item-2 {
            background-color: rgb(219, 219, 219);
            flex-basis: 200px;
            width: 100px;
        }
        .item-3 {
            background-color: rgb(166, 166, 166);
        }
    </style>
</head>
<body>
    <div class="container">
        <div class="item item-1">1</div>
        <div class="item item-2">2</div>
        <div class="item item-3">3</div>
    </div>
</body>
```

Flex container with a width of 600px.

Item 1 has a flex-basis of 100px.

Item 2's flex-basis overrides the width.

Item 3 has no flex-basis set.

**NOTE** All the code for this chapter's listings is available in this book's GitHub repository: https://github.com/paulmcfe/web-dev-math.

The base size is vital mathematically in Flexbox because it's what the browser uses to

- Calculate how much total space the items will take up initially
- Compare that total to the size of the flex container
- Determine whether it needs to grow or shrink items to fit the container

How the browser distributes space within the flex container is where Flexbox really gets interesting. But without a solid understanding of how base sizes are chosen, the calculations the browser uses to grow and shrink items won't make much sense, and the unexpected item sizes in your layouts will have you scratching your head.

**EXERCISES**

**Exercise 5.1:** Fill in the missing CSS to make the flex base size of all items in this container `150px`:

```
.item {
    flex-_____: _____;
}
```

**Exercise 5.2:** Assuming a horizontal main axis, which value will the browser use as the flex base size for the following rule?

```
.item {
    flex-basis: auto;
    height: 200px;
    width: 180px;
}
```

1. `auto`
2. `180px`
3. `200px`
4. content width

## 5.2 Understanding the flex factors

Things get more useful (and more complicated) when you put the "flex" in Flexbox to handle scenarios where your content doesn't fit within the container:

- *Underflow scenario*—If there's unused space, you can use `flex-grow` to expand items until all the space is used.
- *Overflow scenario*—If there's not enough space, you can use `flex-shrink` to reduce items until they fit.

The next two sections discuss the math of these scenarios.

### 5.2.1 The flex-grow calculation

When the container still has unused available space after the browser has allocated space to the items according to their flex base sizes, you can use `flex-grow` to have one or more items expand to fill that space.

The simplest case is when you set `flex-grow` on a single item:

```
.item {
    flex-grow: 1;
}
```

Here, the value `1` is called the item's *flex grow factor.* This declaration tells the browser to expand the item along the primary axis until there's no more unused space in the container. The more interesting (mathematically speaking) scenario is when you set `flex-grow` on two or more items. Here's the math the browser goes through to handle multiple flex grow factors:

1 Sum the initial base sizes of all the items. This is the sum of the initial sizes that the browser allocates according to the procedure from the previous section. Call this value `sum_of_initial_sizes`.

2 Calculate the total unused space in the container:

```
available_unused_space = container_width - sum_of_initial_sizes
```

3 Sum the flex grow factors of all the items. This is the sum of all the `flex-grow` values of the items (bearing in mind that the default `flex-grow` value is 0). Call this value `sum_of_flex_grow_factors`.

4 Calculate what portion of the unused space is allocated to each item (where `item_flex_grow_factor` is the item's `flex-grow` value):

```
item_unused_portion = item_flex_grow_factor / sum_of_flex_grow_factors
```

5 Calculate how much unused space is allocated to each item:

```
item_unused_space = item_unused_portion * available_unused_space
```

6 Calculate the final width of each item:

```
item_final_width = item_initial_size + item_unused_space
```

Here's an example that modifies the three items from listing 5.2 and renders them as shown in figure 5.2.

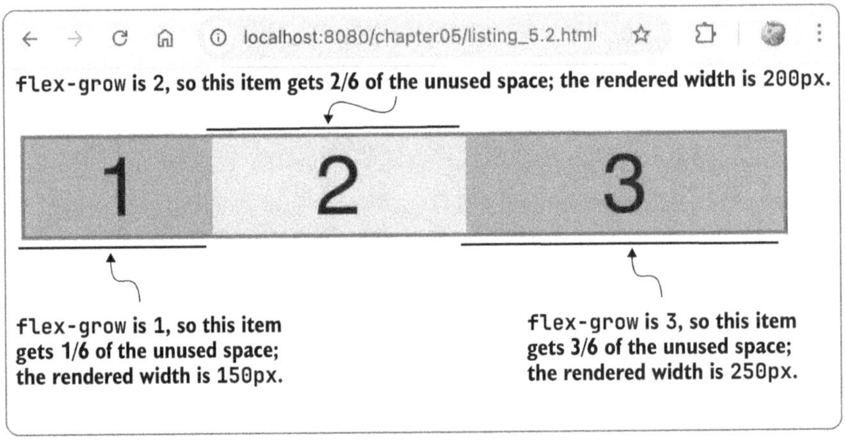


**Figure 5.2** How `flex-grow` works. Notice that there's no longer any unused space in the container.

**Listing 5.2 The `flex-grow` calculation**

```
.container {
    display: flex;
    flex-direction: row;
    width: 600px;
}
.item-1 {
    flex-grow: 1;
    flex-basis: 100px;
}
.item-2 {
    flex-grow: 2;
    flex-basis: 100px;
}
.item-3 {
    flex-grow: 3;
    flex-basis: 100px;
}
```

Here's how the math shakes out:

1. The sum of all the initial main sizes is `100px + 100px + 100px = 300px`.
2. The unused space in the container is `600px - 300px = 300px`.
3. The sum of the flex grow factors is `1 + 2 + 3 = 6`.
4. Here are the portions of the unused space allocated to each item:
   - `item-1`: `1/6 = 0.167`
   - `item-2`: `2/6 = 0.333`
   - `item-3`: `3/6 = 0.5`
5. Here's how much of the unused space is allocated to each item:
   - `item-1`: `0.167 * 300px = 50px`
   - `item-2`: `0.333 * 300px = 100px`
   - `item-3`: `0.5 * 300px = 150px`
6. Here's the final width of each item:
   - `item-1`: `100px + 50px = 150px`
   - `item-2`: `100px + 100px = 200px`
   - `item-3`: `100px + 150px = 250px`

Notice that the total of the final widths (`150px + 200px + 250px`) is equal to the container width (`600px`).

As a practical example, imagine you want to build a landing page for a product that offers three tiers (Basic, Pro, and Enterprise), and Marketing wants to emphasize the Pro tier. One way to do that is to make the Pro card more prominent, which can be done in a Flexbox layout by giving that element a higher `flex-grow` value. Figure 5.3 shows the resulting page, with the Pro card slightly more prominent than the Basic and Enterprise cards. To achieve this layout, use the page code from listing 5.3.

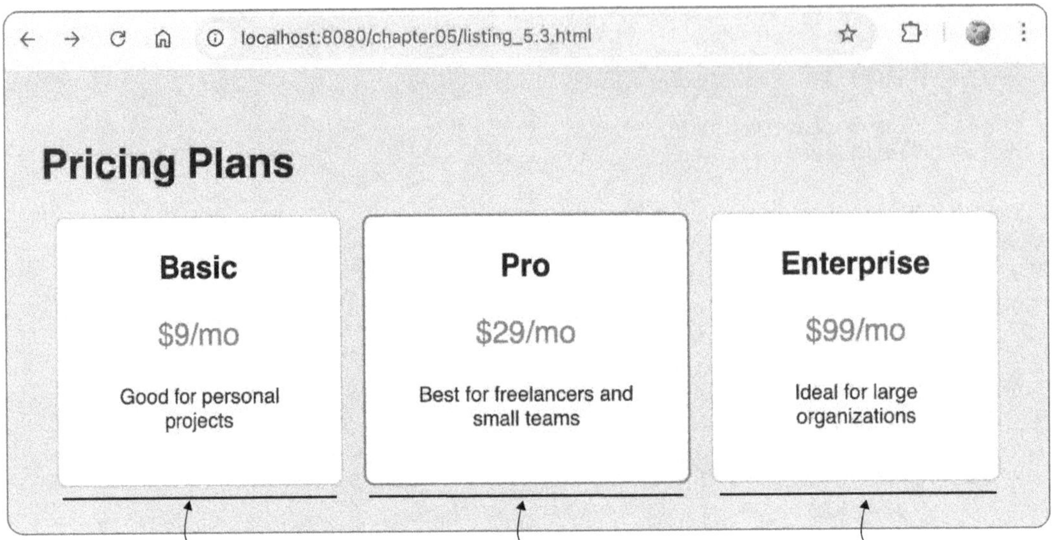


**Figure 5.3** Using `flex-grow` to make a card more prominent

**Listing 5.3 A `flex-grow` example**

```
<head>
    <style>
        .container {
            display: flex;
            width: 750px;
            gap: 1rem;
        }
        .card {
            padding: 1.5rem;
            background-color: white;
            border-radius: 8px;
            border: 2px solid #ccc;
            text-align: center;
        }
        .card-basic {
            flex-grow: 1;
            flex-basis: 200px;
        }
        .card-pro {
            flex-grow: 2;
            flex-basis: 200px;
            border-color: #0077cc;
        }
        .card-enterprise {
            flex-grow: 1;
```

Flex container is 750px wide

Basic and Enterprise cards use flex-grow: 1

Pro card uses flex-grow: 2

```
            flex-basis: 200px;
        }
    </style>
</head>
<body>
    <h1>Pricing Plans</h1>
    <div class="container">
        <div class="card card-basic">
            <h2>Basic</h2>
            <p class="price">$9/mo</p>
            <p>Good for personal projects</p>
        </div>
        <div class="card card-pro">
            <h2>Pro</h2>
            <p class="price">$29/mo</p>
            <p>Best for freelancers and small teams</p>
        </div>
        <div class="card card-enterprise">
            <h2>Enterprise</h2>
            <p class="price">$99/mo</p>
            <p>Ideal for large organizations</p>
        </div>
    </div>
</body>
```

### 5.2.2 The flex-shrink calculation

When the container doesn't have enough space to hold all the items according to their `flex-basis` values, you can use `flex-shrink` to have one or more items contract so that everything fits within the container. In fact, the default value of `flex-shrink` is `1`, so the browser always contracts items to prevent container overflow.

But unlike declaring `flex-grow: 1` on all flex items, which makes them grow by the same amount to fill the unused space in a container, having a default of `flex-shrink: 1` on every flex item does *not* mean that the items shrink by the same amount. That's because when it calculates how much to shrink an item, the browser takes into account both the item's `flex-shrink` value, known inevitably as the *flex shrink factor*, and the item's size along the primary axis (for example, the item's width if the container is using `flex-direction: row`).

This means that the `flex-shrink` calculation is bit more complex than the `flex-grow` calculation:

1. Sum the initial main sizes of all the items. This is the sum of the initial sizes that the browser allocates according to the procedure from the previous section. Call this value `sum_of_initial_sizes`.
2. Calculate the amount by which the items overflow the container:

   ```
   overflow = sum_of_initial_sizes - container_width
   ```

3 Calculate the *weighted shrink factor* for each item, which is the item's width multiplied by its `flex-shrink` value (where `item_flex_shrink_factor` is the item's `flex-shrink` value):

```
item_weighted_shrink_factor = item_width * item_flex_shrink_factor
```

4 Sum the weighted shrink factors of all the items. Call this value `sum_of_weighted_shrink_factors`.

5 Calculate what portion of the overflow is allocated to each item:

```
item_overflow_portion = item_weighted_shrink_factor / sum_of_weighted_
shrink_factors
```

6 Calculate how much overflow space is allocated to each item:

```
item_overflow_space = item_overflow_portion * overflow
```

7 Calculate the final width of each item:

```
item_final_width = item_initial_size - item_overflow_space
```

Figure 5.4 shows an example. To render this layout, use the page code in the following listing.

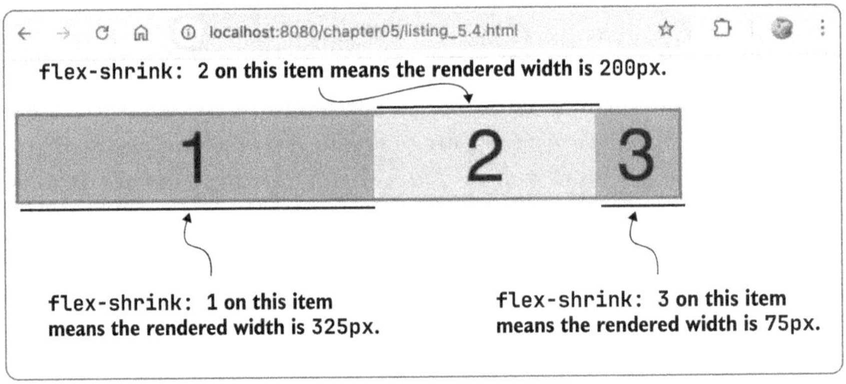


**Figure 5.4** How `flex-shrink` works. Notice that there's no longer any unused space in the container.

**Listing 5.4 The `flex-shrink` calculation**

```
.container {
    display: flex;
    width: 600px;
}
.item-1 {
```

```
    flex-shrink: 1;
    flex-basis: 450px;
}
.item-2 {
    flex-shrink: 2;
    flex-basis: 450px;
}
.item-3 {
    flex-shrink: 3;
    flex-basis: 450px;
}
```

Here's the math the browser uses to determine how much each item must shrink to resolve the container's overflow problem:

1. The sum of all the initial main sizes is `450px + 450px + 450px = 1350px`.
2. The overflow is `1350px - 600px = 750px`.
3. Here are the weighted shrink factors for each item:
   - `item-1`: `450 * 1 = 450`
   - `item-2`: `450 * 2 = 900`
   - `item-3`: `450 * 3 = 1350`
4. The sum of the weighted shrink factors is `450 + 900 + 1350 = 2700`.
5. Here are the portions of the overflow allocated to each item:
   - `item-1`: `450 / 2700 = 0.167`
   - `item-2`: `900 / 2700 = 0.333`
   - `item-3`: `1350 / 2700 = 0.5`
6. Here's how much of the overflow is allocated to each item:
   - `item-1`: `0.167 * 750px = 125px`
   - `item-2`: `0.333 * 750px = 250px`
   - `item-3`: `0.5 * 750px = 375px`
7. Here's the final width of each item:
   - `item-1`: `450px - 125px = 325px`
   - `item-2`: `450px - 250px = 200px`
   - `item-3`: `450px - 375px = 75px`

Happily, the math works out since the total of the final widths (`325px + 200px + 75px`) is equal to the container width (`600px`).

> **NOTE** One takeaway from using weighted shrink factors is that if you want an item to shrink less than the other items, proportionally speaking, set its `flex-shrink` value to a number between, but not including, `0` and `1`. Similarly, if you want an item to shrink more than the other items, again proportionally speaking, set its `flex-shrink` value to a number greater than `1`. (Both of these scenarios assume the other flex items use the default `flex-shrink` value of `1`.)

A good use case for `flex-shrink` is a navigation bar consisting of buttons that you want to shrink when the flex container gets smaller, as shown in figure 5.5. To achieve this layout, use the code in listing 5.5. Each button is rendered at `113.2px` thanks to the following shrink math:

```
button_width = (content_width - gaps - borders - padding) / 5
             = (650px - 48px - 4px - 32px) / 5
             = 566px / 5
             = 113.2px
```

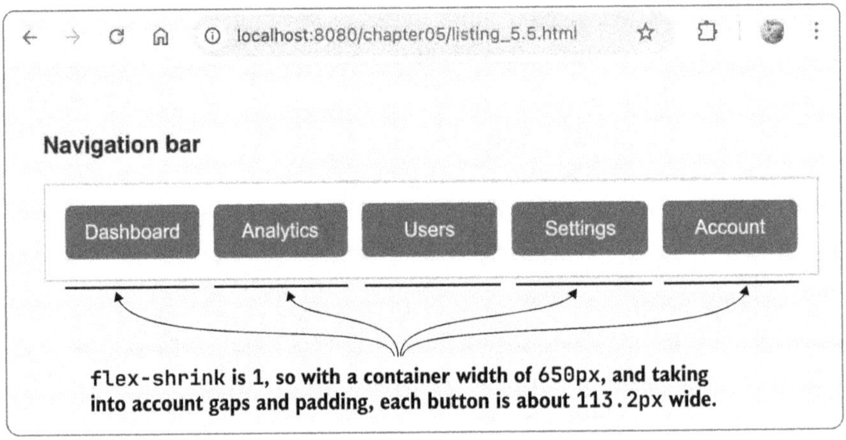


**Figure 5.5 A `flex-shrink` example**

**Listing 5.5 A `flex-shrink` example**

```
<head>
    <style>
        * {
            box-sizing: border-box;
        }
        .toolbar {
            display: flex;
            width: 650px;                    ← Flex container is 650px wide
            gap: 0.75rem;                    ┐ Gaps, borders, and padding
            border: 2px solid #ccc;          │ reduce content area
            padding: 1rem;                   ┘
        }
        .action {
            flex-grow: 0;                    ← Buttons can't grow
            flex-shrink: 1;                  ← Buttons can shrink
            flex-basis: 160px;               ← Base size is 160px
        }
    </style>
</head>
<body>
```

```
    <h3>Navigation bar</h3>
    <div class="toolbar">
        <button class="action">Dashboard</button>
        <button class="action">Analytics</button>
        <button class="action">Users</button>
        <button class="action">Settings</button>
        <button class="action">Account</button>
    </div>
</body>
```

### 5.2.3 *The flex shorthand*

For convenience, CSS offers the `flex` property that lets you set the values of `flex-grow`, `flex-shrink`, and `flex-basis` in a single declaration:

```
flex: flex-grow flex-shrink flex-basis;
```

For example, if you have a menu of navigation icons, you can ensure that they don't grow or shrink with the following rule:

```
nav .icon {
    flex: 0 0 auto;
}
```

With the `flex` property, you can specify one, two, or all three values. However, it's important to understand that if you specify only one or two values, the browser still applies an implicit value, or values, for the "missing" flex properties. Here's the breakdown:

| Shorthand | Equivalent |
|---|---|
| `flex: auto` | **flex: 1 1 auto;** |
| `flex: none` | **flex: 0 0 auto;** |
| `flex: initial` | **flex: 0 1 auto;** |
| `flex:` *`number`* | **flex: number 1 0;** |
| `flex:` *`width`* | **flex: 1 1 width;** |
| `flex:` *`number1 number2`* | **flex: number1 number2 0;** |
| `flex:` *`number width`* | **flex: number 1 width;** |

Because `flex` always applies all three flex properties, sometimes implicitly, it's a common CSS best practice to never use the separate `flex-grow`, `flex-shrink`, and `flex-basis` properties. Instead, always use `flex` to ensure that you know which flex property values you're setting.

### 5.2.4 *Dealing with flex-grow values between 0 and 1*

Some interesting mathematical twists happen when you specify a `flex-grow` factor greater than 0 but less than 1 (negative flex factors are illegal). How the browser handles `flex-grow` values in the range (0, 1) depends on whether their total is greater than or equal to 1 or less than 1.

#### CASE 1: THE SUM OF THE FLEX-GROW VALUES IS GREATER THAN OR EQUAL TO 1

When you have one or more `flex-grow` values in (0, 1), but the total of all the `flex-grow` values is 1 or higher, the math the browser uses is a straightforward variation on the algorithm it uses when all the `flex-grow` values are 1 or more. Figure 5.6 shows an example. To get this layout, use the CSS code in listing 5.6.

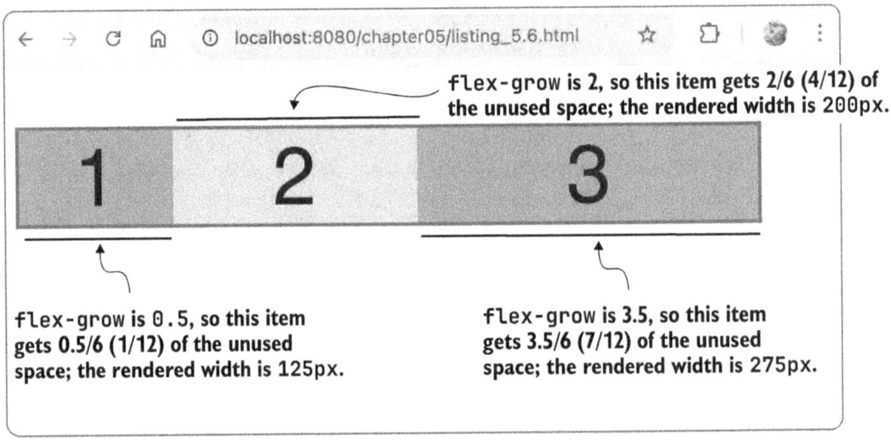


**Figure 5.6 Item 1 has a `flex-grow` value of 0.5.**

**Listing 5.6 The sum of the `flex-grow` values is greater than or equal to 1.**

```
.container {
    display: flex;
    flex-direction: row;
    width: 600px;
}
.item-1 {
    flex-grow: 0.5;        ◄── flex-grow value is between 0 and 1
    flex-basis: 100px;
}
.item-2 {
    flex-grow: 2;
    flex-basis: 100px;
}
.item-3 {
    flex-grow: 3.5;
    flex-basis: 100px;
}
```

Here's the math that produces the item widths shown in the figure:

1. The sum of all the initial main sizes is `100px + 100px + 100px = 300px`.
2. The unused space in the container is `600px - 300px = 300px`.
3. The sum of the flex grow factors is `0.5 + 2 + 3.5 = 6`.
4. Here are the portions of the unused space allocated to each item:
   - `item-1`: `0.5/6 = 1/12 = 0.083`
   - `item-2`: `2/6 = 4/12 = 0.333`
   - `item-3`: `3.5/6 = 7/12 = 0.583`
5. Here's how much of the unused space is allocated to each item:
   - `item-1`: `0.083 * 300px = 25px`
   - `item-2`: `0.333 * 300px = 100px`
   - `item-3`: `0.583 * 300px = 175px`
6. Here's the final width of each item:
   - `item-1`: `100px + 25px = 125px`
   - `item-2`: `100px + 100px = 200px`
   - `item-3`: `100px + 175px = 275px`

Once again, we can confirm these calculations by noting that the total of the final widths (`125px + 200px + 275px`) equals the container width (`600px`).

#### CASE 2: THE SUM OF THE FLEX-GROW VALUES IS LESS THAN 1

When the total of the `flex-grow` factors is 1 or more, the browser treats each `flex-grow` value as a relative ratio. If, say, the sum of the `flex-grow` factors is `8` and one item uses `flex-grow: 2`, the browser interprets that declaration to mean that the item wants one quarter of the available free space in the flex container.

However, when all the `flex-grow` values are in (0, 1) and their total is less than `1`, the browser interprets each `flex-grow` declaration differently. In this case, instead of a relative ratio, each `flex-grow` value is interpreted as a request for a specific percentage of the free space. In other words, the browser skips steps 3 and 4 in the original algorithm and jumps directly to apportioning the free space:

1. Sum the initial main sizes of all the items. This is the sum of the initial sizes that the browser allocates according to the procedure from the previous section. Call this value `sum_of_initial_sizes`.
2. Calculate the total unused space in the container:

   ```
   available_unused_space = container_width - sum_of_initial_sizes
   ```

3. Calculate how much unused space is allocated to each item:

   ```
   item_unused_space = item_flex_grow_factor * available_unused_space
   ```

4 Calculate the final width of each item:

```
item_final_width = item_initial_size + item_unused_space
```

Figure 5.7 shows an example. To achieve this layout, use the CSS code in listing 5.7.

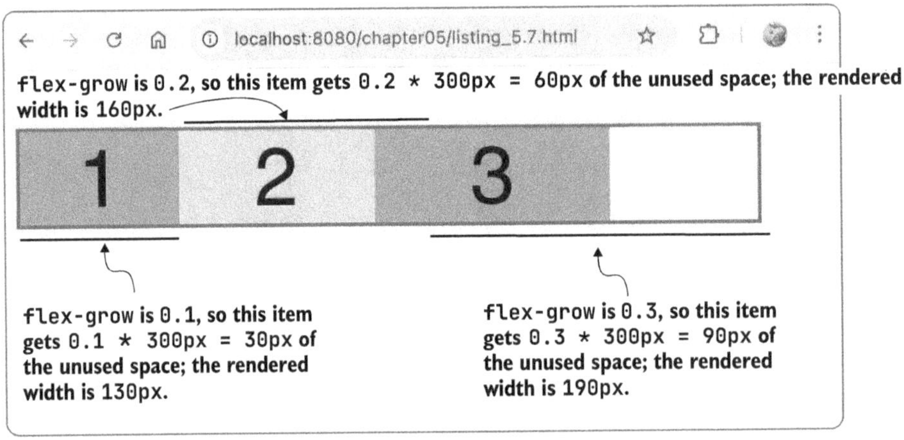


**Figure 5.7** The total of the `flex-grow` factors is less than 1.

**Listing 5.7 The sum of the `flex-grow` values is less than 1.**

```
.container {
    display: flex;
    flex-direction: row;
    width: 600px;
}
.item-1 {
    flex-grow: 0.1;
    flex-basis: 100px;
}
.item-2 {
    flex-grow: 0.2;
    flex-basis: 100px;
}
.item-3 {
    flex-grow: 0.3;
    flex-basis: 100px;
}
```

flex-grow values sum to 0.6

Here's how the math works using the revised algorithm:

1 The sum of all the initial main sizes is `100px + 100px + 100px = 300px`.

2 The unused space in the container is `600px - 300px = 300px`.

3 Here's how much of the unused space is allocated to each item:
   - item-1: `0.1 * 300px = 30px`
   - item-2: `0.2 * 300px = 60px`
   - item-3: `0.3 * 300px = 90px`
4 Here's the final width of each item:
   - item-1: `100px + 30px = 130px`
   - item-2: `100px + 60px = 160px`
   - item-3: `100px + 90px = 190px`

Note that this time we're left with unused space in the container because the total of the final widths (`130px + 160px + 190px = 480px`) is less than the container width (`600px`).

> **NOTE** You might be wondering whether there's a similar algorithm shift when all the `flex-shrink` values are in the range (0, 1) and the total is less than `1`. The short answer is no. The (slightly) longer answer is that, when the flex container is in an overflow state, the entire purpose of `flex-shrink` is to resolve that state, which means all `flex-shrink` values, even those less than `1`, are always treated as relative ratios.

**EXERCISES**

**Exercise 5.3:** Given a flex container, what is the implicit value of the `flex` property on all of the container's flex items?

**Exercise 5.4:** Consider a flex container with `400px` of free space and three flex items with `flex-grow` values of `1`, `1`, and `2`. How much of the container's free space will the third item receive?

1 `100px`
2 `150px`
3 `200px`
4 `300px`

**Exercise 5.5:** Which value determines most how much a flex item shrinks?

1 Its `flex-shrink` value
2 Its base size
3 Its content size
4 Its base size * `flex-shrink` value

**Exercise 5.6:** You declared `flex-shrink: 0` on an item, but it still shrinks. Why?

## 5.3 *Taking min/max constraints into account*

Once the web browser determines each item's flex base size and calculates whether items need to be expanded or contracted to fit in the flex container, it can proceed to the third stage of the flex sizing algorithm: taking any minimum and maximum constraints into account. When the main flex axis is horizontal, these constraints are given by the `min-width` and `max-width` properties. When the main axis is vertical, the constraints are set with the `min-height` and `max-height` properties.

These min/max constraints act like hard stops that limit how small a flex item is allowed to shrink or how large a flex item is able to grow, even when the flex sizing math returns values beyond those limits.

### 5.3.1 Using min-width to limit shrinking

It's often the case that you don't want a flex item to become too small when the browser applies its shrinking algorithm in a flex container overflow scenario. For a horizontal main axis, the way you prevent an item's width from shrinking below a certain size is to declare a `min-width` value on the item.

For example, earlier in listing 5.4, three items were given `flex-shrink` values of `1`, `2`, and `3`, resulting in new widths of `325px`, `200px`, and `75px` (refer to figure 5.4), allowing them to fit inside the `600px` flex container. However, suppose you don't want any item to have a width less than `100px`. In that case, you can constrain the width by setting `min-width` either directly on an item or on a class that applies to all the items, as done in listing 5.8 with the `.item` class (which is applied to all the items; refer to listing 5.1). Figure 5.8 shows an example page. To render this layout, use the CSS classes shown in listing 5.8.

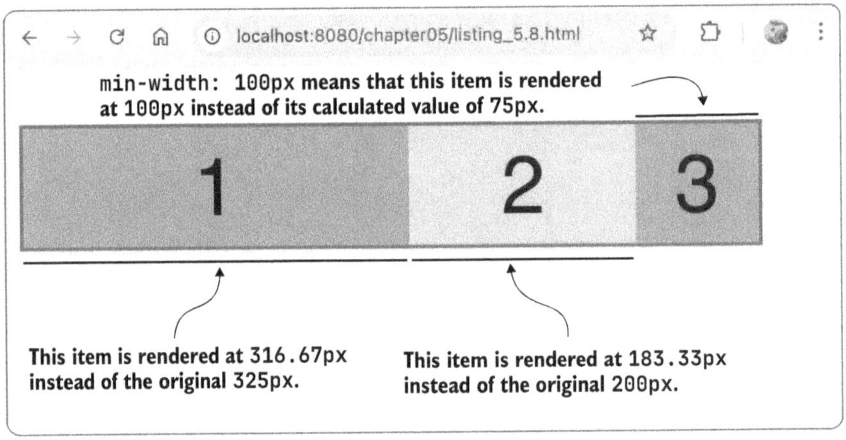


**Figure 5.8 Setting `min-width: 100px` ensures that no item is rendered with a width smaller than that constraint.**

**Listing 5.8 Using `min-width` to limit shrinking**

```
.container {
    display: flex;
    width: 600px;
```

```
}
.item {
    min-width: 100px;        ◄── min-width constraint
}                                applies to all items
.item-1 {
    flex-shrink: 1;
    flex-basis: 450px;
}
.item-2 {
    flex-shrink: 2;
    flex-basis: 450px;
}
.item-3 {
    flex-shrink: 3;
    flex-basis: 450px;
}
```

As shown in figure 5.8, the browser handles the `min-width` constraint by shrinking the other two items a bit more, with that extra shrinking apportioned according to each item's `flex-shrink` value:

1 Run through the `flex-shrink` calculation to determine the proposed width of each item:
   - `item-1`: `325px`
   - `item-2`: `200px`
   - `item-3`: `75px`
2 Apply any `min-width` constraints to the proposed values:
   - `item-1`: `325px`
   - `item-2`: `200px`
   - `item-3`: `100px`
3 Calculate the total widths of the items: `325px + 200px + 100px = 625px`.
4 Calculate the overflow: `625px - 600px = 25px`.
5 Apportion the overflow to the non-constrained items according to their `flex-shrink` values:
   - `item-1`: `flex-shrink: 1;`
   - `item-2`: `flex-shrink: 2;`
   - `total: 3`
   - `item-1 ratio`: `1 / 3 = 0.33`
   - `item-2 ratio`: `2 / 3 = 0.67`
   - `item-1 portion of overflow: 25px * 0.33 = 8.33px`
   - `item-2 portion of overflow: 25px * 0.67 = 16.67px`
6 Adjust to get the rendered widths:
   - `item-1`: `325px - 8.33px = 316.67px`

- `item-2`: `200px - 16.67px = 183.33px`
- `item-3`: `100px`

A quick check shows that `316.67px + 183.33px + 100px = 600px`, so the container no longer overflows, and all constraints have been satisfied.

### 5.3.2 Using max-width to limit growing

A common scenario is not wanting a flex item to become too large when the browser applies its growth algorithm in a flex container underflow situation. For a horizontal main axis, to prevent an item's width from growing beyond a set size, declare a `max-width` value on the item.

For example, earlier in listing 5.2, three items were given `flex-grow` values of `1`, `2`, and `3`, resulting in new widths of `150px`, `200px`, and `250px` (refer to figure 5.2), allowing them to fit inside the `600px` flex container. But suppose you don't want any item to have a width greater than `220px`. In that case, you can constrain the width by setting `max-width` either on an item directly or on a class that applies to all the items, as shown in listing 5.9 with the `.item` class (which is applied to all the items; refer to listing 5.1). Figure 5.9 shows the results of the code.

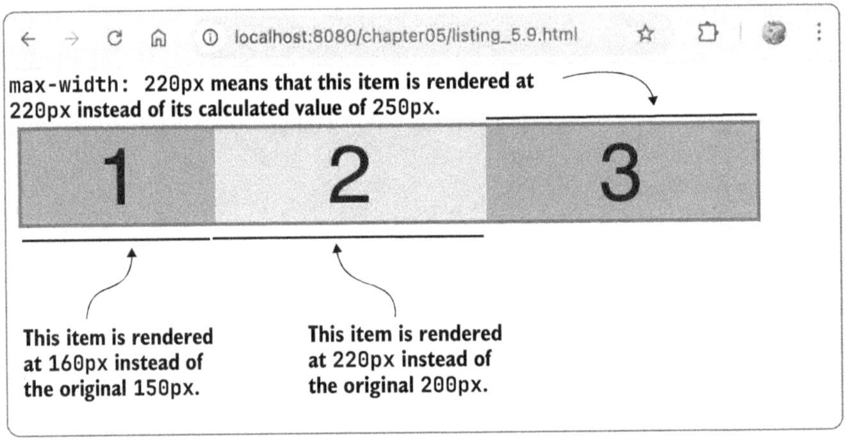


**Figure 5.9 Setting `max-width: 220px` ensures that no item is rendered with a width greater than that constraint.**

**Listing 5.9 Using `max-width` to limit growing**

```
.container {
    display: flex;
    width: 600px;
}
```

```
.item {
    max-width: 220px;
}
.item-1 {
    flex-grow: 1;
    flex-basis: 100px;
}
.item-2 {
    flex-grow: 2;
    flex-basis: 100px;
}
.item-3 {
    flex-grow: 3;
    flex-basis: 100px;
}
```

**max-width constraint applies to all items**

As shown in figure 5.9, the browser handles the `max-width` constraint by growing the other two items a bit more, with that extra growth apportioned according to each item's `flex-grow` value:

1. Run through the `flex-grow` calculation to determine the proposed width of each item:
   - `item-1`: `150px`
   - `item-2`: `200px`
   - `item-3`: `250px`
2. Apply any `max-width` constraints to the proposed values:
   - `item-1`: `150px`
   - `item-2`: `200px`
   - `item-3`: `220px`
3. Calculate the total widths of the items: `150px + 200px + 220px = 570px`.
4. Calculate the underflow: `600px - 570px = 30px`.
5. Apportion the underflow to the non-constrained items according to their `flex-grow` values:
   - `item-1`: `flex-grow: 1;`
   - `item-2`: `flex-grow: 2;`
   - `total: 3`
   - `item-1 ratio`: `1 / 3 = 0.33`
   - `item-2 ratio`: `2 / 3 = 0.67`
   - `item-1 portion of underflow: 30px * 0.33 = 10px`
   - `item-2 portion of underflow: 30px * 0.67 = 20px`
6. Adjust to get the rendered widths:
   - `item-1`: `150px + 10px = 160px`

- item-2: 200px + 20px = 220px
- item-3: 220px

Some quick math shows that `160px + 220px + 220px = 600px`, so the container is no longer in underflow, and all constraints have been satisfied.

**EXERCISES**

**Exercise 5.7:** Consider the following code:

```
.container {
    display: flex;
    width: 800px;
}
.item {
    flex: 0 1 250px;
    min-width: 225px;
}
```

Suppose there are four flex items and that they all use the `.item` class. Will all four items fit into the flex container?

**Exercise 5.8:** Create a rule for a flex item to be used as a column, where each column is flexible but can't be smaller than `100px` or larger than `300px`.

## 5.4 Solutions to Exercises

**Exercise 5.1:** Setting `flex-basis` directly defines the item's base size before any growing or shrinking:

```
.item {
    flex-basis: 150px;
}
```

**Exercise 5.2:** Since `flex-basis` is set to `auto` and the main flex container axis is horizontal, the browser uses `width`, if defined, to set the base size. Therefore, the answer is `180px`.

**Exercise 5.3:** The implicit `flex` property value for all the flex container's items consists of the default values for `flex-grow` (`0`), `flex-shrink` (`1`), and `flex-basis` (`auto`):

```
flex: 0 1 auto;
```

**Exercise 5.4:** The total of the flex grow factor is `1 + 1 + 2 = 4`. Item 3 gets 2/4 of the extra space: `0.5 × 400px = 200px`. Therefore, the answer is `200px`.

**Exercise 5.5:** The answer is 4: its base size * `flex-shrink` value. This is the weighted shrink factor used in the shrink calculation.

**Exercise 5.6:** It's likely that a shorthand declaration such as `flex: 1`, appearing later in your code, is overriding the individual `flex-grow` setting. A declaration such as `flex: 1` sets `flex-grow: 1`, but it also sets `flex-shrink: 1` (and `flex-basis: 0`), so your item shrinks.

**Exercise 5.7:** The answer is no. Since all four items have `min-width: 225px`, the total rendered width will be `4 * 225px = 900px`, which will overflow the `800px` flex container.

**Exercise 5.8:**

```
.column {
    flex: 1 1 200px;
    min-width: 100px;
    max-width: 300px;
}
```

## Summary

- The flex base size is the starting point for all flex calculations and is determined by `flex-basis`, or, if that's `auto`, by `width` or the item's intrinsic size.
- When a flex container has extra space (underflow), the browser distributes it using each item's `flex-grow` value as a proportion of the total grow factors.
- When a container doesn't have enough space (overflow), the browser reduces each item's size using a weighted formula based on the item's width and `flex-shrink` value.
- The `flex` shorthand property sets all three flex properties (`flex-grow`, `flex-shrink`, and `flex-basis`) at once and can override individual settings if not used carefully.
- When all `flex-grow` values are between 0 and 1 and their sum is less than 1, the browser interprets them as absolute percentages of the free space rather than relative ratios.
- Min/max constraints (such as `min-width` and `max-width` for a horizontal main axis) act as hard limits during grow/shrink calculations, forcing the browser to redistribute space when an item hits its bounds.

# 6 The mathematics of responsive design

**This chapter covers**

- The math behind media queries
- Using percentages to create proportional layouts
- Adapting to screen size with viewport units
- Creating fluid layouts with CSS functions

As a web designer or developer, you know that making pages responsive is the right choice because it makes content usable on a wide variety of devices (phones, tablets, desktops, TVs, etc.); ensures that content remains legible and interactive (i.e., *accessible*) without zooming, pinching, or panning; improves performance by avoiding heavy or redundant layouts; enhances search engine optimization since Google favors mobile-friendly designs in search rankings; and increases maintainability because a single responsive codebase is easier to manage than separate versions.

But what you might not realize is that behind every good responsive layout is a foundation of mathematical thinking, and the goal of this chapter is to expose that foundation so that you can make smarter choices when designing and implementing your responsive layouts.

## 6.1 The concept of responsiveness in web design

At its most basic, you could say that responsive design is about *adaptation*. That is, your layout must adapt itself to whatever screen sizes or device capabilities it comes across. This adaptive behavior has many facets, but at its core, it means the following three things:

- Text must remain legible at any viewport size.
- Images must scale without distortion.
- Page components must reorganize to remain usable on any screen size.

Each of these goals involves math, including ratios, percentages, proportions, and conditional logic. (This chapter is all about layout. For info on responsive typography, head over to chapter 8.)

### 6.1.1 Fixed vs. fluid: A visual thought experiment

Imagine you want to display a hero image for a landing page, so you style it as shown in the following listing.

**Listing 6.1 A fixed-width hero image**

```
.hero img {
    display: block;
    width: 1600px;
    height: 900px;
}
```

**NOTE** All the code for this chapter's listings is available in this book's GitHub repository: https://github.com/paulmcfe/web-dev-math.

That fixed width of `1600px` looks great on a desktop monitor, as shown in figure 6.1. But on a tablet, your layout now has an awkward horizontal scrollbar, as shown in figure 6.2. On a phone? It's a disaster, as figure 6.3 illustrates.

Now try this, instead:

```
.hero img {
    display: block;
    width: 100%;
    height: auto;
}
```

Just like that, your hero image scales to fit 100% of whatever container it's in, whether that's a tiny phone screen or an ultra-wide desktop monitor. Now you've got basic proportional math on your side:

- If your container is `1000px` wide, your image automatically scales to `1000px`, and look, there are no scroll bars!
- If your container is `375px` wide, your image automatically scales to `375px`, and look, no disaster!

Figure 6.1 The fixed-width hero image looks good on a desktop.

Figure 6.2 The fixed-width hero image requires a slight scroll on a tablet.

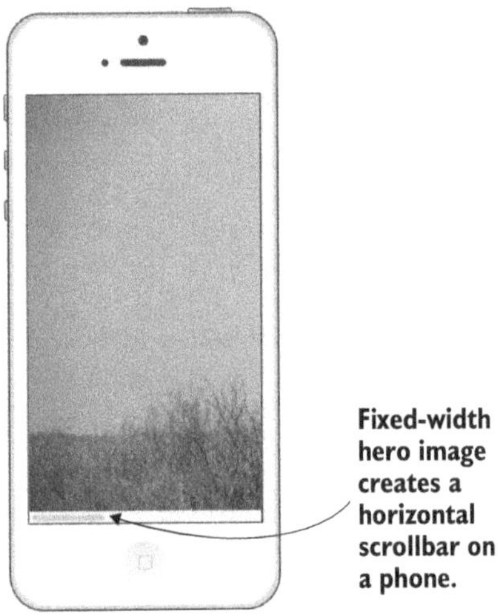


Figure 6.3 The fixed-width hero requires a huge horizontal scroll on a phone.

Just by changing one unit (and by changing `height` to `auto` to ensure your image doesn't distort when it's resized), you've made your layout more responsive.

### 6.1.2 The mathematical mindset

Responsive design calls for a problem-solving mindset where you ask:

- What's the relationship between this element and its parent?

- What should change as the screen gets wider or narrower?
- How can I express this behavior using formulas or ratios?

You'll use math to

- Set breakpoints (e.g., "When the screen is wider than `768px`, do this.")
- Mix units (e.g., calc(100% – 2rem))
- Calculate flexible spacing and positioning
- Adjust layout behavior based on screen size with JavaScript

This mindset helps you avoid brittle layouts that break at unexpected screen widths. Instead, you'll build systems that stretch, shrink, and realign intelligently. Over the rest of this chapter, you'll apply this mindset to breakpoints, proportional layouts, and the CSS and JavaScript tools that make it all work.

## 6.2 Media query logic

One of the key elements of responsive design is the *media query*, a CSS feature that enables you to apply one or more style rules based on a device's features, usually its viewport width. Under the hood, media queries are just conditional logic expressed in CSS, so like all conditional logic, they're grounded in math.

### 6.2.1 Grid and Flexbox as your first responsive tools

Before you reach for a media query, remember that CSS Grid and Flexbox are inherently responsive:

- With Grid, you can define tracks using fractional units (`fr`), use `auto-fit` and `auto-fill`, and build layouts that adapt automatically to the container size (refer to chapter 4).
- With Flexbox, you can make items grow, shrink, or wrap to fit the space available (refer to chapter 5).

For many situations, using one or even both of these layout systems is enough to let you check "responsive" off your design to-do list because these technologies enable creating flexible, fluid designs without needing to ask the browser how wide the viewport is. But sometimes, you need to go further.

### 6.2.2 Why you might still need media queries

Even though modern Grid- and Flexbox-based layout systems are responsive right out of the box, there are still use cases where you'll need to explicitly change the layout rules based on screen size:

- Switching from a multicolumn to a single-column layout
- Adjusting padding or spacing for larger viewports
- Hiding or revealing navigation items

- Starting with a minimal mobile-first design, then progressively adding page elements as the screen size gets larger
- Reducing animation intensity on small or performance-constrained devices or if the user prefers reduced motion

These are layout-level decisions that can't always be solved with percentages, flex containers, or `fr` units. This is where media queries come in.

### 6.2.3 *The math behind media queries*

When you write a media query like

```
@media (min-width: 768px) {
    .sidebar {
        display: block;
    }
}
```

you're telling the browser: "If the viewport is greater than or equal to 768 pixels wide, apply these styles." This is a mathematical comparison expression—specifically, a greater than or equal to (`>=`) check. The basic list of feature expressions used in media queries is shown in Table 6.1.

**Table 6.1 Media query feature expressions**

| Media feature expression | Applies styles when |
|---|---|
| `min-width:` *`value`* | The viewport width is greater than or equal to *value*. |
| `max-width:` *`value`* | The viewport width is less than or equal to *value*. |
| `min-height:` *`value`* | The viewport height is greater than or equal to *value*. |
| `max-height:` *`value`* | The viewport height is less than or equal to *value*. |
| `aspect-ratio:` *`value`* | The viewport width/height equals *value*. |

### 6.2.4 *Using range syntax for cleaner media queries*

The standard media query feature expression targets viewport sizes that are above or below (or equal to) some specified value. But responsive design is often more nuanced than that. For example, you might have some rules to apply only if the viewport is less than or equal to some width *and* greater than or equal to a smaller width.

To handle two media query features in a single expression, modern CSS supports range syntax, which makes multicondition media queries simpler to write and easier to read. Here's how it works:

```
@media (600px <= width <= 1024px) {
    .container {
```

```
        padding: 1rem;
    }
}
```

**NOTE** Range syntax has been supported by all modern browsers since about March 2023. It is safe to use unless you need to support older browsers.

This expression tells the browser, "If the viewport width is greater than or equal to `600px` *and* less than or equal to `1024px`, apply the following styles." Range syntax supports the comparison operators `<`, `<=`, `>`, and `>=`, and it works with the media feature keywords `width` and `height`.

If you need to support older browsers, you can instead use the traditional Boolean operator syntax:

- AND (`and`)

  ```
  @media (min-width: 600px) and (max-width: 1024px)
  ```

- OR (comma-separated)

  ```
  @media (max-width: 600px), (min-width: 1200px)
  ```

- NOT (`not`)

  ```
  @media not all and (hover: hover)
  ```

If you're targeting modern browsers, go with the range syntax for clarity. Otherwise, use Boolean combinations as a fallback.

### 6.2.5 Media query tips

Here are some tips to make your media queries work more predictably:

- Use consistent units. Stick with `em` or `px`, not both. Using `em` ties breakpoints to font size, which can improve accessibility.
- Avoid overlap. Make sure your breakpoints don't conflict. For example, the following could be problematic because the two @rules overlap at exactly `768px`:

  ```
  @media (max-width: 768px) { ... }
  @media (min-width: 768px) { ... }
  ```

The following option is better because there's no overlap:

```
@media (max-width: 767px) { ... }
@media (min-width: 768px) { ... }
```

- Take advantage of your developer tools. Resize your browser window and watch which styles activate. Most dev tools show active media queries in the inspector.

**EXERCISES**

**Exercise 6.1:** Which of the following media queries correctly targets screens that are at least 500 pixels wide and at most 900 pixels wide, using range syntax?

```
1 @media (min-width: 500px) and (max-width: 900px) { ... }
2 @media (500px < width < 900px) { ... }
3 @media (500px <= width <= 900px) { ... }
4 @media (width >= 500px and width <= 900px) { ... }
```

**Exercise 6.2:** Create a media query that switches a `.card-container` class from a single column to a two-column grid when the screen is wider than `700px`, using modern range syntax. Here's the initial class rule:

```
.card-container {
    display: grid;
    grid-template-columns: 1fr;
    gap: 1rem;
}
```

## 6.3 Proportional layouts

A *proportional layout* refers to a layout in which element sizes, spacing, or positioning are defined relative to other elements or to the overall container, rather than with fixed values. Specifically, a proportional layout adapts to different screen or window sizes by using relative units (such as `%`, `vw`, `vh`, `fr`, `rem`, etc.) instead of absolute units (such as `px`).

I cover the `fr` unit in chapter 4, and I tackle viewport units a bit later in this chapter (refer to section 6.4). This section discusses one of the simplest and most powerful tools in responsive design: the humble percentage (`%`). When you use percentages for widths, margins, padding, or positioning, you create layouts in which each element scales along with its container. This lets your designs adapt as screen or window sizes change without resorting to media queries.

### 6.3.1 How percentage-based layouts work

Percentages in CSS are relative to another value:

- For "horizontal" properties such as `width`, `min-width`, `max-width`, `margin-left`, `margin-right`, `padding-left`, or `padding-right`, the percentage is relative to the width of the parent element.
- For "vertical" properties such as `margin-top`, `margin-bottom`, `padding-top`, or `padding-bottom`, the percentage is relative to the width of the parent, *not* the height. This is deeply counterintuitive, so this quirk is worth remembering.
- For `height`, `min-height`, and `max-height`, the percentage is relative to the parent container's height, but only if the parent has an explicit height set. If the parent has no explicit height (i.e., its height is determined by its content), then the

percentage has nothing to resolve against, and the browser will treat `10%` as `auto` or `0`, depending on the layout context.

- For absolutely positioned elements, percentage offsets are relative to the containing block.

**NOTE** I'm using property names such as `margin-top` and `padding-right` for clarity, but the rules I've outlined here also apply to logical block and logical inline properties, such as `margin-block-start` and `padding-inline-end`.

For example,

```
.parent {
    width: 1000px;
}
.child {
    width: 50%;
}
```

The `.child` element will be `500px` wide because `50%` of `1000` is `500`. If you change the parent width to `800px`, the child element automatically adapts its width to `400px`, and the proportions remain the same.

### 6.3.2 Nesting percentages

When you nest percentage-based elements, the math stacks:

```
.outer {
    width: 80%;
}
.inner {
    width: 50%;
}
```

Assume for this code that the `body` element is the parent of the `.outer` element and the `.outer` element is the parent of the `.inner` element. If the browser window is `1000px` wide, then you have the following:

- The `.outer` element is `1000px * 0.8 = 800px` wide.
- The `.inner` element is `800px * 0.5 = 400px` wide.

Understanding this cascading behavior helps you predict how layouts will behave.

### 6.3.3 When to mix percentages with fixed units

Sometimes you want an element to scale but also include a fixed-size gutter. That's where `calc()` comes in:

```
width: calc(100% - 2rem);
```

Here, the element takes up the full container width minus a `2rem` gap. This combination gives you the flexibility of percentages with the control of fixed values.

### 6.3.4 Creating a liquid layout

A fixed-width layout is one where the element widths are set to absolute values. For example, suppose you're designing a page for an article or blog post and you give the `body` element a fixed width. Your page will also likely have an `article` and an `aside` element to which you assign fixed-width values, as demonstrated in figure 6.4. Listing 6.2 shows the code behind this page.

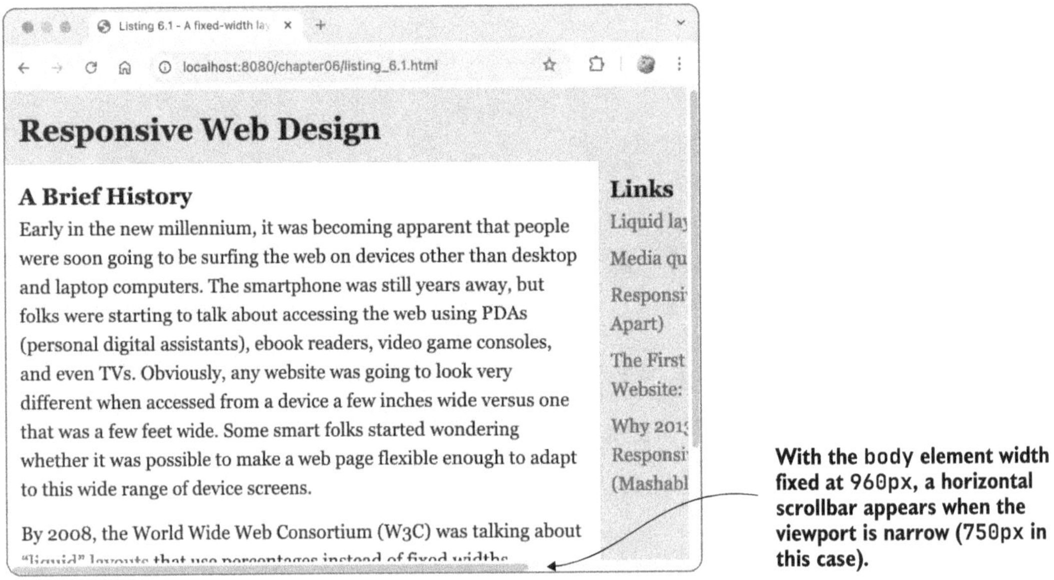


**Figure 6.4 A fixed-width layout isn't adaptable to different screen sizes.**

**Listing 6.2 A fixed-width layout**

```
body {
    width: 960px;
}
header {
    padding: 16px;
}
article {
    width: 640px;
    padding: 16px;
}
aside {
```

- `width: 960px;` — The body element uses a fixed width of 960px.
- `width: 640px;` — The article element uses a fixed width of 640px.

```
    width: 320px;        ← The aside element uses
    padding: 12px;         a fixed width of 320px.
}
```

This type of layout creates all kinds of problems on screens narrower than the fixed width of the `body` element, as shown in figure 6.4. You can fix that by converting your absolute width values to relative widths that use percentages instead of pixels. This is often called a *liquid layout.* Converting a fixed-width layout to a liquid layout is most often a three-stage process.

The first stage is deciding a maximum width for your layout. The goal of a liquid layout is to allow the content to scale down when faced with smaller screen sizes and to scale up when a larger screen comes along. However, most of the time, you don't want the content to get too wide, since that can result in text lines that are too long for comfortable reading. Examine your content, and then decide on the maximum width that still allows for good reading and navigation. With that number in mind, apply the `max-width` property to the outermost container (such as the `body` element). For example, the following declares the `body` element with a maximum width of 960 pixels:

```
body {
    max-width: 960px;
}
```

The second stage is to determine the percentage widths to use for the rest of the elements. By default, any block-level element takes up 100% of its parent's width, so you need to calculate percentages only for elements that you want to use less than the full parent width. For example, if a `main` element is 1,000 pixels wide and a child `div` is declared with `width: 75%`, that `div` will be 750 pixels wide. If the screen is resized so that the `article` element is now 800 pixels wide, the child `div` will automatically scale down to 600 pixels.

To convert your fixed-width elements to percentages, apply the following formula to each:

```
element percentage = (element fixed width / parent fixed width) * 100
```

In the example shown earlier, there were two fixed-width components:

- *An* `article` *element set to 640 pixels wide*—Since the parent (the `body` element) is 960 pixels wide, the `article` element's percentage width value is `(640 / 960) * 100 = 66.67%`.
- *An* `aside` *element set to 320 pixels wide*—Again, the parent (the `body` element) is 960 pixels wide, so the `aside` element's percentage width value is `(320 / 960) * 100 = 33.33%`.

The third stage in converting a fixed-width layout to a liquid layout is to apply the same formula to any other spacing-related items that are part of the layout, such as margins and padding. For example, if an element is declared with `padding: 12px` and its parent is 960 pixels wide, then the liquid padding width becomes `(12 / 960) * 100 = 1.25%`. Figure 6.5 shows the result of these changes. Refer to the revised code in listing 6.3 to understand how to achieve this liquid layout.

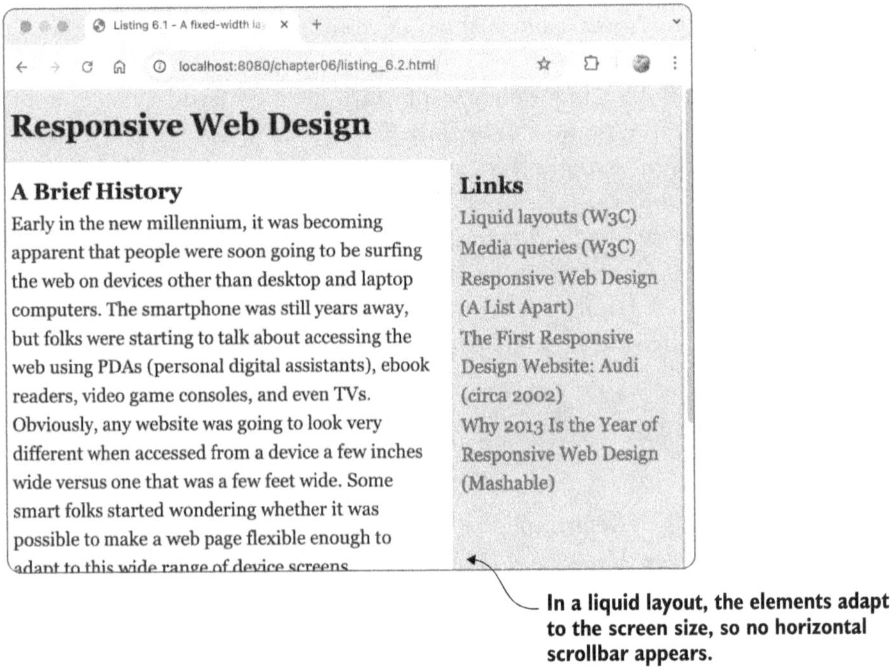


**Figure 6.5** The same page from figure 6.4, now with a responsive liquid layout

**Listing 6.3 A liquid layout**

```
body {
    max-width: 960px;
}
header {
    padding: 1.67%;
}
article {
    width: 66.67%;
    padding: 1.67%;
}
aside {
    width: 33.33%;
    padding: 1.25%;
}
```

- body maximum width is 960px
- article width is 66.67%
- aside width is 33.33%
- padding properties are percentages

**EXERCISES**

**Exercise 6.3:** You have the following layout:

```
.parent {
    width: 800px;
}
.child {
    width: 75%;
}
```

What is the width of `.child` in pixels?

1. 600px
2. 650px
3. 700px
4. 750px

**Exercise 6.4:** When converting a fixed-width layout to a liquid one, you decide on a `800px` maximum width. Your layout has several rules where `padding` is set to `16px`. What percentage value will you substitute for these fixed padding values?

1. 1.6%
2. 2%
3. 2.25%
4. 16%

## 6.4 Viewport-based units

When dealing with percentage units, as described in the previous section, it's important to remember that assigning a percentage width to an element means styling that element as a percentage of its *parent's* width. If a parent element is 800 pixels wide, and you declare `width: 75%` on a child element, that child is 600 pixels wide. It doesn't matter whether the browser's screen width is 2,000 pixels; that child still takes up only 600 pixels across the screen.

What if you want that child element to be 75% of the screen instead of its parent? In that case, you need to switch from percentages to viewport units, which act as percentage-like units that are relative to the entire browser viewport.

### 6.4.1 The classic viewport units

CSS defines four core viewport units, all relative to what the CSS spec calls the *initial containing block*, which is the containing block of the root element. For our purposes, the initial containing block is the browser's viewport. Here are the core viewport units:

- `vw`—The viewport width unit, where `100vw` equals 100% of the current viewport width. If the viewport is 1,600 pixels wide, then `1vw = 1600px / 100 = 16px`.

- `vh`—The viewport height unit, where `100vh` equals 100% of the current viewport height. If the viewport is 1,000 pixels high, then `1vh = 1000px / 100 = 10px`.
- `vmin`—The viewport minimum unit, where `100vmin` equals 100% of the smaller of the two viewport dimensions. If the viewport is 800 pixels wide and 600 pixels high, `1vmin = 600px / 100 = 6px` (because, in this case, the viewport height is the smaller of the two dimensions).
- `vmax`—The viewport maximum unit, where `100vmax` equals 100% of the larger of the two viewport dimensions. If the viewport is 1,200 pixels wide and 1,024 pixels high, `1vmax = 1200px / 100 = 12px` (because the viewport width is the larger of the two dimensions).

Suppose that you want to display an image so that it automatically takes up the entire height of the viewport. You can do that by applying the following rule to the image:

```
.image-full {
    height: 100vh;
    width: auto;
}
```

These units are absolute, meaning they're not relative to any parent. They're always tied to the viewport.

### 6.4.2 Logical viewport units

Just like the `*-block` and `*-inline` properties, viewport units also have logical variants:

- `vb`—The viewport block dimension unit, where `100vb` equals 100% of the current viewport size along the block dimension (such as height in horizontal writing mode)
- `vi`—The viewport inline dimension unit, where `100vi` equals 100% of the current viewport size along the inline dimension (such as width in horizontal writing mode)

Here is an example:

```
section {
    padding-block: 10vb;
    padding-inline: 5vi;
}
```

These units are writing-mode aware, which makes them ideal for multilingual and vertical writing designs.

### 6.4.3 The scrollbar problem

For years, `100vh` caused a subtle but frustrating bug, especially on mobile devices. When you navigate to a page using a mobile browser, the browser calculates the value of `100vh` by taking the full height of the screen, *including* the height of the browser chrome (UI elements such as the address bar and the toolbar). However, those chrome elements appear above or below the viewport—they're not part of the viewport itself. So, for example, you might have the following:

- Total screen height: `844px`
- Height of address bar: `50px`
- Height of toolbar: `90px`
- Viewport height without chrome: `844px - 50px - 90px = 704px`

Suppose your CSS includes a rule that applies `height: 100vh` on an element, as shown in the following listing.

**Listing 6.4 The `100vh` overflow bug**

```
<head>
    <style>
        .fullscreen {
            height: 100vh;
            display: flex;
            flex-direction: column;
            justify-content: space-between;
            align-items: center;
        }
    </style>
</head>
<body>
    <div class="fullscreen">
        <h1>The 100vh overflow bug</h1>
        <p class="bottom">IMPORTANT! Please read before continuing!</p>
    </div>
</body>
```

When the page first loads, `100vh` is going to be `844px` on our example mobile device, but the actual viewport area will be only `704px` tall, so you end up with the dreaded *100vh overflow bug*, as demonstrated in figure 6.6:

- The `.fullscreen` element overflows vertically below the visible screen.
- The `.bottom` element is hidden behind the browser chrome at the bottom of the screen.

And as you scroll a page vertically, browsers often display or hide the chrome, effectively changing the height of the viewport on the fly, but `100vh` doesn't update to compensate, so the visual rhythm is constantly broken.

Developers used various hacks to address this problem in the past (e.g., using JavaScript to get `window.innerHeight` or special CSS properties such as `-webkit-fill-available`), but these were clunky solutions. The good news is that CSS now provides viewport-relative units to handle these scenarios in a cleaner way.

### 6.4.4 New viewport units: the sv*, lv*, and dv* families

To solve the mobile viewport conundrum, the CSS Working Group introduced the concepts of large, small, and dynamic viewports, each with their own set of units. These new units are essentially variations of `vh`, `vw`, and so on, that explicitly account for whether browser UI is present. From a mathematical standpoint, they're still percentages of a certain defined viewport size, but the definition of the viewport can differ:

**Figure 6.6 The `100vh` overflow bug can cause important screen elements to be hidden behind the browser's chrome.**

- *Small viewport* (`sv*`)—The viewport size when the browser's interface elements are fully visible. Think of this as the "minimum content area" viewport. This family consists of the following units:
  - `svw`—1% of the small viewport width
  - `svh`—1% of the small viewport height
  - `svb`—1% of the small viewport block dimension
  - `svi`—1% of the small viewport inline dimension
  - `svmin`—1% of the smaller small viewport dimension
  - `svmax`—1% of the larger small viewport dimension

  If you use `100svh` for an element, it will perfectly fill the visible height when the browser UI is present, ensuring nothing is cut off. This is a safe choice for full-screen sections on mobile devices because it avoids initial overflow. However, if the user scrolls and the toolbars hide (making the viewport taller), that element at `100svh` will now appear shorter than the viewport, potentially leaving blank space at the bottom. In short, `sv*` units give a stable, minimum viewport-relative size with no surprises on load, but they won't expand to fill extra space when toolbars disappear.
- *Large viewport* (`lv*`)—The viewport size when all the browser's UI is hidden. Think of this as the "maximum content area" viewport. This family consists of the following units:
  - `lvw`—1% of the large viewport width
  - `lvh`: 1% of the large viewport height
  - `lvb`—1% of the large viewport block dimension

- `lvi`—1% of the large viewport inline dimension
- `lvmin`—1% of the smaller large viewport dimension
- `lvmax`—1% of the larger large viewport dimension

If you use `100vh` for an element, it will perfectly fill the visible height when the browser UI is hidden. In other words, the `lvh` unit works similarly to the `vh` unit. Use an `lv*` unit when you want to size content for times when the browser UI is out of the way, but be mindful that if the UI is actually visible, part of that content might be obscured.

- *Dynamic viewport* (`dv*`)—The browser's real-time measurement that updates as the browser's UI elements appear and disappear. Think of this as the "always current" viewport. This family consists of the following units:
  - `dvw`—1% of the current viewport width
  - `dvh`—1% of the current viewport height
  - `dvb`—1% of the current viewport block dimension
  - `dvi`—1% of the current viewport inline dimension
  - `dvmin`—1% of the smaller current viewport dimension
  - `dvmax`—1% of the larger current viewport dimension

  If you use `100dvh` for an element, it will perfectly fill the visible viewport at any given moment by dynamically resizing the element as the browser UI comes and goes. This can be great for ensuring an element (like a background or a panel) always covers the whole screen without gaps or overflow in either state. As the following listing and figure 6.7 show, the result when, from listing 6.4, you change `height: 100vh` to `height: 100dvh` on the `.fullscreen` element.

By setting the element height to `100dvh`, the message at the bottom of the screen is no longer hidden behind the browser chrome.

**Figure 6.7 Setting the `.fullscreen` element's height to `100dvh` solves the overflow bug**

**Listing 6.5 The `100dvh` overflow fix**

```
.fullscreen {
   height: 100dvh;
   display: flex;
```

```
    flex-direction: column;
    justify-content: space-between;
    align-items: center;
}
```

Because these viewport units dynamically resize, they can cause content to reflow during scroll, leading to a jarring effect or performance problems if not used sparingly. Browser engines mitigate this a little by throttling dynamic unit updates (e.g., updates don't happen with every single frame of a scroll), but it's still something to use only for crucial elements rather than entire pages of text.

The good news is that these units are well supported in modern browsers. All major engines implemented them around late 2022 or in 2023. In fact, by Chrome 108 (and similarly Firefox 101+ and Safari 15.4+), the `sv*`, `lv*`, and `dv*` units, along with `vi` and `vb`, became available in stable releases. As of mid-2025, roughly 93% of users globally are on browsers that support these new viewport units, so you can use them in production with reasonable confidence (just double-check if you need to support older mobile browsers, as they might not recognize them).

### 6.4.5 *Deciding which viewport unit to use*

From a practical standpoint, all these different viewport units mean that you now have granular control:

- If you want an element to never overflow on mobile initial load, use `svh` (or just use a percentage height if inside a container) for the height so it accounts for the toolbar.
- If you want an element to always cover the full screen even after the user scrolls (like a sticky full-page panel), you might opt for `dvh` to stretch with the viewport. Just be mindful of the reflow effect.
- In many cases, using the default `vh` (which is like `lvh`) is fine on desktops and can be acceptable on mobile devices if a little overflow isn't critical (or if you handle it via padding where the UI overlaps).

Now that you have these new units, you can make a conscious choice. For instance, a common pattern is to use `min-height: 100svh` on a section so it's at least the full visible height on load and can expand if needed.

**EXERCISES**

**Exercise 6.5:** You applied this style to a full-page image on mobile:

```
.fullscreen-image {
    height: 100vh;
}
```

But in some mobile browsers, the image scrolls slightly or is partially cut off. Why does this happen, and how do you fix it?

**Exercise 6.6:** You're designing a multipanel app interface. The screen is split into

- A top toolbar: `10svh`
- A content area: `auto`
- A footer: `8svh`

Using viewport units and CSS Grid, create a layout that honors these constraints on all screen sizes without overflow.

## 6.5 Layout fluidity with CSS functions

Modern CSS provides powerful functions that let developers describe layout relationships mathematically: `calc()`, `min()`, `max()`, and `clamp()`. These tools enable fluid, responsive layouts that scale smoothly with the viewport, without needing dozens of media queries. This section explores how to use these functions to make layouts fluid.

### 6.5.1 Why fluid layouts matter

Traditional responsive design uses breakpoints to switch styles at certain screen widths. That works, but it also creates jumps. An element might go from `width: 100%` to `width: 50%` when the screen changes because of some dynamic behavior (e.g., adding or removing content) that triggers a media query. The result is a sudden layout shift.

Fluid layouts eliminate that. Instead of sudden jumps, elements adjust continuously. A container can start at `width: 100%` on small screens, then gradually morph to `max-width: 500px` on larger ones. Or padding can grow smoothly as the screen gets wider, giving a more natural, proportional look.

To achieve fluid layouts, you can use CSS math functions to express relationships such as

- "Grow this container to `80%` of the screen, but cap it at `1200px`."
- "Give this section horizontal padding that grows from `1rem` to `2rem`, based on viewport width."
- "Place this element a distance from the left edge that scales with the screen size but never gets too large."

Let's get into the math behind the functions that make such fluidity possible.

### 6.5.2 Using clamp() for fluid container widths

Let's say you want a container to be

- `90%` width on small screens
- Fixed at `1200px` on very wide screens
- Somewhere in between as it scales

A common solution would be

```
.container {
   width: 90%;
```

```
    max-width: 1200px;
}
```

This is fine, but it doesn't give you fine-grained control. Instead, you can write:

```
.container {
    width: clamp(300px, 90%, 1200px);
}
```

Now the container scales fluidly between `300px` and `1200px` based on screen size. If the screen is tiny, it won't go below `300px`. If the screen is massive, it won't go above `1200px`. In between, it adjusts smoothly.

### 6.5.3 The math behind custom fluid widths

Suppose you want a container that grows as follows:

- At `500px` viewport width, the container width should be `400px`.
- At `1000px` viewport width, the container width should be `800px`.

This is a linear relationship, so you can model it using algebra's linear equation (`y = mx + b`):

- *Slope* (`m`)—`(800 - 400) / (1000 - 500) = 400 / 500 = 0.8`
- *Intercept* (`b`)—`y - mx = 400 - (0.8 * 500) = 400 - 400 = 0`

So, the formula is

```
width: calc(0.8 * 100vw);
```

This formula grows the container from `400px` to `800px` as the viewport scales from `500px` to `1000px`. Outside that range, you want to cap it, so, use

```
width: clamp(400px, 0.8vw * 100, 800px);
```

Or just use

```
width: clamp(400px, 80vw, 800px);
```

This approach clamps the fluid width within your desired minimum and maximum.

### 6.5.4 Calculating preferred clamp() values

The procedure outlined in the previous section is a linear interpolation formula that you can use to derive any preferred (middle) `clamp()` value. (I explain how linear interpolation works in chapter 12.) To use the formula, assume you already have a minimum (call it `minValue`) and a maximum (call it `maxValue`) value for your property to plug into the `clamp()` function. Now you need to define two more numbers:

- The minimum viewport width (call it `minVW`) at which you want the property to be `minValue`
- The maximum viewport width (call it `maxVW`) at which you want the property to be `maxValue`

Now you can calculate the preferred value in `vw`:

```
preferredValue = (maxValue - minValue) / (maxVW - minVW) * 100
```

Finally, you plug that value into your declaration:

```
property: clamp(minValue, preferredValue, maxValue);
```

For example, suppose you want the following for an element:

- `1rem` (`16px`) margin at `400px` screen width
- `3rem` (`48px`) margin at `1200px` screen width

Plug those values into the linear interpolation formula:

```
preferredValue = (48 - 16) / (1200 - 400) * 100
               = 32 /  800 * 100
               = 3200 / 800
               = 4
```

Your declaration becomes the following:

```
margin: clamp(1rem, 4vw, 3rem);
```

### 6.5.5 *Fluid padding and gaps*

As hinted in the example in the previous section, you can also make spacing responsive. Say you want horizontal padding that

- Is at least `0.25rem` (`4px`) on small screens (say, down to `320px`)
- Grows to `1.75rem` (`28px`) on large screens (say, up to `1280px`)

Now you do the math using the linear interpolation formula:

```
preferredValue = (28 - 4) / (1280 - 320) * 100
               = 24 /  960 * 100
               = 2400 / 960
               = 2.5
```

So, these declarations will get the job done:

```
padding-left: clamp(0.25rem, 2.5vw, 1.75rem);
padding-right: clamp(0.25rem, 2.5vw, 1.75rem);
```

This approach gives you fluid gutters that feel natural on all screen sizes.

### 6.5.6 *How to think about CSS math for layouts*

Here are some takeaways to bear in mind:

- Use `calc()` to build linear equations that scale with viewport size.
- Use `min()` and `max()` to enforce limits.
- Use `clamp()` to combine all three: a preferred value that scales, with defined minimum and maximum bounds.
- Think in terms of slopes: (change in size) / (change in viewport).
- Replace media queries with math when possible to simplify and smooth your layouts.

By using these functions with some basic math, you can create layouts that flex and flow naturally across screen sizes, with no jumpy breakpoints required.

### 6.5.7 *When to bring in JavaScript*

CSS media queries, responsive units (especially percentages and viewport-based units), and CSS functions such as `calc()` and `clamp()` will cover most of your day-to-day responsive design needs. However, there are situations where these CSS techniques aren't up to the task, and you need to bring in the extra muscle of JavaScript. For example, you might need to

- *Apply complex conditional logic*—For example, you might need to completely rearrange DOM elements or toggle UI components based on various conditions, not just screen width. CSS can't easily move an element from one container to another, but JavaScript can (by manipulating the DOM).
- *Calculate sizes dynamically*—For example, you might need to set an element's height to match another element's width or scale a font size continuously with screen size according to a specific formula. CSS has mathematical limits. Sure, it offers `calc()` for relatively simple expressions, but it can't handle more involved runtime calculations or conditional decisions beyond media query breakpoints.
- *Respond to user interactions or real-time data*—For example, you might need to resize a game canvas or an interactive chart based on container dimensions, or you might need to adjust the layout when content changes. JavaScript can listen for events and make on-the-fly adjustments that CSS alone can't trigger.

In essence, JavaScript provides interactivity and flexibility for responsive layouts, enabling features that go beyond what CSS can achieve alone.

For example, suppose you want to build a responsive dashboard, such as the one shown in figure 6.8 and listing 6.6, where each widget has a weight (based, say, on a factor such as relative importance or data volume), and you want the layout engine to calculate how much horizontal space to allocate to each widget based on those weights. Sure, you could do that using pure CSS as long as you know the weights in advance. However, imagine a scenario where you're bringing in the widgets

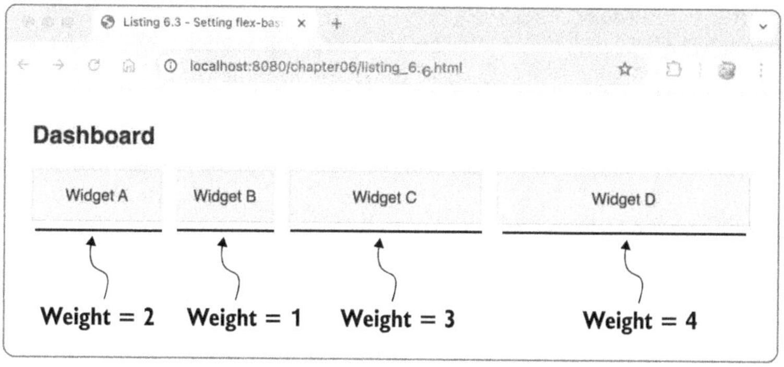


**Figure 6.8 Dashboard widgets where the `flex-basis` was calculated dynamically via JavaScript.**

via an API, so you don't know the weights until you receive the data. This is JavaScript territory.

First, you have a container for your widgets:

```
<h2>Dashboard</h2>
<div class="dashboard" id="dashboard"></div>
```

Next, you apply some styling (only layout-related styles are shown here):

```
.dashboard {
    display: flex;
    gap: 1rem;
}
.widget {
    min-width: 100px;
}
```

Now it's time for JavaScript.

**Listing 6.6 Setting `flex-basis` dynamically**

```
const widgetData = [
    { name: 'Widget A', weight: 2 },
    { name: 'Widget B', weight: 1 },
    { name: 'Widget C', weight: 3 },
    { name: 'Widget D', weight: 4 },
];

const dash = document.getElementById('dashboard');
const gap = parseFloat(getComputedStyle(dash).gap) || 0;

widgetData.forEach(widget => {
    const el = document.createElement('div');
    el.className = 'widget';
```

**Example dashboard data**

**Get gap property value**

**Create and append widgets**

```
    el.textContent = widget.name;
    dash.appendChild(el);
});

const widgets = dash.querySelectorAll('.widget');
const totalWeight = widgetData.reduce((sum, w) =>
                    sum + w.weight, 0);
const widgetCount = widgets.length;

const totalGapWidth = gap * (widgetCount - 1);
const containerWidth = dash.clientWidth;
const usableWidth = containerWidth - totalGapWidth;

widgets.forEach((widget, i) => {
    const weight = widgetData[i].weight;
    const width = (weight / totalWeight) * usableWidth;
    widget.style.flexBasis = `${width}px`;
});
```

Create and append widgets

Sum weights

Calculate total gap space in pixels

Set flex-basis for each widget based on weight

This code uses the weights from the `widgetData` array to dynamically set the `flex-basis` property for each widget (refer to figure 6.8 for the results), something that's just not possible using CSS alone. This pattern is common in data dashboards, media galleries, or any interface that requires proportional sizing beyond fixed rules.

**EXERCISE**

**Exercise 6.7:** Suppose you want to style grid gaps to have the following characteristics:

- The gap is `0.25rem` when the screen is `400px` wide.
- The gap caps at `1rem` when screen is `1600px` wide.

What is the preferred value to use in the `clamp()` function?

## 6.6 Solutions to exercises

**Exercise 6.1:** Here is the explanation:

- 1 is valid but uses the old Boolean syntax.
- 2 is valid but the use of strict inequalities (<) means that the edge cases of `500px` and `900px` are excluded.
- 3 is valid and correctly uses range syntax.
- 4 is not valid CSS media query syntax.

Therefore, the correct answer is 3.

**Exercise 6.2:** Here's the at-rule:

```
@media (width > 700px) {
    .card-container {
        grid-template-columns: 1fr 1fr;
    }
}
```

**Exercise 6.3:** The `.child` element's width is `75%` of its parent's width, which is `800px`: `0.75 * 800px = 600px`. Therefore, the correct answer is `600px`.

**Exercise 6.4:** The maximum width is `800px` and the fixed padding width is `16px`. Therefore, the percentage top use is `16 / 800 = 0.02`, and the answer is `2%`.

**Exercise 6.5:** On some mobile browsers, `100vh` may include space under the dynamic UI that's not visible when the page loads. The fix is to switch to `dvh` to reflect the actual visible viewport height:

```
.fullscreen-image {
    height: 100dvh;
}
```

**Exercise 6.6:** Here's the code:

```
.app {
    display: grid;
    grid-template-rows: 10svh 1fr 8svh;
    height: 100dvh;
}
```

In this case,

- `10svh` ensures the toolbar never grows too large even if UI chrome is hidden.
- `1fr` gives the content area all available remaining space.
- `100dvh` ensures the layout adapts to dynamic screen height changes without overflow.

**Exercise 6.7:** Here's the math:

```
preferredValue = (16 - 4) / (1600 - 400) * 100
               = 12 /  1200 * 100
               = 1200 / 1200
               = 1
```

Therefore, your `gap` declaration will look like this:

```
gap: clamp(0.25rem, 1vw, 1rem);
```

## Summary

- Responsive design is about adaptation, where a layout adapts itself to the current screen size and device features.
- Fixed-width layouts are almost always a problem on mobile devices because once the screen width is less than the fixed-size width, the user must scroll horizontally to read the page.
- Grid and Flexbox offer responsiveness right out of the box, but you might still need extra CSS properties to ensure your layout adapts properly to all screen sizes.

- The media query range syntax is well-supported and should be used unless you need to support legacy browsers.
- When using percentages, remember that with both horizontal properties such as `width` and `padding-right` and vertical properties such as `margin-top` and `padding-bottom` the percentage is relative to the *width* of the parent.
- To create a liquid layout based on percentages, decide on a maximum width for your layout, determine the percentage widths to use for the rest of the elements, and then apply the same formula to any other spacing-related items that are part of the layout, such as margins and padding.
- The standard viewport units `vw` and `vh` are fine in most cases, but consider using newer units such as `svh` and `dvh` if you want more control over your layouts.
- When using `clamp()`, you can calculate a length for the preferred value using the linear interpolation formula: `(maxValue - minValue) / (maxVW - minVW) * 100`.

# 7 The mathematics of color

**This chapter covers**

- Converting color values between models
- Creating harmonious color schemes and accessible colors
- Switching between light and dark mode
- Creating interesting visual effects with blend modes

Most developers start with CSS colors such as `#ff0000` or `hsl(240 100% 50%)` without understanding what's happening under the hood. But colors aren't just pretty decorations. They're mathematical constructs that follow precise rules. Understanding these rules will help you create better color schemes, fix accessibility problems, and implement advanced color effects that would otherwise seem like magic.

Think of this chapter as a bridge between merely knowing how to use CSS colors and understanding how colors work mathematically. By the end of the chapter, you'll be manipulating colors like a pro, creating accessible designs with confidence, and impressing your colleagues with your color wizardry.

## 7.1 Color models and color spaces

To understand the math behind web colors, you first need to learn about color models and color spaces. The next few sections discuss these topics.

### 7.1.1 The RGB color model

RGB is the foundational color model for all digital displays. It's based on additive color mixing where you're literally adding light to create colors. Mathematically, RGB represents colors as triplets (R, G, B), where each component ranges from 0 to 255:

- Each channel represents the intensity of red, green, or blue light.
- The total number of possible colors is $256^3$, or 16,777,216.
- The RGB model forms a cube in 3D space (refer to figure 7.1), where (0, 0, 0) is black, (255, 0, 0) is pure red, (0, 255, 0) is pure green, (0, 0, 255) is pure blue, and (255, 255, 255) is white. The diagonal line connecting black and white represents all the grayscale colors (i.e., where the values for red, green, and blue are equal).

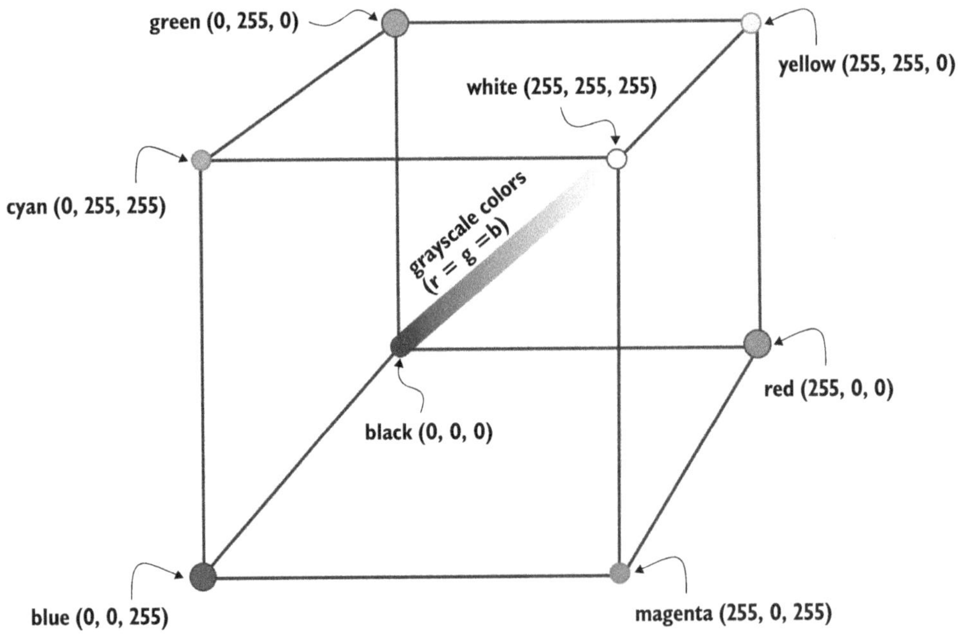


**Figure 7.1 You can visualize the RGB color model as a cube.**

In CSS, you usually specify a color in the RGB model by using the `rgb()` function:

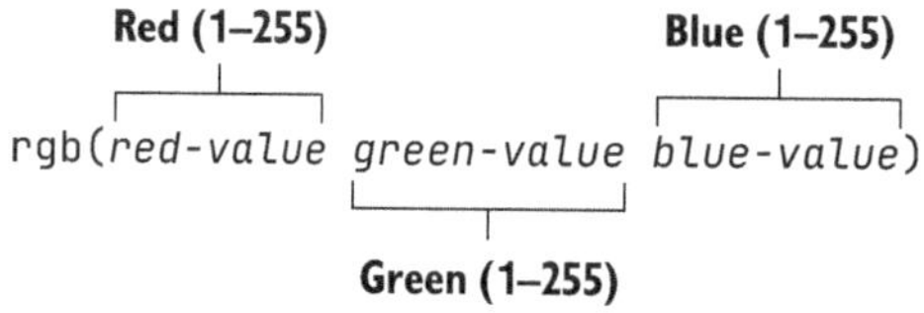


To use this function, replace `red-value` with a number between `0` and `255` to specify the red component, replace `green-value` with a number between `0` and `255` to specify the green component, and replace `blue-value` with a number between `0` and `255` to specify the blue component. For example, you can generate purple by using `128` for red, `0` for green, and `128` for blue. The following snippet shows how to use CSS to display all your `h1` headings with purple text.

```
h1
    color: rgb(128  0 128);
}
```

You can also specify the `rgb()` function's `red-value`, `green-value`, and `blue-value` parameters using percentages, with `100%` specifying the full intensity of the color (equivalent to the decimal value 255) and `0%` specifying the lowest intensity (the same as 0 in decimal notation).

If you want to include an alpha channel to specify the color's transparency, add a slash (/) followed by the alpha value in the range [0, 1] or [0%, 100%], where `0` or `0%` is completely transparent and `1` or `100%` is completely opaque:

```
h1
    color: rgb(128  0 128 / 0.5);
}
```

Rather than using the `rgb()` function to specify a color's red, green, and blue components, you can use the CSS hexadecimal-based method:

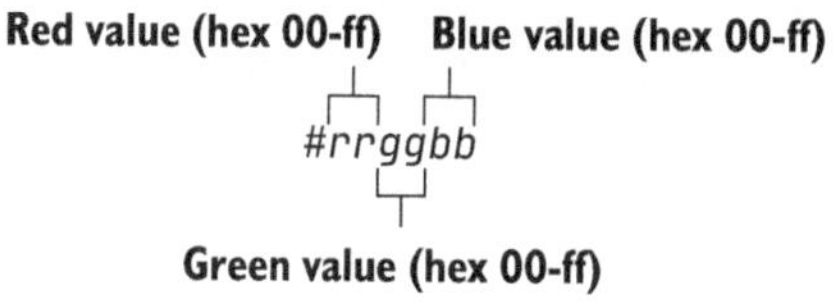


These RGB hex codes always begin with the hash symbol (#), followed by the two-digit hex value for the red component, the two-digit hex value for the green component, and the two-digit hex value for the blue component. (If you want to include an alpha channel to control transparency, use the format `#rrggbbaa`, where `aa` is a two-digit hex value.) In each case, the allowed hex values range from `00` to `ff`. (If you're using the format `#rrggbbaa`, when `aa` is `00`, the color is completely transparent, and when `aa` is `ff`, the color is completely opaque.) Because these codes consist of three hex values, they're often called *hex triplets.*

The following example shows how you'd use this method to apply purple to `h1` text. The hex equivalent of decimal 128 is 80, so for the `color` value, the red component is hex `80`, the green component is hex `00`, and the blue component is hex `80`.

```
h1 {
    color: #800080;
}
```

You can use an even shorter code in certain circumstances. If each of the `rr`, `gg`, and `bb` values consists of repeated characters, such as `00`, `66`, or `ff`, you can use one of the repeated characters for each color. The following two codes are equivalent:

```
#3366cc
#36c
```

The RGB color model is straightforward, but it's not particularly intuitive. That's the main reason most web designers eschew RGB values in favor of the more intuitive HSL color model, discussed next.

### 7.1.2 *The HSL color model*

An often more intuitive method of creating a color involves supplying numeric values for three attributes called hue, saturation, and lightness, so this technique is sometimes termed the *HSL method*:

- *Hue*—This value, which is more or less equivalent to the term *color,* measures the position in degrees on the color wheel, with values between 0 and 359. Hues wrap around in rainbow order. For example, 0° = red, 120° = green, 240° = blue, and 360° ≈ 0° = red again. All intermediate angles give a continuum of colors.
- *Saturation*—This value is a percentage measure of a given hue's purity. A saturation value of 100% means that the hue is a pure color. Lower numbers indicate that more gray is mixed with the hue; at 0%, the color becomes part of the grayscale.
- *Lightness*—This value is also a percentage and measures how light or dark the color is. Lower percentages are darker (with 0% producing black), and higher percentages are lighter (with 100% producing white). 50% lightness is normal brightness.

HSL translates RGB's cube into a more intuitive cylindrical coordinate system (refer to figure 7.2). This is where the math gets interesting:

- Hue is the angle around the cylinder (0°–360°)

- Saturation is the distance from the center axis of the cylinder (0%–100%)
- Lightness is the height on the vertical axis of the cylinder (0%–100%)

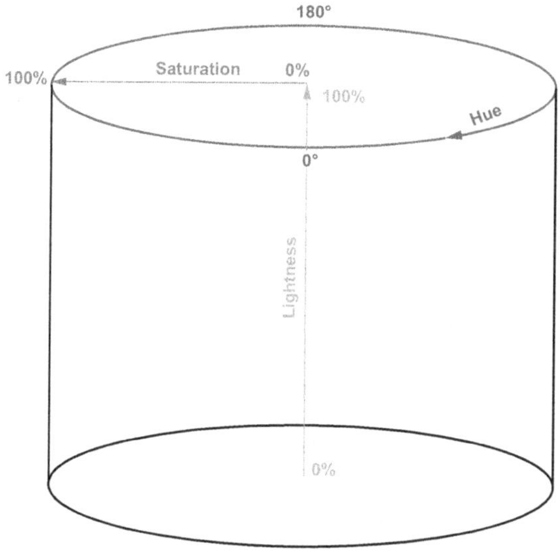


**Figure 7.2 You can visualize the HSL color model as a cylinder.**

HSL is great for designers because adjusting H, S, or L produces intuitive changes. For example, to make a color lighter or darker, you just tweak the lightness value. To get a pastel, you lower saturation and increase lightness. HSL is directly supported in CSS via the `hsl()` function:

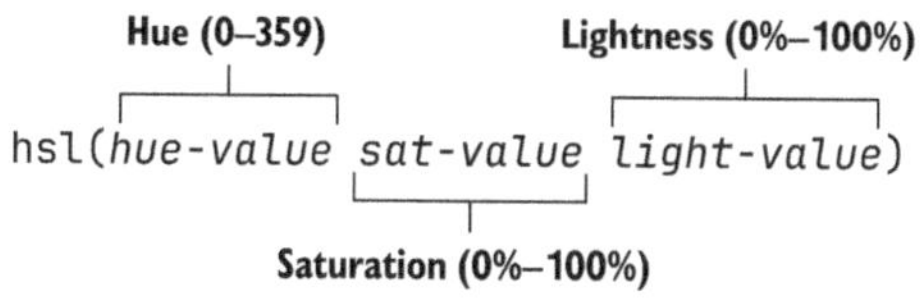


To use this function, replace *`hue-value`* with a number between 0 and 359 to specify the hue component, replace *`sat-value`* with a percentage between 0 and 100 to specify the saturation component, and replace *`light-value`* with a percentage between 0 and 100 to specify the lightness component. Sticking with the purple `h1` text example, the following shows how to use CSS to display all your `h1` headings in purple by using the `hsl()` function.

```
h1 {
    color: hsl(300 100% 25%);
}
```

If you want to include an alpha channel to specify the color's transparency, add a slash (/) followed by the alpha value in the range [0, 1] or [0%, 100%], where `0` or `0%` is completely transparent and `1` or `100%` is completely opaque:

```
h1
    color: hsl(300 100% 25% / 0.75);
}
```

### 7.1.3 The LAB color space

The LAB (also L*a*b* or Lab*) color space represents the full range of color that humans can perceive and is designed so that equal value changes correspond to equal perceived color differences. This perceptual uniformity is crucial for accessibility because it lets you mathematically determine if two colors are distinguishable to human eyes, regardless of the specific type of color vision. This color space was defined by the International Commission on Illumination (CIE), so the space is also often called CIELAB or CIELab. LAB is a spherical coordinate system (refer to figure 7.3) that expresses color as three values:

- *L*—The brightness axis of the coordinate system with values between 0 or 0% (black) and 100 or 100% (white).
- *A*—The green-red axis with values between –125 (green) and 125 (red). Alternatively, you can use percentages from –100 (green) to 100 (red).
- *B*—The blue-yellow axis with values between –125 (blue) and 125 (yellow). Alternatively, you can use percentages from –100 (blue) to 100 (yellow).

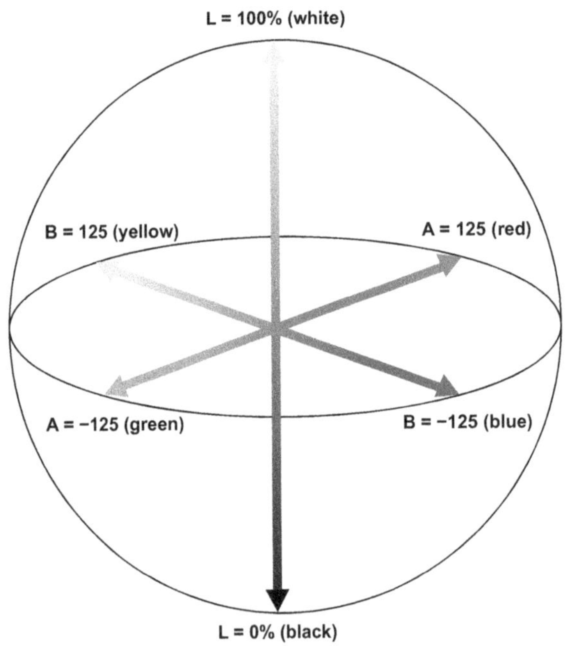


**Figure 7.3** You can visualize the LAB color space as a sphere.

For both the A and B axes, greater absolute values of a and b produce more saturated colors. Smaller absolute values of a and b produce more desaturated colors, with a = b = 0 producing grayscale colors. LAB is directly supported in modern (since early 2023) browsers via the CSS `lab()` function:

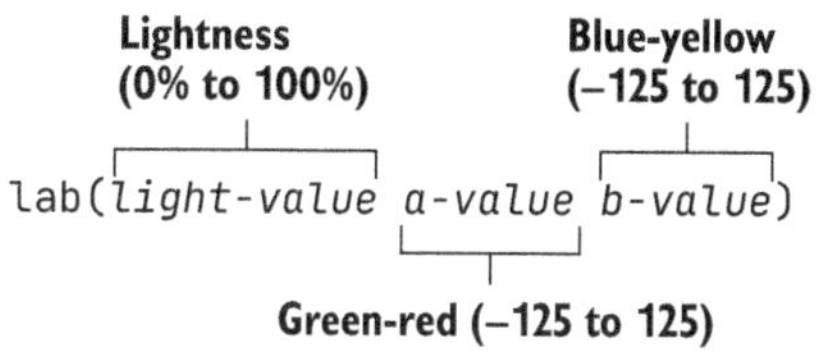


To use this function, replace *`light-value`* with a percentage between 0 and 100 to specify the lightness component, replace *`a-value`* with a number between –125 and 125 (or a percentage between –100 and 100) to specify the green-red component, and replace *`b-value`* with a number between –125 and 125 (or a percentage between –100 and 100) to specify the blue-yellow component. Sticking with the purple `h1` text example, the following snippet shows how you'd use CSS to display all your `h1` headings with purple text using the `lab()` function.

```
h1 {
    color: lab(30% 60 -50);
}
```

To include an alpha channel, add a slash (/) followed by the alpha value in the range [0, 1] or [0%, 100%]:

```
h1
    color: lab(30% 60 -50% / 0.25);
}
```

### 7.1.4 The OKLCH color space

OKLCH (Ottoson-Kim Lightness, Chroma, Hue) combines LAB's perceptual accuracy with HSL's intuitive hue-based approach. Think of it as "HSL that actually works the way your eyes work." OKLCH is a polar coordinate system that expresses color using three values:

- *L*—The brightness axis of the coordinate system with values between 0 or 0% (black) and 1 or 100% (white).
- *C*—The color's *chroma,* a measure of how far the color is from neutral gray (i.e., how intense or vivid it is), with values from 0 (which produces a grayscale color) to about 0.4 to 0.5 (which produces a fully saturated color, depending on the hue and lightness).

- *H*—The color's hue, which is its angle around the color wheel from 0 to 359 degrees. This sounds like the hue value in the HSL color model, but although they generally refer to the same color (e.g., red is hue 0), they're quite different. OKLCH hue is derived from CIELAB, which is based on how humans actually perceive color.

> **WARNING** OKLCH is designed for modern screens that support Display P3, which can handle wide-gamut colors. This means there are OKLCH values that will display perfectly on Display P3 screens but will fail on less capable displays. Therefore, unless you're directly targeting Display P3, always check OKLCH colors on regular monitors to make sure they work.

OKLCH has become increasingly popular not only because it continues the intuitive hue-based approach of HSL, but also because it enables designers to make perceptually uniform hue adjustments. With HSL, when you rotate a hue through the color wheel, the perceived brightness of the color changes. With OKLCH, by contrast, rotating the hue maintains the same perceived brightness.

OKLCH has been directly supported in modern browsers since early 2023 via the CSS `oklch()` function:

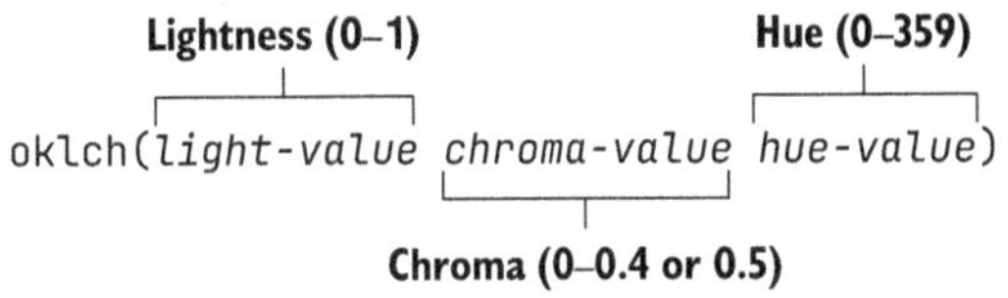


To use this function, replace *`light-value`* with a number between 0 and 1 (or a percentage between 0% and 100%) to specify the lightness component, replace *`chroma-value`* with a number between 0 and about 0.4 or 0.5 to specify the chroma component, and replace *`hue-value`* with a number between 0 and 359 to specify the hue component. The following shows how you'd use CSS to display all your `h1` headings with purple text using the `oklch()` function.

```
h1 {
    color: oklch(0.42 0.2 328);
}
```

To include an alpha channel, add a slash (`/`) followed by the alpha value in the range [0, 1] or [0%, 100%]:

```
h1
    color: oklch(0.42 0.2 328 / 0.5);
}
```

One big advantage that OKLCH offers is predictable lightness because lightness values correspond to actual perceived brightness. For example, imagine you're designing pages for a brand and want to vary the background colors while still referencing the brand's signature raspberry color. One way to do that is to create a color scale that varies the color's lightness using the OKLCH lightness parameter, as listing 7.1 demonstrates. This scheme works by adjusting the lightness value from 0.8 to 0.6 to 0.4. By using the OKLCH color space, you can be sure that these changes create uniformly different variations of the base hue, as shown in figure 7.4.

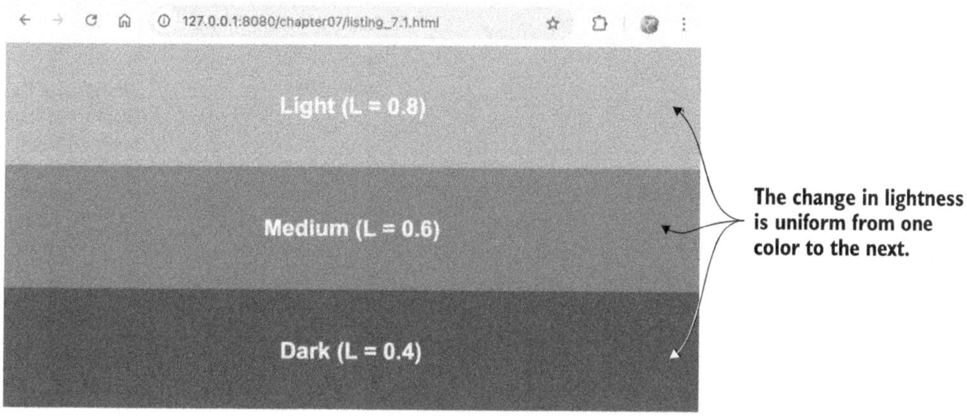


**Figure 7.4 A color scale that uses different lightness values on the same hue**

**Listing 7.1 Creating a color scale by varying lightness in the OKLCH color space**

```
.brand-light   { background: oklch(0.8 0.15 350); }
.brand-medium  { background: oklch(0.6 0.15 350); }
.brand-dark    { background: oklch(0.4 0.15 350); }
```

**NOTE** All the code for this chapter's listings is available in this book's GitHub repository: https://github.com/paulmcfe/web-dev-math.

Making these kinds of uniform adjustments in other color models doesn't produce uniformly different colors. But with OKLCH, each step on the color scale looks equally different, resulting in a perfectly even visual progression—a designer's dream come true!

OKLCH also provides reliable chroma control because increasing chroma always makes colors more vibrant, regardless of hue. OKLCH also gives you chroma adjustments that work consistently across all hues. For example, suppose your brand customer wants a page that supports a wider gamut of their signature raspberry. With OKLCH in your toolbox, you can satisfy the client's request by creating a color scale that holds the lightness steady, keeps the hue at 350, but varies the chroma, as Listing

7.2 demonstrates. This scale does the job by adjusting the chroma values from 0.05 (low chroma, which gives a muted color) to 0.2 (medium-high chroma, which gives a vivid color) to 0.4 (very high chroma, which gives an intense color). By using the OKLCH color space, you can be assured that these changes create uniform changes to the base hue, as shown in figure 7.5.

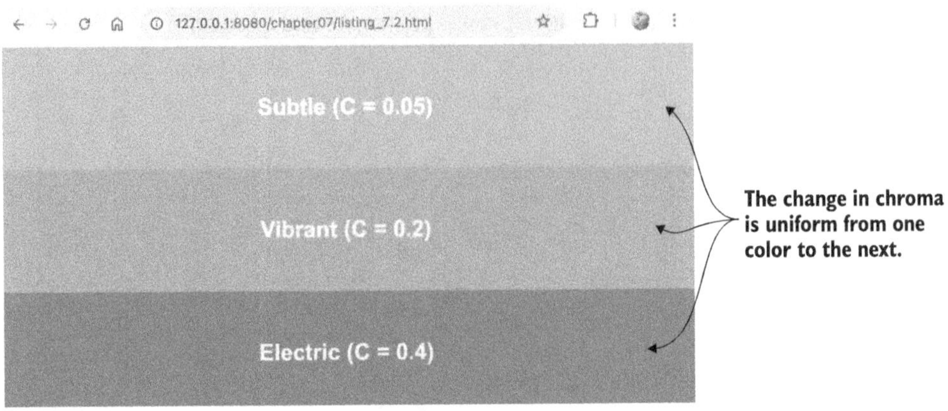


**Figure 7.5 A color scale that uses different chroma values on the same hue.**

**Listing 7.2 Creating a color scale by varying chroma in the OKLCH color space**

```
.brand-subtle    { background: oklch(0.8 0.05 350); }
.brand-vibrant   { background: oklch(0.8 0.2 350); }
.brand-electric  { background: oklch(0.8 0.4 350); }
```

**EXERCISES**

**Exercise 7.1:** Which of the following CSS color values uses a perceptually uniform color space?

1 `rgb(255 128 64)`
2 `hsl(30 100% 50%)`
3 `lab(60% 40 -30)`
4 `#ff8040`

**Exercise 7.2:** Which statement about color models is incorrect?

1 RGB uses additive color mixing where adding all channels at full intensity produces white.
2 HSL represents colors using a cylindrical coordinate system with hue as the angle.
3 LAB provides perceptually uniform lightness adjustments across all hues.
4 OKLCH has a smaller gamut than sRGB and cannot represent colors outside the visible spectrum.

**Exercise 7.3:** Fill in the missing values to create a vivid green color using OKLCH:

```
color: oklch(___ ___ 145);
```

## 7.2 Converting between color models

Converting between color models is where the real mathematical heavy lifting happens. The next few sections discuss the most important conversions.

### 7.2.1 Converting RGB to grayscale

It's not uncommon to work with grayscale colors instead of saturated blends of red, green, and blue. If you have existing RGB colors, however, converting them to grayscale isn't straightforward. Naively, you might think you could get away with totaling the values of R, G, and B, dividing that sum by 3, and then applying the result to all three parameters of the `rgb()` function. That approach won't work because RGB values don't correspond linearly to perceived brightness: our eyes are relatively more sensitive to green and relatively less sensitive to blue. So, instead, you need to calculate a weighted average between the colors, as shown in the following listing.

**Listing 7.3 Converting RGB to grayscale using a weighted average**

```
function rgbToGrayscale(r, g, b) {
    return 0.299 * r + 0.587 * g + 0.114 * b;    // Values weighted based on human perception
}
```

This function returns a weighted grayscale value from 0 (black) to 255 (white), representing how bright this color appears to human eyes:

```
console.log(rgbToGrayscale(255, 0, 0));    // 76.255 (fairly dark gray)
console.log(rgbToGrayscale(0, 255, 0));    // 149.69 (medium gray)
console.log(rgbToGrayscale(0, 0, 255));    // 29.07 (dark gray)
```

You can use the value returned by the function directly as an RGB grayscale color:

```
const grayValue = rgbToGrayscale(255, 100, 50);
const grayColor = `rgb(${grayValue} ${grayValue} ${grayValue})`;
```

### 7.2.2 Converting RGB to HSL

If you have RGB colors and you prefer to work with the more intuitive HSL color model, you can convert your colors using the following algorithm:

1. *Normalize R, G, and B.* Divide R, G, B by 255 to get values in the range [0, 1]. Call these normalized values $R_n$, $G_n$, and $B_n$.

2 *Find the minimum and maximum of the color values.* Let `min = min(R`$_n$`,G`$_n$`,B`$_n$`)` and `max = max(R`$_n$`,G`$_n$`,B`$_n$`)`. This tells you the range of the color.

3 *Calculate the chroma (C).* Chroma is a measure of the colorfulness of the color and is calculated by taking the difference between the `max` and `min`: `C = max - min`.

4 *Calculate the lightness (L).* Lightness is the average of the `max` and `min` values: `L = (max + min) / 2`. The result is a value between 0 and 1.

5 *Check for a grayscale color.* If C = 0, it means we're dealing with a grayscale color, so set H and S to 0, multiply L by 100, then stop.

6 *Calculate the saturation (S).* Saturation represents the intensity of chroma (C) relative to the lightness (L), which means scaling C according to the following formula:

$$S = \frac{C}{1 - |2L - 1|}$$

7 *Calculate the hue (H).* This depends on which $R_n$, $G_n$, and $B_n$ is the maximun because that channel dominates the color:

- If `max` = $R_n$:

$$H = \frac{G_n - B_n}{C} + 6$$

  (but only add 6 if $G_n < B_n$)

- If `max` = $G_n$:

$$H = \frac{B_n - R_n}{C} + 2$$

- If `max` = $B_n$:

$$H = \frac{R_n - G_n}{C} + 4$$

- The result of these is in sector units, meaning that each formula gives a number between 0 and 6, corresponding to 6 sectors of the color wheel. Multiply the result by 60° to get an angle.
- If the calculated H is negative, add 360°.

The following listing translates this algorithm into JavaScript.

**Listing 7.4 Converting RGB to HSL**

```
function rgbToHsl(r, g, b) {
    r /= 255;
    g /= 255;
    b /= 255;
```

Normalize the color values

```
    const max = Math.max(r, g, b);
    const min = Math.min(r, g, b);
    const diff = max - min;
    const l = (max + min) / 2;       ◀ Lightness is the average of max and min.

    if (diff === 0) {                 ◀ Is color a shade of gray?
        return {h: 0, s: 0, l: Math.round(l * 100)};   ◀ If so, returns HSL grayscale values
    }

    const s = diff / (1 - Math.abs(2 * l - 1));   ◀ Calculates saturation
    let h;
    switch (max) {
        case r:
            h = ((g - b) / diff) + (g < b ? 6 : 0);
            break;
        case g:
            h = (b - r) / diff + 2;
            break;
        case b:
            h = (r - g) / diff + 4;
            break;
    }                                  ◀ Hue calculation depends on which channel is dominant.
    h *= 60;                           ◀ Converts to an angle
    if (h < 0) h += 360;               ◀ Handles a negative hue

    return {
        h: Math.round(h),
        s: Math.round(s * 100),
        l: Math.round(l * 100)
    };
}
```

The `rgbToHsl()` function takes three values between 0 and 255 representing the red, green, and blue RGB values you want to convert. The code then implements the RGB-to-HSL algorithm and returns a JavaScript object with the converted values stored in the `h`, `s`, and `l` keys. Here's an example that uses this function:

```
const r = 128;
const g = 0;
const b = 128;
const { h, s, l } = rgbToHsl(r, g, b);
const hslString = `hsl(${h} ${s}% ${l}%)`;        ◀ hsl(300 100% 25%)
document.body.style.backgroundColor = hslString;
```

### 7.2.3 Converting HSL to RGB

If you have HSL colors and you need to use the RGB color model, you can convert your colors using the following algorithm:

1 *Normalize H, S, and L.* To get values in the range [0, 1], divide H by 360 and divide S and L by 100. Call these normalized values $H_n$, $S_n$, and $L_n$.

2. *Check for a grayscale color.* If $S_n = 0$, the color is a shade of gray, so scale the lightness level back to the RGB range ($L_n$ * 255); set the red, green, and blue components equal to the scaled value; then stop.
3. *Calculate temporary values for chromatic colors.* Compute two intermediate values, *p* and *q*, based on lightness and saturation:
   - If lightness < 0.5, then `q = lightness × (1 + saturation)`.
   - Otherwise, `q = lightness + saturation - lightness × saturation`.
   - Then, compute `p = 2 × lightness - q`.
4. *Convert the hue to temporary RGB components.* Adjust the hue into three positions for red, green, and blue channels by adding or subtracting 1⁄3. For each position, apply the following rules:
   - If the adjusted hue is less than 0, add 1.
   - If it's greater than 1, subtract 1.
   - Next, use conditional logic to compute the interpolated value based on the relative position within the color wheel sector.
5. *Scale the RGB components.* Multiply each of the resulting red, green, and blue values by 255.

The following listing translates this algorithm into JavaScript.

**Listing 7.5 Converting HSL to RGB**

```
function roundToDecimals(num, decimals) {
    const factor = 10 ** decimals;
    return Math.round(num * factor) / factor;
}

function hslToRgb(h, s, l) {
    h = h / 360;
    s = s / 100;
    l = l / 100;
    if (s === 0) {
        const gray = Math.round(l * 255);
        return { r: gray, g: gray, b: gray };
    }
    const q = l < 0.5
        ? l * (1 + s)
        : l + s - l * s;
    const p = 2 * l - q;
    function hueToRgb(p, q, t) {
        if (t < 0) t += 1;
        if (t > 1) t -= 1;
        if (t < 1/6) return p + (q - p) * 6 * t;
        if (t < 1/2) return q;
        if (t < 2/3) return p + (q - p) * (2/3 - t) * 6;
        return p;
    }
    const r = roundToDecimals(hueToRgb(p, q, h + 1 / 3), 1);
```

Annotations:
- Rounds num to the specified decimals
- Normalizes the H, S, and L values
- Is the color a shade of gray?
- If so, returns RGB grayscale values
- Calculates temp values for colors
- Converts H to temp RGB components

```
    const g = roundToDecimals(hueToRgb(p, q, h), 1);
    const b = roundToDecimals(hueToRgb(p, q, h - 1 / 3), 1);
    return {
        r: Math.round(r * 255),
        g: Math.round(g * 255),
        b: Math.round(b * 255)
    };
}
```

Scales and returns RGB components

**EXERCISES**

**Exercise 7.4:** The following function attempts to normalize RGB values but contains a bug. What's wrong?

```
function normalizeRGB(r, g, b) {
    return {
        r: r / 100,
        g: g / 100,
        b: b / 100
    };
}
```

**Exercise 7.5:** In the following code, supply a value for the `rgbString` variable to apply the converted RGB color to the `body` element's `background-color` property:

```
const h = 300;
const s = 100;
const l = 25;
const { r, g, b } = hslToRgb(h, s, l);
const rgbString = ____________________;
document.body.style.backgroundColor = rgbString;
```

## 7.3 Creating harmonious color schemes with math

When selecting colors for a web page, you need to give some thought to how your colors work together. Some colors naturally clash and, when used together, will make your page look terrible. Fortunately, every hue has one or more colors that blend well, resulting in harmonious designs that are pleasing to your visitors' eyes. Note that harmonious doesn't mean boring! Depending on the colors you choose, the result can be anything from soothing to vibrant, so the color scheme you go with is a reflection of what you want your site to say.

Happily, you don't have to guess which colors will do the job. You can use the math tricks described in the following sections.

### 7.3.1 Complementary colors

Complementary colors lie opposite each other on the color wheel. In terms of the `hsl()` function, complementary colors are those with hue values that are 180 degrees apart. For example, red, `hsl(0 100% 50%)`, is the complement of cyan, `hsl(180 100%`

50%). To build a simple complementary color scheme, you take a base hue (H) and use the following formula to find the complementary color (C):

```
C = (H + 180) % 360
```

For example, if H is 240, here's the calculation:

```
C = (240 + 180) % 360
  = 420 % 360
  = 60
```

So, the complement of hsl(240 100% 50%) is hsl(60 100%, 50%), which is yellow.

You can implement a complementary color scheme in CSS using variables and calc(), as shown in the following listing.

**Listing 7.6 Implementing complementary colors in CSS**

```
:root {
    --base-hue: 39;
    --main-color: hsl(var(--base-hue) 100% 50%);
    --comp-color: hsl(calc(var(--base-hue) + 180) 100% 50%);
}
```

Note that CSS handles the modulo for you automatically.

### 7.3.2 Analogous colors

*Analogous colors* lie near to each other on the color wheel. With the hsl() function, analogous colors are the two colors whose hue values are a relatively small number of degrees above or below the main color, typically 30. For example, hsl(30, 100%, 50%), a shade of orange, is analogous to both hsl(60, 100%, 50%), yellow, and hsl(0, 100%, 50%), red. The following listing shows this analogous color scheme implemented in CSS using variables and calc().

**Listing 7.7 Implementing analogous colors in CSS**

```
:root {
    --base-hue: 30;
    --main-color: hsl(var(--base-hue) 100% 50%);
    --analagous-color-1: hsl(calc(var(--base-hue) + 30) 100% 50%);
    --analagous-color-2: hsl(calc(var(--base-hue) - 30) 100% 50%);
}
```

If you prefer even less contrast (i.e., you want colors that are closer to each other), you can create an analogous scheme by using colors that are 15 degrees apart.

### 7.3.3 Triadic colors

*Triadic colors* are three colors that lie an equal distance from one another on the color wheel. In terms of the hsl() function, triadic colors are those with hue values that are

120 degrees apart. For example, red, `hsl(0 100% 50%)`, is triadic to both `hsl(120 100% 50%)` and `hsl(240 100% 50%)`. The following listing shows this triadic color scheme implemented in CSS using variables and `calc()`.

**Listing 7.8 Implementing triadic colors in CSS**

```
:root {
    --base-hue: 30;
    --main-color: hsl(var(--base-hue) 100% 50%);
    --triadic-color-1: hsl(calc(var(--base-hue) + 120) 100% 50%);
    --triadic-color-2: hsl(calc(var(--base-hue) - 120) 100% 50%);
}
```

### 7.3.4 Split-complementary colors

A *split-complementary* color scheme is similar to a complementary color scheme, except that instead of using the opposite hue on the color wheel, you use the two colors that lie 30 degrees to either side of that opposite color. For example, red, `hsl(0, 100%, 50%)`, is split-complementary with both `hsl(150, 100%, 50%)` and `hsl(210, 100%, 50%)`. The following listing shows this split-complementary color scheme implemented in CSS using variables and `calc()`.

**Listing 7.9 Implementing split-complementary colors in CSS**

```
:root {
    --base-hue: 30;
    --main-color: hsl(var(--base-hue) 100% 50%);
    --split-comp-color-1: hsl(calc(var(--base-hue) + 150) 100% 50%);
    --split-comp-color-2: hsl(calc(var(--base-hue) + 210) 100% 50%);
}
```

**EXERCISES**

**Exercise 7.6:** Which of the following hue shifts creates a triadic scheme?

1. ±30°
2. ±90°
3. ±120°
4. ±180°

**Exercise 7.7:** Given a base hue of 45° (orange), which set of colors would create a split-complementary color scheme?

1. 45°, 165°, 285°
2. 45°, 75°, 15°
3. 45°, 165°, 225°
4. 45°, 195°, 255°

## 7.4 Specifying accessible colors with math

Web designers and developers need to ensure that page text is easily readable against its background. Sure, you can just examine the page and decide whether its text seems readable to you, but that's not good enough. The Web Content Accessibility Guidelines (WCAG) define readability in terms of a *contrast ratio*, a mathematical measure of the difference in brightness between two colors. Instead of relying on subjective judgment, you can use a formula to calculate color contrast and ensure it meets the minimum accessibility levels outlined by the WCAG. The following sections delve into the math behind contrast ratios and how to apply it with CSS and JavaScript.

### 7.4.1 The WCAG contrast requirements (AA vs. AAA)

The WCAG defines two levels of acceptable contrast for text: AA is the minimum acceptable level, and AAA is the enhanced level:

- *Normal text*—Defined as regular text below `18px`. Here are the required contrast ratios:
  - *AA:* 4.5:1 or higher.
  - *AAA:* 7:1 or higher.
- *Large or bold text*—Defined as regular text set at `18px` or higher, or bold text set at `14px` or higher. Here are the required contrast ratios:
  - *AA:* 3:1 or higher.
  - *AAA:* 4.5:1 or higher.

These numbers mean that light gray text on white (with a contrast ratio about 2.5:1) would fail, whereas black text on white (contrast ratio 21:1) easily passes even AAA.

In practice, meeting AAA for regular text is quite strict. For instance, a medium gray such as `hsl(0 0% 46%)` on white yields a contrast ratio of 4.54:1, which is just enough to meet AA, but isn't close to the 7:1 required by AAA. A darker gray such as `hsl(0 0% 35%)` on white has a contrast ratio of 7:1, which meets AAA. Designers need to decide which level to target and choose colors accordingly.

### 7.4.2 The contrast ratio formula

The contrast ratio is defined mathematically by the WCAG. First, you compute each color's relative luminance, which is the color's perceived brightness normalized on a 0 to 1 scale; refer to the next section for the details. With those two values in hand, you calculate the contrast ratio CR by plugging the values into the following formula:

$$CR = \frac{L_1 + 0.05}{L_2 + 0.05}$$

where $L_1$ is the relative luminance of the lighter color, and $L_2$ is the relative luminance of the darker color. (The 0.05 is a fixed adjustment factor to account for the perception of absolute black and absolute white.) This formula yields a value between 1:1 (which means no contrast, such as you'd get with white text on a white background) and 21:1 (which is the maximum contrast, such as you'd get with black text on a white background).

Note that this computed ratio is independent of which color is text and which is background. The ratio is determined by color lightness/darkness. For example, black on white and white on black both give the same ratio of 21:1. It's the numeric ratio that must meet the guideline (such as normal text having a contrast ratio greater than or equal to 7:1 to meet the AAA threshold), regardless of the foreground and background assignment of the color.

### 7.4.3 Calculating relative luminance from color

How do we get the luminance (L) for a given color? WCAG uses the sRGB color space (a standardized color space based on RGB, defining specific intensities, gamma, and white point to make colors look consistent across devices) and a specific formula to account for human perception. It involves converting the standard RGB values into a linear light intensity, then taking a weighted sum of the R, G, and B components. Here's how it works:

1. *Normalize RGB to the range [0–1].* Convert each channel to a decimal between 0 and 1 by dividing by 255. For example, pure red—`rgb(255 0 0)` or `#ff0000`—becomes $R_n$=1, $G_n$=0, $B_n$=0.
2. *Apply gamma correction.* The sRGB values aren't linear, so have to we linearize them. For each normalized component,
   - If the value is less than or equal to 0.04045, divide by 12.92.
   - Otherwise, apply the formula

   $$\left(\frac{value + 0.055}{1.055}\right)^{2.4}$$

   This piecewise formula is applied to $R_n$, $G_n$, and $B_n$, respectively, to yield the linearized values $R_l$, $G_l$, and $B_l$.
3. *Calculate the luminance L.* Once we have $R_l$, $G_l$, and $B_l$, the relative luminance is a weighted sum of these components:

$$L = 0.2126 \times R_l + 0.7152 \times G_l + 0.0722 \times B_l$$

The coefficients in the luminance formula reflect the human eye's higher sensitivity to green light and lower sensitivity to blue, and they come from the standard luminance definition for sRGB. The result L ranges between 0 (perceived black) and 1 (perceived white).

As a quick example, consider pure blue—`rgb(0 0 255)` or `#0000FF`:

1. Normalized, it's (0,0,1), so $R_n$=0, $G_n$=0, $B_n$=1.

2 Applying gamma correction, we get
   - $R_n = 0$, so

$$R_l = \frac{R_n}{12.92} = 0$$

   - $G_n = 0$, so

$$G_l = \frac{F_n}{12.92} = 0$$

   - $B_n = 1$, so

$$B_l = \left(\frac{1 + 0.055}{1.055}\right)^{2.4} = 1$$

3 $L = 0.2126 \times 0 + 0.7152 \times 0 + 0.0722 \times 1 = 0.0722$

Now we can calculate the contrast ratio. If the other color is white (L = 1), then we have

```
CR = (1 + 0.05) / (0.0722 + 0.05) = 1.05 / 0.1222 = 8.59
```

So, blue text on a white background produces high-contrast text that exceeds the WCAG AAA level. Contrast (pun intended) this with a red background. For pure red—`rgb(255 0 0)` or `#FF0000`—L = 0.2126, so we have

```
CR = (0.2126 + 0.05) / (0.0722 + 0.05) = 0.2626 / 0.1222 = 2.15
```

Thus, blue text on a red background produces low-contrast text that falls below even the WCAG AA level.

**NOTE** When plugging values into the contrast ratio formula, use the higher L value as the numerator ($L_1$) and the lower L value as the denominator ($L_2$).

### 7.4.4 Calculating contrast ratios with JavaScript

Yes, these are complex calculations that are far too time-consuming to work through by hand. Fortunately, you can throw some JavaScript at the problem by implementing a few functions that take two RGB hex codes (such as the codes returned by the HTML `input` element when the `type` attribute is set to `color`) and return their contrast ratio, as shown in the following listing.

**Listing 7.10 JavaScript code to calculate a contrast ratio**

```
function hexToRgb(hex) {
    hex = hex.replace(/^#/, "");
```

Converts hex color code to {r,g,b} object

Strips the leading #

```
    if (hex.length === 3) {
        hex = hex.split("").map(ch => ch + ch).join("");
    }
    const num = parseInt(hex, 16);
    return {
        r: (num >> 16) & 255,
        g: (num >> 8) & 255,
        b: num & 255
    };
}
function relativeLuminance(r, g, b) {
    let R_n = r / 255, G_n = g / 255, B_n = b / 255;
    const toLinear = (c) =>
        c <= 0.04045 ?
        c / 12.92 :
        ((c + 0.055) / 1.055) ** 2.4;
    const R_l = toLinear(R_n);
    const G_l = toLinear(G_n);
    const B_l = toLinear(B_n);
    return 0.2126 * R_l + 0.7152 * G_l + 0.0722 * B_l;
}
function getContrastRatio(color1, color2) {
    const rgb1 = hexToRgb(color1);
    const rgb2 = hexToRgb(color2);
    const L1 = relativeLuminance(rgb1.r, rgb1.g, rgb1.b);
    const L2 = relativeLuminance(rgb2.r, rgb2.g, rgb2.b);

    const lighter = Math.max(L1, L2);
    const darker = Math.min(L1, L2);

    const ratio = (lighter + 0.05) / (darker + 0.05);
    return ratio;
}
function checkCompliance(cr, isLargeText = false) {
    const thresholds = {
        aa: { normal: 4.5, large: 3.0 },
        aaa: { normal: 7.0, large: 4.5 }
    };

    const textType = isLargeText ? 'large' : 'normal';

    return {
        aa: cr >= thresholds.aa[textType],
        aaa: cr >= thresholds.aaa[textType]
    };
}
```

**Converts 3-digit hex to 6-digit hex**

**Returns the red, green, and blue bytes**

**Calculates relative luminance of an RGB color**

**Normalizes to [0,1]**

**Linearizes each component**

**Returns weighted sum**

**Calculates the contrast ratio between two hex colors**

**Ensures L1 is the luminance of lighter color**

**Applies contrast ratio formula**

**Checks contrast ratio compliance**

**WACG thresholds**

**True if ratio meets AA standard**

**True if ratio meets AAA standard**

The code in listing 7.10 consists of four functions:

- `hexToRgb(hex)`—Converts a 3- or 6-digit RGB hex code into decimal RGB values (between 0 and 255).
- `relativeLuminance(r, g, b)`—Applies the relative luminance algorithm to the red, green, and blue components of a color.

- `getContrastRatio(color1, color2)`—Applies the contrast ratio formula to two colors.
- `checkCompliance(cr, isLargeText = false)`—Checks whether the passed contrast ratio meets the WACG AA and AAA guidelines for accessible contrast.

Here's an example use where `textHexString` and `bgHexString` are RGB hex codes (as strings) for the text and background, respectively:

```
const contrastRatio = getContrastRatio(textHexString, bgHexString).toFixed(2);
const wacg = checkCompliance(contrastRatio, false);
const result = Object.entries(wacg)
    .map(([key, value]) => `${value ? '✅' : '❌'} ${key.toUpperCase()}`)
    .join(', ');
crText.textContent = `Contrast ratio: ${contrastRatio}: ${result}`;
```

Figure 7.6 shows the web page for listing 7.10, which uses this code as part of an app to calculate and check the contrast ratio of two colors. See the listing on GitHub for the complete code for this page.

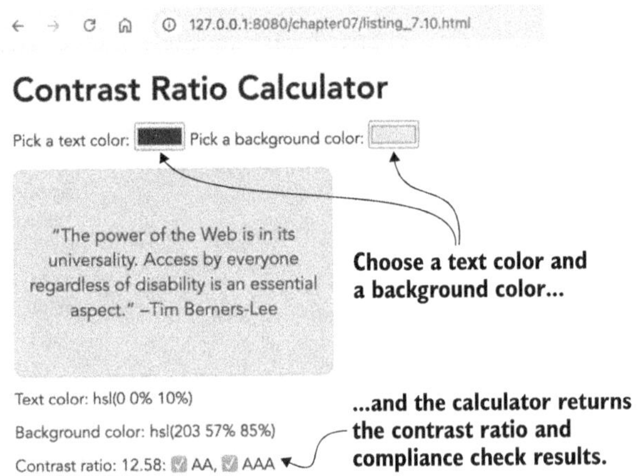


**Figure 7.6 A JavaScript-based contrast ratio calculator.**

### EXERCISES

**Exercise 7.8:** Consider the following CSS rule:

```
.element {
    background-color: hsl(185 64% 33%);
    color: hsl(0 0% 0%);
    font-size: 20px;
    font-weight: bold;
}
```

The contrast ratio of the text and background colors is 4.5. Which WCAG requirement does this meet, if any?

**Exercise 7.9:** True or false? The contrast ratio between two colors depends on the one in the background.

## 7.5 Light mode and dark mode mathematics

A common component on many web pages these days is a setting or toggle that enables the user to switch between light and dark modes. Similarly, it's common now to use the `prefers-color-scheme` media query to check whether the user has enabled dark mode via their operating system or browser. But that mode switch doesn't just involve inverting colors. To get it right requires thoughtful color transformations to preserve visual hierarchy, maintain contrast ratios, and ensure brand consistency. When you switch from light mode to dark mode (or vice versa), you're flipping the lightness distribution across your UI. But to avoid jarring results, the key is preserving the relationships between elements:

- Text should remain readable.
- Backgrounds must maintain depth and separation.
- Accent colors should retain their relative prominence.

To accomplish this, your transformations must maintain or exceed required contrast ratios (as described in the previous section), preserve the perceptual order of lightness and saturation, and apply aesthetic adjustments, especially to make things look good in dark mode.

All of this is highly mathematical because these transformations depend heavily on math-related concepts such as luminance, contrast preservation, hue shifts, and even perceptual lightness. This section discusses how to approach these transformations both programmatically and mathematically.

### 7.5.1 Why basic inversion doesn't work

For a quick-and-dirty mode switch, you might be tempted to apply a simple inversion of the RGB values:

```
:root {
    --light-r: 194;
    --light-g: 123;
    --light-b: 160;
    --dark-r: calc(255 - var(--light-r));
    --dark-g: calc(255 - var(--light-g));
    --dark-b: calc(255 - var(--light-b));
}
```

Or, in JavaScript,

```
const inverted = {
    r: 255 - r,
    g: 255 - g,
    b: 255 - b
};
```

Either way, you end up with the mathematical inverse of a color, but it often leads to undesirable results, such as muted colors in light mode becoming garish in dark mode and the relative contrast between UI elements becoming distorted.

Instead of naively (lazily?) inverting colors, you'll get much better results by making more sophisticated adjustments of lightness and luminance, while keeping the hue and saturation in check.

### 7.5.2 A better approach: Inverting perceptual lightness

One effective strategy is to use a perceptual color space such as HSL and invert the lightness by subtracting the current value from 100:

```
function invertHslColor(h, s, l) {
    return {
        h: h,
        s: s,
        l: 100 - l      ◄── Inverts the lightness value
    };
}
```

This maintains the original hue and saturation while flipping the brightness axis. In CSS, we have

```
:root {
    --bg-light: hsl(0, 0%, 95%);       | Light mode
    --text-light: hsl(0, 0%, 10%);     |

    --bg-dark: hsl(0, 0%, 5%);         | Dark mode
    --text-dark: hsl(0, 0%, 90%);      |
}
```

This approach gives you control, while preserving color identity across modes.

OKLCH is better than HSL for perceptual fidelity, and you can invert the lightness by subtracting the current value from 1:

```
function invertOklchColor(l, c, h) {
    return {
        l: 1 - l,      ◄── Inverts lightness only
        c: c,
        h: h
    };
}
```

This gives dark mode versions that feel consistent because the OKLCH lightness axis is perceptually uniform. For example, 10% OKLCH lightness is perceived as equally "dark" as 90% is "light."

### 7.5.3 Hue and saturation adjustments for aesthetic consistency

Dark mode often calls for a slightly different mood: cooler, less saturated, and softer tones. For example, a small hue shift can make a big visual difference:

- Blues can skew slightly cyan.
- Reds can skew toward magenta or purple.
- Grays can be warmed or cooled based on brand tone.

You can model hue shifts like this:

```
function mod(dividend, divisor) {
    return ((dividend % divisor) + divisor) % divisor;
}

function shiftHue(hue, amount) {
    return mod(hue + amount, 360);
}
```

This code uses the `mod()` helper function (refer to chapter 2) because if `amount` is negative, then the expression `hue + amount` might return a negative value, which you don't want.

If you're using HSL colors, a related adjustment for dark mode is to reduce the saturation a little, which helps match the darker tone. Applying hue shifts of plus or minus 15°–30° and reducing saturation by 10%–30% (or, if you're using OKLCH, multiplying the light mode chroma by 0.4 to 0.6) will give you a more atmospheric dark palette.

### 7.5.4 Generating a paired light/dark palette

For an automated light/dark theme generation, follow this process:

1. Start with a base light-mode palette in HSL or OKLCH.
2. Transform each color:
   - Invert the lightness.
   - Reduce saturation or chroma.
   - Apply a small hue shift.
3. Test each pair's contrast ratio against its new background (refer to the previous section).

Here's a basic HSL example:

```
function transformToDarkMode(h, s, l) {
    const newH = shiftHue(h, 15);
    const newS = s * 0.8;
    const newL = 100 - l;
    return {
        h: newH,
        s: newS,
        l: newL
    };
}
```

### 7.5.5 CSS implementation with media queries

Once your color math is defined, you can use CSS variables and a `prefers-color-scheme` media query to switch between modes:

```
:root {
    --bg: hsl(240, 30%, 80%)
    --text: hsl(0, 0%, 10%);
}
@media (prefers-color-scheme: dark) {
    :root {
        --bg: hsl(255, 24%, 20%)
        --text: hsl(0, 0%, 90%);
    }
}
```

For dynamic JavaScript-driven themes, you can calculate and assign values based on user preferences or toggles using the color math functions described previously. For an example, refer to the code for listing 7.11 on this book's GitHub repo.

**EXERCISES**

**Exercise 7.10:** Given `hsl(210, 60%, 85%)` in light mode, use the transformation function to compute the dark mode equivalent with:

- Hue shift: 20°
- Saturation reduction: 10%
- Lightness inversion

**Exercise 7.11:** Why is OKLCH preferred over HSL for generating dark mode color variants?

1. It uses CMYK channels.
2. It always makes colors warmer.
3. It maintains perceptual brightness across hue shifts.
4. It's faster to compute.

## 7.6 The math behind blend modes and opacity

Sometimes a straight-up color just doesn't get the job done. For those situations, CSS blend modes can create interesting visual effects by mathematically combining colors. Think of blend modes as recipes for mixing colors. Each mode follows a specific set of instructions for combining two colors into a new result. Understanding these recipes helps you choose the right blend mode for your design goals and predict what effects you'll get.

### 7.6.1 How blending works

In CSS, a *blend mode* defines how the colors of two overlapping layers of content combine visually based on mathematical rules. It's a way to control how colors from different layers interact, similar to blending tools in Photoshop or other graphics software. Setting a blend mode on an element causes the browser to composite it in a special way. Technically, the element creates a new stacking context and blends with the backdrop of the parent stacking context. This means the element is rendered onto its parent background using the specified formula. All standard blend modes from graphic design (like multiply, screen, overlay, etc.) are available in CSS. (I cover the math for these modes shortly.) This happens for every single pixel where your elements overlap.

> **NOTE** All blend mode math happens with normalized color values between 0 and 1, where 0 represents black and 1 represents white. Your browser automatically converts regular RGB values (0–255) to this range, applies the blend formula, and then converts back to display colors.

Understanding blend mode math helps

- Predict how things will look color-wise before writing any CSS
- Choose which blend mode is appropriate to achieve your design goals
- Create more sophisticated visual effects with confidence
- Troubleshoot unexpected color results in your pages

### 7.6.2 Alpha compositing

Before exploring the various blend modes in CSS, it's crucial to understand *alpha compositing*, also known as *alpha blending*. This is the foundation of how any transparency is handled in graphics. Whenever you have a semitransparent element over a background, the browser calculates the pixel colors using alpha compositing: the process of combining a foreground color with a background color given the foreground's transparency (alpha). The result is as if the foreground were painted on glass: you see a mix of the foreground and background. Formally, each output pixel color is a weighted average of the source (foreground) and backdrop (background) colors, weighted by the alpha value. Mathematically, if we denote

- $C_s$—The source color (as a normalized RGB triple between 0 and 1)
- $\alpha_s$—The source alpha (a value from 0 to 1)
- $C_b$—The backdrop color (as a normalized RGB triple between 0 and 1)
- $\alpha_b$—The backdrop alpha (a value from 0 to 1)

then the normal blend (which is known as *source-over compositing*) result is calculated per channel as follows:

$$C_{out} = C_s\alpha_s + C_b\alpha_b(1 - \alpha_s)$$

This is how the browser renders a normal layered element. Each channel (red, green, blue) of the output color is the source channel scaled by its opacity, plus the background channel scaled by whatever "weight" remains. That is, the background contributes in proportion to $(1 - \alpha_s)$.

If the background is fully opaque, then $\alpha_b = 1$, so the equation simplifies to

$$C_{out} = C_s\alpha_s + C_b(1 - \alpha_s)$$

This is essentially a linear interpolation between the two colors, controlled by the alpha value. As an example, imagine a semitransparent blue square, `rgb(0 0 255 / 0.5)`, over a solid red background—`rgb(255 0 0)`. In normalized terms, you have the following:

- $C_s$—(0, 0, 1)
- $\alpha_s$—0.5
- $C_b$—(1, 0, 0)
- $\alpha_b$—1

Plugging these values into the formula, you get

- Red channel equals `0 * 0.5 + 1 * (1 - 0.5) = 0 + 0.5 = 0.5`.
- Green channel equals `0 * 0.5 + 0 * (1 - 0.5) = 0 + 0 = 0`.
- Blue channel equals `1 * 0.5 + 0 * (1 - 0.5) = 0.5 + 0 = 0.5`.

The resulting color is the normalized RGB value (0.5, 0, 0.5), or `rgb(128 0 128)`, which is purple, something you'd expect when blending blue and red.

What's the alpha value of the result? That's given by the following formula:

$$\alpha_{out} = \alpha_s + \alpha_b(1 - \alpha_s)$$

For the example, $\alpha_{out} = 0.5 + 1(1 - 0.5) = 0.5 + 0.5 = 1$. That is, the resulting color is a fully opaque purple.

### 7.6.3 *Blending in CSS*

Before digging into the math behind blending, you should know the basics of applying blends in your CSS code. Understanding the blending-related properties will enable you to create layered visual effects similar to those in image editors. The two primary properties are `mix-blend-mode` and `background-blend-mode`.

#### MIX-BLEND-MODE

The `mix-blend-mode` property specifies how an element's content blends with the content behind it, meaning its parent background or other overlapping elements. That is, when elements overlap, `mix-blend-mode` determines the color mix formula for the top element against its backdrop. By default, elements simply paint over those beneath ("normal" blending). But with `mix-blend-mode`, you can achieve effects like multiply, screen, and so on directly in the browser.

In listing 7.11, the image inside `.container` will blend with the red background using the `darken` blend mode. This means the overlapping areas of the image and the red backdrop will only show the darker color values of the two. Visually, it looks like the image is being filtered through a dark red lens.

**Listing 7.11 Using `mix-blend-mode`**

HTML:

```
<div class="container">
    <img src="pink-flamingo.png" alt="Photo" class="blended-image">
</div>
```

CSS:

```
.container {
    background-color: rgb(255, 0, 0);
}
.blended-image {
    mix-blend-mode: darken;
}
```

#### BACKGROUND-BLEND-MODE

The `background-blend-mode` property controls blending of multiple background layers within a single element. Normally, if you stack multiple background images or colors using CSS `background-image` and `background-color`, they just paint over each other. By applying `background-blend-mode`, those layers blend together in various ways before the element's content is drawn.

For example, suppose a `div` has two background images and a background color. You can blend the bottom image with the color, then blend the top image with the result, each with different modes. In the following listing, the second background (`pink-flamingo.png`, beneath) will blend with the orange color using `multiply` mode, and then the first background (`texture.png`, on top) will blend with that result using `screen` mode:

**Listing 7.12 Using `background-blend-mode`**

```
.container {
    background-color: hsl(239 100% 50%);
    background-image: url("pink-flamingo.png"), url("texture.png");
    background-blend-mode: screen, multiply;
}
```

The `multiply` blend with orange will tint the photo darker (since `multiply` darkens by multiplying color values), and then the texture image on top screens with the result, lightening it in highlights. The outcome is a composite background with a nuanced, layered appearance, all achieved in a single element. An important detail is that an element's background layers don't blend with the element's content, which is isolated to the element itself.

### 7.6.4 The separable blend modes

*Separable blend modes* operate on each color channel (R, G, B) independently. The blend formula is applied separately to the red, green, and blue components to produce a final color. These modes are akin to mixing colors by their individual channels, without cross-coupling between channels. Most common blend modes fall in this category.

In the sections that follow, the formulas use the following values:

- $C_b$—The backdrop color (as a normalized RGB triple between 0 and 1)
- $C_s$—The source color (as a normalized RGB triple between 0 and 1)
- $B(C_b, C_s)$—The specific blending function, which varies by blend mode.

For each blend mode, the math operates on normalized 0–1 values and then converts them back to 0–255. Table 7.1 takes you through the separable blend modes.

**Table 7.1 The separable blend modes**

| Blend mode | $B(C_b, C_s)$ | Description |
|---|---|---|
| `normal` | $C_s$ | The "no-blend" mode that leaves the source color as is. The result is just the source color replacing the backdrop in the overlap area. |
| `multiply` | $C_b * C_s$ | Multiplies the source and backdrop channel values. Multiplying by black (0) yields black; multiplying by white (1) leaves the color unchanged. For every other value, the result is always darker than the original colors because multiplying any two values *a* and *b* in the range (0, 1) always returns a value smaller than both *a* and *b*, and with RGB colors, smaller values represent darker colors. |
| `screen` | $1 - (1 - C_b) * (1 - C_s)$ or $C_b + C_s - (C_b * C_s)$ | "Lights" the backdrop by blending as if projecting slides on a screen, making this blend mode essentially the opposite of multiply. Screening by white (1) produces white; screening by black (0) leaves the color unchanged. For every other value, the result is always lighter than the original colors. |
| `darken` | $\min(C_b, C_s)$ | The backdrop color is replaced with the source color wherever the source is darker; otherwise, the backdrop is left unchanged. |
| `lighten` | $\max(C_b, C_s)$ | The backdrop color is replaced with the source color wherever the source is lighter; otherwise, the backdrop is left unchanged. |
| `color-dodge` | $\min(1, C_b / (1 - C_s)$ | Brightens the backdrop to the source color by decreasing contrast in darker areas. Returns 0 if the backdrop color is 0; returns 1 if the source color is 1. |
| `color-burn` | $\min(1, (1 - C_b) / C_s)$ | Darkens the backdrop to the source color by increasing contrast in dark areas. Returns 1 if the backdrop color is 1; returns 0 if the source color is 0. |
| `hard-light` | if $(C_s <= 0.5)$ $C_b * 2C$ s else $2C_b + 2C_s - 2C_bC_s - 1$ | Applies a multiply or screen blend depending on the source color. |

**Table 7.1 The separable blend modes (*continued*)**

| Blend mode | $B(C_b, C_s)$ | Description |
|---|---|---|
| `soft-light` | $\text{if } (C_s <= 0.5)\ \ C_b - (1 - 2C_s) * C_b * (1 - 2C_b)\ \ \text{else}\ \ C_b + (2C_s - 1) * (D(C_b) - C_b)$ $\text{where}\ \ \text{if } (C_b <= 0.25)\ \ D(C_b) = ((16 - C_b - 12) * C_b + 4) * C_b\ \ \text{else}\ \ D(C_b) = \text{sqrt}(C_b)$ | A more complex, gentler version of hard-light. It also darkens or lightens based on source, but in a softer, less contrasty way. |
| `overlay` | $\text{if } (C_b <= 0.5)\ C_s * 2C_b\ \text{else}\ 2C_s + 2C_b - 2C_bC_s - 1$ | This is the inverse of the hard-light blend mode. |
| `difference` | $\lvert C_b - C_s \rvert$ | The absolute value of the difference of the channel values, which creates high-contrast results since identical pixels become black (no difference) and very different pixels produce bright colors. |
| `exclusion` | $C_b + C_s - 2C_bC_s$ | Creates a lower contrast version of the difference mode. |

For example, suppose you have a black-and-white photo and want to impart a sepia tone to the image. Sure, you could set `filter: sepia(80%)` on the `img` element for a quick-and-dirty effect. But if you want more artistic control, you can specify your preferred sepia tone as a background color and use the `multiply` blend mode, as shown in the following listing.

**Listing 7.13 Using the `multiply` blend mode to apply a sepia tone**

HTML:

```
<div class="sepia-image">
    <img src="old-bicycle.png" alt="Photo" class="sepia-image">
</div>
```

CSS:

```
.sepia-image {
    position: relative;
    display: inline-block;
}
.sepia-image img {
    display: block;
    width: 100%;
    height: auto;
}
.sepia-image::after {                     ◄── Sepia effect added as an overlay
    content: "";
    position: absolute;
    top: 0;
    left: 0;
    width: 100%;
    height: 100%;
    background-color: hsl(30 60% 50%);   ◄── Warm brown color for sepia tone
```

```
    mix-blend-mode: multiply;        ← Applies the multiply blend mode
    opacity: 0.4;                    ← Adjust opacity to control intensity
}
```

These separable blends are the workhorses of design. By combining foreground and background in mathematically defined ways, you can achieve various visual outcomes. For example,

- If you want to increase the contrast and vibrancy of a background image, place a duplicate of the image or a color layer above it and apply the `overlay` or `hard-light` blend mode.
- To soften an image, you might use a solid fill with the `soft-light` blend mode.
- To create a unified color tone, put a semitransparent layer of a single color with `multiply` (for a dark tint) or `screen` (for a light wash).

The math ensures predictable results: `multiply` and `color-burn` modes drive colors darker by proportional or fractional relationships, while `screen` and `color-dodge` drive them brighter.

### 7.6.5 The nonseparable blend modes

*Nonseparable blend modes* don't operate on R, G, B channels independently but, instead, they treat any color as an integrated whole. What this means in practice is that each nonseparable blend mode runs through the following high-level procedure:

1. Convert the backdrop and source colors from their original color space into a representation based on hue, saturation, and luminosity.
2. Take certain hue, saturation, and luminosity components from one color and others from the second color, then combine them into a new color.
3. Convert the result back to the original color space.

To perform the combining in step 2, the nonseparable blend mode formulas use the following auxiliary functions (note that these are pseudocode, not JavaScript, and come from the W3C's Compositing and Blending Level 1 spec):

```
Lum(C) = 0.3Cred + 0.59Cgreen + 0.11Cblue

ClipColor(C)
    L = Lum(C)
    n = min(Cred, Cgreen, Cblue)
    x = max(Cred, Cgreen, Cblue)
    if(n < 0)
        C = L + (((C - L) * L) / (L - n))

    if(x > 1)
        C = L + (((C - L) * (1 - L)) / (x - L))

    return C

SetLum(C, l)
```

```
    d = l - Lum(C)
    Cred = Cred + d
    Cgreen = Cgreen + d
    Cblue = Cblue + d
    return ClipColor(C)

Sat(C) = max(Cred, Cgreen, Cblue) - min(Cred, Cgreen, Cblue)

SetSat(C, s)
    if(Cmax > Cmin)
        Cmid = (((Cmid - Cmin) * s) / (Cmax - Cmin))
        Cmax = s
    else
        Cmid = Cmax = 0
    Cmin = 0
    return C;
```

In the `SetSat()` function, the subscripts `min`, `mid`, and `max` refer to the color components of the passed color value `C` that have the minimum, middle, and maximum values. For example, if the passed color is RGB(128, 0, 64), then $C_{min}$ = 0, $C_{mid}$ = 64, and $C_{max}$ = 128. The function-modified version of these values is then applied to the same components: the calculated value of $C_{min}$ is applied to G, the calculated value of $C_{mid}$ is applied to B, and the calculated value of $C_{max}$ is applied to R. Table 7.2 lists the nonseparable blend modes.

Nonseparable modes are perfect for controlled color adjustments. Want to quickly re-hue an icon or graphic? Hue or Color mode with a solid fill can do that. Need to dial up the intensity of colors in a photo? Overlay a copy of it or another image with Saturation mode to boost or dampen vibrancy. Have a light/shadow map (like a texture) you want to apply to an element? Luminosity mode can transfer those light levels.

**Table 7.2 The nonseparable blend modes**

| Blend mode | $B(C_b, C_s)$ | Description |
|---|---|---|
| hue | $SetLum(SetSat(C_s, Sat(C_b)), Lum(C_b))$ | Blends the hue of the source with the saturation and luminosity of the backdrop |
| saturation | $SetLum(SetSat(C_b, Sat(C_s)), Lum(C_b))$ | Blends the saturation of the source with the hue and luminosity of the backdrop |
| color | $SetLum(C_s, Lum(C_b))$ | Blends the hue and saturation of the source with the luminosity of the backdrop |
| luminosity | $SetLum(C_b, Lum(C_s))$ | Blends the luminosity of the source with the hue and saturation of the backdrop |

## 7.7 Solutions to exercises

**Exercise 7.1:** `lab(60% 40 -30)` uses the LAB color space, which is designed to be perceptually uniform, so the answer is 3.

**Exercise 7.2:** OKLCH color space actually represents the full range of colors that humans can perceive and has a much larger gamut than sRGB. OKLCH was designed to encompass all visible colors, while sRGB is a subset designed for typical computer monitors.

**Exercise 7.3:** Use a medium lightness and high chroma to make the green vivid:

```
color: oklch(0.7 0.3 145);
```

**Exercise 7.4:** The RGB values should be divided by 255, not 100. Here's the corrected function:

```
function normalizeRGB(r, g, b) {
    return {
        r: r / 255,
        g: g / 255,
        b: b / 255
    };
}
```

**Exercise 7.5:** Here's the completed code:

```
const h = 300;
const s = 100;
const l = 25;
const { r, g, b } = hslToRgb(h, s, l);
const rgbString = `rgb(${r} ${g} ${b})`;
document.body.style.backgroundColor = rgbString;
```

**Exercise 7.6:** ±120° creates a triadic scheme (three evenly spaced hues), so the answer is 3.

**Exercise 7.7:** A split-complementary scheme uses the base color plus the two colors that are 30° on either side of its complement. The complement of 45° is 45° + 180° = 225°. The two split-complementary colors would be 225° – 30° = 195° and 225° + 30° = 255°. Therefore, the answer is 4.

**Exercise 7.8:** The text and background colors meet both the AA and AAA requirements of the WCAP because the text is bold and the text size is over `18px`.

**Exercise 7.9:** False. The contrast formula is symmetric—it uses the brighter and darker luminance values, regardless of which is foreground or background.

**Exercise 7.10:** Here's the function implementing the required adjustments:

```
function transformToDarkMode(h, s, l) {
    const newH = shiftHue(h, 20);
    const newS = s * 0.9;
    const newL = 100 - l;
    return {
        h: newH,
        s: newS,
```

```
        l: newL
    };
}
```

**Exercise 7.11:** OKLCH maintains perceptual brightness across hue shifts, so the answer is 3.

## Summary

- Color models are mathematical constructs where RGB uses additive mixing in a cube, HSL uses cylindrical coordinates, LAB uses spherical coordinates to represent the full range of color that humans can perceive, and OKLCH provides perceptually uniform adjustments that maintain consistent brightness across all hues.
- OKLCH provides superior color control for designers because its lightness values correspond to actual perceived brightness, enabling uniform color scales and consistent chroma adjustments across all hues.
- Converting between color spaces requires specific algorithms including weighted averages for RGB-to-grayscale transformations that account for human eye sensitivity.
- Color harmony follows mathematical rules based on hue relationships: complementary colors are 180° apart, triadic colors are 120° apart, and analogous colors are typically 30° apart on the color wheel.
- Accessible color contrast has precise mathematical requirements using the WCAG formula, which calculates relative luminance and requires ratios of 4.5:1 for AA compliance and 7:1 for AAA compliance.
- Relative luminance calculations account for human perception using gamma correction and weighted coefficients that reflect the eye's sensitivity to different colors.
- Effective dark mode requires perceptual mathematics, not simple RGB inversion by inverting lightness values, while reducing saturation by 10%–30% and optionally applying small hue shifts for better atmospheric effects.
- Alpha compositing uses a weighted average formula where each channel (red, green, blue) of the output color is the source channel scaled by its opacity, plus the background channel scaled by whatever weight remains, forming the mathematical foundation for all CSS opacity effects.
- CSS blend modes follow specific mathematical formulas in which `multiply` always darkens, `screen` always lightens, and each mode has a precise calculation method.

# 8 Text and typography math

**This chapter covers**

- Mathematical relationships between font size, line height, and spacing for optimal readability
- Using CSS math functions for fluid, responsive typography
- Implementing modular scales and mathematical ratios in type systems

Typography on the web is fundamentally a mathematical craft. While designers often make typographic decisions based on visual intuition, the most readable and aesthetically pleasing text arrangements follow specific mathematical relationships that have been refined over decades of digital typography research and over centuries of print design.

When you land on a web page that you find aesthetically pleasing, you might be responding to the color scheme or to the use of images, but I'm willing to bet that what you're in fact responding to is the typography of the page. If that is surprising, then it means the person who did the page typography has done a great job because it's a general design rule that the better the typography, the less noticeable it is.

It's entirely possible that the source of that great-looking text was nothing more than the designer's innate sense of what looks good on the page. But even if that's true, there's a reason why some page text is a pleasure to read and other is a slog—the mathematics of typography. When web page typography works well, it's because there's math behind the design, math that ensures a harmonious, readable, and accessible flow of text across the page. In this chapter, you'll learn all about that math so that you can put it to good use making your own page text swoon-worthy.

## 8.1 The math behind the typographic trinity

If you visit a web page and you notice something "off" about the text, the likely culprit can be found in one or more of three fundamental typographic qualities: the type size, the line height (that is, the vertical spacing between lines in the same paragraph), and the line length. These three properties are the troublemakers of the typography world because they're behind almost every typography failure that you come across. The good news, though, is that if you can get these three aspects of your page into harmony, then they switch from being typographic troublemakers into the typographic trinity, giving you the foundation for a great-looking page.

### 8.1.1 General readability considerations

Combining font size, line height, and line length mathematically is all about enhancing the readability of the page text. That readability depends on a balance in which each value ideally falls within its optimal range:

- *Font size*—Arguably, the biggest problem with web typography is that most page text is simply too small. Most people slap up a page with body text that uses the browser's default text size, which is `16px` on all modern browsers. That's too small, especially when seen on a desktop monitor that's a foot or two away from your eyes. Web page body text should be set to at least `1.25rem` (`20px` assuming the default of `16px` hasn't been changed by the user).
- *Line height*—In CSS, line height is defined as the element's `font-size` value plus the following (refer to figure 8.1):
  - Half of the distance between the ascender line of the current line and the descender line of the line above the current line
  - Half of the distance between the descender line of the current line and the ascender line of the line below

**NOTE** An *ascender* is a stroke that extends above the x-height (the height above the baseline of the typeface's lowercase letter *x*) in lowercase letters such as b, d, and f. A *descender* is a stroke or bowl that extends below the baseline in lowercase letters such as g, p, and y.

**Figure 8.1 Line height in CSS**

Another common web typography woe is that all web browsers have a disappointingly small default `line-height` value, usually between `1.15` and `1.2`. (In practice, the browser applies the `line-height` value by multiplying it by the element's font size.) These values render text in a tightly packed bunch that's hard to read. For optimum readability, web body text should have a line height of around `1.4` or `1.5`.

- *Line length*—This value, which, when measured in characters, is also called the *measure* of the line, is a crucial metric because line lengths that are too short create a choppy read that causes your eyes to shift back and forth too frequently, resulting in eyestrain (and overall annoyance), while line lengths that are too long cause eye fatigue because you're required to scan each line for too long. Also, really long lines make it difficult to quickly locate the beginning of the next line (more annoyance!). To improve readability, line lengths should be no less than about 45 characters and no more than about 75 characters. An easy way to implement such a length is to set the text element's `max-width` to a value using the `ch` unit. Here, `1ch` is equal to the width of the `0` character in the element's font family:

```
.element {
    max-width: 65ch;
}
```

These considerations assume that font size, line height, and line length operate independently, but they're tightly bound to each other, and modifying one almost always requires modifying the other two to maintain the readability of your page text. The next three sections take you through the math.

### 8.1.2 When you know the font size you want to use

For a given type size (as given by the `font-size` property), you maintain readability by adjusting the line height and line length as follows:

- With larger type sizes, you should use smaller line heights and longer line lengths.
- With smaller type sizes, you should use larger line heights and shorter line lengths.

So, mathematically, you want to scale the element's line height along with the element's known font size. Given the following:

- `ELH`—The scaled element line height to be calculated.
- `BLH`—The web page's base line height.
- `EFS`—The element's known font size.
- `BFS`—The web page's base font size (usually `16px` or `1rem`).
- `LHF`—The line height factor, which depends on the `font-size` unit: use `100` for `px` or `6.67` for `rem` or `em`.
- `EW`—The scaled element width to be calculated.
- `BW`—The web page's base width, which you set to `BFS` (in pixels) times `30` (so, it's usually `480px`).
- `WF`—The width factor, which depends on the `font-size` unit: use `BLH / BFS` for `px` or the value of `BLH` for `rem` or `em`.

Now you can use the following formula to scale the line height:

```
ELH = BLH - (EFS - BFS) / LHF
```

To scale the line length based on the font size, you can use the following formula:

```
EW = BW + (EFS - BFS) * WF
```

Implementing these formulas in CSS is tricky because most browsers reject `line-height` formulas that combine values with and without units. So, given a font, you can use CSS variables to scale line height and line length with unitless values. For example, if you want to apply a `24px` font size to the `article` element, and if you're using a base `line-height` value of `1.45` and a base `font-size` value of `16px`, you can scale the article element's line height and line length as follows:

```
:root {
    --base-font-value: 16;
    --base-line-height: 1.45;
    --base-width: calc(var(--base-font-value) * 30);
}
article {
    --article-font-value: 24;
    font-size: calc(var(--article-font-value) * 1px);
    line-height: calc((var(--base-line-height) -
➥ (var(--article-font-value) - var(--base-font-value))
➥ / 100);
    max-width: calc(var(--base-width) +
➥ (var(--article-font-value) - var(--base-font-value))
➥ * 30) * 1px);
```

**These represent pixel values**

**Line height factor is 100 when using pixels.**

**Width factor is 480px / 16 = 30px when using pixels.**

In this example, given a `24px` `font-size` value, `line-height` scales to `1.37` and `max-width` scales to `720px`. Table 8.1 presents a few other results.

**Table 8.1 Calculated line heights and maximum widths based on different font sizes**

| Font size | Calculated line height | Calculated maximum width |
|---|---|---|
| 12px | 1.49 | 360px |
| 16px | 1.45 | 480px |
| 20px | 1.41 | 600px |
| 24px | 1.37 | 720px |
| 28px | 1.33 | 840px |
| 32px | 1.29 | 960px |

### 8.1.3 When you know the line height you want to use

For a given line height (as given by the `line-height` property), you maintain readability by adjusting the font size and line length as follows:

- With bigger line heights, you should use smaller type sizes and shorter line lengths.
- With smaller line heights, you should use larger type sizes and longer line lengths.

A bit of algebra applied to the element line height formula from the previous section reveals the corresponding formula for calculating the element font size (`EFS`) based on the known element line height (`ELH`):

```
ELH = BLH - (EFS - BFS) / LHF
ELH - BLH = -(EFS - BFS) / LHF
(ELH - BLH) * LHF = -(EFS- BFS)
(ELH - BLH) * LHF = BFS - EFS
(ELH - BLH) * LHF - BFS = -EFS
EFS = BFS - (ELH - BLH) * LHF
```

I know, that's a lot of math! But there's nothing here you need to memorize. These operations are provided in case you're curious to learn more about the algebraic process that's involved. If you're not, they can be safely ignored.

To determine the mathematical connection between a set line height and an adjustable line length, first examine the minimum and maximum values from table 8.1 in the previous section:

- For `line-height`, the minimum value was `1.29` and the maximum value was `1.49`.
- For `max-width`, the minimum value was `360px` and the maximum value was `960px`.

Therefore, given that the `line-height` range of `0.2` (`1.49 - 1.29`) corresponds to the `max-width` range of `600px` (`960px - 360px`), we solve for the multiplier `x`:

```
0.2x = 600
x = 600 / 0.2
x = 3000
```

This gives us the element line length (`ELL`) formula given a known element line height (`ELH`), a base line height (`BLH`), and a base font size (`BFS`):

```
EW = BW + (BLH - ELH) * 3000
```

Now all this can be implemented using CSS as follows:

```
:root {
    --base-line-height: 1.45;
    --base-font-value: 16;
    --base-width: calc(var(--base-font-value) * 30);
}
article {
    --article-line-height: 1.37;
    line-height: var(--article-line-height);
    font-size: calc((var(--base-font-value) -
➥ ((var(--article-line-height) - var(--base-line-height))
➥ * 100)) * 1px);
    max-width: calc((var(--base-width) +
➥ (var(--base-line-height) - var(--article-line-height))
➥ * 3000) * 1px);
}
```

In this example, given a `1.37` `line-height` value, `font-size` scales to `24px` and `max-width` scales to `720px`. Table 8.2 displays a few other results.

**Table 8.2 Calculated font sizes and maximum widths based on different line heights**

| Line height | Calculated font size | Calculated maximum width |
|---|---|---|
| 1.49 | 12px | 360px |
| 1.45 | 16px | 480px |
| 1.41 | 20px | 600px |
| 1.37 | 24px | 720px |
| 1.33 | 28px | 840px |
| 1.29 | 32px | 960px |

### 8.1.4 *When you know the line length you want to use*

For a given line length (as determined by the element's `width` or `max-width` properties), you maintain readability by adjusting the font size and line height as follows:

- With longer line lengths, you can get away with larger type sizes and bigger line heights.
- With shorter line lengths, you can use smaller type sizes and shorter line heights.

To connect a given line length and an adjustable font size mathematically, use algebra on the `EW` formula from section 8.1.2 (the steps of which are left as an exercise for the reader; refer to exercise 8.2) to derive the equation for the scaled element font size:

```
EFS = BFS + (EW - BW) / WF
```

To connect a set line length with a flexible line height, you apply some algebra to the `EW` formula from section 8.1.3 (again, the algebraic manipulations are left as an exercise; refer to exercise 8.2) to derive the equation for the scaled element line height:

```
ELH = BLH - (EW - BW) / 3000
```

Here's some CSS to implement this:

```
:root {
    --base-line-height: 1.45;
    --base-font-value: 16;
    --base-width: calc(var(--base-font-value) * 30);
}

article {
    --article-width: 600;
    max-width: calc(var(--article-width) * 1px);
    font-size: calc((var(--base-font-value) +
➥((var(--article-width) - var(--base-width))
➥/ 30)) * 1px);
    line-height: calc(var(--base-line-height) -
➥(var(--article-width) - var(--base-width))
➥/ 3000);
}
```

In this example, given a `600px` `max-width` value, `font-size` scales to `24px` and `line-height` scales to `1.41`. Table 8.3 displays a few other results.

**Table 8.3 Calculated font sizes and line heights based on different maximum widths**

| Maximum width | Calculated line height | Calculated font size |
|---|---|---|
| 360px | 1.49 | 12px |
| 480px | 1.45 | 16px |
| 600px | 1.41 | 20px |
| 720px | 1.37 | 24px |
| 840px | 1.33 | 28px |
| 960px | 1.29 | 32px |

### 8.1.5 Putting the formulas to work

To ground all this in the real world, imagine that you've been tasked with turning the humdrum, hard-to-read post shown in figure 8.2 (with the partial code shown in listing 8.1) into something that looks better and reads more easily.

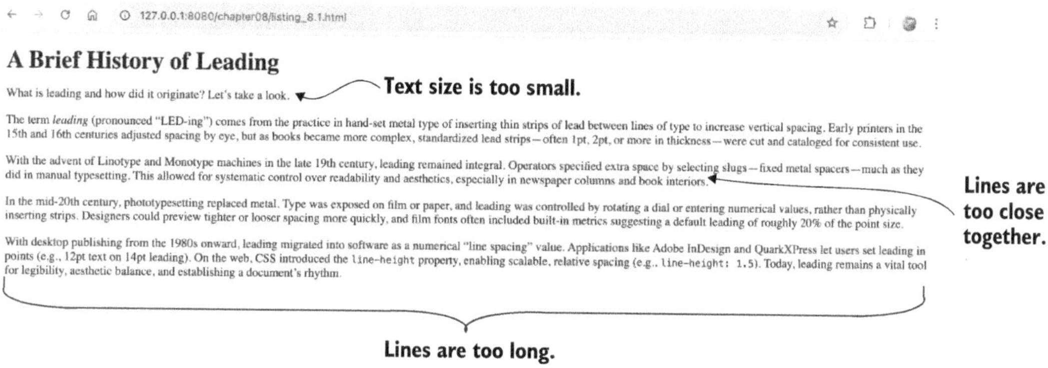


**Figure 8.2 Your job is to make this typographically inept post into something harmonious and readable.**

**Listing 8.1 An article with hard-to-read text**

```
<head>
    <style>
        * {
            margin: 0;
            padding: 0;
            box-sizing: border-box;
        }

        h1,
        p {
            margin: 1rem;
        }
    </style>
</head>

<body>
    <h1>A Brief History of Leading</h1>
    <article>
        <p>
            What is leading and how did it originate? Let's take a look.
        </p>
        <p>
            The term <i>leading</i> (pronounced "LED-ing") comes from
            the practice in hand-set metal type of inserting thin strips
            of lead between lines of type to increase vertical spacing.
            Early printers in the 15th and 16th centuries adjusted
```

```
            spacing by eye, but as books became more complex,
            standardized lead strips—often 1pt, 2pt, or more in
            thickness—were cut and cataloged for consistent use.
        </p>
        ...
    </article>
</body>
```

**NOTE** All the code for this chapter's listings is available in this book's GitHub repository: https://github.com/paulmcfe/web-dev-math.

When you examine the page, you can detect three major flaws in the design:

- *The text size is too small.* The text in figure 8.2 uses the browser default `font-size` value of `16px`, and it's just too small to be read comfortably.
- *The lines within each paragraph are too close together.* The lines are rendered with the browser's default `line-height` value of 1.2, which scrunches the lines too close together, making them difficult to read.
- *The line lengths are too long.* The element that holds the text inherits the body tag's default width of `100%`, so the lines are far too long to scan.

To fix these problems, you begin by choosing which of the three main typographical properties you want to set: `font-size`, `line-height`, or `max-width`. With that done, you then apply the formulas to calculate the other two properties using the previous sections in this chapter.

Suppose that you select a font size of `20px`. The following listing implements that size and scales the line height and line length accordingly.

**Listing 8.2 Improving the article with a set font size and scaled line heights and line lengths**

```
:root {
    --base-font-value: 1;
    --base-line-height: 1.45;
    --base-width: calc(var(--base-font-value) * 480);
}

article {
    --article-font-value: 1.25;
    font-size: calc(var(--article-font-value) * 1px);
    line-height: calc(var(--base-line-height) -
    (var(--article-font-value) - var(--base-font-value))
    / 6.67);
    max-width: calc((var(--base-width) +
    (var(--article-font-value) - var(--base-font-value))
    * 480) * 1px);
}
```

**Represents a rem value**

**Width factor for rem units is 16 * 30 = 480.**

**Line height factor for rem units is 6.67.**

Figure 8.3 shows the result, which uses a `1.25rem` font size, a `1.41` line height, and a `600px` maximum width, all of which serve to make the page text much more readable.

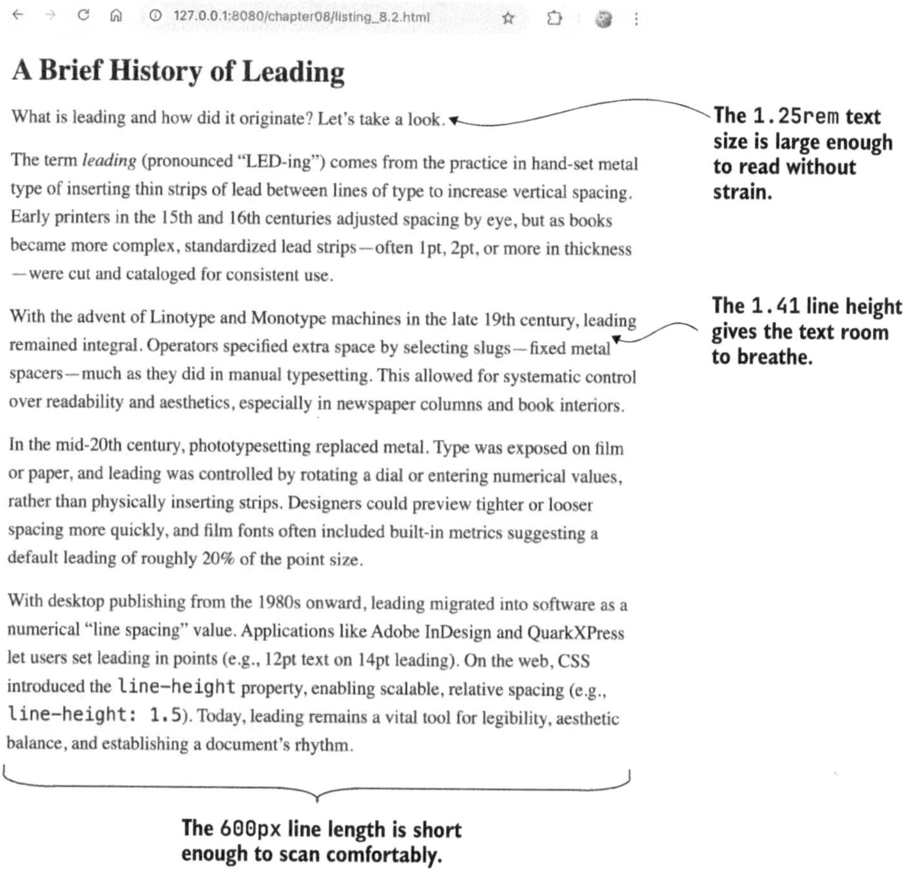


**Figure 8.3 A much more readable and harmonious page, all thanks to math**

For the other two scenarios (i.e., when you know the line height you want to use and when you know the line length you want to use) refer to the files listing_8.3.html and listing_8.4.html in this book's GitHub repo.

#### EXERCISES

**Exercise 8.1:** When you increase the font size on an element, how should the line height and length scale to maintain readability? Pick one of the following:

1. Larger line heights and longer line lengths
2. Smaller line heights and longer line lengths

3 Larger line heights and shorter line lengths
4 Smaller line heights and shorter line lengths

**Exercise 8.2:** Start with the formulas for calculating an element's scaled width (`EW`) based on a known font size and a known line height:

```
EW = BW + (EFS - BFS) * WF
EW = BW + (BLH - ELH) * 3000
```

Use algebra to derive the formulas for an element's scaled font size (`EFS`) and line height (`ELH`):

```
EFS = BFS + (EW - BW) / WF
ELH = BLH - (EW - BW) / 3000
```

## 8.2 Fluid typography with CSS math functions

In the old days of web development, designers often defined font sizes in absolute terms (`px`) or maybe used responsive units such as `em` or `rem` along with breakpoints to bump text sizes up or down based on screen widths. But modern CSS has powerful math functions and relative units that let us create *fluid typography*: text that scales smoothly across screen sizes without abrupt jumps. This section explores how to make font sizes adjust to the viewport using CSS alone, including viewport width and height units (`vw` and `vh`); functions such as `calc()`, `min()`, and `max()`; and the incredibly useful `clamp()`. You'll also learn how to create a responsive typographic scale that ensures your text sizes scale harmoniously, and how to ensure your headings shrink or grow proportionally across devices. All of this can be done with pure CSS math, no JavaScript required.

### 8.2.1 Using vw and vh for scalable text sizes

CSS provides several viewport-relative units that allow property values to scale relative to the browser window. The units relevant to typography are `vw` (viewport width) and `vh` (viewport height), where `1vw` is `1%` of the viewport's width, and `1vh` is `1%` of the viewport's height. Using these units for `font-size` can make text scale automatically as the browser window changes size. For example,

- Setting `font-size: 2vw` will make the text size `2%` of the viewport's width. On a `1000px` wide screen, `2vw = 20px`. On a `375px` wide mobile screen, `2vw = 7.5px`, which is way too small to read! This indicates that using `vw` (or `vh`) to scale font size isn't a great standalone strategy, but that gets fixed in the next section when I introduce more CSS functions into the mix.
- Setting `font-size: 5vh` would size text based on `5%` of the viewport height. This technique is rarely used for text, since width usually constrains text more than height, but it can be useful for text that needs to fill a vertical space.

If you use viewport units, test extreme cases. A pure `2vw` font size could be unreadably small on a phone. Meanwhile, `5vw` might be enormous on an ultrawide monitor. The web has a vast range of screen sizes, so while tying text to viewport size is simple and easy because the browser does all the work, it's rarely one-size-fits-all. You usually need to restrict the values to sensible minimums and maximums.

### 8.2.2 Setting constraints on dynamic font scaling

A few CSS math functions let you express relationships and boundaries for values, which is perfect for fluid typography. The most useful functions here are `calc()`, `min()`, `max()`, and especially `clamp()`. Here's how each can help with font sizing:

- `calc()`—This function allows basic arithmetic with mixed units. For example, `calc(2vw + 1rem)` means "combine a value that grows with viewport width (`2vw`) with a base value of `1rem`." If `1rem` is `16px`, and on a particular screen `2vw` is, say, `20px`, then the computed `font-size` would be `36px`. On a smaller screen where `2vw` is `10px`, `font-size` computes to `26px`. So, `calc()` is great for creating a formula for font-size that has a responsive part and a static part.
- `min()` and `max()`—These are helpful for setting an upper or lower bound in isolation. For example, `font-size: min(5vw, 24px)` means the font size will be set to `5vw`, but it won't grow any bigger than `24px`. On a small screen, such as a `320px` wide phone, `5vw` is `16px`, which is under `24px`, so that `16px` will be used. On a larger screen, such as a `1024px` tablet, `5vw` is `51.2px`, quite a bit larger than `24px`, so the font size will cap at `24px`. Similarly, `font-size: max(2vw, 16px)` ensures the font is at least `16px` even when `2vw` on a small screen computes to a value less than `16px`.
- `clamp(min, preferred, max)`—This is the star for fluid typography. It lets you specify a minimum value, a preferred (ideal) value, and a maximum value all in one declaration. The browser will take the `preferred` value unless it's out of bounds, in which case it uses the `min` or `max`. For fluid text, you often make the `preferred` value one that scales with viewport (using `vw`), and set `min` and `max` in `rem` or `px` to keep things reasonable. For example, `font-size: clamp(1rem, 0.5rem + 2vw, 2rem)`. Let's dissect this:
  - *`min`* = `1rem`—The font size will never be smaller than `1rem` (`16px` if the browser's default font size hasn't been changed).
  - *`preferred`* = `0.5rem + 2vw`—This is a formula that grows with viewport width.
  - *`max`* = `2rem`—The font size will never exceed `2rem` (`32px` if the browser's default is still `16px`).

  On a small screen, such as a `320px` wide phone, `2vw` is `6.4px`, so `0.5rem + 6.4px = 8px + 6.4px = 14.4px`. This is smaller than the minimum value (assuming `1rem = 16px`), so the text would be rendered at the `1rem` minimum. On a large screen, such as a `1600px` desktop monitor, `2vw` is `32px`, so `0.5rem + 32px = 8px + 32px = 40px`. This is larger than the maximum value (assuming `2rem = 32px`), so the text would be rendered at the `2rem` maximum. In between these extremes, the `clamp()` function offers smooth, viewport-based changes to the font size.

### 8.2.3 Calculating the preferred clamp() formula for font sizes

In section 8.2.2, where did the `clamp()` function's preferred value formula of `0.5rem + 2vw` come from? The `0.5rem` part comes from the general rule that, for font sizes, the preferred value should begin at half the minimum value. In the previous section's `clamp()` example, the minimum value was `1rem`, so the formula starts at `0.5rem`.

To determine the formula's `vw` scaling value, you can use a linear interpolation formula. First, assuming you already have a minimum (call it `minFontSize`) and a maximum (call it `maxFontSize`) value for the `font-size` property to plug into the `clamp()` function, you then need to define two more numbers:

- The minimum viewport width (call it `minVW`) at which you want the `font-size` property to be `minValue`
- The maximum viewport width (call it `maxVW`) at which you want the `font-size` property to be `maxValue`

Now you can calculate the scale value in `vw`:

```
scaleVW = (maxFontSize - minFontSize) / (maxVW - minVW) * 100
```

Finally, you plug that value into your declaration:

```
font-size: clamp(minFontSize, minFontSize / 2 + scaleVW, maxFontSize);
```

For example, suppose you want the following for an element:

- `1rem (16px) font-size` value at `400px` screen width
- `2rem (32px) font-size` value at `1200px` screen width

Plug those values into the linear interpolation formula:

```
scaleVW = (32 - 16) / (1200 - 400) * 100
        = 16 /  800 * 100
        = 1600 / 800
        = 2
```

Therefore, your declaration becomes the following:

```
font-size: clamp(1rem, 0.5rem + 2vw, 2rem);
```

### 8.2.4 Example: Hero text for a landing page

As a practical example, imagine you've been tasked to style the text for a landing page that contains a full-screen hero image. Figure 8.4 shows the existing page with

**Figure 8.4 This hero page needs text that fills the screen much like the image does.**

its underwhelming `h1` element set at its default size (refer to listing_8.5.html in this book's GitHub repo).

Your only directives are

- No other text appears on the screen.
- The text must appear to "fill" the screen.
- Supported screen sizes range from `320px` to `1600px`.

You begin by using your browser's dev tools to change the screen width to `320px`, and you notice that a `font-size` value of `4rem` makes the `h1` text fill the screen, so that's your minimum value. Similarly, at `1600px`, a `font-size` value of `8rem` makes the `h1` text fill the screen, so that's your maximum value. Now you can calculate the `vw` scaling factor:

```
scaleVW = (128 - 64) / (1600 - 320) * 100
        = 64 /  1280 * 100
        = 6400 / 1280
        = 5
```

So, now you have your fluid `font-size` value:

```
font-size: clamp(4rem, 2rem + 5vw, 8rem);
```

Figure 8.5 shows how the text scales down to fit a phone screen, and figure 8.6 shows how the text scales up to fit a laptop display (refer to listing_8.6.html in this book's GitHub repo).

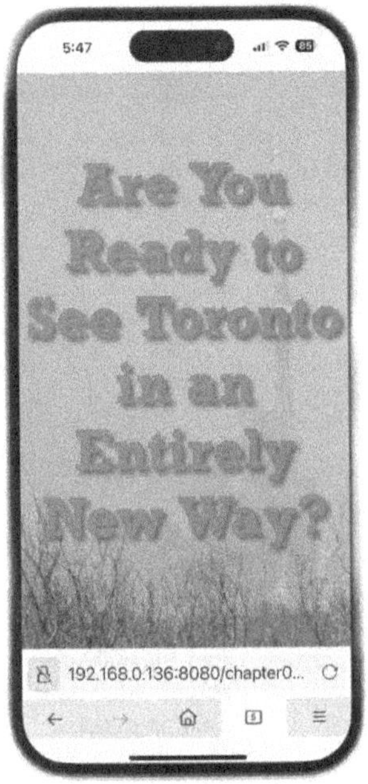


**Figure 8.5 The `clamp()` function scales the text down to fit this phone display.**

**Figure 8.6 The `clamp()` function scales the text up to fit this laptop display.**

#### EXERCISES

**Exercise 8.3:** When settling on a font size for a page element, imagine that you want to use `1.5rem` for small- to medium-size screens (say, up to about `1200px` wide), and then the text can become arbitrarily large as the screen width increases from there. What CSS function would you use to set the element's `font-size` property and what arguments would you pass to the function?

**Exercise 8.4:** Suppose you want to style an element's font size to have the following characteristics:

- The font size minimum is `2rem` when the screen is `400px` wide.
- The font size caps at `4rem` when the screen is `1200px` wide.

What is the formula to use as the preferred value in the `clamp()` function?

## 8.3 Applying a modular scale to text

When you visit some web pages, you might notice that the text, even though it's set with a nice typeface and is large enough to read comfortably, feels off in some way. That slightly negative feeling likely comes from the page designer choosing font sizes that are either chosen seat-of-the-pants style, for example, arbitrarily setting the body text at `20px`, `h2` text at `26px`, `h1` text at `30px`, and so on, or determined by a rigid step formula, such as body text at `20px`, `h2` text at `24px`, `h1` text at `28px`, and so on. Setting text size either willy-nilly or with rigid step differences rarely produces harmonious text.

In contrast, for some pages you visit, you might notice that all the text—the body text, the headings and subheadings, the image captions, and so on—has a certain rhythm that just feels right in a way that's hard to define. That feel-good rhythm almost certainly comes from the page designer using some sort of modular scale for the type sizes. A *modular scale* is a set of font sizes based on a specified ratio. In other words, a typographical modular scale is akin to a musical scale, where successive notes sound right because they're separated by a predefined distance that creates harmony.

You can create a similar harmony in your web pages by implementing a modular scale on all your font sizes. Using a modular scale ensures that all your text sizes have a deliberate relationship based on established principles that create more balanced and pleasing designs.

### 8.3.1 Creating a modular scale from a scaling factor

A typographical modular scale is a set of `font-size` property values that are all derived by repeatedly applying a scaling factor (also called a ratio) that starts with a base size. Here's the general equation:

$$S_n = B * F^n$$

where

- `n` is the nth value in the modular scale set; `n` is `0` for the base value (`B`), positive for increasing font sizes, and negative for decreasing font sizes.
- `S` is the calculated font size for this value of `n`.
- `B` is the base size.
- `F` is the scaling factor.

So, a typical modular scale might consist of the following set:

$$S_{-2} = B * F^{-2}$$
$$S_{-1} = B * F^{-1}$$
$$S_0 = B * F^0$$
$$S_1 = B * F^1$$
$$S_2 = B * F^2$$
$$S_3 = B * F^3$$

For example, suppose your base is `20px` (so `B = 20`), and your scaling factor is `1.5` (so `F = 1.5`). This produces the following modular scale:

$$S_{-2} = 20 * 1.5^{-2} = 20 * 0.44 = 8.89px$$
$$S_{-1} = 20 * 1.5^{-1} = 20 * 0.67 = 13.33px$$
$$S_0 = 20 * 1.5^0 = 20 * 1 = 20px$$
$$S_1 = 20 * 1.5^1 = 20 * 1.5 = 24px$$
$$S_2 = 20 * 1.5^2 = 20 * 2.25 = 36px$$
$$S_3 = 20 * 1.5^3 = 20 * 3.375 = 67.5px$$

This scale is demonstrated in figure 8.7, the code for which is shown in listing 8.3.

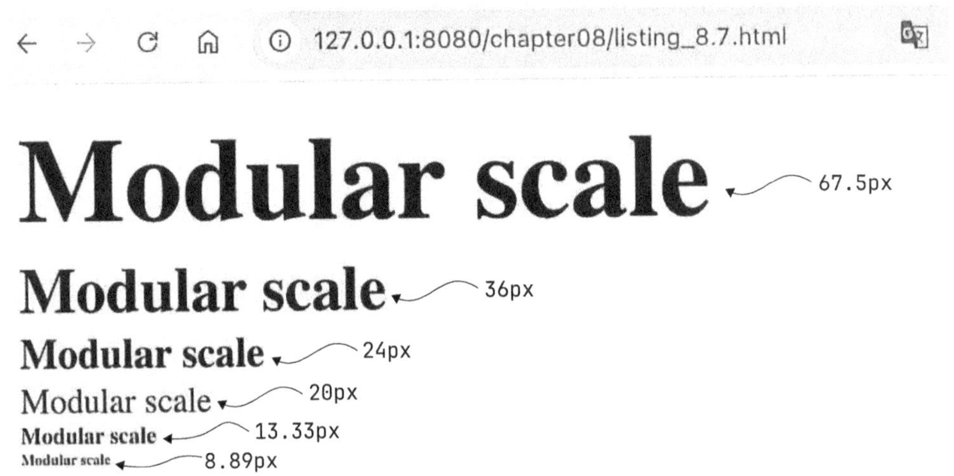


**Figure 8.7 A modular scale based on the ratio 1.5**

**Listing 8.3 A modular scale based on the ratio 1.5**

```
<head>
    <style>
        h1 { font-size: 67.5px; }
        h2 { font-size: 36px; }
        h3 { font-size: 24px; }
        p { font-size: 20px; }
        h4 { font-size: 13.33px; }
        h5 { font-size: 8.89px; }
    </style>
</head>
<body>
    <h1>Modular scale</h1>
    <h2>Modular scale</h2>
    <h3>Modular scale</h3>
    <p>Modular scale</p>
    <h4>Modular scale</h4>
    <h5>Modular scale</h5>
</body>
```

Choosing a modular scale ratio can feel a little arbitrary, but there are several ratios based on mathematical and musical principles that are commonly used in design circles that can remove some of the guesswork.

### 8.3.2 Choosing a modular scale ratio

Rather than just guessing which ratio would work best with your modular scale, you can follow these guidelines to narrow your choices:

- If you want subtle changes from one step to the next, choose a ratio `r` in the range `1 < r <= 1.2`.
- If you want to emphasize readability, choose a ratio `r` in the range `1.2 < r <= 1.5`.
- If you want dramatic changes from one step to the next, choose a ratio `r` in the range `1.5 < r <= 1.75`.

However, there are also several traditional ratios that designers have used for centuries and that have proven track records for creating harmonious, pleasing text sizes. For example, the `1.5` ratio I used in the previous section is based on the musical notion of the *perfect fifth*. It refers to the interval between two notes where the higher note's frequency is `1.5` times that of the lower note. If one note has a frequency of 200 Hz, a note a perfect fifth above it would be 300 Hz (`200 * 1.5`). Table 8.4 lists a few other common ratios from math and music.

**Table 8.4 Traditional modular scale ratios based on ideas in math and music**

| Name | Ratio | Example scales (base = `20px`) |
|---|---|---|
| Minor third | 1.125 | `15.8px 17.78px 20px 22.5px 25.31px 28.48px` |
| Major third | 1.2 | `13.89px 16.67px 20px 24px 28.8px 34.56px` |
| Perfect fourth | 1.25 | `12.8px 16px 20px 25px 31.25px 39.06px` |
| Augmented fourth | 1.33 | `11.31px 15.04px 20px 26.6px 35.38px 47.05px` |
| Square root of two | 1.414 | `10px 14.14px 20px 28.28px 39.99px 56.54px` |
| Minor sixth | 1.6 | `7.81px 12.5px 20px 32px 51.2px 81.92px` |
| Golden ratio | 1.618 | `7.64px 12.36px 20px 32.36px 52.36px 84.72px` |
| Major sixth | 1.67 | `7.17px 11.98px 20px 33.4px 55.78px 93.15px` |
| Octave | 2 | `5px 10px 20px 40px 80px 160px` |

Each of these scales creates a different typographical rhythm. Smaller ratios such as the minor and major third generate `font-size` values that are closer together, which creates a subtler hierarchy. Larger ratios such as the minor sixth and the golden ratio generate `font-size` values that are dramatically different, which creates a bolder hierarchy. Fortunately, there's no such thing as a single correct ratio. Which one you choose depends on the visual effect you're looking to achieve.

### 8.3.3 Implementing typographic scales with CSS variables

Suppose you're designing a website, and the client insists that you use the golden ratio (approximately 1.618) as much as possible. This preference isn't all that unusual since people have believed that the golden ratio has special aesthetic properties for a very long time (e.g., the dimensions of the Parthenon's facade are based on the golden ratio). Where does this ratio come from? Often denoted by the Greek letter φ (phi), the golden ratio is an irrational number that appears when a line is divided into two parts so that the ratio of the whole length to the longer part is the same as the ratio of the longer part to the shorter part. That is, if a line is divided into segments `a` and `b`, where `a` is the longer segment and `b` is the shorter one, then

$$\frac{a+b}{a} = \frac{a}{b} = \varphi$$

The actual value is the unending irrational number `1.6180339887…`, which is usually shortened to `1.618` for design work. Here's the scale generated by the golden ratio when the base is `1.25rem`:

```
S-2 = 1.25 * 1.618-2 = 1.25* 0.38 = 0.48rem
S-1 = 1.25 * 1.618-1 = 1.25* 0.62 = 0.77rem
S0 = 1.25 * 1.6180 = 1.25* 1 = 1.25rem
S1 = 1.25 * 1.6181 = 1.25* 1.62 = 2.02rem
S2 = 1.25 * 1.6182 = 1.25* 2.62 = 3.27rem
S3 = 1.25 * 1.61853 = 1.25* 4.24 = 5.29rem
```

Rather than hard-coding these as `font-size` values as done in listing 8.3, a more flexible approach is to use CSS variables as follows:

- Define a variable to hold the ratio.
- Define a variable to hold the base font size.
- For each step of the scale you want to implement, create a variable that either divides (for font sizes smaller than the base) or multiplies (for font sizes larger than the base) the value of the previous step. (CSS doesn't have an exponentiation operator, so you have to use division and multiplication here.)

An example scale based on the golden ratio is shown in figure 8.8, and the following listing shows the code behind it.

**Listing 8.4 A modular scale based on the golden ratio (1.618)**

```
<head>
    <style>
        :root {
            --ratio: 1.618;
            --base: 1.25rem;
            --step-1: calc(var(--base) / var(--ratio));
            --step-2: calc(var(--step-1) / var(--ratio));
            --step1: calc(var(--base) * var(--ratio));
            --step2: calc(var(--step1) * var(--ratio));
            --step3: calc(var(--step2) * var(--ratio));
        }
```

**The golden ratio** (`--ratio: 1.618;`)

**The base font size** (`--base: 1.25rem;`)

**Divides by the ratio to get smaller font sizes** (`--step-1`, `--step-2`)

**Multiplies by the ratio to get larger font sizes** (`--step1`, `--step2`, `--step3`)

```
        h1 { font-size: var(--step3); }
        h2 { font-size: var(--step2); }
        h3 { font-size: var(--step1); }
        p { font-size: var(--base); }
        h4 { font-size: var(--step-1); }
        h5 { font-size: var(--step-2); }
    </style>
</head>

<body>
    <h1>Golden ratio scale</h1>
    <h2>Golden ratio scale</h2>
    <h3>Golden ratio scale</h3>
    <p>Golden ratio scale</p>
    <h4>Golden ratio scale</h4>
    <h5>Golden ratio scale</h5>
</body>
```

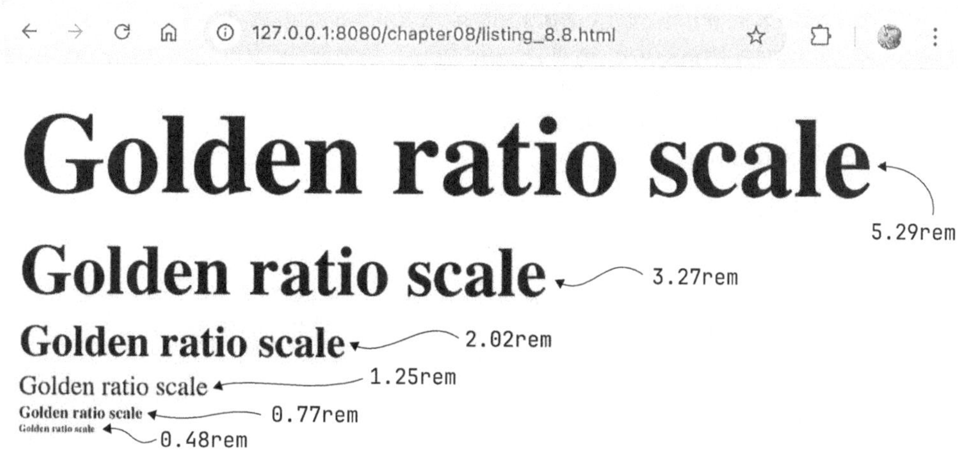


**Figure 8.8 A modular scale based on the golden ratio**

The golden ratio provides dramatic contrasts between steps, so it's suitable for a bold design that demands large headings.

**EXERCISE**

**Exercise 8.5:** You want to create a modular scale for a website where the base font is `22px`, and you choose a ratio based on the square root of two: `1.414`. What would be the next three larger font sizes on that scale? Show the calculations.

## 8.4 Solutions to exercises

**Exercise 8.1:** As you increase the font size, you maintain readability by making the line height smaller and the line length shorter. Therefore, the answer is 2.

**Exercise 8.2:** Here are the algebraic steps required to transform the scaled element width (`EW`) formula for a known font size into the formula for determining an element's scaled font size (`EFS`) given a known element width:

```
EW = BW + (EFS - BFS) * WF
EW - BW = (EFS - BFS) * WF
(EW - BW) / WF = EFS - BFS
EFS = BFS + (EW - BW) / WF
```

Here's the algebra that transforms the scaled element width (`EW`) formula for a known line height into the formula for determining an element's scaled line height (`ELH`) given a known element width:

```
EW = BW + (BLH - ELH) * 3000
EW - BW = (BLH - ELH) * 3000
(EW - BW) / 3000 = BLH - ELH
ELH = BLH - (EW - BW) / 3000
```

**Exercise 8.3:** When you need a font size to always be larger than some value, you use the CSS `max()` function. In this example, `1.5rem` is the lower bound constraint, so you can use that as one argument for the `max()` function. For the other argument, you want the lower bound to be constant until the screen width exceeds `1200px`, so you solve for the scale factor `x`:

```
1200x = 24
x = 24 / 1200
x = 0.02
```

That is, you want the font size to scale as `0.02` of the screen width, which is `2vw`. Here's the `font-size` declaration you need:

```
font-size: max(1.5rem, 2vw)
```

**Exercise 8.4:** Here's the math:

```
scaleVW = (64 - 32) / (1200 - 400) * 100
        = 32 /  800 * 100
        = 3200 / 800
        = 4
```

Therefore, your `font-size` declaration will look like this:

```
font-size: clamp(2rem, 1rem + 4vw, 4rem);
```

**Exercise 8.5:** Given a base `font-size` value of `22px` and a ratio of `1.414`, here are the next three larger `font-size` values:

```
S1 = 22 * 1.4141 = 22 * 1.414 = 31.1px
S2 = 22 * 1.4142 = 22 * 2 = 44px
S3 = 22 * 1.4143 = 22 * 2.83 = 62.2px
```

## Summary

- The typographic trinity consists of font size, line height, and line length, each of which depends mathematically on the others to achieve readable and balanced text.
- A typographically unbalanced page is one that uses a body text font size that's too small (particularly the browser default of `16px`), a line height that's too small (particularly the browser default of 1.2), and a line length that's too long (particularly the default element width of `100%` of the parent width in a wide browser window).
- For readable text, shoot for body text set to at least `1.25rem` (usually `20px`), line height around `1.4` or `1.5`, and line lengths of `45` to `75` characters.
- Line height should scale inversely with the font size and line length should scale with the font size.
- Both font size and line length should scale inversely with the line height.
- Both font size and line height should scale with the line length.
- Use CSS fluid units for responsive text. Viewport-relative units (`vw`, `vh`) and functions such as `calc()` and `clamp()` enable text that scales smoothly across screen sizes without media queries. In particular, using `clamp(min, preferred, max)` can constrain font sizes to maintain legibility.
- A modular scale is a great way to bring harmony to page font sizes. Choose a ratio (e.g., `1.25`, `1.5`, or `1.618`) and derive all text sizes from it. This produces font sizes that feel related and balanced.
- CSS custom properties simplify modular scale math. You can store base sizes and ratios in variables and use `calc()` to compute each modular scale step. This makes it easy to adjust one value (e.g., the ratio or the base font size) and have all related sizes update automatically.

# 9 Trigonometry for web developers

**This chapter covers**

- The trig you need to know for web dev work
- Building circular layouts and animations
- Applying wave effects
- Making directional calculations

Trigonometry, the mathematics of angles and triangles, might seem too esoteric to be useful in frontend web development. But modern browsers now offer tools that enable anyone to use trigonometric concepts to create rich visual effects, dynamic layouts, and smooth animations. From using CSS to rotate or skew elements to using JavaScript to animate elements along a curved path, trig stalwarts such as sine, cosine, and tangent make these and other frontend effects easier to implement and customize to your design requirements.

## 9.1 The basics of trigonometry for web design

Before the code starts flying, let's first take a step back and understand a few fundamentals for implementing trigonometric calculations in frontend web development work.

### 9.1.1 Sine, cosine, and tangent

Trigonometry is all about the relationships that exist within a triangle, particularly a *right-angled triangle*, where one of the angles is 90°, as shown in figure 9.1. The trig workhorses in frontend work are the three primary trig functions of sine (`sin`), cosine (`cos`), and tangent (`tan`). Each defines a relationship between an angle θ (theta) and the ratios of the triangle's sides:

- *sin(θ) = opposite / hypotenuse*—The sine of θ is a measure of the verticalness of that angle. As shown in figure 9.1, with the angle θ at the center (0, 0) of a circle, sin(θ) tells you how far up (in this case) the point (*x*, *y*) is from the center. You can write the sine of θ as sin(θ), sin θ, or sinθ.
- *cos(θ) = adjacent / hypotenuse*—The cosine of θ is a measure of the horizontalness of that angle. As shown in figure 9.1, with the angle θ at the center (0, 0) of a circle, cos(θ) tells you how far right (in this case) the point (*x*, *y*) is from the center. You can write the cosine of θ as cos(θ), cos θ, or cosθ.
- *tan(θ) = opposite / adjacent = sin / cos*—The tangent of θ is a measure of the steepness of that angle. As shown in figure 9.1, with the angle θ at the center (0, 0) of a circle, tan(θ) tells you the slope of the line joining (0, 0) to the point (*x*, *y*). You can write the tangent of θ as tan(θ), tan θ, or tanθ.

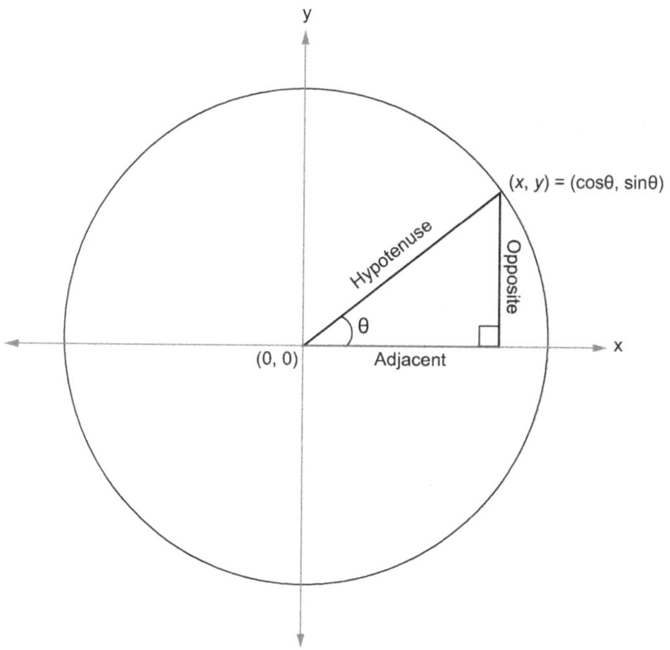


**Figure 9.1 A right triangle and its sides relative to the angle theta (θ)**

The simplest case to examine is the so-called *unit circle*, which has radius 1 and is centered on (0, 0). For the unit circle, a point ($x$, $y$) on the circle at angle θ in the upper-right quadrant (`0 ≤ x ≤ 1, 0 ≤ y ≤ 1`) will have the following coordinates:

```
x = cos(θ)
y = sin(θ)
```

Table 9.1 lists a few representative values for each trig function as you go around the unit circle.

**Table 9.1 Representative values for sin, cos, and tan around the unit circle**

| θ | cos(θ) | sin(θ) | tan(θ) |
|---|---|---|---|
| 0° | 1 | 0 | 0 |
| 45° | 0.707 | 0.707 | 1 |
| 90° | 0 | 1 | not defined |
| 135° | -0.707 | 0.707 | -1 |
| 180° | -1 | 0 | 0 |
| 225° | -0.707 | -0.707 | 1 |
| 270° | 0 | -1 | not defined |
| 315° | 0.707 | -0.707 | -1 |
| 360° (=0°) | 1 | 0 | 0 |

A key takeaway from table 9.1 is that the values of cos(θ) and sin(θ) oscillate smoothly within the range [–1, 1], so that when you graph, say, sin(θ), the result is a regular, repeating wave pattern, as shown in figure 9.2. The graph for cos(θ) has the same shape, but it's shifted horizontally by 90° (π/2 radians).

Note that in figure 9.2, the units are listed in radians instead of degrees. Refer to section 9.1.2 to learn more about radians and to section 9.1.3 to learn how to convert between degrees and radians. For now, it's enough to know that a full circle (360°) is equivalent to 2π radians.

The tan(θ) graph (refer to figure 9.3) is quite a bit different than the ones for sin(θ) and cos(θ). Since tan(θ) = sin(θ) / cos(θ), the value of tan(θ) grows toward infinity (or negative infinity) as cos(θ) approaches 0, which happens at 90° and 270° (that is, π/2 and 3π/2). So, each of these angles represents an *asymptote*, a line that the graph approaches but never quite touches or crosses, even as the values head toward infinity (∞). In practice, you won't work with raw tangent values, except when you need to calculate certain angles or slopes.

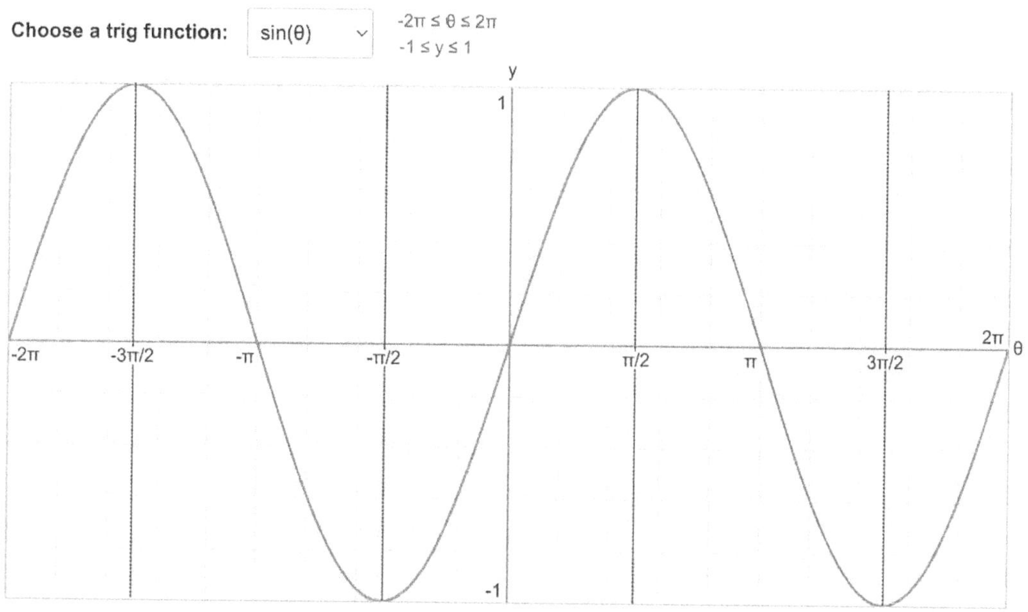


**Figure 9.2 The graph of sin(θ) for $-2\pi \leq \theta \leq 2\pi$**

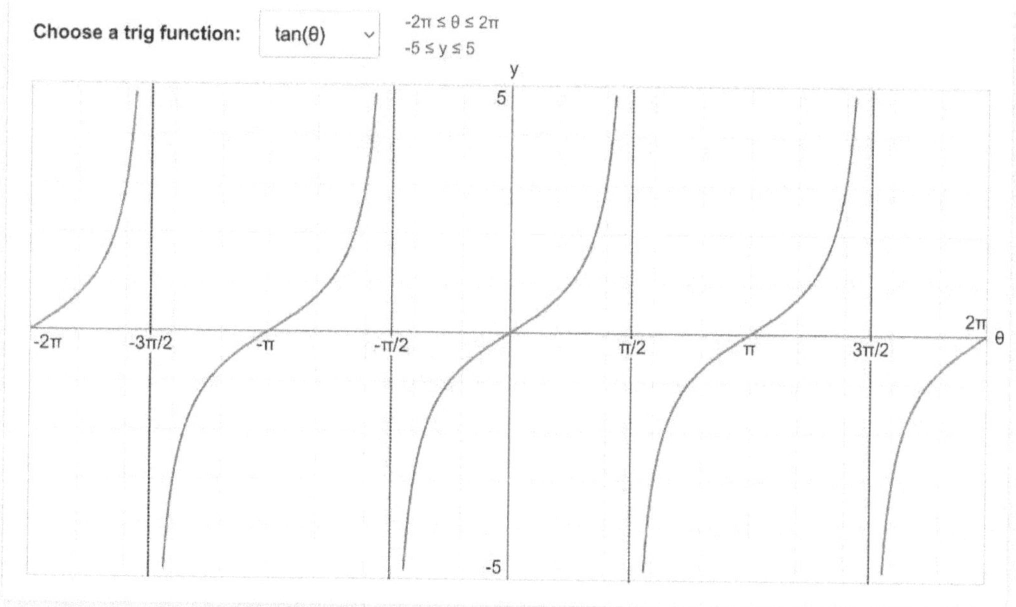


**Figure 9.3 The graph of tan(θ) for $-2\pi \leq \theta \leq 2\pi$**

Another key takeaway for getting the most out of trig in web dev is that when you're working with a circle with radius `r` centered at the point (`centerX, centerY`), for any `angle`, you can calculate the *x* and *y* coordinates of that point on the circle as follows:

```
x = centerX + r * cos(angle)
y = centerY + r * sin(angle)
```

These two equations form the foundation for all kinds of trig-powered effects, from circular menus to spiral animations.

### 9.1.2 Trigonometric units

All the trig functions accept values in trigonometric units as input, and many of those functions also return results expressed in trig units. A trig unit is an angle, and in CSS, there are four ways to express any angle:

- `deg`—The angle expressed as the number of degrees, where one complete circle is represented by `360deg`.
- `rad`—The angle expressed as the number of radians, where `1rad = 180deg/π` and one complete circle is represented by `2πrad`.
- `grad`—The angle expressed as the number of gradians, where one complete circle is represented by `400grad`.
- `turn`—The angle expressed as the number of turns, where one complete circle is represented by `1turn`.

All these values wrap around every turn of the circle. For example, `deg` values wrap around every 360 degrees, so `360deg = 0deg`, `450deg = 90deg`, and so on. Negative values have positive equivalents, so `-90deg = 270deg`, `-180deg = 180deg`, and so on.

### 9.1.3 Converting between degrees and radians

Most of the time, you'll use the `deg` unit in your CSS properties (e.g., `transform: rotate(45deg)`), but JavaScript's `Math` object trig functions require a unitless value that represents radians (e.g., `const x = Math.cos(Math.PI / 4)`). The connection between degrees and radians is that a radian is based on the circle's radius: you take that radius and imagine wrapping it along the circle's circumference. The length that the radius takes up along the circumference equals 1 radian. Since the circumference of a circle is given by `2πr` and there are 360° in the circumference, it follows that

```
2πr = 360°
r = 360° / 2π
r ≈ 57.3°
```

That is, 1 radian is approximately 57.3 degrees. Equivalently, since there are $2\pi$ radians in a circle (360°),

```
360° = 2π
180° = π
1° = π / 180
```

That is, there are $\pi/180$ radians in a degree.

You can use the following formulas to convert between degrees and radians:

```
radians = degrees * (Math.PI / 180)
degrees = radians * (180 / Math.PI)
```

In both formulas, the constant `Math.PI` is JavaScript's representation of $\pi$ (the ratio of the circumference of a circle to its diameter, which is approximately 3.1415926535897932).

### 9.1.4 The inverse trig functions

Sometimes, you have a ratio and need the angle that produced it. The inverses of sin, cos, and tan are, respectively, asin, acos, and atan (where the *a* is short for *arc*, as in arcsin). These return an angle (in radians in JavaScript) given a ratio. For example, suppose you have the ratio 0.5, and you want to know the angle $\theta$ for which $\sin(\theta) = 0.5$ is true. That's the job of the asin function, where asin(0.5) returns $\theta \approx 0.524$ radians, which is 30°.

The most useful in practice is atan2, the two-argument arctan. `Math.atan2(y, x)` takes a *y* and an *x* (such as a vector or a coordinate) and gives the angle of that vector relative to the positive *x*-axis. Unlike a normal atan, atan2 considers the sign of both inputs to return the correct angle in all four quadrants, in the –180° to +180° range. This is extremely handy for finding the angle between points or the orientation of a direction vector, as you'll learn later. For example, if you have a target at coordinates $(x, y) = (3, 2)$ relative to an object, atan2(2, 3) gives the angle (in radians) that the object should face to point directly at that target.

### 9.1.5 Trig functions in CSS and JavaScript

Seven functions—`sin()`, `cos()`, `tan()`, `asin()`, `acos()`, `atan()`, and `atan2()`—were introduced as part of the CSS Values and Units Level 4 spec and gained full mainstream browser support starting in March 2023. All these functions are now supported in all the major evergreen browsers (including Chrome 111+, Firefox 108+, and Safari 15.4+).

JavaScript includes these seven functions as methods of the `Math` object, as well as several other trig functions (the so-called hyperbolic trig functions) that are used rarely (if at all) in frontend work, so they are ignored in this chapter. Table 9.2 summarizes the seven trig functions available in both CSS and JavaScript.

**Table 9.2 The seven trig functions**

| Function | Argument(s) accepted | What it returns | Examples |
|---|---|---|---|
| CSS: `sin(angle)`<br>JS: `Math.sin(angle)` | An angle or number | A number between −1 and 1, representing the sine of `angle` | `sin(0deg) = 0`<br>`sin(45deg) = ~0.707`<br>`sin(90deg) = 1` |
| CSS: `cos(angle)`<br>JS: `Math.cos(angle)` | An angle or number | A number between −1 and 1, representing the cosine of `angle` | `cos(0deg) = 1`<br>`cos(45deg) = ~0.707`<br>`cos(90deg) = 0` |
| CSS: `tan(angle)`<br>JS: `Math.tan(angle)` | An angle or number | A number between −∞ and ∞, representing the tangent of `angle` | `tan(0deg) = 0`<br>`tan(45deg) = 1`<br>`tan(90deg) = undefined` |
| CSS: `asin(number)`<br>JS: `Math.asin(number)` | A number between −1 and 1 | An angle between −90deg and 90deg, representing the inverse sine of `number` | `asin(0) = 0deg`<br>`asin(0.5) = 30deg`<br>`asin(1) = 90deg` |
| CSS: `acos(number)`<br>JS: `Math.acos(number)` | A number between −1 and 1 | An angle between 0deg and 180deg, representing the inverse cosine of `number` | `acos(0) = 90deg`<br>`acos(0.5) = 60deg`<br>`acos(1) = 0deg` |
| CSS: `atan(number)`<br>JS: `Math.atan(number)` | A number | An angle between -90deg and 90deg, representing the inverse tangent of `number` | `atan(0) = 0deg`<br>`atan(1) = 45deg`<br>`atan(infinity) = 90deg` |
| CSS: `atan2(y, x)`<br>JS: `Math.atan2(y, x)` | Two numbers | A value between −180deg and 180deg (CSS) or between −π and π radians (JS), representing the angle between the positive *x*-axis and the point `( x, y)` | `atan2(0, 0) = 0deg`<br>`atan2(3,2) = ~56.3deg`<br>`atan2(1, 0) = π / 2` |

**EXERCISES**

**Exercise 9.1:** What is the value of $\tan(270°)$?

1. 0
2. 1
3. 0.707
4. undefined

**Exercise 9.2:** An angle θ is given as 135°. What is θ in radians?

## 9.2 Circular layouts and animations

Perhaps the most natural and obvious use of trig is to lay out or animate page elements along a circular path. There are many ways to use trig here, and the next few sections outline the most useful of them.

### 9.2.1 Creating a circular menu

Imagine the following scenario. For a special promotional page, Marketing wants to get rid of the traditional inline page nav bar and requires the menu items arranged in a circle. Here are the items:

```
<nav class="menu">
    <div class="menu-item">Home</div>
    <div class="menu-item">Products</div>
    <div class="menu-item">Blog</div>
    <div class="menu-item">Contact</div>
    <div class="menu-item">About</div>
    <div class="menu-item">Help</div>
</nav>
```

And here is the relevant CSS:

```
.menu {
    position: relative;
    width: 300px;
    height: 300px;
}

.menu-item {
    display: flex;
    justify-content: center;
    align-items: center;
    border-radius: 50%;
    position: absolute;
    left: 105px;
    top: 105px;
    height: 90px;
    width: 90px;
}
```

You can satisfy Marketing's circular menu requirement using trig and either JavaScript or pure CSS.

#### CREATING A CIRCULAR MENU WITH JAVASCRIPT

To get your menu items arranged along a circular path using JavaScript, you can wield the `Math.cos()` and `Math.sin()` methods. Figure 9.4 shows the results and listing 9.1 offers the code that makes it happen.

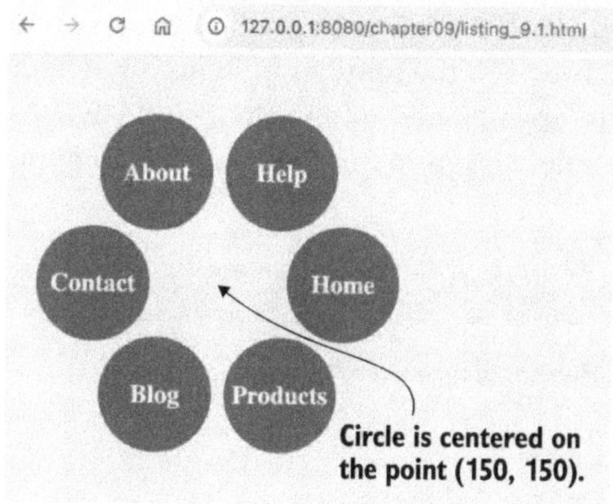


**Figure 9.4 Arranging menu items in a circle using JavaScript**

**Listing 9.1 Circular menu with JavaScript**

```
function generateCircularMenu(items, centerX, centerY, radius) {
    const angleStep = (2 * Math.PI) / items.length;        // Calculates angle change between each item

    items.forEach((item, index) => {        // Runs through the items
        const angle = angleStep * index;        // Calculates item's angle

        const x = centerX + radius * Math.cos(angle);        // Uses trig to calculate the item's
        const y = centerY + radius * Math.sin(angle);        // (x, y) point on the circle

        item.style.left = x + 'px';        // Positions the element
        item.style.top = y + 'px';        // on the circle
        item.style.transform = 'translate(-50%, -50%)';
    });
}

const items = document.querySelectorAll('.menu-item');        // Defines the menu
const radius = 100;        // parameters
const centerX = 150;
const centerY = 150;

generateCircularMenu(items, centerX, centerY, radius);        // Generates the menu
```

**NOTE** All the code for this chapter's listings is available in this book's GitHub repository: https://github.com/paulmcfe/web-dev-math.

The core of listing 9.1 is the `generateCircularMenu()` function, which takes a list of menu elements (`items`), the circle's center point (`centerX` and `centerY`), and its radius (`radius`). The function first calculates the angle step between items by dividing $2\pi$ (the full circle) by the number of items. It then iterates through the items. In the loop, it calculates each item's angle on the circle, then pulls out the trig tools to calculate the item's *x*-coordinate (using `Math.cos(angle)`) and *y*-coordinate (using `Math.sin(angle)`). The function then uses these values to absolutely position the item on the circle (and applies a CSS `transform` to bring the center of each item to the circle point).

#### CREATING A CIRCULAR MENU WITH CSS

Using JavaScript to arrange elements in a circle, as shown in the previous section, works when the number of items can vary. However, if the number of items is fixed, instead of bringing out the big JavaScript guns to arrange menu items in a circle, you can make Marketing happy with pure CSS. The rules shown in the following listing generate the same menu shown in figure 9.4.

**Listing 9.2 Circular menu with CSS**

```
:root {
    --total-items: 6;        /* Number of menu items */
    --radius: 100px;        /* Defines the menu parameters */
    --centerX: 150px;
    --centerY: 150px;
```

```
    --angle-step: calc(360deg / var(--total-items));
}
.menu-item {
    --snip-
    transform: translate(-50%, -50%);
}
.menu-item:nth-child(1) {
    left: calc(var(--centerX) +
               var(--radius) *
               cos(var(--angle-step) * 0));
    top: calc(var(--centerY) +
              var(--radius) *
              sin(var(--angle-step) * 0));
}
.menu-item:nth-child(2) {
    left: calc(var(--centerX) +
               var(--radius) *
               cos(var(--angle-step) * 1));
    top: calc(var(--centerY) +
              var(--radius) *
              sin(var(--angle-step) * 1));
}
.menu-item:nth-child(3) {
    left: calc(var(--centerX) +
               var(--radius) *
               cos(var(--angle-step) * 2));
    top: calc(var(--centerY) +
              var(--radius) *
              sin(var(--angle-step) * 2));
}
.menu-item:nth-child(4) {
    left: calc(var(--centerX) +
               var(--radius) *
               cos(var(--angle-step) * 3));
    top: calc(var(--centerY) +
              var(--radius) *
              sin(var(--angle-step) * 3));
}
.menu-item:nth-child(5) {
    left: calc(var(--centerX) +
               var(--radius) *
               cos(var(--angle-step) * 4));
    top: calc(var(--centerY) +
              var(--radius) *
              sin(var(--angle-step) * 4));
}
.menu-item:nth-child(6) {
    left: calc(var(--centerX) +
               var(--radius) *
               cos(var(--angle-step) * 5));
    top: calc(var(--centerY) +
              var(--radius) *
              sin(var(--angle-step) * 5));
}
```

**Calculates angle change between each item**

**Centers each item on circle**

**Uses cos() to calculate x (left) coordinate**

**Uses sin() to calculate y (top) coordinate**

This code sets up a few CSS variables, then uses `nth-child()` to position each menu item on the circle, with `cos()` setting each item's `left` property and `sin()` setting its `top` property.

### 9.2.2 *Animating circular motion*

As shown in section 9.2.1, a static circular arrangement is a useful pattern, but trig really comes into its own in web dev when used to animate one or more elements along a circular path. Once again, you have two options: JavaScript or CSS.

#### ANIMATING CIRCULAR MOTION IN JAVASCRIPT

Animating an element around a circle essentially means continuously repeating the technique from the previous section to place an element on a circle at point ($x$, $y$) using `Math.cos()` for the *x*-coordinate and `Math.sin()` for the *y*-coordinate. The following listing presents a JavaScript function that animates an element around a center point in a circle with a specified radius.

**Listing 9.3 Circular path animation with JavaScript**

```
function animateInACircle(element, centerX, centerY, radius, speed) {
    let angle = 0;

    function animate() {
        angle += speed;
        const x = centerX + radius * Math.cos(angle);
        const y = centerY + radius * Math.sin(angle);

        element.style.transform = `translate(${x}px, ${y}px)`;

        requestAnimationFrame(animate);
    }

    animate();
}
```

Angle increases by the value of speed

Uses cos() to calculate x coordinate

Uses sin() to calculate y coordinate

Sets the new position

Requests the next frame

The `animateInACircle()` function takes an element (`element`), the center point of the circle (`centerX` and `centerY`), the radius of the circle (`radius`), and a pacing constant (`speed`). The interior `animate()` function writes each frame of the animation by doing four things:

- The `angle` variable is incremented by the value of `speed`. Smaller values of `speed` (say, less than `0.05`) slow down the motion, while higher values speed it up. Negative values reverse the direction.
- The element's next *x*-coordinate is calculated using `Math.cos(angle)`.
- The element's next *y*-coordinate is calculated using `Math.sin(angle)`.
- A CSS `transform` is applied to the element to translate it to the new *x*- and *y*-coordinates.

The `animate()` function then calls `requestAnimationFrame(animate)` to get the next frame, and the process repeats endlessly.

#### ANIMATING CIRCULAR MOTION IN CSS

The JavaScript method for animating an element around a circle gives control over speed, and you could easily add interactivity, such as clicking to stop or even reverse the animation. If you just need a simple circular animation, then pure CSS is the way to go. Given the following HTML,

```
<div class="orbiting">
    <div class="orbiting-element"></div>
</div>
```

you can animate `.orbiting-element` using CSS as shown in the following listing.

**Listing 9.4 Circular path animation with CSS**

```
@property --angle {
    syntax: "<angle>";
    initial-value: 0deg;
    inherits: true;
}

@keyframes orbit {
    from { --angle: 0deg; }
    to   { --angle: 360deg; }
}

.orbiting {
    --angle: 0deg;
    --radius: 100px;
    position: relative;
    animation: orbit 5s linear infinite;
    --snip--
}

.orbiting-element {
    position: absolute;
    left: calc(50% + var(--radius) *
              cos(var(--angle)) - 10px);
    top:  calc(50% + var(--radius) *
              sin(var(--angle)) - 10px);
    --snip--
}
```

- @property block: **Tells CSS about the --angle custom property**
- @keyframes from/to: **The keyframes interpolate --angle**
- --radius: 100px: **Sets the circle radius**
- animation: orbit 5s linear infinite: **Sets the animation parameters**
- left: … cos(var(--angle)) - 10px: **Uses cos() to calculate x coordinate**
- top: … sin(var(--angle)) - 10px: **Uses sin() to calculate y coordinate**

This code works by interpolating the custom `--angle` variable from `0deg` to `360deg`, followed by using that changing angle to position the element using `cos()` and `sin()`.

If you want to reverse the animation, change the plus sign (+) to a minus sign (-) in the `top` property value:

```
top:  calc(50% - var(--radius) * sin(var(--angle)) - 10px);
```

### 9.2.3 Creating an animated spinner

You're a web developer, and you've been tasked to come up with a simple spinner: an animated effect where a collection of small elements orbits a central point, used most often to signal to the user that an operation is pending. Listing 9.5 presents the JavaScript for such a spinner. Note that the starting HTML is an empty div element:

```
<div class="spinner-container" id="spinner-container"></div>
```

**Listing 9.5 Animated spinner**

```
let dots = [];
let rotationAngle = 0;
const centerX = 50;
const centerY = 50;

function createSpinner(container, dotCount, radius) {      ◄ Creates the spinner
    const angleStep = (2 * Math.PI) / dotCount;             ◄ Positions the elements evenly around the circle

    for (let i = 0; i < dotCount; i++) {                    ◄ Creates each spinner element
        const dot = document.createElement('div');
        dot.className = 'spinner-dot';

        const dotInfo = {
            element: dot,
            baseAngle: angleStep * i,                       Stores dot info for animation
            radius: radius
        };

        dots.push(dotInfo);
        container.appendChild(dot);
    }
}

function animateSpinner() {
    rotationAngle += 0.05;                                  ◄ Updates rotation angle

    dots.forEach(dotInfo => {
        const currentAngle = dotInfo.baseAngle + rotationAngle;
        const x = centerX +
                  dotInfo.radius *
                  Math.cos(currentAngle);                   ◄ Uses cos() to calculate x coordinate
        const y = centerY +
                  dotInfo.radius *
                  Math.sin(currentAngle);                   ◄ Uses sin() to calculate y coordinate

        dotInfo.element.style.left = x + 'px';
        dotInfo.element.style.top = y + 'px';               Sets the new position
    });
    requestAnimationFrame(animateSpinner);                  ◄ Requests the next frame
}
```

```
const container = document.getElementById('spinner-container');
createSpinner(container, 10, 20);
animateSpinner();
```

Initializes and starts spinner

The `createSpinner()` function initializes the spinner elements, including creating a `dotInfo` object for each element that stores the element, its base angle, and its radius. The `animateSpinner()` function is essentially the same code as the `animate()` function in listing 9.3, except here each frame iterates over the spinner's collection of elements (stored in the `dots` array).

**EXERCISES**

**Exercise 9.3:** You can convert the circular path animation in listing 9.3 to a spiral animation by varying the `radius` value in each frame: incrementing `radius` causes the element to spiral outward; decrementing `radius` causes the element to spiral inward. Modify the `animate()` function from listing 9.3 to cause the element to spiral in toward the center point. You get bonus points for stopping the animation when the `radius` value hits `0`.

**Exercise 9.4:** You change a circular orbit animation into an elliptical orbit by using different radius values for the *x* and *y* calculations. Modify the `animateInACircle()` function from listing 9.3 to accept different radius values for *x* and *y*, then modify the expressions that calculate these coordinates.

## 9.3 Wave effects

Since the sin and cos functions graph as waves, you might be wondering whether you can take advantage of that to arrange elements in a wave pattern. Easier done than said! Well, almost.

### 9.3.1 Arranging elements along a wave path

You learned earlier (refer to section 9.1.1) that `y = sin(θ)` graphs to a smooth, repeating wave. You can modify that wave in two main ways:

- *Modify the amplitude*—The *amplitude* of the curve is the maximum vertical offset from the horizontal axis. For the graph of sin on the unit circle, the amplitude is 1 because maxima occur at `sin(90°) = 1` and `sin(270°) = -1`. To increase the amplitude, multiply `a * sin(θ)` for `a > 1`; to decrease the amplitude, multiply `a * sin(θ)` for `0 < a < 1`.
- *Modify the frequency*—The *frequency* of the curve is a measure of how fast the sine wave cycles. To increase the frequency, multiply `sin(f * θ)` for `f > 1`; to decrease the frequency, multiply `sin(f * θ)` for `0 < f < 1`.

For example, suppose your company has a summer promotion coming up, and they want some text on the home page to tie in with that. Here's the text:

```
<div id="wave-text">ARE YOU READY TO MAKE WAVES?</div>
```

Your job is to arrange the letters of this text into a wave pattern. That essentially boils down to creating a vertical offset for each letter,

```
offset = a * sin(f * θ)
```

where

- `a` = amplitude
- `f` = frequency

Figure 9.5 shows the result, and listing 9.6 provides the code behind this effect.

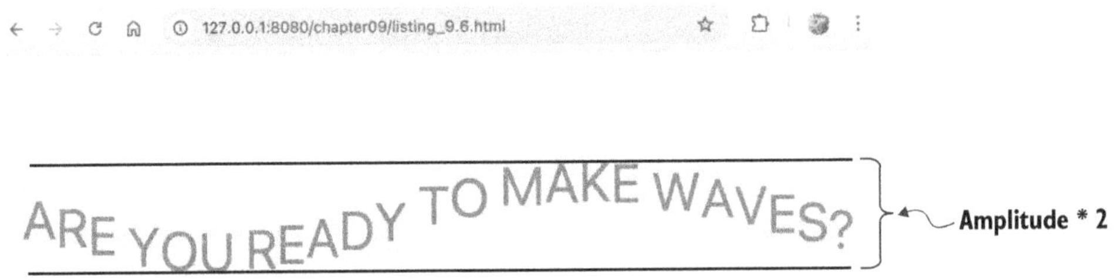


**Figure 9.5 Arranging letters along a wave path using sin**

**Listing 9.6 Arranging letters along a wave shape**

```
const textElement = document.getElementById('wave-text');
const text = textElement.textContent;
textElement.textContent = '';

const letters = text.split('').map(char => {
    const span = document.createElement('span');
    span.textContent = char === ' ' ? '\u00A0' : char;
    span.classList.add('letter');
    textElement.appendChild(span);
    return span;
});

const amplitude = 30;
const frequency = 0.25;

letters.forEach((letter, index) => {
    const offset = amplitude *
                   Math.sin(frequency * index);
    letter.style.transform = `translateY(${offset}px)`;
});
```

Annotations: Gets the text and clears the element; Splits the text into letter spans; Sets up the sine wave parameters; Modifies the amplitude; Modifies the frequency; Applies the transform

This code splits the text by letter and loads each letter into its own `span` element. The collection is stored in the `letters` array. The `amplitude` and `frequency` values are then set, and the `forEach()` loop iterates through the letters, generating an `offset` value calculated by `Math.sin()` and modified by the `amplitude` and `frequency` values.

### 9.3.2 Animating elements with a wave effect

Your boss loves the wavy letters but feels that the page needs more oomph in the form of having the letters animated with a wave effect. This feature requires a slightly different kind of vertical offset:

$$\text{offset} = a \times \sin(ft + \phi)$$

where

- $a$ = amplitude
- $f$ = frequency
- $t$ = time
- $\varphi$ = phase shift (offset between letters)

The phase shift makes each letter animate slightly out of sync, which gives the effect a more realistic feel. The following listing shows the JavaScript function that animates the letters in this way.

**Listing 9.7 Animating letters with a wave effect**

```
function waveText(letters, amplitude, frequency) {
    let time = 0;

    function animate() {
        time += 0.25;                                      ← Time controls the frequency.
        letters.forEach((letter, index) => {               ← Iterates through the letters
            const offset = amplitude *                     ← Modifies amplitude
➥ Math.sin(time * frequency + index * 0.5);              ← Modifies frequency based
            letter.style.transform =                         on time, with a phase shift
➥ `translateY(${offset}px)`;                             ← Sets the new position
        });
        requestAnimationFrame(animate);                    ← Requests the next frame
    }

    animate();
}

--snip--

waveText(letters, 20, 0.3);                                ← Launches the animation
```

`waveText()` takes the `letters` array (the code for creating this array is the same as in listing 9.6), an `amplitude` value, and a `frequency` value. The function iterates through `letters`, animating each with the `animate()` function, which calculates each letter's new position using the equation `a * sin(ft + φ)`.

### 9.3.3 Animating an element with a pendulum effect

You can simulate a pendulum by using the following simplified equation of motion for a pendulum:

$$\theta(t) = \theta_{max} \times \cos(\omega t + \phi)$$

where

- $\theta(t)$ = angular displacement (in radians) at time t
- $\theta_{max}$ = maximum angular displacement (amplitude)
- $\omega$ = angular frequency (oscillation speed)
- $\phi$ = phase shift

In other words, a pendulum's angle over time follows a cosine wave, so you can simulate a pendulum for a swinging sign by rotating an element back and forth using the `Math.cos()` function:

```
const swing = maxAngle * Math.cos(speed * t);
```

For example, suppose your page has the following element:

```
<div class="swing" id="pendulum">Swing Into Summer!</div>
```

The following listing shows the JavaScript code that swings the `div` back and forth in a pendulum motion.

**Listing 9.8 Animating an element with a pendulum effect**

```
const pendulumElement = document.getElementById("pendulum");
const maxAngle = 45 * Math.PI / 180;        // 45 degrees maximum swing
const speed = 1.5;                          // Oscillation speed
const pivotX = window.innerWidth / 2;       // Pivot point
const pivotY = 0;
const amplitude = 200;

let t = 0;

function animate() {
    t += 0.02;                              // Time factor

    // Calculate the current swing angle using cosine for pendulum motion
    const currentAngle = maxAngle * Math.cos(speed * t);    // The pendulum equation

    // Calculate the bob position at the end of the string
    const bobX = pivotX +
                 amplitude * Math.sin(currentAngle);
    const bobY = pivotY +
                 amplitude * Math.cos(currentAngle);
    // Calculates element position at end of pendulum
```

```
    pendulumElement.style.left = `${bobX}px`;
    pendulumElement.style.top = `${bobY}px`;     Sets the new position

    requestAnimationFrame(animate);   ◄── Requests the next frame
}

animate();  ◄── Starts the animation
```

This code sets up the maximum angle, the speed, the position of the pivot point, and the initial time. Then the `animate()` function uses the cosine equation of motion for a pendulum to set the new angle (`currentAngle`), which is then used to calculate the position of the bob (i.e., the element) at the end of the pendulum.

**EXERCISE**

**Exercise 9.5:** Modify the code in listing 9.8 to show a rod running from the pivot point to the top-center of the bob (the `div` element) and that swings along with the bob (picture the swinging pendulum in a grandfather clock). Here's the HTML to get you started:

```
<div class="pendulum-rod" id="rod"></div>
```

And here's the CSS:

```
.pendulum-rod {
    position: absolute;
    width: 2px;
    background-color: #666;
    transform-origin: top center;
}
```

Hint: The length of the rod is the same as the pendulum's amplitude.

## 9.4 Directional calculations

A common need in interactive UIs is to calculate an angle between two objects. For example, you might need to make an element point toward the cursor, rotate an arrow toward a particular element on the page, or in a game setting, have a character sprite rotate toward a target. This is where the JavaScript method `Math.atan2(y, x)` is your friend.

Imagine you have two points: a source (such as the center of a dial) and a target (such as the mouse cursor position or another element's center). Let the source point be $(x1, y1)$ and the target point be $(x2, y2)$. To get the angle between them, you can use the following JavaScript function:

```
function getAngle(x1, y1, x2, y2) {
    const deltaY = y2 - y1;
    const deltaX = x2 - x1;
    const angleRadians = Math.atan2(deltaY, deltaX);
```

```
    const angleDegrees = angleRadians * (180 / Math.PI);

    return angleDegrees;
}
```

Now you have the angle in degrees. If the function return value is stored in a variable named `angleDeg`, you can apply this to rotate the source element:

```
element.style.transform = `rotate(${angleDeg}deg)`;
```

And the source is now rotated to face the target.

The use of `atan2` ensures the angle is correct in all quadrants. For example, suppose both `deltaX` and `deltaY` are equal to `-1`, which you can interpret to mean that the target is down and to the left of the source. If you used `Math.atan(deltaX / deltaY)`, you'd get,

```
Math.atan(deltaX / deltaY)
= Math.atan(-1 / -1)
= Math.atan(1)
= 45 degrees
```

In other words, regular `atan` thinks the angle is up and to the left! By contrast, `atan2` preserves the signs of the deltas and gets the correct angle:

```
Math.atan2(deltaY, deltaX)
= Math.atan2(-1, -1)
= -135 degrees
```

Using `atan2` for directional calculations is useful for things such as rotating arrows or pointers, making eyes or cameras follow the cursor, drag-and-drop where an element rotates according to move direction, or calculating the sweep of an arc. In canvas drawings or games, you'd use `atan2` to point bullets or to find the angle between two objects. In UI, you might use it for something like a knob the user can drag around: you take the mouse position relative to the knob center, compute `atan2`, and set the knob's rotation accordingly. Another example is determining the angle between two DOM elements to draw a connecting line at the correct angle.

Okay, let's put it all to work by building a simple page with an arrow that always points to the mouse cursor. You'll learn about capturing the mouse cursor position in chapter 13, but for now, I can tell you that when you implement a `mousemove` event listener, the `Event` object returns the current position of the cursor as the point `(clientX, clientY)`. Given any element on the page, you can use `getBoundingClientRect()` to determine its center point. The element center is the source point, and the cursor position is the target point, so now it's just a matter of using `Math.atan2()` and the earlier `getAngle()` function to get the angle between them. Figure 9.6 shows the result, and listing 9.9 shows how it was done.

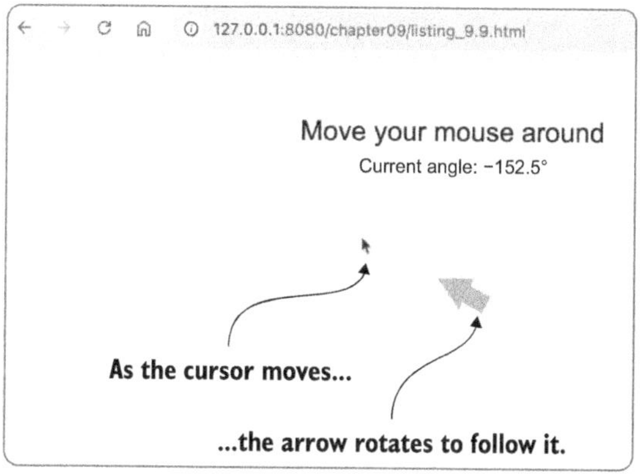


**Figure 9.6 Using `Math.atan2()` to get the arrow to follow the cursor**

**Listing 9.9 Rotating an element to always face the cursor**

```
function pointAtCursor(element) {
    let prevAngle = null;                                    // Tracks previous raw angle (−180..180)
    let rotation = 0;                                        // Tracks continuous rotation (can exceed 360)
    document.addEventListener('mousemove', (e) => {          // Listens for the mousemove event
        const rect = element.getBoundingClientRect();
        const elCenterX = rect.left + rect.width / 2;        // Calculate element center
        const elCenterY = rect.top + rect.height / 2;

        const angle = getAngle(elCenterX, elCenterY,
                               e.clientX, e.clientY);        // Gets angle between element and cursor

    if (prevAngle === null) {
        rotation = angle;
    } else {
        let delta = angle - prevAngle;
        if (delta > 180) delta -= 360;                       // Handle sign change
        if (delta < -180) delta += 360;
        rotation += delta;
    }
    prevAngle = angle;

        element.style.transform = `rotate(${degrees}deg)`;   // Rotates the arrow
        document.querySelector('.angle-output').textContent =
            `Current angle: ${degrees.toFixed(1)}°`;         // Displays the angle
    });
}

const arrow = document.getElementById('pointer');
pointAtCursor(arrow);                                        // Initializes arrow to point at cursor
```

With `clientX`, `clientY` for the mouse and known coordinates for the arrow's center, the code passes the values to the `getAngle()` function (shown earlier), then it applies `transform: rotate()` to turn the arrow to the cursor position. This happens each time the mouse moves, so the arrow will rotate smoothly, following the cursor.

**EXERCISE**

**Exercise 9.6:** In figure 9.6, notice that even though the cursor is above and to the left of the arrow, the displayed angle is negative. Why?

## 9.5 Solutions to exercises

**Exercise 9.1:** The angle 270° is vertical, so it's asymptotic for tan. Therefore, the correct answer is 4, undefined.

**Exercise 9.2:** Use the following formula to convert degrees to radians:

```
radians = degrees * (π / 180)
        = 135 * (π / 180)
        = 135 * (3.14159 / 180)
        = 3 * (3.14159 / 4)
        = 2.356
```

As the second-last line of the calculation shows, 135° is equivalent to $3\pi/4$ radians. This makes intuitive sense because the angle 135° is midway between 90° ($\pi/2$) and 180° ($\pi$).

**Exercise 9.3:** Here's a revised version of the `animate()` function from listing 9.3 that causes the element to spiral inward and then stop when the `radius` value hits `0`:

```
function animate() {
    angle += speed;
    radius += -0.25;                          // Decrements the radius in each frame
    if (radius <= 0) {                        // Is radius now <= 0?
        cancelAnimationFrame(animationId);    // If so, cancel the
        return;                               // animation and return.
    }
    const x = centerX + radius * Math.cos(angle);
    const y = centerY + radius * Math.sin(angle);

    element.style.transform = `translate(${x}px, ${y}px)`;

    animationId = requestAnimationFrame(animate);   // Need to save the animation ID to cancel it
}
```

**Exercise 9.4:** Here's the revised `animateInACircle()` function:

```
function animateInACircle(element, centerX, centerY,
                          radiusX, radiusY,      // Function now accepts radiusX
                          speed) {               // and radiusY arguments
    let angle = 0;

    function animate() {
        angle += speed;
        const x = centerX + radiusX * Math.cos(angle);   // Math.cos() now multiplied by radiusX
        const y = centerY + radiusY * Math.sin(angle);   // Math.sin() now multiplied by radius
```

```
        element.style.transform = `translate(${x}px, ${y}px)`;

        const animationId = requestAnimationFrame(animate);
    }

    animate();
}
```

**Exercise 9.5:** The JavaScript code in listing 9.8 requires just two modifications to show a rod running from the pivot point to the top-center of the bob and swings along with the bob. First, you get a reference to the rod element:

```
const rodElement = document.getElementById("rod");
```

Then, in the `animate()` function, you update the position of the rod as follows:

```
rodElement.style.left = `${pivotX}px`;
rodElement.style.top = `${pivotY}px`;
rodElement.style.height = `${amplitude}px`;
rodElement.style.transform = `rotate(${-currentAngle}rad)`;
```

**Exercise 9.6:** The negative angle happens because of how browser coordinates work.

In the browser coordinate system, the origin (0,0) is at the top-left corner, which means that *x* increases to the right (positive direction) and *y* increases downward (positive direction). So when the cursor is above (negative direction) and to the left (negative direction) of the arrow, both deltas are negative, and the angle is negative.

## Summary

- Trigonometry deals with the relationships that exist within a triangle, particularly a right-angled triangle, where one of the angles is 90 degrees.
- The sine is the opposite over the hypotenuse, so it's a measure of the vertical component of the angle.
- The cosine is the adjacent over the hypotenuse, so it's a measure of the horizontal component of the angle.
- The tangent is the opposite over the adjacent, so it's a measure of the steepness of the angle.
- The values of $\cos(\theta)$ and $\sin(\theta)$ oscillate smoothly within the range $[-1, 1]$, so that when you graph $\sin(\theta)$ or $\cos(\theta)$, the result is a regular, repeating wave pattern.
- To convert from degrees to radians, use `degrees * (Math.PI / 180)`. To convert from radians to degrees, use `radians * (180 / Math.PI)`.
- There are seven main trig functions—`sin()`, `cos()`, `tan()`, `asin()`, `acos()`, `atan()`, and `atan2()`—available in both CSS and JavaScript. The JavaScript versions are methods of the `Math` object (`Math.sin()`, `Math.cos()`, etc.).

- You can use sin and cos to arrange page elements along a circle. For a circle with radius `r` centered at the point (`centerX`, `centerY`), for any angle, you calculate the *x*- and *y*-coordinates of that point on the circle using `x = centerX + r * cos(angle)` and `y = centerY + r * sin(angle)`.
- The trig functions are useful for arranging page elements along a curved path. Multiply cos or sin to modify the amplitude of the curve, which is the maximum vertical offset from the horizontal axis. Multiply the angle to modify the frequency, which is a measure of how fast the wave cycles.
- When working with directional calculations, use `atan2` to ensure the angle is correct in all quadrants.

# 10 Vectors and geometry in UI design

**This chapter covers**

- The fundamentals of vectors and geometry in web dev
- Using geometry to manipulate the DOM
- Working with vectors in JavaScript
- Creating sophisticated geometric shapes and animations in CSS

When you examine a web page from the perspective of a frontend web developer or designer, you know that underneath that surface is a bunch of HTML tags, CSS rules, and JavaScript statements. But below all that code, there's another, even more fundamental layer: the math that makes the code work. In particular, modern web browsers use concepts from vectors and geometry to position elements, rotate and scale graphics, animate UI components, and define shapes for layouts.

## 10.1 Mathematical foundations: Points, vectors, and bounding boxes

For the rest of this chapter to make sense, and for you to use its concepts and examples to improve your own web page code, there are a few basics about vectors and geometry you need to know. I'm going to keep things relatively simple by focusing on 2D geometry here since most web content is laid out on a flat (two-dimensional) plane (your browser window). Here are the key concepts you'll need for this chapter:

- *Points and coordinates*—A point is a single location in 2D space. Web development often uses (*x*, *y*) coordinates to describe a point's position on the page. The browser uses a coordinate system with an origin at the top-left corner of a container (for the page overall, the origin is the top-left of the viewport). A point's *x*-coordinate increases to the right, and its *y*-coordinate increases downward. In other words, (0, 0) is the top-left, and (100, 150) would be a point `100px` to the right and `150px` down from the origin. All window coordinates in the DOM are measured from the top-left corner.
- *Vector*—Unlike regular numbers that only represent magnitude, vectors represent both magnitude and direction, which makes them perfect for describing element movement, positioning, and transformations within the document. Think of vectors as instructions for element movement. Instead of saying something vague such as "move that element five pixels" (which direction?), you say "move that element right three pixels and up four pixels." This precision becomes crucial when creating smooth animations and element relationships, or positioning elements dynamically in response to user interactions.
- *Vector values*—A vector in 2D is basically a pair of numbers [*x*, *y*], where *x* is called the *abscissa,* and *y* is called the *ordinate.* They represent a direction and distance. You can think of a vector as an arrow from one point to another, or simply as an offset. For example, the vector [50, 20] essentially means "move `50px` to the right and `20px` down." In code, you might represent this as an array or object with *x* and *y* key–value pairs. Vector values enable you to code movement and position changes. If you have a starting point at, say, (100, 100) and you add a vector [50, 20], you end up at (150, 120). This addition is just adding $x_1$ to $x_2$ and $y_1$ to $y_2$. In fact, much of what CSS and JavaScript do for positioning is essentially adding or modifying vectors behind the scenes.

**NOTE** Don't confuse the point (*x*, *y*) with the vector [*x*, *y*]. A point (*x*, *y*) represents a location in space, whereas a vector [*x*, *y*] represents a direction and a magnitude, like an arrow pointing somewhere. A point is where something is; a vector is how something moves.

- *Vector magnitude*—Vectors have a length, also called *magnitude.* This is the straight-line distance the vector covers. If a vector is [*x*, *y*], its magnitude is given by the Pythagorean formula: `magnitude =` $\sqrt{x^2 + y^2}$. For example, a vector [3, 4] has length 5, because $\sqrt{3^2 + 4^2} = \sqrt{9 + 16} = \sqrt{25} = 5$. The magnitude tells you how far the vector moves in total. This concept is useful if you need to know a distance (e.g., how far an element moved).

- *Vector direction*—Besides magnitude, a vector has a direction, expressed as an angle. For example, a vector pointing directly to the right is at 0° (or 0 radians) relative to the horizontal, and a vector pointing straight down is at 90°. In web terms, 0° usually means pointing parallel to the positive *x*-axis (rightward), and angles increase clockwise (because *y*-axis values increase downward). An angle of 45° would point down and to the right. You can get the angle of a vector [*x*, *y*] using `Math.atan2(y, x)` in JavaScript (which returns radians) or `atan2(y, x)` in CSS (which returns degrees). Conversely, if you have an angle θ and a length, you can get a vector via trigonometry:

  ```
  x = length * Math.cos(θ)
  y = length * Math.sin(θ)
  ```

  For example, a `100px` movement at `30°` from horizontal corresponds to `x = 100 * Math.cos(30°) = 86.6px` and `y = 100 * Math.sin(30°) = 50px`, so the resulting vector is [86.6, 50]. Refer to chapter 9 for information about cos, sin, atan2, and other trigonometric functions.
- *Line*—A straight, one-dimensional figure extending infinitely in both directions. A *line segment* is a portion of a line that connects two points. In web layout, you usually deal with line segments, which could be the edge of an element or a movement path. You can describe a line segment by referencing its two end points, but you can also reference one point and a direction vector. For example, an element moving from point A to point B traces a line segment; the vector from A to B describes that movement.
- *Bounding box*—A rectangle that encloses an element. A bounding box is typically described by the coordinates of its top-left corner (*x*, *y*) and its width and height. You can also think of this as one point plus a vector. For example, a rectangle can be defined by its top-left corner at (*x*, *y*) and a size vector (width, height) extending to the bottom-right. In JavaScript, the `getBoundingClientRect()` method gives an element's bounding box in terms of the coordinates, width, height (or equivalently left, top, right, bottom). Later, this chapter describes how to use these return values for layout calculations in JavaScript.

## 10.2 DOM geometry: Measuring and aligning elements with JavaScript

When it comes to positioning and aligning elements on the page, CSS is the usual technology of choice as it provides myriad tools for laying out elements. However, you might be required to calculate element positions, sizes, or alignments dynamically. For example, you might need to modify the layout based on user interaction. As with all things related to dynamic content in web dev, JavaScript is the way to go. And when it comes to geometric manipulations in the DOM, JavaScript offers an essential tool: the `getBoundingClientRect()` method for an element.

When you call `element.getBoundingClientRect()`, the method returns a `DomRect` (DOM rectangle) object with the following properties (refer to figure 10.1):

- `x`—The horizontal distance from the left edge of the viewport to the left edge of the element.
- `left`—Same as `x`.
- `y`—The vertical distance from the top edge of the viewport to the top edge of the element.
- `top`—The same as `y`.
- `right`—The horizontal distance from the left edge of the viewport to the right edge of the element.
- `bottom`—The vertical distance from the top edge of the viewport to the bottom edge of the element.
- `width`—The element's width. This value includes the element's horizontal padding and borders. If you're using `box-sizing: border-box`, then this value is the same as the value of the element's `width` property.
- `height`—The element's height. This value includes the element's vertical padding and borders. If you're using `box-sizing: border-box`, then this value is the same as the value of the element's `height` property.

Essentially, `getBoundingClientRect()` gives you the bounding box of the element in the viewport coordinate system. This method answers the question, "Where is this element right now, and how big is it?" This function is incredibly useful for moving or aligning elements in scripts.

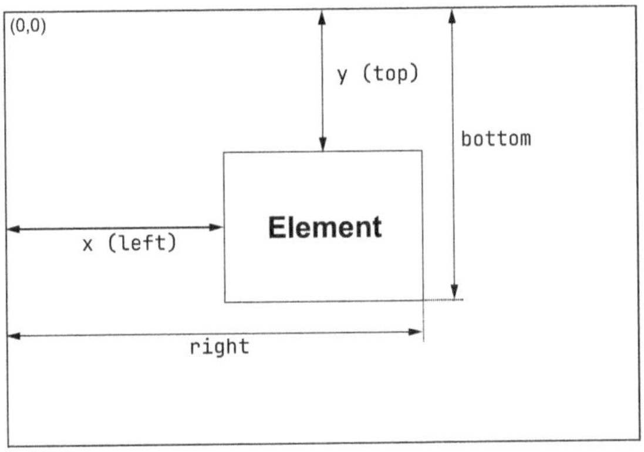


Figure 10.1 The return values of `getBoundingClientRect()`

### 10.2.1 Calculating the center point of an element

Perhaps the most common use for the data returned by `getBoundingClientRect()` is to determine the point $(x, y)$ that represents the exact center of the element:

```
x = (left + right) / 2
y = (top + bottom) / 2
```

or,

```
x = left + width / 2
y = top + height / 2
```

In code, you can do the following:

```
const myElement = document.querySelector('#my-element');
const rect = myElement.getBoundingClientRect();
const centerX = (rect.left + rect.right) / 2;
const centerY = (rect.top + rect.bottom) / 2;
```

Or, you can do this:

```
const myElement = document.querySelector('#my-element');
const rect = myElement.getBoundingClientRect();
const centerX = rect.left + rect.width / 2;
const centerY = rect.top + rect.height / 2;
```

Either way, the point (`centerX`, `centerY`) represents the exact center of the element in the viewport.

Having the center point in hand is useful if you want to align another element, such as a tooltip or an overlay, on that point (refer to section 10.2.2). In chapter 9, listing 9.9, the code that rotated an arrow to always face the cursor used the center point of the arrow to get the correct angle between the arrow and the cursor.

### 10.2.2 Aligning one element relative to another

A common UI requirement is to overlay a pop-up or tooltip over another element, such as a button, where the overlay element is perfectly centered over the button. Getting the bounding boxes of the two elements and applying a bit of math makes this a straightforward proposition. Specifically, you get the button's bounding box, the overlay's bounding box, then set the overlay's `left` and `top` properties to center it over the button. Figure 10.2 shows a button and a perfectly centered tooltip that appears when the user hovers the mouse over the button. To implement this pattern, use the code in listing 10.1.

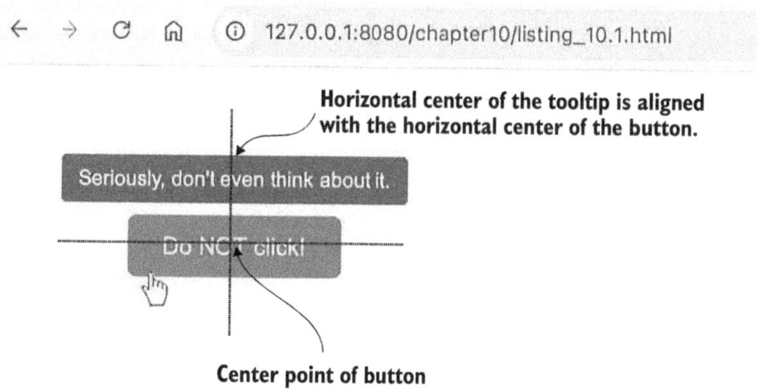


**Figure 10.2 A button with a perfectly centered tooltip**

**Listing 10.1 Perfectly centering a tooltip over a button**

HTML:

```
<button id="demoButton" class="demo-button">
    Do NOT click!
</button>

<div id="tooltip" class="tooltip">
    Seriously, don't even think about it.
</div>
```

CSS:

```
.tooltip {
    visibility: hidden;
}
.tooltip.visible {
    opacity: 1;
    visibility: visible;
}
```

JavaScript:

```
const button = document.getElementById('demoButton');
const tooltip = document.getElementById('tooltip');

function positionTooltip() {
    const buttonRect = button.getBoundingClientRect();      // Gets the bounding
    const tooltipRect = tooltip.getBoundingClientRect();    // box data

    const buttonCenterX = (buttonRect.left +
                          buttonRect.right) / 2;            // Horizontal center of button
    tooltip.style.left = buttonCenterX -
                         tooltipRect.width / 2 + 'px';      // Centers the tooltip

    tooltip.style.top = buttonRect.top -
                        tooltipRect.height - 8 + 'px';      // Positions tooltip above
                                                            // button with 8px margin
}

button.addEventListener('mouseenter', () => {
    tooltip.classList.add('visible');                       // Shows the tooltip
    positionTooltip();
});

button.addEventListener('mouseleave', () => {
    tooltip.classList.remove('visible');                    // Hides the tooltip
});
```

**NOTE** All the code for this chapter's listings is available in this book's GitHub repository: https://github.com/paulmcfe/web-dev-math.

This code uses `getBoundingClientRect()` to return the position and size of the button and the tooltip. The code determines the horizontal center (`buttonCenterX`) of the button, then centers the tooltip on that value with `buttonCenterX - tooltipRect .width / 2`. The tooltip is then placed vertically above the button with `buttonRect.top - tooltipRect.height - 8`, which gives an `8px` gap between them.

### 10.2.3 Geometric hover effects

You can use the goldmine of data returned by `getBoundingClientRect()` to achieve some eye-catching effects, all with a bit of geometry-based math, and with a little trig thrown in for the wow factor.

For example, suppose you're working on a card layout that uses CSS Grid for responsiveness but is lacking the pizzazz that the sales team is bugging your boss to add. You decide to add a rotation hover effect to each card, one where the degree of rotation varies with how close the mouse is to the center of the element. In figure 10.3 (a composite image), the top-left card shows the mouse pointer near the edge of the card for the full rotational effect, while the top-right card shows the mouse pointer closer to the center for a lesser effect. The implementation of this geometry-based hover effect is shown in listing 10.2.

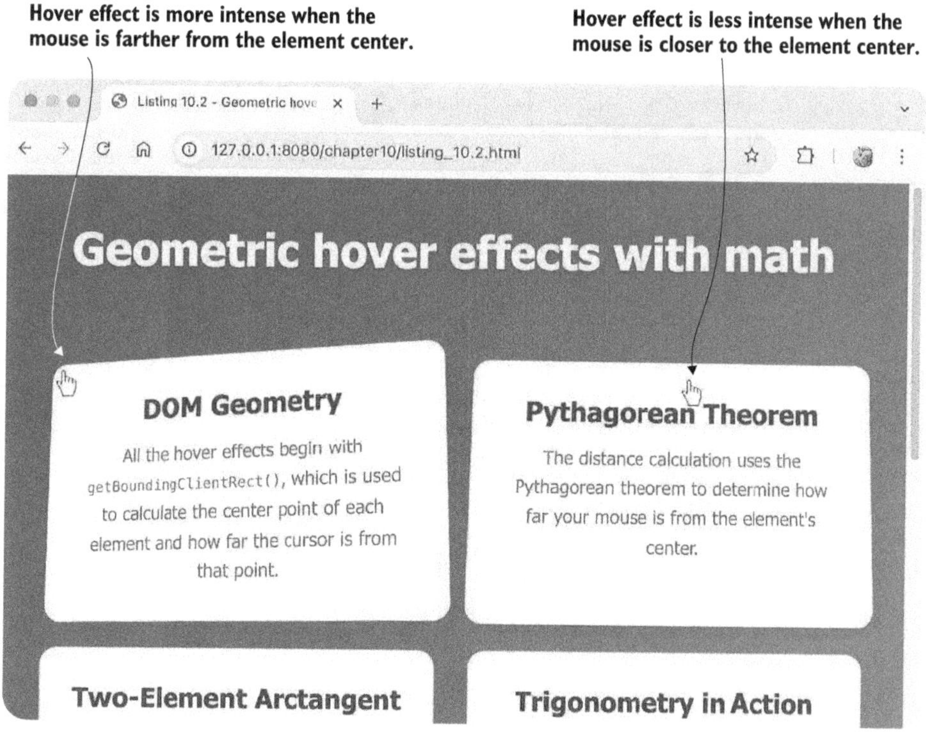


Figure 10.3 The farther the mouse from the center of the element, the more intense the hover effect

**Listing 10.2 Geometric hover effects**

```
class GeometricHoverEffect {
    constructor(element) {
        this.element = element;
        this.rect = element.getBoundingClientRect();    ◄── getBoundingClientRect() is the basis.
        this.setUpEventListeners();
        element.geometricHoverEffect = this;
    }

    setUpEventListeners() {
        this.element.addEventListener('mousemove', (event) => {
            this.handleMouseMove(event);    ◄── Calls handleMouseMove() on hover
        });

        this.element.addEventListener('mouseleave', () => {
            this.reset();    ◄── Calls reset() when mouse leaves
        });
    }

    handleMouseMove(event) {
        const centerX = this.rect.left +
                        this.rect.width / 2;
        const centerY = this.rect.top +
                        this.rect.height / 2;

        const mouseX = event.clientX - centerX;
        const mouseY = event.clientY - centerY;
        // Calculates mouse position relative to element center

        const angle = Math.atan2(mouseY, mouseX);    ◄── Calculates angle with atan2
        const distance = Math.sqrt(mouseX * mouseX +
                                   mouseY * mouseY);
        // Calculates distance with Pythagorean theorem
        const maxDistance = Math.sqrt(
            (this.rect.width / 2) ** 2 +
            (this.rect.height / 2) ** 2
        );
        // Calculates max possible distance from center

        const tiltIntensity = Math.min(distance /
                                 maxDistance, 1) * 20;
        const rotationX = Math.sin(angle) *
                          tiltIntensity;
        const rotationY = Math.cos(angle) *
                          tiltIntensity;
        // Calculates geometric transformation based on mouse position

        this.element.style.transform = `
            perspective(1000px)
            rotateX(${-rotationX}deg)
            rotateY(${rotationY}deg)
            scale(${1 + distance / maxDistance * 0.05})
        `;
        // Adds the transformation
    }

    reset() {
        this.element.style.transform = 'perspective(1000px)
                                         rotateX(0deg)
```

```
                                        rotateY(0deg)
                                        scale(1)';
    }

    updateRect() {
        this.rect = this.element.getBoundingClientRect();
    }
}

document.querySelectorAll('.geometric-hover')
        .forEach(element => {
            new GeometricHoverEffect(element);
});

window.addEventListener('resize', () => {.
    document.querySelectorAll('.geometric-hover').forEach(element => {
        if (element.geometricHoverEffect) {
            element.geometricHoverEffect.updateRect();
        }
    });
});
```

Applies effect to elements

Updates element rectangles on window resize

To make it easy to apply the hover effect on multiple elements, this code creates a `GeometricHoverEffect` class that has two attributes: the element (`element`) and the `DomRect` object (`rect`) returned by `getBoundingClientRect()`. Here's a summary of the math used in the `handleMouseMove()` function:

- The element's center point (`centerX`, `centerY`) is calculated from the `rect` object's `left`, `width`, `top`, and `height` properties.
- The mouse position (`mouseX`, `mouseY`) relative to the element center is calculated using `event.clientX - centerX` and `event.clientY - centerY`.
- The angle (`angle`) between the element center and the mouse pointer is calculated using the two-element arctan: `Math.atan2(mouseY, mouseX)`.
- The distance (`distance`) between the element center and the mouse is calculated using the Pythagorean theorem: `Math.sqrt(mouseX * mouseX + mouseY * mouseY)`.
- The Pythagorean theorem is used again to calculate the maximum distance (`maxDistance`) the mouse pointer can be from the element center: `Math.sqrt((this.rect.width / 2) ** 2 + (this.rect.height / 2) ** 2)`.
- The intensity of the rotation (`tiltIntensity`) is calculated using `(distance / maxDistance) * 20`. This is a scaling factor that increases as the mouse moves farther from the element center.
- The horizontal (`rotationX`) and vertical (`rotationY`) rotation values are calculated with `Math.cos()` and `Math.sin()`, respectively, and multiplied by the `tiltIntensity` scaling factor.
- A subtle zoom effect is applied using `scale(${1 + distance / maxDistance * 0.05})`. The `scale` value is 1 at the center (where `distance = 0`, so `1 + distance`

`/ maxDistance * 0.05 = 1 + 0 / maxDistance * 0.05 = 1 + 0 * 0.05 = 1`), and rises to `1.05` at the edge (where `distance = maxDistance`, so `1 + distance / maxDistance * 0.05 = 1 + 1 * 0.05 = 1.05`).

### 10.2.4 Parallax scrolling with geometric precision

*Parallax scrolling* refers to background or layered content moving at different speeds to create a depth effect while scrolling. A classic example is the background image that moves slower than the foreground content, which makes it seem distant. This effect is essentially about moving things in proportion to the scroll offset, often using a scaled-down vector of the scroll movement.

One way to implement parallax scrolling is to provide each background element and content section with a `data-parallax` attribute set to a value in the range (0, 1), where values under 0.5 move faster during scrolling, and values over 0.5 move slower. Here's an example:

```
<div class="content-wrapper" data-parallax="0.85">
```

To simplify working with so many elements, you can set up a class for the effect:

```
class GeometricParallax {
    constructor() {
        this.layers = this.initializeLayers();
        this.setUpEventListeners();
        this.isScrolling = false;
    }
    --snip--
}

// Initialize parallax system with safety checks
document.addEventListener('DOMContentLoaded', () => {
    const parallax = new GeometricParallax();
});
```

Within that class, for each element that uses the `data-parallax` attribute, you create an array of layers, a scroll event listener, and a function for updating the parallax effect, all shown in listing 10.3.

> **WARNING** Parallax scrolling can create problems for people with vestibular problems and is also tough to implement on mobile interfaces. When you examine the full code for listing 10.3, you'll notice that I include code that shuts off parallax scrolling for users who have the `prefers-reduced-motion: reduce` media query set, and it also implements parallax scrolling only on larger screens.

**Listing 10.3 Geometric parallax scrolling**

```
initializeLayers() {
    return Array.from(document
```

```
        .querySelectorAll('[data-parallax]'))        ◄── Gets all elements with
                                                          data-parallax attribute
        .map(element => {
            const depth = parseFloat(element.dataset
                          .parallax) || 1;                  Extracts attribute value
            const rect = element.getBoundingClientRect();  ◄── Gets element's
                                                                bounding box
            return {
              element: element,
              depth: depth,
              initialY: rect.top + window.scrollY,        Gets element's initial
              initialX: rect.left                          top-left point
          };
      });
}

setUpEventListeners() {
    window.addEventListener('scroll', () => {   ◄── Listens for scrolling
        if (!this.isScrolling) {
            requestAnimationFrame(() => {          Updates parallax on scroll
                this.updateParallax();
                this.isScrolling = false;
            });
            this.isScrolling = true;
        }
    }, { passive: true });
}

updateParallax() {                                 How much has
    const scrollTop = window.scrollY;          ◄── the page scrolled?
    const windowHeight = window.innerHeight;   ◄── Gets the window height

    this.layers.forEach(layer => {
        const elementTop = layer.initialY - scrollTop;
        const elementBottom = elementTop +                Calculates element's
                              layer.element.offsetHeight;  current top and bottom

        if (elementBottom >= -windowHeight &&      Only animates elements in
            elementTop <= windowHeight * 2) {      or near viewport

            const parallaxOffset = scrollTop *         Calculates parallax
                                   (1 - layer.depth);  offset based on depth

            let transform = `translate3d(0, ${parallaxOffset}px, 0)`;
            layer.element.style.transform = transform;
        }
    });                                                 Applies the transform
}
```

The `initializeLayers()` function returns an array of all the elements with the `data-parallax` attribute, where each array item is an object that includes the element (`element`), the element's `data-parallax` value (`depth`), and the element's initial top-left corner (`initialX`, `initialY`), which is determined via `getBoundingClientRect()`.

The `setUpEventListeners()` function creates a listener for the `scroll` event that, when fired, calls the `updateParallax()` function (throttled via the `requestAnimationFrame()` method).

The `updateParallax()` function determines how much the page has been scrolled (`scrollTop`), gets the window height, then runs through each layer. The loop calculates the layer's top and bottom, makes sure the element is within the viewport, then runs the fundamental parallax calculation:

```
const parallaxOffset = scrollTop * (1 - layer.depth);
```

From this expression, you can understand why smaller `depth` values result in a faster parallax effect. Finally, the element's `transform` property is updated with `translate3d()` based on the value of `parallaxOffset`.

**EXERCISES**

**Exercise 10.1:** Which of the following is *not* a property returned by the `getBoundingClientRect()` method?

1. `y`
2. `bottom`
3. `center`
4. `height`

**Exercise 10.2:** Modify the `positionTooltip()` JavaScript code in listing 10.1 so that the tooltip is aligned with the bottom-right corner of the button.

## 10.3 Manipulating vectors in JavaScript

Basic vector arithmetic directly translates to common DOM manipulation tasks. For example, vector addition involves movements down and to the right. If an element moves right 3 pixels and down 4 pixels in one animation frame and right 1 pixel and down 2 pixels in the next, the total movement is right 4 pixels and down 6 pixels:

```
[3, 4] + [1, 2] = [3 + 1, 4 + 2] = [4, 6]
```

Vector subtraction is similar:

```
[10, 15] - [5, 10] = [10 - 5, 15 - 10] = [5, 5]
```

And vector multiplication is used to scale the vector:

```
[100, 200] * 2 = [100 * 2, 200 * 2] = [200, 400]
[100, 200] * 0.5 = [100 * 0.5, 200 * 0.5] = [50, 100]
```

These basic arithmetic operations make vectors ideal for cumulative transformations and smooth animations.

### 10.3.1 Essential vector operations for DOM developers

If you're going to be working with vectors a lot in your JavaScript code, it helps to set up a class that includes all the essential operations you can perform on a vector:

```
class Vector2 {
    constructor(x = 0, y = 0) {           ← Constructor defaults to [0, 0].
        this.x = x;
        this.y = y;
    }
    add(vector) {
        return new Vector2(this.x + vector.x, this.y + vector.y);
    }
    subtract(vector) {
        return new Vector2(this.x - vector.x, this.y - vector.y);
    }
    multiply(scalar) {
        return new Vector2(this.x * scalar, this.y * scalar);
    }
    magnitude() {
        return Math.sqrt(this.x * this.x + this.y * this.y);
    }
    normalize() {                          ← Creates a unit vector
        const mag = this.magnitude();
        return mag > 0 ? new Vector2(this.x / mag, this.y / mag) :
                         new Vector2(0, 0);
    }
    clone() {
        return new Vector2(this.x, this.y);
    }
    toCSSTranslate() {
        return `translate(${this.x}px, ${this.y}px)`;   ← Converts vector to CSS translate string
    }
}
```

Vector normalization creates a unit vector with magnitude 1 that preserves the vector direction, while standardizing the magnitude. Normalized vectors are commonly used for directional calculations, such as determining which way an element should move, calculating perpendicular directions, or creating consistent movement speeds regardless of target distance (refer to section 10.3.3 for an example).

### 10.3.2 Using vectors to have an element follow the mouse

A simple demonstration of the power of vectors is to have an element follow along with the mouse, as shown in figure 10.4. This is basically a matter of determining the current mouse position, adding an offset vector, and then applying that vector to the follower element. You begin with the HTML:

```
<div id="demoArea">
    <div class="follower"></div>
</div>
```

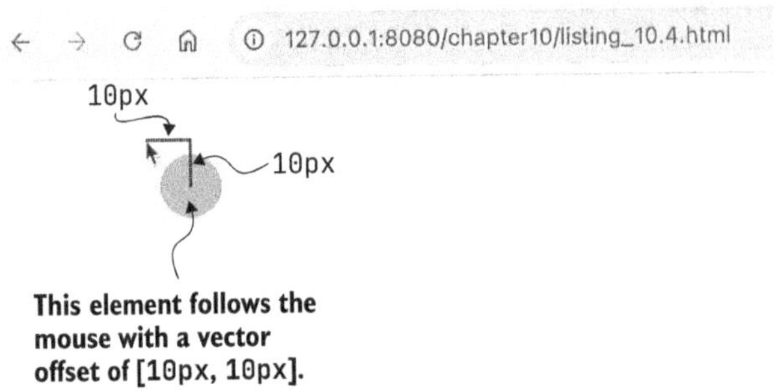


Figure 10.4 The dot follows the mouse with an offset of [10px, 10px].

From there, you implement the follow-the-mouse behavior using the JavaScript code in the following listing.

**Listing 10.4 Having an element follow the mouse**

```
const demoArea = document.getElementById('demoArea');
const follower = document.querySelector('.follower');
const offset = new Vector2(10, 10);    // Vector to offset the element from the mouse

demoArea.addEventListener('mousemove', event => {    // Listens for mouse moves
    const rect = demoArea.getBoundingClientRect();    // Gets the demoArea bounding box
    const mousePos = new Vector2(
        event.clientX - rect.left,
        event.clientY - rect.top
    );    // Gets a vector for the mouse position within demoArea

    const newPos = mousePos.add(offset);    // Adds the offset vector
    follower.style.transform = newPos.toCSSTranslate();    // Uses the vector to translate the follower element
});
```

This code uses three vectors: `offset` is a [10, 10] vector that specifies the horizontal and vertical offset of the `follower` element, `mousePos` is a vector that specifies the mouse position within the `demoArea` element, and `newPos` is a vector created by adding `offset` to `mousePos`. Each time the `mousemove` event fires, the `follower` element uses the `newPos` vector to translate to its new position relative to the mouse.

### 10.3.3 Animating an element to a mouse-click position using vectors

A slightly more advanced example of vector manipulation with JavaScript is to have an element animate to the spot where the mouse was clicked. You begin with some HTML and CSS:

HTML:

```
<div class="chaser"></div>
```

CSS:

```
.chaser {
    position: absolute;
    width: 30px;
    height: 30px;
    background: hsl(84 74% 44%);
    border-radius: 50%;
    transform: translate(0, 0);
    will-change: transform;
}
```

This code creates a circle with diameter `30px`. As illustrated in figure 10.5, clicking anywhere within the viewport causes the `.chaser` element to animate to the click point. Listing 10.5 shows how to implement this effect using vector operations in JavaScript.

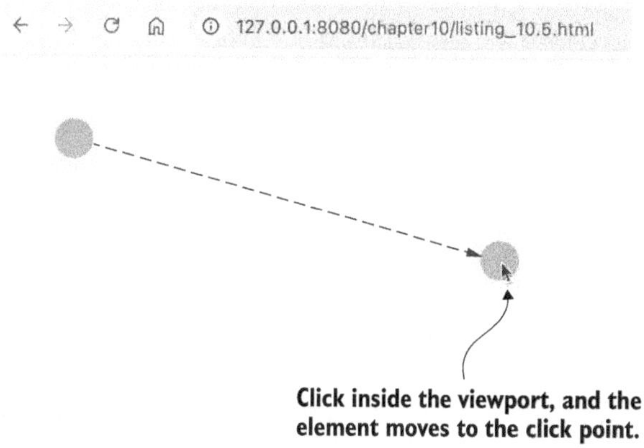


**Figure 10.5** Click inside the viewport, and the chaser dot animates to the click point.

**Listing 10.5 Animating an element to the click point with vectors**

```
const chaserEl = document.querySelector('.chaser');
let position = new Vector2(50, 50);
chaserEl.style.transform = position.toCSSTranslate();
let target;

document.addEventListener('click', e => {
    target = new Vector2(e.clientX - 15, e.clientY - 15);
    animate();
});

const SPEED = 10;

function animate() {
    const toTarget = target.subtract(position);
    const dist = toTarget.magnitude();
```

Initializes the chaser position

Listens for clicks

Creates target vector at click point

Starts animation

Moves 10px per frame toward target

Creates vector from chaser to target

Calculates distance

```
    if (dist > SPEED) {
        const step = toTarget.normalize().multiply(SPEED);
        position = position.add(step);
        chaserEl.style.transform = position.toCSSTranslate();
        requestAnimationFrame(animate);
    } else if (dist > 0) {
        position = target.clone();
        chaserEl.style.transform = position.toCSSTranslate();
    }
}
```

Moves SPEED pixels toward the target

Snaps exactly to the target

Here's a summary of all the vector operations happening in this short piece of code:

- The `.chaser` element's initial position (`position`) is set with `new Vector2(50, 50)`.
- The click point (`target`) vector is set with `new Vector2(e.clientX - 15, e.clientY - 15)`. (Refer to exercise 10.3 to consider why `15` is subtracted from both the *x* and *y* component of this vector.)
- The vector from the `.chaser` element to the click point (`toTarget`) is set using the `subtract` method of the `Vector2` class: `toTarget = target.subtract(position)`.
- The distance (`dist`) from the element to the click point is calculated using the `magnitude` method of the `Vector2` class: `dist = toTarget.magnitude()`.
- Each step of the animation (`step`) is derived by normalizing the `toTarget` vector (using the `normalize` method of the `Vector2` class), then multiplying (using the `multiply` method of the `Vector2` class) that unit vector by the `SPEED` variable: `step = toTarget.normalize().multiply(SPEED)`.
- The element is moved toward the target using the `add` method of the `Vector2` class: `position = position.add(step)`.
- The new position is applied using a CSS transform via the `toCSSTranslate` method of the `Vector2` class.
- When the element is less than `SPEED` pixels from the target, the code for the final frame of the animation snaps the element to the target by cloning the target (using the `clone` method of the `Vector2` class) and then translating the element to that final position.

### 10.3.4 Dragging with geometric constraints

A common UI pattern is allowing an element to be dragged, but only within a specified area. If that area is a figure such as a square, rectangle, or circle, then it's called a *geometric constraint*. Suppose you're part of a team building a web-based game that will involve dragging elements to different parts of the game board. It's important that the user not be able to drag any elements outside of the board's edges, so assuming the board is rectangular, you have to create a geometric constraint for the drag behavior. Your task is to prototype this behavior with a rectangular page area and a draggable element.

You begin with some HTML and CSS:

HTML:

```
<div class="game-board" id="game-board">
    <div class="game-piece" id="game-piece"></div>
</div>
```

CSS:

```
.game-board {
    position: relative;
    width: 400px;
    height: 300px;
    border: 2px solid #888;
    background: #fff;
}
. game-piece {
    position: absolute;
    width: 50px;
    height: 50px;
    background: hsl(322, 100%, 31%);
    cursor: grab;
    transform: translate(0, 0);
}
. game-piece:active {
    cursor: grabbing;
}
```

The .game-board element is the rectangle constraint, and the .game-piece element is the square to be dragged. As illustrated in figure 10.6, you can drag the square anywhere within .game-board, but not beyond its borders. The implementation of this prototype uses a combination of vector manipulations and geometry, as shown in listing 10.6.

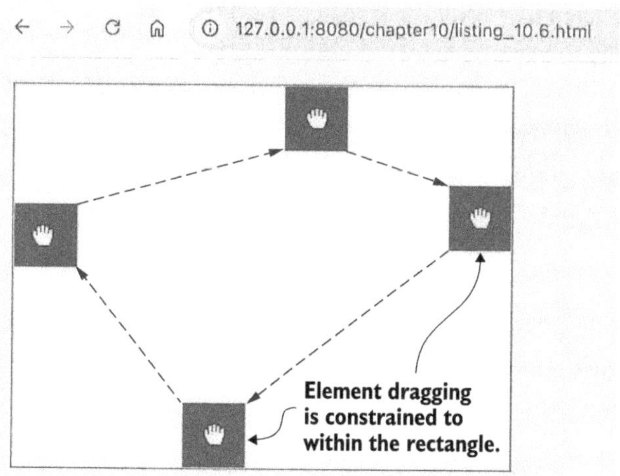


**Figure 10.6 You can drag the square anywhere within, but not outside of, the rectangular area.**

**Listing 10.6 Dragging with a geometric constraint**

```
const board = document.getElementById('game-board');
const piece = document.getElementById('game-piece');

const boardRect = board.getBoundingClientRect();    // Gets the bounding boxes
const pieceRect = piece.getBoundingClientRect();    // for the board and piece

const min = new Vector2(boardRect.left, boardRect.top);   // Minimum possible position is game board top-left.
const max = new Vector2(
  boardRect.left + boardRect.width - pieceRect.width - 4,
  boardRect.top + boardRect.height - pieceRect.height - 4
);   // Maximum possible position is game board bottom-right.

let dragging = false;
let pointerOffset;
let piecePos;

piece.addEventListener('mousedown', e => {   // Listens for the mouse being pressed
    dragging = true;
    const pieceRect = piece.getBoundingClientRect();
    const pieceTopLeft = new Vector2(pieceRect.left, pieceRect.top);
    const pointerPos = new Vector2(e.clientX, e.clientY);
    pointerOffset = pieceTopLeft.subtract(pointerPos);   // Calculates pointer offset from top-left of game piece
    document.body.style.cursor = 'grabbing';
});

window.addEventListener('mousemove', e => {   // Listens for the mouse moving
    if (!dragging) return;

    const pointerPos = new Vector2(e.clientX, e.clientY);   // Gets the new pointer position
    let reqPos = pointerPos.add(pointerOffset);   // Gets the piece position requested by the pointer

    reqPos.x = Math.min(Math.max(reqPos.x, min.x), max.x);   // Constrains the request
    reqPos.y = Math.min(Math.max(reqPos.y, min.y), max.y);   // to within the board's max and min

    piecePos = reqPos.subtract(new
              Vector2(boardRect.left, boardRect.top));   // Converts to a board-relative vector
    piece.style.transform = piecePos.toCSSTranslate();   // Moves the piece
});

window.addEventListener('mouseup', () => {
    if (dragging) {
        dragging = false;
        document.body.style.cursor = '';
    }
});
```

This code implements the geometric constraint of the rectangular game board by doing two things. First, it uses the following to set the vectors that represent the minimum and maximum board points:

```
const min = new Vector2(boardRect.left, boardRect.top);
const max = new Vector2(
```

```
  boardRect.left + boardRect.width - pieceRect.width - 4,
  boardRect.top + boardRect.height - pieceRect.height - 4
);
```

The `min` value is just the board's top-left corner. For the `max` value, you take the board's bottom-right value, subtract the width and height of the game piece, then subtract 4 (refer to exercise 10.4).

Second, the code uses the following to ensure the piece can't be dragged beyond the edges of the board:

```
const pointerPos = new Vector2(e.clientX, e.clientY);
let reqPos = pointerPos.add(pointerOffset);
reqPos.x = Math.min(Math.max(reqPos.x, min.x), max.x);
reqPos.y = Math.min(Math.max(reqPos.y, min.y), max.y);

piecePos = reqPos.subtract(new Vector2(boardRect.left, boardRect.top));
piece.style.transform = piecePos.toCSSTranslate();
```

As the pointer moves, it essentially says to the browser, "Okay, I've moved to a new position (`pointerPos`) and I'd like to request that this game piece I'm dragging be moved to my position (`pointerPos`) plus how much the piece's top-left corner is offset from me (`pointerOffset`)." That requested position for the piece (`reqPos`) might be outside of the game board, so the code performs a min/max check that brings the `reqPos` vector back within the bounds of the game board (if needed). That vector is expressed in viewport-relative units, so the code subtracts the board's top-left corner (using the `subtract` method of the `Vector2` class) to convert it to a board-relative vector (`piecePos`).

#### EXERCISES

**Exercise 10.3:** In listing 10.5, examine the code for the `click` event handler:

```
document.addEventListener('click', e => {
    target = new Vector2(e.clientX - 15, e.clientY - 15);
    animate();
});
```

Why does this code subtract `15` from both the *x* and *y* components of the vector?

**Exercise 10.4:** In listing 10.6, consider again the following code for determining the maximum board point:

```
const max = new Vector2(
  boardRect.left + boardRect.width - pieceRect.width - 4,
  boardRect.top + boardRect.height - pieceRect.height - 4
);
```

Why does this code subtract `4` from both the *x* and *y* components of the vector?

## 10.4 Geometric clipping and motion paths

So far we've looked at transforms and positioning, which deal with moving or aligning whole elements. CSS also has features that let us define shapes and paths, which are pure geometry. These include clipping paths and motion paths for animation. Here's how vectors and geometry come into play with the `clip-path` and `offset-path` properties.

### 10.4.1 Clipping elements

The `clip-path` property lets you define a shape for an element so that only the part of the element inside that shape is visible and everything outside is clipped (i.e., hidden). This shape can be basic (a circle, an ellipse, a rectangle, a polygon, etc.) or an SVG path. For example, you can make an image appear as a circle by using `clip-path: circle(50% at 50% 50%)`, which creates a circular clip path of radius 50% at the element's center.

More obscurely, you can define a polygon. For example, here's some HTML:

```
<div>
</div>
<div class="diamond">
</div>
<div class="arrow">
</div>
```

In this case, you have a `div` without a class, followed by a `div` with class `diamond` and a `div` with class `arrow`. Figure 10.7 shows what happens when you define `clip-path` on the `diamond` and `arrow` elements. Listing 10.7 takes you through the code that produces these shapes.

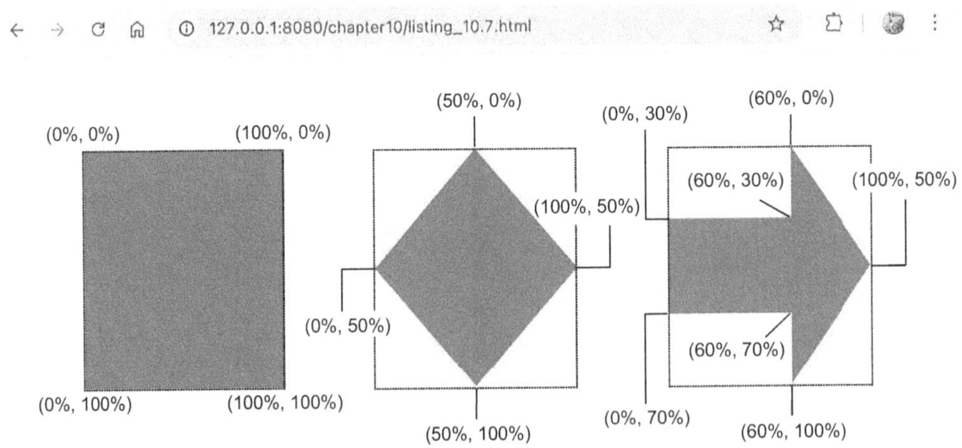


**Figure 10.7 Using `clip-path` to create a diamond shape and an arrow shape**

**Listing 10.7 Using `clip-path` to define a polygon**

```
div {
    width: 200px;
    height: 200px;
    background-color: hsl(23 100% 40%);
}
.diamond {
    clip-path: polygon(
        50% 0%,
        100% 50%,
        50% 100%,
        0% 50%
    );
}
.arrow {
    clip-path: polygon(
        0% 30%,
        60% 30%,
        60% 0%,
        100% 50%,
        60% 100%,
        60% 70%,
        0% 70%
    );
}
```

The idea behind `clip-path` is that every element has a box around it, with the default being `border-box`. The box is given a kind of mini coordinate system, with (0%, 0%) marking the top-left corner, (100%, 0%) marking the top-right corner, (0%, 100%) marking the bottom-left corner, and (100%, 100%) marking the bottom-right corner. In figure 10.7, refer to the default figure on the left.

When you set a `clip-path` value using the `polygon()` shape function, you specify a series of points in this mini coordinate system. For example, to create a diamond shape (refer to the `diamond` class in listing 10.7 and the middle shape in figure 10.7), you specify four points:

```
50% 0%
100% 50%
50% 100%
0% 50%
```

The browser connects these points to create the shape, then clips everything outside of that shape.

Points in a `polygon()` function are essentially vectors from the top-left corner (0%, 0%). Under the hood, these percentage vectors are converted to absolute pixel coordinates based on the element's size. It's pure geometry, with the browser figuring out the intersection of the element with the polygon shape.

### 10.4.2 Motion paths

The CSS motion path lets you animate an element along a custom path. The animation requires two properties:

- `offset-path` defines the path along which you want the element to move. As with `clip-path`, you can use a shape function such as `circle()`, `ellipse()`, `rect()`, or `polygon()`, or the `path()` function with an SVG path. You can also use a keyword such as `border-box` to define the path as the parent element's border.
- `offset-distance` specifies a position along an `offset-path` for an element to be placed, so you animate an element's progress along the path by animating this property.

A motion path is a high-level way to do something that would otherwise require JavaScript or complex keyframes. For example, in chapter 9, listing 9.3 showed how to use JavaScript to animate an element in a circle. The following listing re-creates the same animation with pure CSS.

**Listing 10.8 Circular path animation with CSS**

HTML:

```
<div class="container">
    <div class="orbiting-element"></div>
</div>
```

CSS:

```
.container {
    width: 200px;
    height: 200px;
    border-radius: 50%;        ◄── Container is a circle.
}
.orbiting-element {
    width: 20px;
    height: 20px;
    background-color: #f00;
    border-radius: 50%;
    offset-path: border-box;              ◄── Offset path is the parent border.
    animation: move 3s infinite linear;   ◄── Specifies the keyframes to use
}
@keyframes move {
    from {
        offset-distance: 0%;
    }                                  Motion path is all the
    to {                               way around the circle.
        offset-distance: 100%;
    }
}
```

Motion paths let you specify complex animations without manual calculations. Before this feature, developers often used JavaScript with `requestAnimationFrame()` to update an element's position along a mathematical path, essentially doing the same thing but manually computing the path's ($x$, $y$) points using equations. Now you can offload all that work to CSS, as long as you know the path.

**EXERCISES**

**Exercise 10.5:** What kind of geometric figure is created with the following `clip-path` declaration?

```
clip-path: polygon(
    30% 0%,
    70% 0%,
    100% 30%,
    100% 70%,
    70% 100%,
    30% 100%,
    0% 70%,
    0% 30%
);
```

1. Heptagon (seven-sided figure)
2. Octagon (eight-sided figure)
3. Nonagon (nine-sided figure)
4. Decagon (ten-sided figure)

**Exercise 10.6:** The following HTML and CSS code define a diamond motion path for the `mover` element inside the `container` element:

HTML:

```
<div class="container">
    <div class="mover"></div>
</div>
```

CSS:

```
.container {
    width: 300px;
    height: 300px;
}
.mover {
    width: 20px;
    height: 20px;
    offset-path: polygon(
        50% 0%,
        100% 50%,
        50% 100%,
        0% 50%
    );
```

```
    animation: move 4s infinite linear;
}

@keyframes move {
    from {
        offset-distance: 0%;
    }
    to {
        offset-distance: 100%;
    }
}
```

The code works, but the `mover` element partially crosses each border as it reaches each point of the diamond. How would you modify the code to prevent the `mover` element from crossing any of the borders?

## 10.5 Solutions to exercises

**Exercise 10.1:** The `getBoundingClientRect()` method returns the properties `x`, `left`, `y`, `top`, `right`, `bottom`, `width`, and `height`. It does not return a property named `center`, so the correct answer is 3.

**Exercise 10.2:** Here's the modified `positionTooltip()` code that aligns the tooltip with the bottom-right corner of the button:

```
function positionTooltip() {
    const buttonRect = button.getBoundingClientRect();
    const tooltipRect = tooltip.getBoundingClientRect();

    tooltip.style.left = buttonRect.right + 'px';
    tooltip.style.top = buttonRect.bottom + 'px';
}
```

**Exercise 10.3:** The code subtracts `15` because that value is half the width and half the height of the `.chaser` element:

```
.chaser {
    --snip-
    width: 30px;
    height: 30px;
    --snip-
}
```

This subtraction ensures that, at the end of the animation, the center point of the element rests exactly on the click point.

**Exercise 10.4:** It's necessary to subtract `4` from both the *x* and *y* components of the `max` vector to account for the `4px` of horizontal border and `4px` of vertical border that the `game-piece` element is styled with:

```
.game-board {
    --snip--
```

```
    border: 2px solid #888;
    --snip--
}
```

**Exercise 10.5:** The correct answer is 2, an octagon, as shown in figure 10.8.

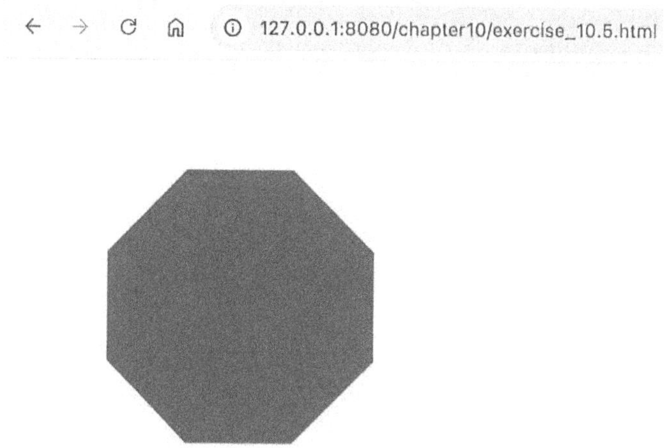


**Figure 10.8 The `clip-path` value in exercise 10.5 produces an octagon.**

**Exercise 10.6:** You need to adjust the `polygon()` value to replace each instance of `0%` with `10px` (half the height and width of the `mover` element) and each instance of `100%` with `calc(100% - 10px)`:

```
offset-path: polygon(
    50% 10px,
    calc(100% - 10px) 50%,
    50% calc(100% - 10px),
    10px 50%
);
```

## Summary

- The browser uses a coordinate system with the origin (0, 0) at the top-left corner of a container (or the viewport). A point's *x*-coordinate increases to the right, and its *y*-coordinate increases downward.
- A vector in 2D is a pair of numbers [*x*, *y*] that represent a direction (as an angle) and distance (also known as the magnitude).
- For a vector [*x*, *y*], its magnitude is given by the Pythagorean formula: `magnitude` `=` $\sqrt{x^2 + y^2}$.
- An element's bounding box is a rectangle that encloses an element and is described by its top-left corner (*x*, *y*) and its width and height. In JavaScript, the

`getBoundingClientRect()` method gives you an element's bounding box in terms of *x*, *y*, width, height (or equivalently, left, top, right, bottom).

- Given a variable `rect` that holds an element's bounding box object as returned by `getBoundingClientRect()`, the center of the element (`centerX`, `centerY`) is given by `centerX = (rect.left + rect.right) / 2` and `centerY = (rect.top + rect .bottom) / 2`.
- Vector operations in JavaScript, such as addition, multiplication, and finding magnitude, correspond to CSS translations that you can use to move and animate elements and apply geometric constraints.
- Use the `clip-path` property to define a shape for an element such that only the part of the element inside that shape is visible.
- In CSS, use the `offset-path` property to define the path along which you want an element to move, such as a circle, or by following the element's border.
- To animate an element along an offset path, manipulate the `offset-distance` property.

# 11 Using Bézier curves for smooth animation

**This chapter covers**

- The mathematical foundation of Bézier curves
- Working with cubic Bézier curves in CSS animations
- Creating custom easing functions for more natural motion

As you surf the web, you occasionally encounter pages with beautifully crafted interface transitions and other animated effects. You can't quite put your finger on why these effects work; you only know that they somehow feel just right. This chapter explains why certain effects create such a positive response. And there is a good chance the math behind those effects involves Bézier curves.

## 11.1 Introduction to Bézier curves

Before diving into CSS syntax and implementations of Bézier curves, it's crucial to understand what Bézier curves are and how they work mathematically. Think of a Bézier curve as a mathematical recipe for creating smooth, flowing lines between points. These lines can be gentle and gradual or sharp and dramatic, depending on how you configure them.

### 11.1.1 What is a Bézier curve?

Bézier curves are elegant mathematical constructs that describe smooth, flowing motion through space and time. The name might sound intimidating, but they're actually one of the most intuitive mathematical tools in web development. Named after French engineer Pierre Bézier, who used them in automotive design, these curves have become the foundation for how browsers create smooth, natural animations. Whether you're making a button gently bounce into view or creating a complex multistep animation sequence, understanding the math behind Bézier curves will help you craft animations that feel polished and professional.

Imagine you're working on an e-commerce site where product cards need to slide in from the side upon scrolling. A constant (linear) motion would feel mechanical and jarring, so you've been tasked to make the cards enter more naturally. A Bézier curve lets you create motion that, for example, starts slow, builds momentum, then settles gently into place. Now the card entrances feel more natural because they mimic how objects move in the real world under the influence of forces such as friction or gravity.

### 11.1.2 The mathematical construction of Bézier curves

You don't need to memorize complex formulas to use Bézier curves effectively in your web dev work. However, understanding their mathematical foundation will make you a more confident and capable developer, so this section provides a bit of Bézier background.

A Bézier curve is constructed using a parameter `t` that varies from `0` to `1`, where `t = 0` represents the start of the curve and `t = 1` represents the end. For any value of `t` between `0` and `1`, the curve's position is calculated using a weighted average of the control points. A *control point* is a point that affects the curve shape and direction, although the curve usually does not pass through it:

- In a quadratic Bézier curve, there's one control point, which pulls the curve toward itself between the start and end points.
- In a cubic Bézier curve, there are two control points (refer to figure 11.1), which act like handles that shape how the curve leaves the starting point and approaches the ending point.

Control points act like magnets that bend the path of the Bézier curve, defining its curvature and smoothness. The key insight is that as `t` changes from `0` to `1`, the influence of different control points grows and shrinks in a mathematically predictable way.

Consider a simple quadratic Bézier curve with three points: $P_0$ (start), $P_1$ (control), and $P_2$ (end). The mathematical formula is

$$B(t) = (1-t)^2 P_0 + 2(1-t)tP_1 + t^2 P_2$$

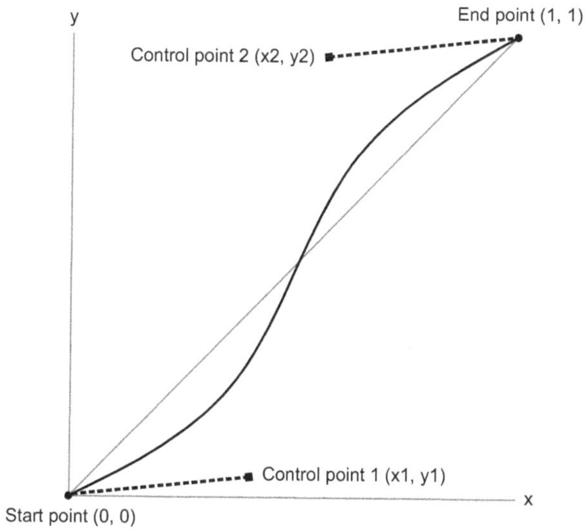


**Figure 11.1 A cubic Bézier curve has two control points.**

This formula might look complex, but it's actually telling a straightforward story:

- When `t = 0`, the curve is at $P_0$ (the start point).
- When `t = 1`, the curve is at $P_2$ (the end point).
- For values between `0` and `1`, the curve is pulled toward $P_1$ with varying strength.

From the perspective of a web developer looking to create animations with a natural feel, the beautiful aspect of this construction is that the curve is always smooth and continuous. There are no sharp corners or discontinuities. The mathematical properties of this formula guarantee that the resulting motion will feel natural and flowing.

### 11.1.3 Quadratic vs. cubic Bézier curves

In web development, you'll encounter two main types of Bézier curves: quadratic and cubic. Understanding the difference is crucial for choosing the right tool for your animation needs:

- Quadratic Bézier curves use three points: a start point, a control point, and an end point. These create simple, elegant curves that are perfect for basic animations. However, they have a limitation: you can't independently control how the curve behaves at the beginning and at the end. The single control point influences the entire curve shape.
- Cubic Bézier curves use four points: a start point, two control points, and an end point. This additional control point gives greater flexibility. You can make the curve start slowly but end quickly, start quickly but end slowly, or create more complex S-shaped curves. This flexibility is why cubic Bézier curves became the standard for web animations.

The mathematical difference lies in the degree of the polynomial. Quadratic curves use second-degree polynomials (involving $t^2$), while cubic curves use third-degree polynomials (involving $t^3$):

$$B(t) = (1 - t)^3 P_0 + 3(1 - t)^2 t P_1 + 3(1 - t) t^2 P_2 + t^3 P_3$$

This higher degree gives cubic curves more bending power, so they can create more complex shapes, while maintaining mathematical smoothness.

For web animations, CSS exclusively uses cubic Bézier curves because they provide the flexibility needed to create natural motion that can accelerate or decelerate independently at the beginning and end of an animation.

### 11.1.4 The role of cubic Bézier curves in animations

In web animations, cubic Bézier curves serve as timing functions. That is, they define how an animated property progresses from its starting to its ending value over the duration of the animation. The horizontal axis represents time (from `0` to `1`, where `1` is the animation's total duration), and the vertical axis represents progress (from `0` to `1`, where `1` is the final property value).

The key here is that the slope of the Bézier curve is mapped to the animation speed. That is, when the curve has a steep slope, the animation speed will be fast; when the curve has a shallow slope, the animation will be slow. By shaping the curve, you control the rhythm and character of the animation. This mapping creates a powerful tool for controlling the feel of animations.

The mathematical elegance of cubic Bézier curves makes them perfect for this role because

- *They're bounded*—The curve generally stays within the `0-1` range for both time and progress, but later you'll learn that breaking out of that range on the progress axis can create some interesting and useful effects.
- *They're smooth*—There are no abrupt changes that would cause jarring motion.
- *They're flexible*—Two control points provide enough degrees of freedom to create virtually any timing feel.
- *They're efficient*—Browsers can calculate curve values quickly using optimized mathematical algorithms.

In CSS timing functions, a cubic Bézier describes a curve where $x$ = time and $y$ = progress. The four control points of a cubic Bézier curve in CSS animations have specific roles:

- $P_0$ `(0, 0)`—Always the start point: the beginning of the animation and the starting value of the property
- $P_1$ $(x_1, y_1)$—First control point, which influences the beginning behavior
- $P_2$ $(x_2, y_2)$—Second control point, which influences ending behavior
- $P_3$ `(1, 1)`—Always the end point: the end of the animation and the final property value

The two inner control points $(x_1, y_1)$ and $(x_2, y_2)$ determine the acceleration, that is, how progress changes as time flows. If the start of the curve gently bows downward, you get a slow start (called an *ease-in*). If the end of the curve gently bows upward, you get a soft landing (an *ease-out*). If the curve has both of these properties and forms a shallow S, you get a classic Bézier curve called an *ease-in-out* (the curve shown in figure 11.1).

> **NOTE** When the control points $(x_1, y_1)$ and $(x_2, y_2)$ are equally distant from the center point `(0.5, 0.5)`, the resulting curve produces *symmetrical easing*, where the second half of the animation mirrors the first half.

For example, imagine you're a web developer tasked with making a toggle switch animation that feels snappy and realistic because the default toggle feels stiff and unnatural. You need the animation to start fast so the switch moves briskly, but then you want the switch to slow to a clean stop at the end. A cubic Bézier with a strong first handle (i.e., a steep slope created by a relatively high *y*-value and a relatively low *x*-value) and a softer second handle (i.e., a shallow slope created by a very high *y*-value [close to 1] and a very low *x*-value [close to 0]) gives you exactly that profile.

**EXERCISES**

**Exercise 1:** Which statement best describes why cubic Bézier curves are preferred over quadratic ones for web animations?

1. Cubic curves are faster to calculate.
2. Cubic curves provide independent control over beginning and ending behavior.
3. Cubic curves use less memory.
4. Cubic curves are supported by more browsers.

**Exercise 2:** Fill in the blanks. In a cubic Bezier curve used for CSS animations, on the *x*-axis, the parameter `t` represents ________, and it varies from ___ to ___.

## 11.2 Cubic Bézier curves in CSS

CSS provides built-in support for cubic Bézier curves through the `cubic-bezier()` function and several predefined timing function keywords. Understanding how to work with these tools effectively requires grasping both the syntax and the mathematical meaning behind the numbers.

### 11.2.1 The cubic-bezier() function

In CSS, the `cubic-bezier()` function gives you a compact way to define a Bézier curve to control animation timing. Here's the general syntax:

```
cubic-bezier(x1, y1, x2, y2)
```

where $(x_1, y_1)$ specifies the first control point and $(x_2, y_2)$ specifies the second control point. Browsers fix the endpoints at `(0,0)` and `(1,1)` and compute the curve between.

Here are a couple of points to bear in mind when building your `cubic-bezier()` functions:

- $x_1$ and $x_2$ must stay within the range [0, 1].
- $y_1$ and $y_2$ generally stay within [0, 1], but are allowed to wander out of that range to create anticipation ($y$-values below 0) or overshoot ($y$-values above 1).

Let's return to our web developer from the previous section, who was tasked to make a toggle switch animation feel snappy and realistic. The following listing shows the code.

**Listing 11.1 Applying a cubic Bézier curve to a toggle button animation**

HTML:

```
<label>
    <input type="checkbox" />
    <span class="switch"></span>
</label>
```

CSS:

```
.switch {
    position: relative;
    width: 50px;
    height: 28px;
    background: #ccc;
    border-radius: 14px;
    cursor: pointer;
    display: inline-block;
}
.switch::after {
    content: "";
    position: absolute;
    top: 3px;
    left: 3px;
    width: 22px;
    height: 22px;
    background: white;
    border-radius: 50%;
    transition: transform 1000ms cubic-bezier(0.2, 0.9, 0.1, 1.0);
}
input {
    display: none;
}
input:checked+.switch {
    background: #5b9df9;
}
input:checked+.switch::after {
    transform: translateX(22px);
}
```

**NOTE** All the code for this chapter's listings is available in this book's GitHub repository: https://github.com/paulmcfe/web-dev-math.

The key line here is the `transition` declaration:

```
transition: transform 1000ms cubic-bezier(0.2, 0.9, 0.1, 1.0);
```

This animates the `transform` property (which, in this example, is a horizontal translation) with a `1000ms` duration using the specified `cubic-bezier()` function as the timing function. (The `1000ms` duration is deliberately long to help you see the effect. In a production page, you'll want to keep the animation crisp with a shorter duration of, say, `250ms`.) Figure 11.2 shows the cubic Bézier curve. Notice the steep slope at the beginning, which gives the animation a fast start, then the relatively level slope at the end, which brings the animation to a slow finish.

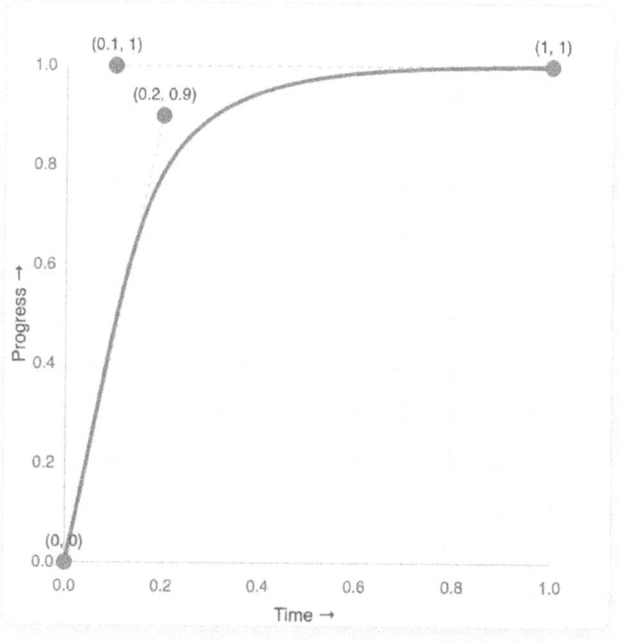


**Figure 11.2 The cubic Bézier curve defined by `cubic-bezier(0.2, 0.9, 0.1, 1.0)`**

**NOTE** The graph in figure 11.2 and the other cubic Bézier visualizations in this chapter were generated by the Cubic Bezier Curve Generator (cubic-bezier-visualizer.html), available with this chapter's code. A second version (cubic-bezier-visualizer-plus.html) handles *y* values below 0 and greater than 1.

### 11.2.2 Understanding the four control point values

Each of the four control point values in a `cubic-bezier()` function has a specific mathematical role in shaping the animation curve. Understanding these roles helps you predict how changes will affect the animation feel.

The first control point ($x_1$, $y_1$) affects the beginning of the animation:

- $x_1$ *controls when the initial acceleration happens*—Use a smaller value for an earlier acceleration, or a larger value for a later acceleration.
- $y_1$ *controls the extent of the initial acceleration*—Use a larger value for a more aggressive start, or a smaller value for a gentler start. Note that a negative value creates negative acceleration (i.e., backward motion).

The second control point ($x_2$, $y_2$) affects the end of the animation:

- $x_2$ *controls when the deceleration begins*—Use a smaller value for an earlier deceleration, or a larger value for a later deceleration.
- $y_2$ *controls the final approach behavior*—Use a larger value for a gentler finish, or a smaller value for a faster finish. Note that a value greater than 1 creates an overshoot effect.

Here are some practical examples with mathematical explanations:

- Gentle ease-in-out (figure 11.3)

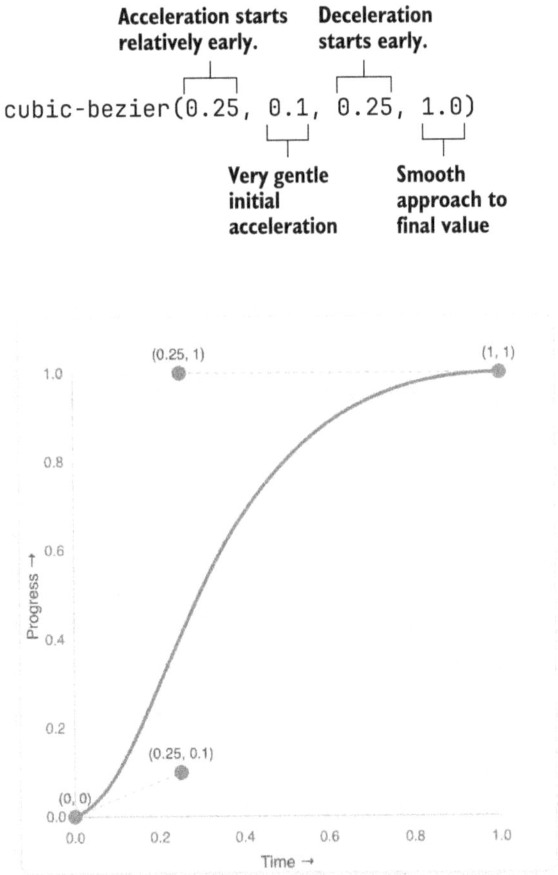


**Figure 11.3** The cubic Bézier curve defined by `cubic-bezier(0.25, 0.1, 0.25, 1.0)`

- Aggressive ease-out (figure 11.4)

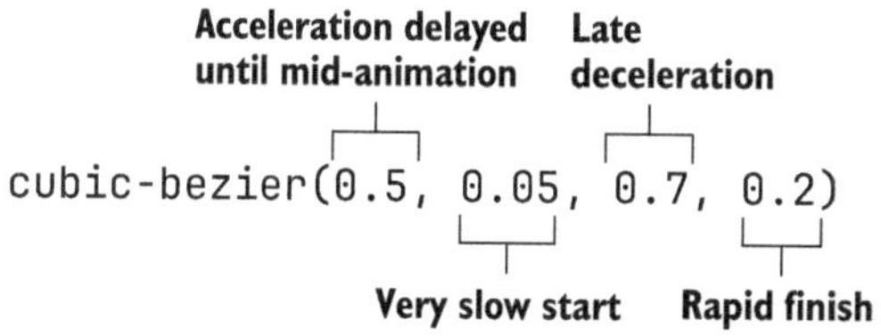


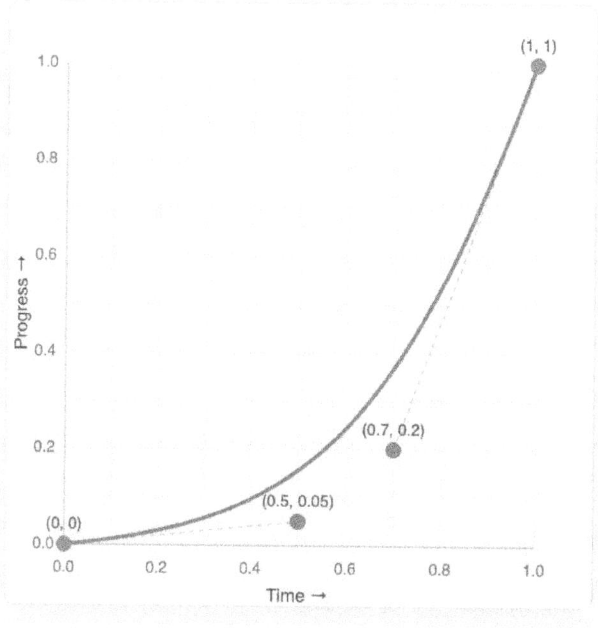


**Figure 11.4 The cubic Bézier curve defined by `cubic-bezier(0.5, 0.05, 0.7, 0.2)`**

- Bounce effect (figure 11.5)

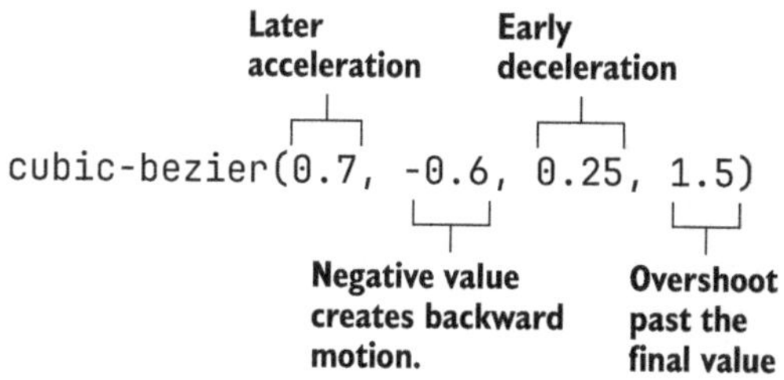

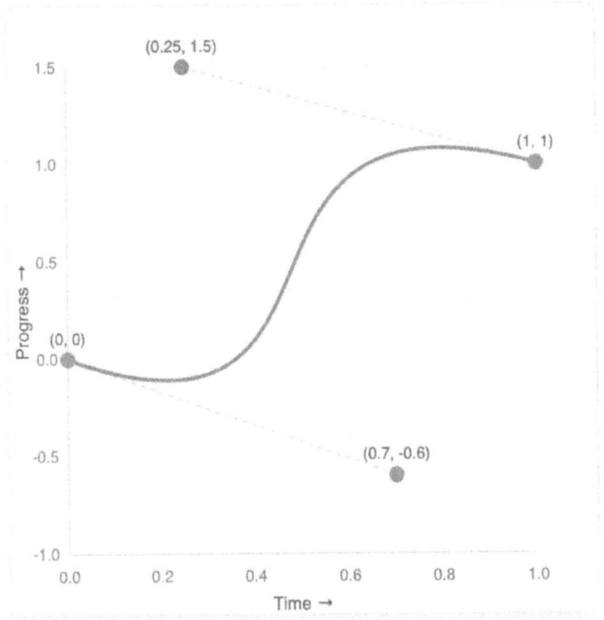


**Figure 11.5 The cubic Bézier curve defined by `cubic-bezier(0.7, -0.6, 0.25, 1.5)`**

The mathematical relationships between these values create predictable patterns. When $y_1$ and $y_2$ are both positive and less than 1, you get standard easing. When *y*-values exceed 1, you get overshoot effects. When *y*-values are negative, you get anticipation effects, where the animation briefly moves in the opposite direction before proceeding to the target.

### 11.2.3 Built-in CSS easing keywords

An *easing function* is a mathematical curve that defines how an animation progresses over time, controlling the speed of change rather than moving at a constant rate. Instead of interpolating values in a straight line (linear motion), easing functions make animations feel more natural by adding acceleration and deceleration.

Easing functions are the practical application of Bézier curve mathematics in web animation. They determine not just how an animation looks, but how it feels to users. The mathematical properties of different easing curves create distinct psychological and aesthetic effects that can make the difference between an animation that feels natural and one that feels robotic or jarring.

Handily, CSS comes with several predefined timing function keywords that correspond to specific cubic Bézier curves. These keywords represent mathematically optimized curves that have been tested extensively for creating natural motion.

Here are the built-in easing functions related to cubic Bézier curves and their mathematical equivalents:

- `linear`—Creates a straight diagonal line from (0, 0) to (1, 1), as shown in figure 11.6. Mathematically, this means the rate of change is constant, so there's no acceleration or deceleration. While this motion might seem pure, it often feels mechanical and unnatural because real-world motion rarely maintains perfectly constant velocity. This keyword is equivalent to

```
cubic-bezier(0, 0, 1, 1)
```

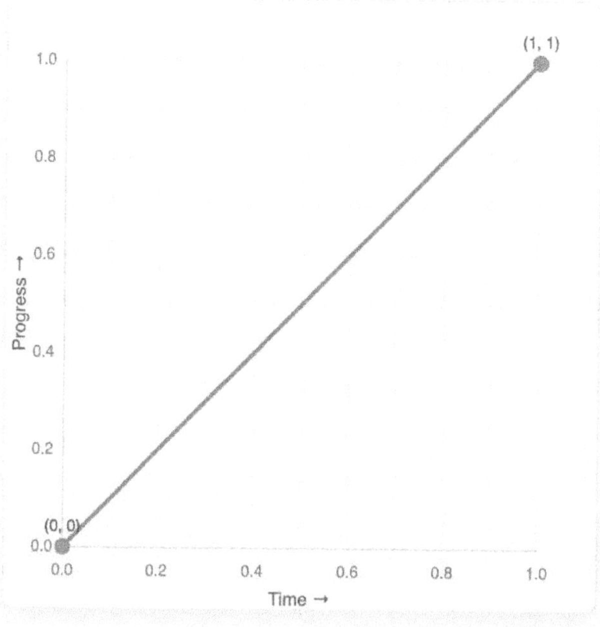


**Figure 11.6 The cubic Bézier curve defined by the `linear` keyword or `cubic-bezier(0, 0, 1, 1)`**

- `ease`—Uses control points that create a gentle S-curve, as shown in figure 11.7. The mathematical curve starts with mild acceleration, reaches peak velocity around the middle, then gradually decelerates, which mimics how humans expect motion to behave: starting and ending gently. This keyword is equivalent to

```
cubic-bezier(0.25, 0.1, 0.25, 1)
```

- `ease-in`—Creates a curve that stays close to the bottom-left, then rises sharply, as shown in figure 11.8. Mathematically, most of the change happens near the end of the animation in this case. It's like watching something fall under gravity: slow at first, then accelerating rapidly. This keyword is equivalent to

```
cubic-bezier(0.42, 0, 1, 1)
```

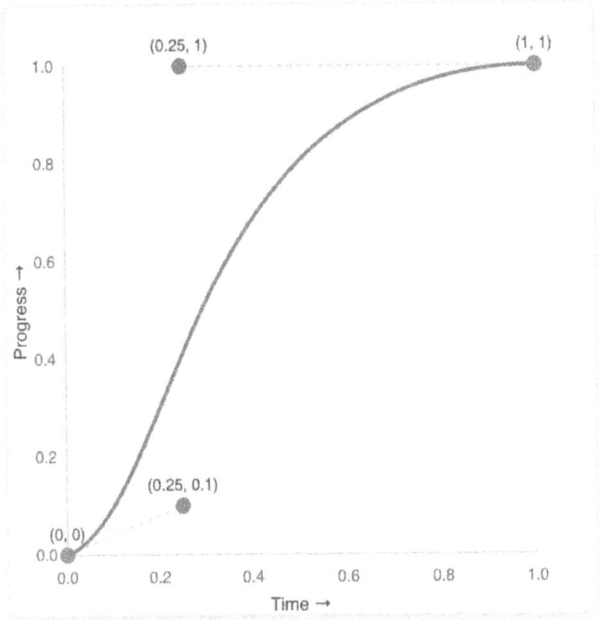


**Figure 11.7 The cubic Bézier curve defined by the `ease` keyword or `cubic-bezier(0.25, 0.1, 0.25, 1)`**

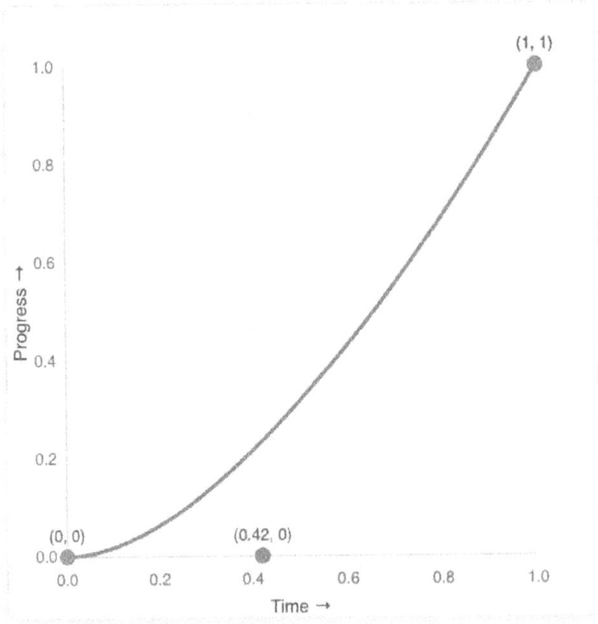


**Figure 11.8 The cubic Bézier curve defined by the `ease-in` keyword or `cubic-bezier(0.42, 0, 1, 1)`**

- `ease-out`—Creates a curve with a sharp initial rise that gradually levels off, as shown in figure 11.9. Most change happens at the beginning, then the animation settles slowly into its final state, which mimics objects sliding to a stop due to friction. This keyword is equivalent to

  ```
  cubic-bezier(0, 0, 0.58, 1)
  ```

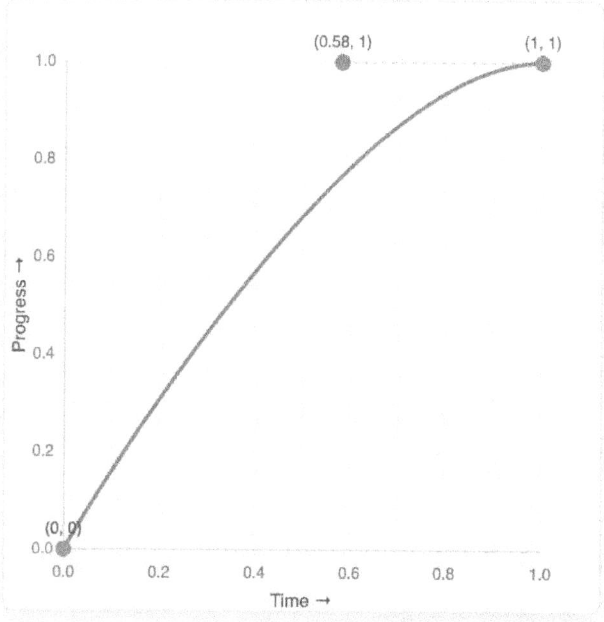


**Figure 11.9 The cubic Bézier curve defined by the `ease-out` keyword or `cubic-bezier(0, 0, 0.58, 1)`**

- `ease-in-out`—Creates an S-curve that accelerates at the beginning and decelerates at the end, as shown in figure 11.10. The control points are symmetric about the center of the curve, and this symmetry makes the curve feel balanced and natural for many types of motion. This keyword is equivalent to

  ```
  cubic-bezier(0.42, 0, 0.58, 1)
  ```

Imagine you've been tasked with creating a mobile menu that appears when the user taps a hamburger icon. You don't want the menu to suddenly materialize onscreen, which would be too jarring. Instead, your job is to find a better way to bring the menu onscreen. The `ease` function is likely the best bet here because it provides a natural feel. The menu starts sliding in at a gentle pace that doesn't startle users, accelerates to show clear motion. It then decelerates as it reaches its final position, creating a sense of the menu settling into place. Listing 11.2 shows the code.

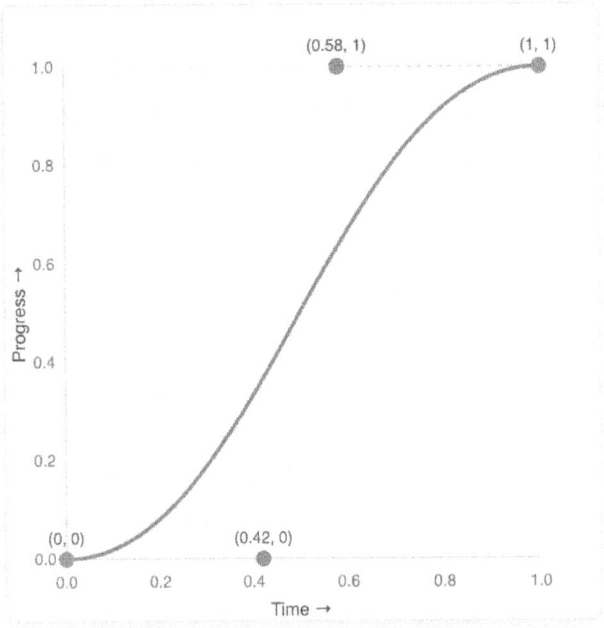


Figure 11.10 The cubic Bézier curve defined by the `ease-in-out` keyword or `cubic-bezier(0.42, 0, 0.58, 1)`

**Listing 11.2 Using the ease function to animate a mobile menu**

HTML:

```
<header>
    <h1>My App</h1>
    <button class="menu-button" id="menuToggle">
        &#9776;
    </button>
</header>

<nav id="sideMenu">
    <ul>
        <li><a href="#">Home</a></li>
        <li><a href="#">Features</a></li>
        <li><a href="#">About</a></li>
        <li><a href="#">Contact</a></li>
    </ul>
</nav>
```

The hamburger menu

The side menu

JavaScript:

```
const toggleButton = document.getElementById('menuToggle');
const sideMenu = document.getElementById('sideMenu');

toggleButton.addEventListener('click', () => {
    sideMenu.classList.toggle('open');
});
```

Clicking hamburger menu toggles open class

CSS (partial):

```
.menu-button {
    font-size: 1.5rem;
    background: none;
    border: none;
    color: white;
    cursor: pointer;
}
nav {
    position: fixed;
    top: 0;
    left: 0;
    height: 100vh;
    width: 250px;
    background: #444;
    padding: 2rem 1rem;
    transform: translateX(-100%);     ◄── Side menu is initially offscreen.
    transition: transform 0.5s ease;  ◄── transition animation uses ease function.
    z-index: 1000;
}
nav.open {
    transform: translateX(0);    ◄── open class brings menu onscreen
}
```

#### Exercises

**Exercise 3:** Examine this CSS rule and predict what kind of animation motion it will create:

```
.element {
    transition: transform 1s cubic-bezier(0.17, 0.67, 0.83, 0.33);
}
```

1. Fast start, slow end
2. Slow start, fast end
3. Smooth, symmetrical easing
4. Bounce with overshoot

**Exercise 4:** Fill in the `cubic-bezier()` values to create an animation that starts very slowly, then accelerates dramatically toward the end:

```
.slow-start-fast-end {
    animation: slide 2s cubic-bezier(__, __, __, __);
}
```

**Exercise 5:** Debug this CSS. The developer wants a gentle bounce effect, but the animation feels too aggressive:

```
.bounce-element {
    transition: transform 0.3s cubic-bezier(0.25, 2.5, 0.75, -1.5);
}
```

**Exercise 6:** Match each CSS easing function—`ease`, `ease-in`, `ease-out`, `ease-in-out`, `linear`—with its best-use case:

1. A loading spinner that should rotate at constant speed
2. A modal dialog appearing on screen
3. A notification sliding away after being dismissed
4. A button scaling up when hovered
5. A page transition where one page slides out while another slides in

## 11.3 Customizing animations with Bézier curves

Creating custom easing curves is where the mathematical understanding of Bézier curves becomes a practical superpower. Instead of being limited to predefined easing functions, you can craft curves that perfectly match your design vision and create unique motion signatures that set your interfaces apart.

Different types of user interface elements and interactions benefit from different mathematical curve characteristics. Understanding these patterns lets you make informed decisions about easing functions based on the psychological and functional requirements of each animation.

### 11.3.1 Entrance animations

Animations that bring an element onto the screen should feel welcoming and attention grabbing without being jarring. The curve characteristics that work well are

- Moderate to fast initial acceleration ($y_1$-values between `0.3` and `0.8`)
- Gentle deceleration ($y_2$-values between `0.6` and `1.0`)
- Timing that completes the motion in the first 60% to 80% of the duration.

For example, suppose you're working on a web page that brings a dialog onto the screen when the user clicks a button. You use the mentioned curve characteristics to bring the dialog onscreen in a welcoming way, as shown in the following listing.

**Listing 11.3 Bringing a dialog onscreen**

HTML:

```
<button id="showBoxBtn">Click Me!</button>
<div id="container">
    <div id="helloDialog"
         class="dialog"
         style="display:none;">
        <div class="dialog-message">Thanks for clicking me!</div>
        <button id="hideBoxBtn">OK</button>
    </div>
</div>
```

**Dialog hidden by default**

JavaScript:

```
function showBox() {
    const dialog = document.getElementById('helloDialog');
    dialog.style.display = 'flex';
    dialog.classList.add('enter-animation');    <-- Clicking button adds enter-animation class to dialog
}

function hideBox() {
    const dialog = document.getElementById('helloDialog');
    dialog.style.display = 'none';
    dialog.classList.remove('enter-animation');
}
document.getElementById('showBoxBtn')
    .addEventListener('click', showBox);
document.getElementById('hideBoxBtn')
    .addEventListener('click', hideBox);
```

CSS (partial):

```
.enter-animation {
    animation: slideIn 0.3s cubic-bezier(0.25, 0.5, 0.5, 0.9);
}
                                        enter-animation class runs
@keyframes slideIn {                    slideIn animation on a curve
    from {
        transform: translateX(-100%);
    }
    to {
        transform: translateX(0);
    }
}
```

Figure 11.11 shows a visualization of the curve defined by `cubic-bezier(0.25, 0.5, 0.5, 0.9)`.

Now your boss checks out your effect and decides that something more attention grabbing is required. This is where *y* values outside of [0, 1] can make a big difference. A negative $y_1$-value creates backward motion, while a $y_2$-value greater than `1` creates an overshoot. For the dialog, you decide that applying these *y* values to bounce the `scale` property is just the thing: the dialog shrinks slightly at first, then expands briefly beyond its normal size before settling down. The following listing shows the CSS involved.

**Listing 11.4 Bouncing a dialog onto the screen**

```
.attention-grabbing {
    animation: bounceIn 0.6s cubic-bezier(0.7, -0.5, 0.25, 1.5);
}
                                        attention-grabbing class runs
@keyframes bounceIn {                   bounceIn animation on a curve
    0% {
        transform: scale(0.7);
        opacity: 0;
    }
```

```
    60% {
        transform: scale(1.05);
        opacity: 1;
    }
    80% {
        transform: scale(0.95);
    }
    100% {
        transform: scale(1);
    }
}
```

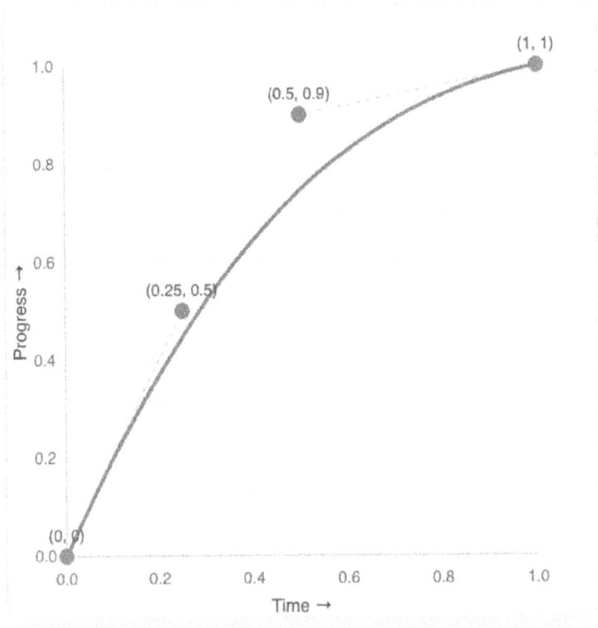


**Figure 11.11 The cubic Bézier curve defined by `cubic-bezier(0.25, 0.5, 0.5, 0.9)`**

Figure 11.12 shows a visualization of the curve defined by `cubic-bezier(0.7, -0.5, 0.25, 1.5)`.

### 11.3.2 Exit animations

Animations that send elements offscreen should feel smooth and nondisruptive, clearing the way for new content. Effective mathematical patterns include

- Gentle initial motion ($y_1$-values between `0` and `0.4`)
- Strong acceleration toward the end ($y_2$-values between `0.0` and `0.3`)
- Faster overall timing to avoid blocking user flow

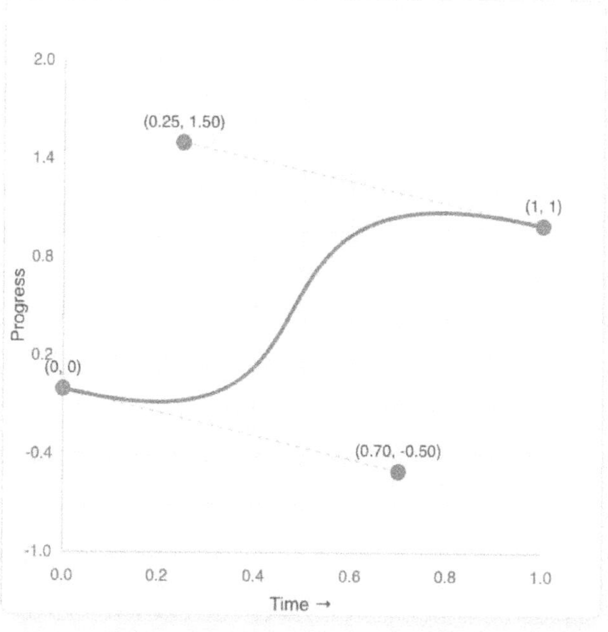


**Figure 11.12 The cubic Bézier curve defined by `cubic-bezier(0.7, -0.5, 0.25, 1.5)`**

For example, going back to your original dialog animation (listing 11.3), you like the way the dialog slides onto the screen, but when the user clicks OK, the dialog just disappears. Now your job is to fix that by animating the dialog off the screen. The following listing shows the CSS that uses a `cubic-bezier()` function to supply the easing curve for the `slideOut` animation.

**Listing 11.5 Animating a dialog off the screen**

```
.exit-animation {
    animation: slideOut 0.2s cubic-bezier(0.5, 0.05, 0.75, 0.2);
}

@keyframes slideOut {
    from {
        transform: translateX(0);
    }
    to {
        transform: translateX(-100%);
    }
}
```

**exit-animation class runs slideOut animation on a curve**

Figure 11.13 shows a visualization of the curve defined by `cubic-bezier(0.5, 0.05, 0.75, 0.2)`.

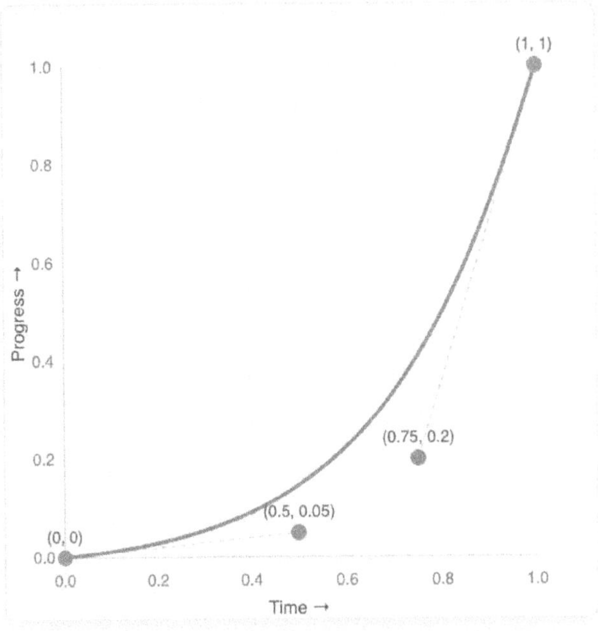


**Figure 11.13 The cubic Bézier curve defined by `cubic-bezier(0.5, 0.05, 0.75, 0.2)`**

Another way to animate an element off the screen is to fade it out. In this case, we have

- Moderate initial motion ($y_1$-values between `0.4` and `0.6`)
- Gentle acceleration toward the end ($y_2$-values between `0.7` and `1`)
- Fast overall timing to provide immediate feedback to the user

This effect is useful when something is being removed or deleted, but you could also use it to animate the dialog version from listing 11.4. The following listing shows the CSS that uses a `cubic-bezier()` function to provide the easing curve for the `fadeOut` animation.

**Listing 11.6 Fading a dialog off the screen**

```
.fade-away {
    animation: fadeOut 0.5s cubic-bezier(0.25, 0.5, 0.5, 0.95);
}

@keyframes fadeOut {
    0% {
        opacity: 1;
    }
    100% {
        opacity: 0;
    }
}
```

**fade-away class runs fadeOut animation on a curve**

Figure 11.14 shows a visualization of the curve defined by `cubic-bezier(0.25, 0.5, 0.5, 0.95)`.

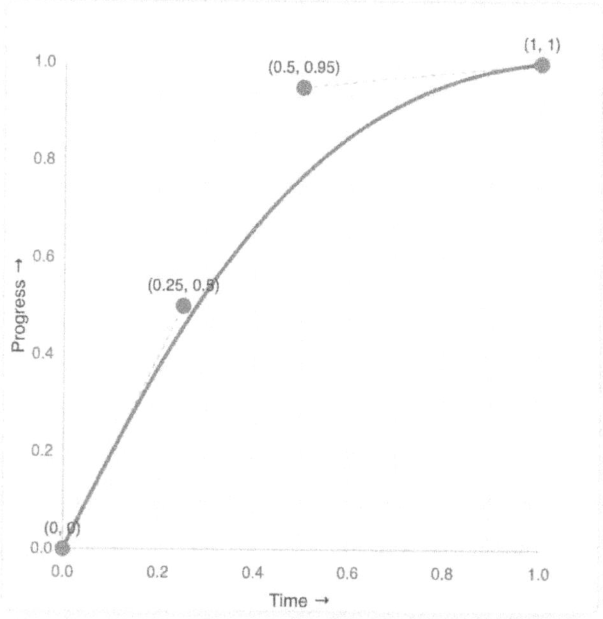


**Figure 11.14 The cubic Bézier curve defined by `cubic-bezier(0.25, 0.5, 0.5, 0.95)`**

### 11.3.3 *Interactive feedback animations*

When you provide animated interactive feedback, the effect needs to feel immediate and responsive. The mathematical requirements are

- Very fast initial response ($y_1$-values of `0.5` or more)
- Quick completion (short duration)
- Often symmetrical curves for reversible interactions

For example, suppose your animated menu triggered by clicking a hamburger button (refer to listing 11.2) was a rousing success. Now your project manager wants to reduce user confusion by having a tooltip appear when the user hovers the mouse over the hamburger menu. The following listing shows the HTML and CSS used to achieve this effect.

**Listing 11.7 Animatating a tooltip**

HTML:

```
<header>
    <h1>My App</h1>
```

```
    <div class="menu-container">
        <button class="menu-button" id="menuToggle">&#9776;</button>
        <div class="menu-tooltip">Open the navigation menu</div>
    </div>
</header>
```

CSS:

```
.menu-tooltip {
    visibility: hidden;
    opacity: 0;
    background: #333;
    color: #fff;
    text-align: center;
    border-radius: 4px;
    padding: 8px 14px;
    position: absolute;
    left: 50%;
    transform: translateX(-80%) translateY(5px);
    top: 100%;
    width: max-content;
    z-index: 1;
    font-size: 15px;
    pointer-events: none;
    transition: all 0.15s cubic-bezier(0.4, 0.0, 0.2, 1);
}

.menu-container:hover .menu-tooltip,
.menu-container:focus-within .menu-tooltip {
    visibility: visible;
    opacity: 1;
    transform: translateX(-90%) translateY(5px);
    pointer-events: auto;
}
```

Figure 11.15 shows a visualization of the curve defined by `cubic-bezier(0.4, 0.0, 0.2, 1)`.

### EXERCISES

**Exercise 7:** You need to create an animation for a shopping cart icon that briefly scales up when items are added. Which cubic Bézier curve would be most appropriate?

1. `cubic-bezier(0.7, -0.5, 0.25, 1.5)`—A bounce with overshoot effect
2. `cubic-bezier(0.25, 0.4, 0.5, 0.95)`—A smooth ease-out effect
3. `cubic-bezier(0.4, 0, 1, 1)`—An ease-in acceleration effect
4. `cubic-bezier(0.55, 0.05, 0.7, 0.2)`—An aggressive ease-in effect

**Exercise 8:** Debug this animation curve. The developer wants a smooth, professional fade-in effect, but users report the animation feels jumpy:

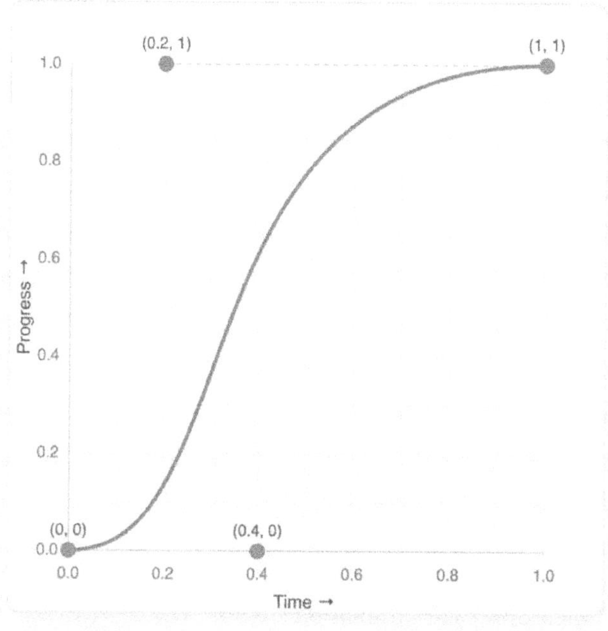


**Figure 11.15 The cubic Bézier curve defined by `cubic-bezier(0.4, 0.0, 0.2, 1)`**

```
.fade-in {
    animation: fadeIn 0.3s cubic-bezier(0.95, 0.05, 0.8, 0.04);
}
```

Identify the problem and suggest a better curve.

## 11.4 Answers to exercises

**Exercise 1:** Cubic curves provide independent control over beginning and ending behavior. The two control points in a cubic Bézier curve let you shape independently how the animation starts and how it ends, while quadratic curves only have one control point that affects the entire curve shape. Therefore, the correct answer is 2.
**Exercise 2:** In a cubic Bézier curve used for CSS animations, the parameter `t` represents time (or animation progress), and it varies from `0` to `1`.
**Exercise 3:** The correct answer is 3—smooth, symmetrical easing. The control points `(0.17, 0.67)` and `(0.83, 0.33)` are symmetrical around the center of the curve, creating a smooth S-curve that first accelerates then decelerates symmetrically.
**Exercise 4:** Here's one possible solution:

```
.slow-start-fast-end {
    animation: slide 2s cubic-bezier(0.7, 0, 0.8, 0);
}
```

This code creates a curve where the first control point `(0.7, 0)` delays acceleration until late in the animation, and the second control point `(0.8, 0)` defines a very steep curve to the end, creating dramatic final acceleration.

**Exercise 5:** The *y*-values are too extreme. For a gentle bounce, try this:

```
.bounce-element {
    transition: transform 0.3s cubic-bezier(0.25, 0.5, 0.75, 1.2);
}
```

**Exercise 6:** The answers are as follows:

1. Use `linear` to achieve the spinner's constant rotation speed.
2. Use `ease-out` so that the modal appears quickly and settles gently.
3. Use `ease-in` so that the notification starts slow, then accelerates away.
4. Use `ease` or `ease-out` to give the button a gentle, welcoming motion.
5. Use `ease-in-out` to achieve balanced motion for the transition's coordinated elements.

**Exercise 7:** The best choice here is `cubic-bezier(0.7, -0.5, 0.25, 1.5)`, the bounce with overshoot effect. The shopping cart animation should provide satisfying feedback that an item was successfully added. The bounce effect with slight overshoot creates a celebratory feel that confirms the action and makes the interaction feel responsive and delightful.

**Exercise 8:** The problem is that the curve delays almost all motion until the very end ($x_1$ = `0.95`, which gives a very late start), then tries to complete everything rapidly ($y_2$ = `0.04`, which is a very slow finish). This creates a jumpy effect where nothing happens, and then everything happens at once.

Here's a better curve:

```
.fade-in {
    animation: fadeIn 0.3s cubic-bezier(0.25, 0.46, 0.45, 0.94);
}
```

This provides smooth, gradual acceleration with gentle deceleration, which is perfect for professional fade effects.

## Summary

- A Bézier curve is a mathematically defined curve generated from a set of control points acting like magnets that pull the curve into a particular shape.
- A quadratic Bézier curve has one control point, while a cubic Bézier curve has two control points.
- With two control points, a cubic Bézier curve lets you control the shape of the curve at both the beginning (using the first control point) and the end (using the second), so CSS animations use these curves almost exclusively.

- The animation segment will be fast where the Bézier curve has a steep slope and slow where it has a shallow slope.
- The first control point ($x_1$, $y_1$) influences the beginning of the animation, where $x_1$ controls when the initial acceleration happens and $y_1$ controls the amount of initial acceleration.
- The second control point ($x_2$, $y_2$) influences the end of the animation, where $x_2$ controls when the deceleration begins and $y_2$ controls the final deceleration.
- $y_1$ and $y_2$ generally stay within [0, 1], but are allowed to wander out of that range to create anticipation ($y$-values below 0) or overshoot ($y$-values above 1).
- An *easing function* is a mathematical curve that defines how an animation progresses over time.
- CSS offers the following five predefined easing functions based on cubic Bézier curves: `linear`, `ease`, `ease-in`, `ease-out`, and `ease-in-out`.

# 12 Physics-based animations

**_This chapter covers_**

- Using real-world physics to improve user experience in animations
- Applying velocity and acceleration equations in JavaScript
- Simulating gravity and bouncing effects with mathematical precision
- Implementing spring- and friction-based animations using physics formulas

When you watch a leaf fall from a tree, a ball bounce on the ground, or a pendulum swing back and forth, your brain instinctively recognizes these movements as natural and proper in some hard-to-define way. That's because these motions follow the fundamental laws of physics that govern everything in our world. When you bring these same principles into your web animations, something magical happens: your interfaces start to feel more intuitive, more responsive, and more delightful to use.

The secret isn't just in making things move but making them move the way users expect based on their experience with the physical world. A modal dialog that slides into view with constant velocity feels robotic and artificial. But a modal that starts fast and gradually slows down as it settles into place feels natural, because that's how objects behave when they're subject to friction and momentum in the real world.

This chapter explores the mathematical foundations of physics-based animations and shows you how to implement them in JavaScript. You'll learn to think like a physicist when designing motion, using equations for velocity, acceleration, gravity, springs, and friction to create animations that not only look good, but also feel right. By the end of this chapter, you'll understand how a few simple mathematical formulas can transform static interfaces into dynamic, engaging experiences that users love to interact with.

## 12.1 Understanding motion in UI design

The difference between a good and a great animation often comes down to physics. When elements on your page move with realistic acceleration, deceleration, and momentum, they feel tangible, as if they have weight and substance. This section introduces the fundamental physics concepts that make animations feel natural and explores why your brain expects digital objects to behave like physical ones.

### 12.1.1 How real-world physics improves user experience

Your brain has spent a lifetime observing how objects move in the physical world. When you drop an object, it accelerates as it falls. When you push something across a table, it gradually slows down due to friction. When you pull back and release a spring, it oscillates before settling into place. These patterns are so deeply ingrained that when digital objects violate these expectations, the movement feels wrong, even if you can't quite articulate why.

Imagine you're a web developer tasked with creating a dialog that slides in from the top of the screen. Figure 12.1 shows the completed animation.

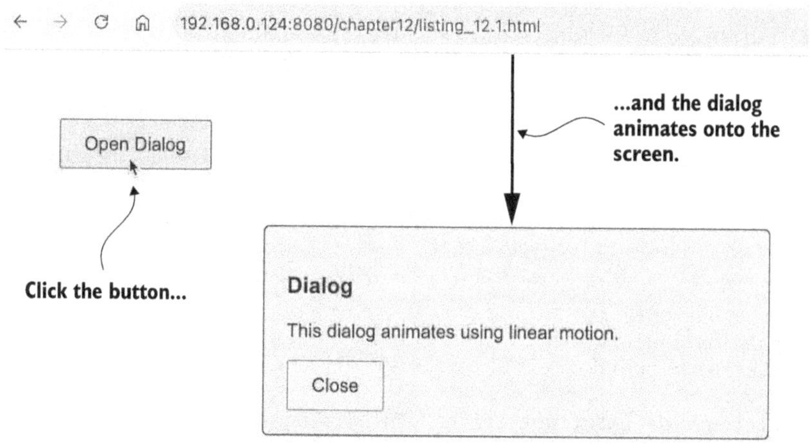


**Figure 12.1 The completed animation of a dialog entering from the top of the viewport. This example uses linear motion (i.e., a constant speed).**

If you animate the dialog with a linear transition (constant speed), as shown in the following listing, it will look mechanical and abrupt.

**Listing 12.1 Animating a dialog onto the screen with linear motion**

```
function openDialog() {
    if (isAnimating) return;
    isAnimating = true;

    let dialog = document.getElementById('dialog');
    let start = -300;
    let end = (window.innerHeight / 2)
            - (dialog.offsetHeight / 2);
    let distance = end - start;
    let duration = 1000;
    let startTime = Date.now();

    function animate() {
        let elapsed = Date.now() - startTime;
        let progress = elapsed / duration;

        if (progress >= 1) {
            isAnimating = false;
            return;
        }

        let currentTop = start + distance * progress;
        dialog.style.top = currentTop + 'px';

        requestAnimationFrame(animate);
    }

    animate();
}
```

Dialog starts offscreen

Dialog ends mid-screen

The distance it travels

The animation duration

Start timing

Elapsed time

Portion of animation complete

Checks for end of animation

Adjusts dialog position using constant (linear) speed

**NOTE** All the code for this chapter's listings is available in this book's GitHub repository: https://github.com/paulmcfe/web-dev-math.

However, if you apply acceleration at the start and deceleration at the end to mimic how a physical panel might slide, as shown in the following listing, the animation feels smooth and professional.

**Listing 12.2 Animating a dialog onto the screen with an ease-out curve**

```
function openDialog() {
    if (isAnimating) return;
    isAnimating = true;

    let dialog = document.getElementById('dialog');
    let start = -300;
    let end = (window.innerHeight / 2) - (dialog.offsetHeight / 2);
    let distance = end - start;
```

```
    let duration = 1000;
    let startTime = Date.now();

    function animate() {
        let elapsed = Date.now() - startTime;
        let progress = elapsed / duration;

        if (progress >= 1) {
            isAnimating = false;
            return;
        }
        const eased = 1 - Math.pow(1 - progress, 3);
        let currentTop = start + eased * distance;
        dialog.style.top = currentTop + 'px';

        requestAnimationFrame(animate);
    }

    animate();
}
```

**Ease-out curve: fast start, gradual deceleration**

What makes the difference is physics: real objects don't instantly achieve full speed or stop on a dime. This physics-based version creates a natural acceleration and deceleration using a cubic ease-out function:

```
(1 - Math.pow(1 - progress, 3))
```

This simple change makes the animation feel like it has momentum that gradually dissipates. I discuss JavaScript implementations of easing functions a bit later in section 12.1.3.

### 12.1.2 Why animations feel natural when physics is applied

Animations feel natural when they match your expectations from the physical world. Your brain is constantly predicting how objects should move, based on countless observations, and when animations align with these predictions, they feel right. Here are the key physics principles that make animations feel natural:

- *Inertia*—Objects resist changes in motion. They don't start or stop instantly.
- *Momentum*—Moving objects want to keep moving in the same direction.
- *Friction*—Motion gradually slows down due to resistance.
- *Gravity*—Objects accelerate downward (or appear to have weight).
- *Elasticity*—Objects can store and release energy when compressed or stretched.

You'll see how to implement these as you progress through this chapter.

### 12.1.3 JavaScript easing functions for natural motion

As discussed in chapter 11, CSS handles many animation needs elegantly, particularly when you use the `cubic-bezier()` function to create custom easing curves. However,

JavaScript gives complete mathematical control over timing functions and enables complex, interactive animations that respond to user input, data changes, or complex logic. Understanding how to implement mathematical easing functions in JavaScript opens up unlimited creative possibilities.

#### LINEAR INTERPOLATION AND OTHER EASING FORMULAS

At the heart of all animation mathematics is *linear interpolation* (often shortened to *lerp*), which is the process of finding intermediate values between two known values. In animation, linear interpolation calculates the current property value based on the animation's progress.

The fundamental linear interpolation formula is

```
function lerp(start, end, progress) {
    return start + (end - start) * progress;
}
```

This function takes the following three parameters:

- `start`—The initial value
- `end`—The target value
- `progress`—A number between 0 and 1 representing how much of the animation is complete

The beauty of this formula is in its simplicity and universality. Whether you're animating position, opacity, color values, or any other numeric property, linear interpolation provides the foundation.

#### BUILDING ON LINEAR INTERPOLATION WITH EASING FUNCTIONS

Easing functions transform the linear progress value into a modified progress value that creates different motion characteristics. Given a progress value represented by `t`, here are a bunch of easing functions implemented in JavaScript code:

```
function linear(t) {
    return t;                    ← Linear easing (no change to progress)
}

function easeInQuad(t) {
    return t * t;                ← Quadratic ease-in (t²)
}

function easeOutQuad(t) {
    return 1 - (1 - t) * (1 - t);    ← Quadratic ease-out (1 – (1–t)²)
}

function easeInOutQuad(t) {
    return t < 0.5 ? 2 * t * t : 1 -
➥       Math.pow(-2 * t + 2, 2) / 2;    ← Quadratic ease-in-out
}

function easeInCubic(t) {
    return t * t * t;            ← Cubic ease-in (t³)
```

```
}

function easeOutCubic(t) {
    return 1 - Math.pow(1 - t, 3);          // ← Cubic ease-out (1 – (1–t)^3)
}

function easeInOutCubic(t) {
    return t < 0.5 ? 4 * t * t * t : 1 -
        Math.pow(-2 * t + 2, 3) / 2;        // ← Cubic ease-in-out
}

function easeInSine(t) {
    return 1 - Math.cos(t * Math.PI / 2);   // ← Sine wave easing
}

function easeOutSine(t) {
    return Math.sin(t * Math.PI / 2);       // ← Sine wave easing
}

function easeInExpo(t) {
    return t === 0 ? 0 : Math.pow(2, 10 * (t - 1));   // ← Exponential easing
}

function easeOutExpo(t) {
    return t === 1 ? 1 : 1 - Math.pow(2, -10 * t);    // ← Exponential easing
}

function easeInCirc(t) {
    return 1 - Math.sqrt(1 - t * t);                  // ← Circular easing
}

function easeOutCirc(t) {
    return Math.sqrt(1 - Math.pow(t - 1, 2));         // ← Circular easing
}
```

For example, imagine you're working on a web page where you want the page title to animate in from offscreen left to the center of the page. Figure 12.2 shows the title

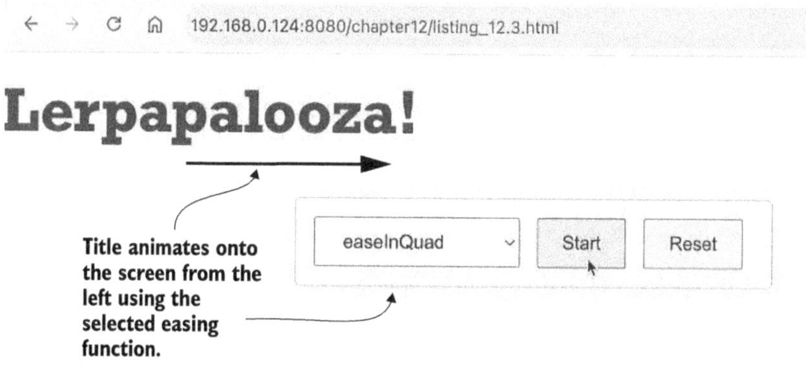


**Figure 12.2** The page title in mid-animation as it enters from the left side of the viewport. The dropdown list lets you try different JavaScript easing functions for the animation.

entering the screen mid-animation. The listing that follows presents a function that takes one of the easing functions as an argument and animates an object (the page title, in this case) using linear interpolation on the eased value.

**Listing 12.3 JavaScript easing functions**

```
function animateTitle(easingFunc) {                    ◄── The easing function is passed.
    if (isAnimating) return;
    isAnimating = true;

    let title = document.getElementById('title');
    let start = -400;
    let end = window.innerWidth - title.offsetWidth;
    let duration = 1000;
    let startTime = Date.now();

    title.style.left = start + 'px';

    function animate() {
        let elapsed = Date.now() - startTime;          ◄── Gets elapsed time
        let progress = elapsed / duration;             ◄── Calculates animation progress

        if (progress >= 1) {                           ◄── Checks for animation end
            title.style.left = end + 'px';
            isAnimating = false;
            return;
        }

        const eased = easingFunc(progress);            ◄── Applies the easing function
        let currentLeft = lerp(start, end, eased);     ◄── Gets new position via linear interpolation
        title.style.left = currentLeft + 'px';         ◄── Moves the object

        requestAnimationFrame(animate);
    }

    animate();
}
```

Easing functions mimic physical reality by creating motion that looks natural. But JavaScript lets you go beyond by implementing actual physics principles and formulas in your animations, such as those for velocity and acceleration, which you'll explore next.

## 12.2 Velocity and acceleration in JavaScript

I don't think I'm going out on much of a limb when I say that velocity and acceleration are the building blocks of realistic motion. Understanding how to implement these concepts in JavaScript gives you the power to create animations that feel natural and responsive to user input.

### 12.2.1 Applying the velocity equation in animations

The fundamental relationship between velocity, distance, and time is expressed as follows:

$$v = \frac{d}{t}$$

That is, velocity equals distance divided by time. In animation contexts, this equation means that the faster something is moving, the farther it will travel in a given time period.

In JavaScript animations, you'll often work with this equation in its rearranged form:

$$d = v \times t$$

That is, distance equals velocity multiplied by time. This version of the equation tells you how far to move an object in each animation frame based on its current velocity.

For example, suppose you've been tasked to code a notification so that it enters the screen from the left and then stops in the center. Figure 12.3 shows the effect in mid-animation. You want to experiment with different velocities to find out which one feels the best. Listing 12.4 presents a simple way to approach velocity.

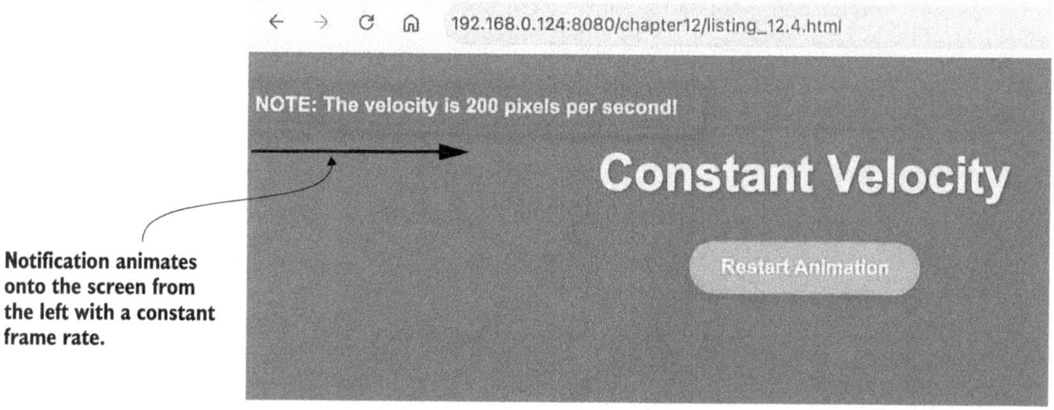


**Figure 12.3 The notification in mid-animation as it enters from the left side of the viewport. The notification enters with a constant velocity of 200 pixels per second.**

**Listing 12.4 Applying the velocity equation with a constant frame rate**

```
const notification = document.getElementById('notification');
const notificationWidth = notification.offsetWidth;
const centerPosition = (window.innerWidth / 2) -
                       (notificationWidth / 2);
```

```
let position = -notificationWidth;
const velocity = 200;                      // Pixels per second
const timePerFrame = 1 / 60;               // Assumes each frame is 1/60th of a second (16.67ms)

function animate() {
    position += velocity * timePerFrame;   // Moves the element: distance = velocity × time
    notification.style.transform = `translateX(${position}px)`;   // 200 * (1/60) = 3.33 pixels per frame

    // Stop the animation when the notification gets to the center
    if (position < centerPosition) {       // Ends when notification is centered
        requestAnimationFrame(animate);
    }
}

requestAnimationFrame(animate);
```

This simple approach works, but it has a major flaw: it assumes the animation always runs at exactly 60 frames per second (fps). However, `requestAnimationFrame()` adapts to the display's refresh rate, which can vary significantly. Here are some common refresh rates:

- *60Hz displays*—60fps. This is the most common rate, used on most laptops and standard monitors.
- *120Hz displays*—120fps. This rate is used with gaming monitors and some mobile devices.
- *144Hz displays*—144fps. This is a common rate on gaming monitors.
- *240Hz displays*—240fps. This rate shows up on high-end gaming monitors.
- *Variable refresh*—This refresh rate fluctuates based on performance.

In addition, `requestAnimationFrame()` can also modify the frame rate based on conditions such as

- *Performance issues*—Heavy computational loads can cause frame drops.
- *Background tabs*—Browsers often throttle background animation to 1fps or pause them entirely.
- *Power saving*—Mobile devices may reduce frame rates to save battery power.

In your animation, if the frame rate drops to, say, 30fps due to a busy CPU, the element will move only half as fast because it's getting half as many updates per second. This makes the animation inconsistent across different devices and performance conditions.

The solution is to use timestamps to measure the time that has passed between frames and implement that in your calculations, as shown in the following listing.

**Listing 12.5 Applying the velocity equation using timestamps**

```
const notification = document.getElementById('notification');
const notificationWidth = notification.offsetWidth;
```

```
const centerPosition = (window.innerWidth / 2) -
                       (notificationWidth / 2);
let position = -notificationWidth;
const velocity = 200;
let lastTime = 0;

function animate() {
    const currentTime = performance.now();        // Gets elapsed time since page load
    if (lastTime === 0) lastTime = currentTime;   // Initializes the previous time
    const deltaTime = (currentTime - lastTime) / 1000;   // Gets the difference in seconds
    lastTime = currentTime;                       // Updates the previous time

    position += velocity * deltaTime;             // Updates position based on time delta
    notification.style.transform = `translateX(${position}px)`;

    if (position <= centerPosition) {
        requestAnimationFrame(animate);
    }
}
```

The key here is that this code calculates the time difference between each frame, instead of assuming a fixed time per frame. Here's how this works:

- At 60fps, each frame occurs ~16.67ms apart, so `deltaTime` = 0.0167 seconds.
- At 30fps, each frame occurs ~33.33ms apart, so `deltaTime` = 0.0333 seconds.

If an element has a velocity of 200 pixels per second,

- At 60fps, it moves 200 × 0.0167 = 3.33 pixels per frame.
- At 30fps, it moves 200 × 0.0333 = 6.66 pixels per frame.

Notice that even though the 30fps animation moves further per frame, both animations cover exactly 200 pixels per second of real time. The slower frame rate is compensated by larger movement per frame, keeping the overall speed consistent.

This frame-rate independence is crucial for creating professional, reliable animations that perform consistently across different devices, browsers, and performance conditions.

### 12.2.2 Handling acceleration

Things get more interesting when you introduce acceleration. Acceleration modifies velocity, which in turn modifies the position. To implement acceleration, you create another variable for acceleration and update it on every frame, just before you update the position. Figure 12.4 shows the accelerated version of the notification in mid-animation, and the following listing shows you how to handle acceleration in your code.

**Listing 12.6 Increasing velocity with acceleration**

```
const notification = document.getElementById('notification');
const notificationWidth = notification.offsetWidth;
let position = -notificationWidth;
```

```
const centerPosition = (window.innerWidth / 2) -
                       (notificationWidth / 2);

let velocity = 200;
const acceleration = 10;

let lastTime = 0;

function animate() {
    const currentTime = performance.now();
    if (lastTime === 0) lastTime = currentTime;
    const deltaTime = (currentTime - lastTime) / 1000;
    lastTime = currentTime;

    velocity += acceleration;
    position += velocity * deltaTime;
    notification.style.transform = `translateX(${position}px)`;

    if (position <= centerPosition) {
        requestAnimationFrame(animate);
    }
}
```

**Initializes velocity** (`let velocity = 200;`)

**Sets acceleration** (`const acceleration = 10;`)

**Adds acceleration to velocity** (`velocity += acceleration;`)

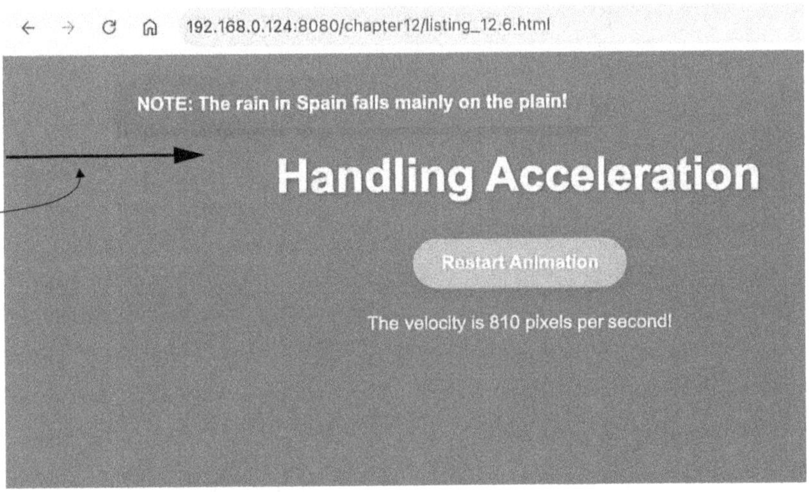


**Notification animates onto the screen from the left with an accelerating frame rate.**

**Figure 12.4 The notification in mid-animation as it enters from the left side of the viewport. The notification speed increases as it enters due to acceleration.**

This simple, layered approach, where acceleration affects velocity and velocity affects position, is the foundation of all the physics-based effects discussed in this chapter.

### EXERCISES

**Exercise 12.1:** Given the following code and the `animate()` function from listing 12.6, what is the position of the element after three frames?

```
let position = 0;
let velocity = 5;
const acceleration = -1;
```

**Exercise 12.2:** Troubleshoot the following code. The goal is for the box to move to the right. Why is it moving to the left instead?

```
const box = document.getElementById('box');
    let position = 100;
    let velocity = -3;

    function animate() {
        position += velocity;
        box.style.transform = `translateX(${position}px)`;
        requestAnimationFrame(animate);
    }

    animate();
```

## 12.3 Simulating gravity and bouncing effects

Gravity is a force that can be simulated with constant acceleration. In a typical screen-based coordinate system where the *y*-axis increases downward, gravity is a positive value that you continuously add to an object's vertical velocity. This makes it accelerate toward the ground (usually the bottom of its container or the viewport).

The magic happens when you add a collision check. When the object hits the ground, you can create a bounce by reversing its vertical velocity and reducing the velocity in each frame to simulate a loss of energy.

### 12.3.1 How to create a bouncing-ball animation

For example, imagine you're building a game where the player drops items into a basket. To make the interaction feel fun and realistic, you can apply a gravity constant to each item so that it falls naturally. When the item lands, you can use a small, negative bounce factor to make it settle in a visually pleasing way. The code in the next listing prototypes this effect using a simple bouncing-ball animation, and figure 12.5 shows the prototype effect in mid-animation.

**Listing 12.7 A bouncing-ball animation**

```
const ball = document.getElementById('ball');
const floor = 490;                    ← y-position of top of floor
let y = 0;
let vy = 0;                           ← Vertical velocity
const gravity = 0.5;                  ← The force of gravity
const bounceFactor = 0.7;             ← Energy retained after a bounce (70%)
let animationId = null;

function animate() {
```

```
        vy += gravity;          ◄── Applies gravity to vertical velocity
        y += vy;           ◄── Applies velocity to position

        if (y > floor) {          ◄── Checks for collision with the floor
            y = floor;
            vy *= -bounceFactor;   ◄── Reverses and reduces velocity to create a bounce
        }

        ball.style.transform = `translateX(-50%) translateY(${y}px)`;
        animationId = requestAnimationFrame(animate);
    }

    animationId = requestAnimationFrame(animate);
```

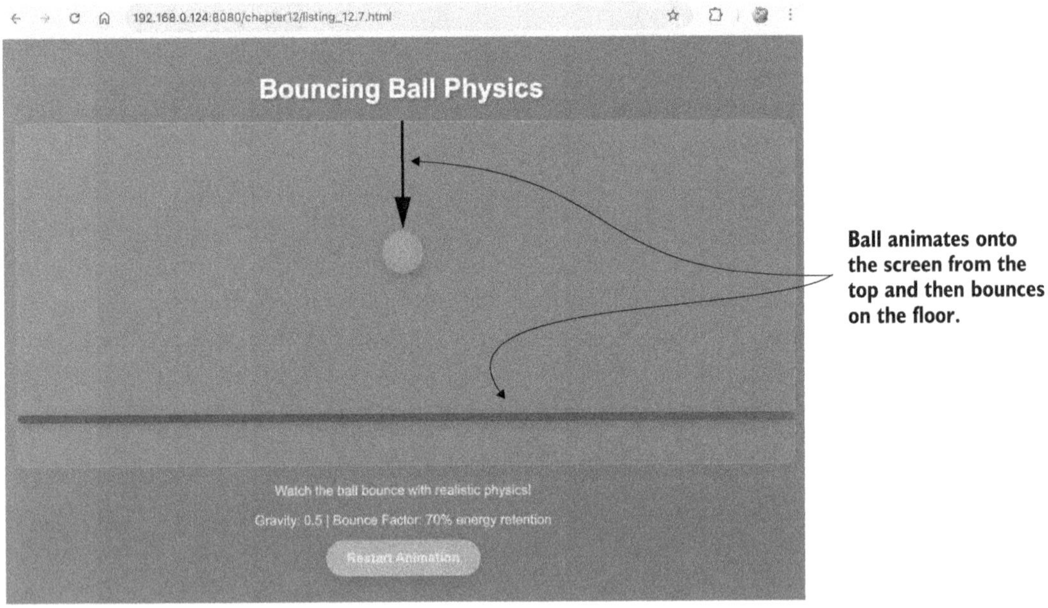


Figure 12.5 A prototype of a realistic bouncing-ball animation. The ball enters from the top of the container and then bounces a few times when it hits the floor.

### 12.3.2 Using Math.sin() for pendulum-like motion

Not all natural motion is in a straight line. Many real-world movements are cyclical or oscillatory, such as the waving of a flag, the gentle bobbing of a boat, or the swing of a pendulum. For these, you can use one of the most useful tools in a developer's math kit: the sine wave (refer to figure 12.6).

The JavaScript function `Math.sin()` is perfect for this task. It takes a single argument—an angle in radians—and returns a value that oscillates smoothly and continuously between –1 and 1.

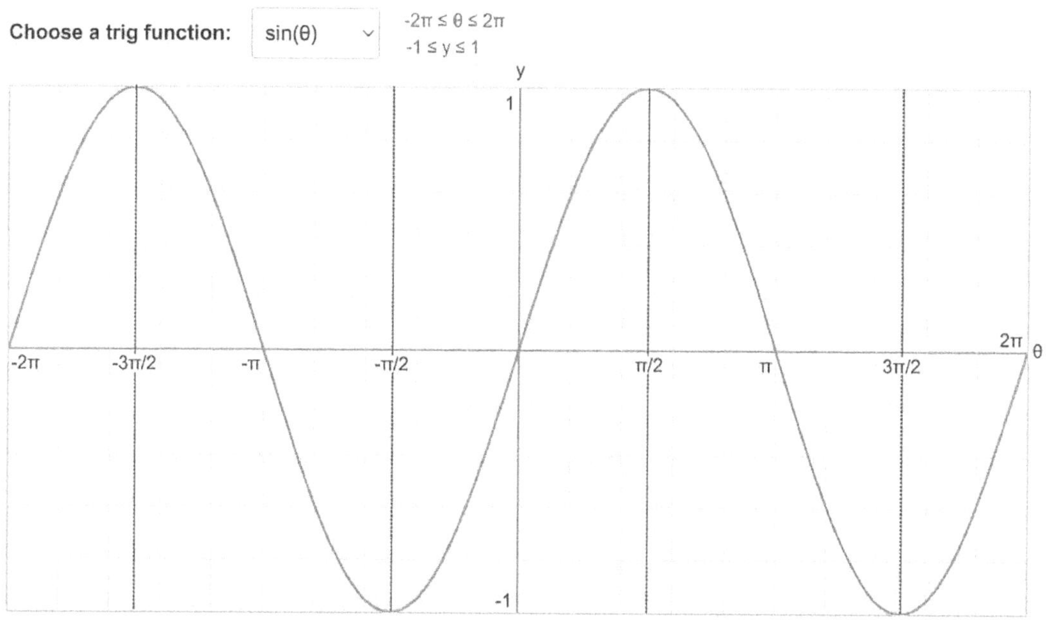


**Figure 12.6 A sine wave oscillates smoothly and continuously between 1 and –1. This oscillatory movement makes a sine wave ideal for modeling pendulum-like motion.**

To use this for animation, you don't need to think too hard about the angle itself. Instead, you can create a variable that increases by a small amount on every frame of your animation loop. As this number increases, feeding it into `Math.sin()` produces a seamless wave. You can then multiply the result by an amplitude to control how wide or tall the oscillation is.

For example, imagine the Marketing Department has come up with a "Wipe the Slate Clean" promotion that waives all user fees for a period of time. They want a windshield washer effect, and you've been asked to prototype it. The code in the following listing takes the first step: a pendulum effect created by applying the sine wave's output to an element's `rotate` transform, as shown in figure 12.7.

**Listing 12.8 Simulating a pendulum**

```
const pendulum = document.getElementById('pendulum');

let angle = 0;
const speed = 0.05;          ← How fast the pendulum swings
const amplitude = 45;        ← Maximum swing angle

function animate() {
    const rotation = amplitude * Math.sin(angle);      ← Gets oscillating value from Math.sin() and scales it
```

```
    pendulum.style.transform = `rotate(${rotation}deg)`;

    angle += speed;

    requestAnimationFrame(animate);
}

requestAnimationFrame(animate);
```

Applies rotation to the element

Increments angle for next frame

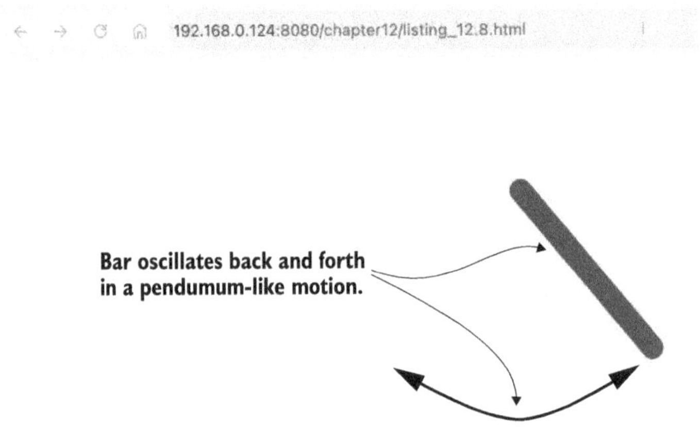


**Figure 12.7 A prototype of a windshield washer effect. The bar oscillates back and forth thanks to the power of the `Math.sin()` function.**

### 12.3.3 Simulating weight and elasticity

You can make your animations feel even more realistic by simulating physical properties such as weight and elasticity. These aren't new concepts but rather new ways of thinking about the physics variables you're already using.

Weight in a UI animation can be thought of as the magnitude of your gravity variable. An element that feels heavy is one with a higher gravity value, causing it to accelerate downward more quickly. A light object would have a lower gravity value, making it seem to float or drift down more slowly.

Elasticity is directly correlated with the bounce factor from the bouncing-ball example. An object that's highly elastic, such as a rubber ball, retains most of its energy after a collision. In your code, this would be a bounce factor close to 1 (say, from 0.7 to 0.9, with higher values producing more bounce). An object with low elasticity, such as a billiard ball, loses most of its energy after a collision. This is simulated with a bounce factor close to 0 (say, from 0.1 to 0.3, with lower values producing less bounce).

By tweaking these two variables, gravity and the bounce factor, you can make your interfaces feel more diverse and dynamic by giving different UI elements distinct physical personalities, as demonstrated in figure 12.8, where each ball is given a different weight and elasticity. Listing 12.9 shows how to implement this effect.

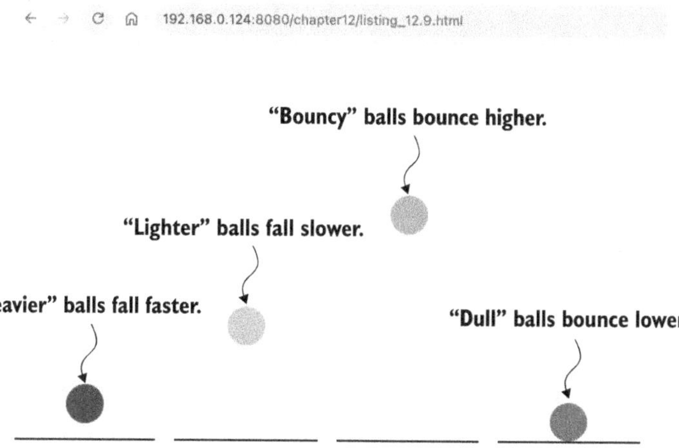


**Figure 12.8** Each ball is given a different weight (gravity) and elasticity (bounce factor).

**Listing 12.9 Simulating weight and elasticity**

```
<body>
    <div class="container">
        <div id="heavyBall" class="ball heavy-ball"></div>
    </div>
    <div class="container">
        <div id="lightBall" class="ball light-ball"></div>
    </div>
    <div class="container">
        <div id="bouncyBall" class="ball bouncy-ball"></div>
    </div>
    <div class="container">
        <div id="dullBall" class="ball dull-ball"></div>
    </div>

    <script>
        function createBallAnimator(elementId, gravity, bounceFactor) {
            const ball = document.getElementById(elementId);
            const floor = 360;
            let y = 0;
            let vy = 0;

            function animate() {
                vy += gravity;
                y += vy;

                if (y > floor) {
                    y = floor;
                    vy *= -bounceFactor;
                }

                ball.style.transform = `translateY(${y}px)`;
                requestAnimationFrame(animate);
            }
```

Container height – ball height

```
            animate();
        }

        createBallAnimator('heavyBall', 0.8, 0.7);
        createBallAnimator('lightBall', 0.2, 0.7);

        createBallAnimator('bouncyBall', 0.5, 0.9);
        createBallAnimator('dullBall', 0.5, 0.3);
    </script>

</body>
```

**Heavy vs. light: Different gravity, same elasticity**

**Bouncy vs. dull: Same gravity, different elasticity**

**EXERCISE**

**Exercise 12.3:** In the bouncing-ball example, what would happen if the bounce factor is changed from `0.7` to `1.1`?

- The ball would bounce lower each time.
- The ball would stop bouncing immediately.
- The ball would bounce higher each time.
- The ball would fall through the floor.

## 12.4 Spring- and friction-based animations

Springs and friction are the secret ingredients that make animations feel organic and satisfying. Springs provide elastic, bouncy motion that overshoots and settles, while friction gradually dissipates energy to bring motion to a natural stop. This section explores how to implement these forces to create animations that feel responsive and alive.

### 12.4.1 Using Hooke's law for spring motion

Spring animations are incredibly popular in UI design because they feel snappy and responsive. They're based on Hooke's law, which states that the force a spring exerts is proportional to how far it's stretched or compressed:

$$F = -k \times x$$

where

- $F$ is the force.
- $k$ is the spring constant (a measure of the spring's stiffness).
- $x$ is the displacement from rest.

In your code, you implement spring motion using the following general steps:

1. Calculate the distance (or *displacement*) between the object's current position and its target position.
2. Use Hooke's law to calculate an acceleration proportional to that distance. The further away the object is, the stronger the pull toward the target.

3. Add that acceleration to the object's velocity.
4. Multiply the velocity by a damping effect, a number between 0 and 1, that determines how quickly the spring settles. (You'll learn more about damping and friction in section 12.4.2.)

Applying Hooke's law in this way creates an effect where the object rushes toward its target, often overshooting it slightly, then getting pulled back and oscillating a few times before the damping causes it to settle at the target position.

For example, suppose your project manager isn't satisfied with the navigation buttons on your company's web pages. She wants the buttons to be animated in a fun, engaging, but also natural way. You immediately think, "Ah, that's a perfect use case for Hooke's law, because I can use it to make each button compress and spring back slightly when clicked." The code for that is in the following listing.

**Listing 12.10 Applying simulated spring motion when clicking a button**

HTML:

```
<button id="springBtn">Click Me</button>
```

JavaScript:

```
const button = document.getElementById("springBtn");

let scale = 1;                  // Initializes the physics parameters
let velocity = 0;
const target = 1;               // The target scale
const k = 0.1;                  // The spring stiffness
const damping = 0.9;            // How quickly it settles

let animating = false;

function animate() {
    if (!animating) return;

    let x = scale - target;     // Calculates displacement from rest
    let force = -k * x;         // Applies Hooke's law (F = -k * x)
    velocity += force;          // Adds force to velocity
    velocity *= damping;        // Adds damping
    scale += velocity;

    button.style.transform = `scale(${scale})`;    // Scales the button

    if (Math.abs(scale - target) < 0.001 &&
        Math.abs(velocity) < 0.001) {
        scale = target;
        velocity = 0;
        animating = false;
        button.style.transform = `scale(${scale})`;
        return;                 // Stops if close enough to target
```

```
    }

    requestAnimationFrame(animate);
}

button.addEventListener("click", () => {
    scale = 0.85;                          ← Initial squish
    velocity = 0;
    animating = true;
    requestAnimationFrame(animate);
});
```

### 12.4.2 Simulating inertia with damping and friction

*Inertia* is the tendency of a moving object to stay in motion. In user interfaces, this is most commonly seen in scrollable lists or draggable elements. When you flick a list on your phone, it doesn't stop the instant your finger leaves the screen; it continues to scroll, gradually slowing down. This coasting effect is inertia.

The force that causes the coasting to slow down and eventually stop is *friction* (also called *damping*). You can simulate it by creating an animation loop that reduces the element's velocity on every frame. The most common way to do this is to multiply the velocity by a *friction coefficient*, which is a number between 0 and 1, but usually slightly less than 1. For example, multiplying the velocity by 0.95 on each frame reduces its speed by 5% every 16 milliseconds or so. This causes the element to slow down rapidly at first and then more gradually, which results in a smooth, natural stop.

This technique is crucial for making drag-and-drop interactions and swipeable galleries feel fluid and responsive. For example, suppose you're part of a team building a web-based game that includes draggable elements that represent puzzle pieces. Right now, dragging a piece from one part of the game to another feels stiff and unnatural. You've been tasked with making drag-and-drop interactions more engaging and visually appealing.

The solution is to introduce inertia so that when the user releases a dragged element, it continues to slide as though it has some momentum, but then settles into place quickly thanks to applied friction. The code is in the following listing.

**Listing 12.11 Applying inertia to a draggable element**

HTML:

```
<div id="draggable">Drag Me!</div>
JavaScript:
const draggable = document.getElementById('draggable');

let isDragging = false;
let startX, startY;
let x = 0, y = 0;
let vx = 0, vy = 0;           ← Horizontal (vx) and vertical (vy) velocity
```

```
let lastX, lastY;
const friction = 0.95;                    ◀── Friction coefficient
let inertiaAnimation;

draggable.addEventListener('mousedown', (e) => {   ◀── Handle drag start
    isDragging = true;
    draggable.style.cursor = 'grabbing';
    startX = e.clientX - x;
    startY = e.clientY - y;
    vx = 0;
    vy = 0;
    lastX = e.clientX;
    lastY = e.clientY;
    cancelAnimationFrame(inertiaAnimation);
});

window.addEventListener('mousemove', (e) => {   ◀── Handle drag
    if (!isDragging) return;
    x = e.clientX - startX;
    y = e.clientY - startY;
    vx = e.clientX - lastX;
    vy = e.clientY - lastY;
    lastX = e.clientX;
    lastY = e.clientY;
    draggable.style.transform = `translate(${x}px, ${y}px)`;
});

window.addEventListener('mouseup', () => {   ◀── Handle drop
    if (!isDragging) return;
    isDragging = false;
    draggable.style.cursor = 'grab';
    applyInertia();                    ◀── Applies inertia effect
});

function applyInertia() {
    vx *= friction;         | Applies friction
    vy *= friction;         |
    x += vx;                                                     | Update position
    y += vy;                                                     |
    draggable.style.transform = `translate(${x}px, ${y}px)`;     |
    if (Math.abs(vx) > 0.1 || Math.abs(vy) > 0.1) {
        inertiaAnimation = requestAnimationFrame(applyInertia);
    }
}
```

#### EXERCISES

**Exercise 12.4:** In Hooke's law (`F = -kx`), what does the negative sign indicate?

1. The force is always downward.
2. The force is in the same direction as the displacement.
3. The force opposes the displacement.
4. The spring is broken.

**Exercise 12.5:** To make a spring animation bouncier (i.e., overshoot the target more), should you increase or decrease the stiffness value?

**Exercise 12.6:** Troubleshoot the following code. The goal is for the element to slow down and stop, but it keeps moving at a constant speed. What's wrong?

```
let position = 0;
let velocity = 10;
let target = 300;
const k = 0.5;
const damping = 1.0;

let animating = false;

function animate() {
    let x = target - position;
    let force = -k * x;
    velocity += force;
    velocity *= damping;
    // The rest of the animation logic appears here...
```

## 12.5 Answers to exercises

**Exercise 12.1:** The position is updated in each frame as follows:

```
velocity += acceleration;
position += velocity;
```

Therefore,

- For frame 1, `velocity` becomes 4, and `position` becomes 4.
- For frame 2, `velocity` becomes 3, and `position` becomes 7.
- For frame 3, `velocity` becomes 2, and `position` becomes 9.

The final position is 9.

**Exercise 12.2:** The `velocity` is initialized to a negative number (`-3`). For the box to move right, the velocity needs to be positive.

**Exercise 12.3:** The ball would bounce higher each time. A `bounceFactor` greater than `1` means the ball gains energy with each bounce, which is unrealistic but demonstrates the principle.

**Exercise 12.4:** The answer is 3. The force opposes the displacement. The negative sign ensures that the spring force always pulls toward the equilibrium position, creating the characteristic oscillating motion.

**Exercise 12.5:** You should increase the stiffness. A higher stiffness value means a stronger spring force, which will create a larger acceleration, causing the element to move faster and overshoot its target by a greater amount.

**Exercise 12.6:** The `damping` value is `1`. Multiplying any number by `1` doesn't change it, so multiplying `velocity` by `damping` doesn't slow down the element. To create a slowing effect, the `damping` value must be less than `1` (such as `0.95`).

## Summary

- Physics-based animations feel more natural because they mimic how objects behave in the real world, meeting user expectations.
- Velocity is the rate of change of an object's position in a certain direction, while acceleration is the rate at which that velocity changes.
- You can simulate gravity by applying a constant positive acceleration to an object's vertical velocity.
- A bounce effect is created by reversing an object's velocity upon collision and multiplying it by a `bounceFactor` less than 1 to simulate energy loss.
- Oscillating motion, like a pendulum, can be modeled using the `Math.sin()` function.
- Spring animations are based on Hooke's law, where an acceleration proportional to the distance from a target is applied, creating a snappy, bouncy effect.
- Friction (or damping) is simulated by multiplying velocity by a factor slightly less than 1 on each frame, which causes the object to slow down.

# 13 Interactivity and gesture-based UI math

**This chapter covers**

- Handling mouse and touch events
- Crafting custom slider controls
- Building scroll-based animations

The static web is dead. Modern surfers now expect web experiences defined by *interactivity*. They want elements that react to their cursor, interfaces they can drag and swipe, and animations that start or change as they scroll. Including this rich layer of user interaction to your pages adds a touch of magic to your site, but there's nothing magical about the implementation. It's made possible by capturing user input, whether it's a click, a touch, or a scroll, and using math to translate that input into a visual change.

## 13.1 Mouse and touch event calculations

Every time a user moves their mouse, drags a finger along a touchpad, or touches the screen, the browser generates events packed to the brim with numerical data. The most fundamental pieces of data are the coordinates: the $x$ and $y$ positions of the pointer or touch point. Understanding how to capture and use these coordinates is the first step toward building any interactive feature.

### 13.1.1 Capturing the cursor position

The most common way to get a cursor's position is through the `mousemove` event. The event object passed to your listener function contains several coordinate properties, but the most useful are `clientX` and `clientY`. These properties give you the pointer's horizontal and vertical coordinates, respectively, relative to the viewport. The viewport is the visible area of the browser window and its origin point, `(0, 0)`, is the top-left corner of this visible area.

Knowing the pointer's coordinates is extremely useful for effects that depend on the pointer's position within the window, regardless of how far the user has scrolled. For example, suppose you're a web developer who has been tasked with creating a custom tooltip that follows the user's cursor. The tooltip should appear near the cursor but offset slightly so it doesn't cover what the user is hovering over, as shown in figure 13.1. Listing 13.1 shows how to implement this effect.

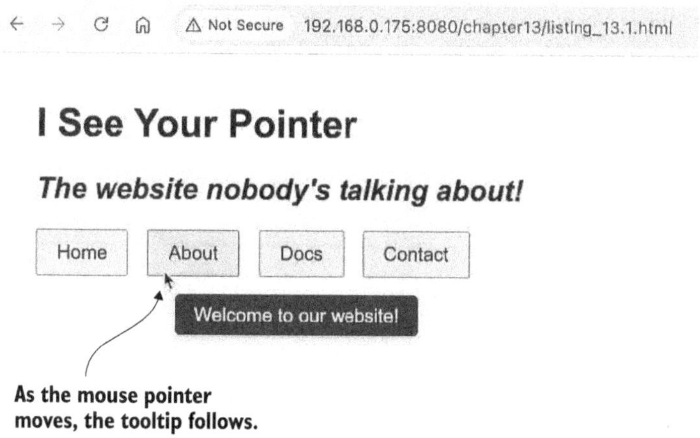


**Figure 13.1 A tooltip that follows the user's pointer**

**Listing 13.1 A tooltip that follows the mouse pointer**

HTML:

```
<h1>I See Your Pointer</h1>
<h2>The website nobody's talking about!</h2>
<nav>
    <button>Home</button>
    <button>About</button>
    <button>Docs</button>
    <button>Contact</button>
```

```
</nav>
<div id="tooltip">Welcome to our website!</div>
```

JavaScript:

```
document.addEventListener('mousemove', (event) => {     ◄── Listens for mousemove events
    const x = event.clientX;                            ── Gets cursor position
    const y = event.clientY;                               relative to viewport

    const tooltip = document.getElementById('tooltip');
    const offsetX = 10;                                 ◄── Offsets to the right
    const offsetY = 20;        ◄── Offsets down

    tooltip.style.left = (x + offsetX) + 'px';          ── Positions the tooltip
    tooltip.style.top = (y + offsetY) + 'px';
});
```

**NOTE** All the code for this chapter's listings is available in this book's GitHub repository: https://github.com/paulmcfe/web-dev-math.

But `clientX` and `clientY` aren't the only options. Mouse events provide multiple coordinate systems:

```
element.addEventListener('click', (e) => {
    console.log('Client coords:', e.clientX, e.clientY);     ◄── Viewport
    console.log('Page coords:', e.pageX, e.pageY);           ◄── Document
    console.log('Screen coords:', e.screenX, e.screenY);     ◄── Monitor
    console.log('Offset coords:', e.offsetX, e.offsetY);     ◄── Target element
});
```

Each coordinate system serves a different purpose:

- Client coordinates measure from the viewport's top-left corner.
- Page coordinates measure from the document's top-left corner (accounting for scroll).
- Screen coordinates measure from the monitor's top-left corner.
- Offset coordinates measure from the target element's top-left corner.

In particular, the mathematical relationship between client and page coordinates is connected to scroll position:

```
const pageX = event.clientX + window.scrollX;     ── Converting between client
const pageY = event.clientY + window.scrollY;        and page coordinates

const clientX = event.pageX - window.scrollX;     ── Converting between page
const clientY = event.pageY - window.scrollY;        and client coordinates
```

Refer to section 13.3 for more on using scroll position to animate page elements.

### 13.1.2 Detecting touch gestures

On touch-enabled devices, you'll work with `TouchEvent` objects instead of `MouseEvent` objects. Touch events are more complex because a user can be touching the screen in multiple places at once (e.g., by pinching or spreading two fingers to zoom out or in).

The `TouchEvent` object contains lists of touch points. The most useful property is `event.touches`, which is a list of all fingers currently on the screen. Each item in this list is a `Touch` object with its own `clientX` and `clientY` properties.

By measuring the properties of these touch points over time, you can detect gestures. For example, a pinch gesture involves two fingers moving closer together, while a spread gesture involves two fingers moving farther apart. You can measure this by calculating the distance between the two touch points in the `event.touches` list on each `touchmove` event. Here's a function that, given two points `a` and `b`, represented by the points `(ax, ay)` and `(bx, by)` and derived from the `clientX` and `clientY` properties of each of the two fingers, returns the distance between them using the Pythagorean theorem:

```
function distance(x1, y1, x2, y2) {
    const dx = x2 - x1;
    const dy = y2 - y1;
    return Math.sqrt(dx * dx + dy * dy);
}
```

As an example, suppose you have a photo on a page, and you want touch-enabled devices to be able to use gestures to zoom in and out on the photo. The following listing shows the code that will do it.

**Listing 13.2 Scaling a photo based on pinch and spread gestures**

HTML:

```
<img src="/images/flower.jpg" alt="Flower" class="photo">
```

JavaScript:

```
const photo = document.querySelector('.photo');
let startDist = 1;

photo.addEventListener('touchstart', (e) => {       ← Listens for touch on photo
    if (e.touches.length === 2) {                   ← Makes sure it's two fingers
        const [a, b] = e.touches;                   ← Gets the touch points
        startDist = distance(a.clientX, a.clientY,
                             b.clientX, b.clientY);   Calculates distance between them
    }
}, { passive: true });

photo.addEventListener('touchmove', (e) => {        ← Listens for touch moves
```

```
    if (e.touches.length === 2) {
        const [a, b] = e.touches;
        const d = distance(a.clientX, a.clientY,
                           b.clientX, b.clientY);
        const raw = d / startDist;
        const scale = Math.min(5, Math.max(0.5, raw));
        photo.style.transform = `scale(${scale})`;
    }
}, { passive: true });
```

Makes sure it's two fingers

Gets the touch points

Calculates distance between them

Calculates scale factor

Clamps scale to range [0.5, 5]

Scales photo

This code uses the earlier `distance()` function to determine the distance between the two fingers throughout the gesture. The ratio of that value to the original distance between the fingers determines the scale factor. It is clamped to the range `[0.5, 5]` to prevent things from getting too out of hand, zoom-wise.

### 13.1.3 Converting screen coordinates to local element coordinates

Often, you need to know where within a specific element the user clicked or touched. To find this out, it is necessary to convert viewport coordinates to element-relative coordinates.

The go-to JavaScript tool here is `getBoundingClientRect()`, which returns an element's position and size relative to the viewport. To get the mouse pointer's current horizontal ($x$) position within the element, you take `event.clientX` in whatever `MouseEvent` you're listening to and subtract the element's `left` property as returned by `element.getBoundingClientRect()`:

```
element.addEventListener('click', (event) => {
    const rect = element.getBoundingClientRect();

    const elementX = event.clientX - rect.left;
    const elementY = event.clientY - rect.top;

    const percentX = (elementX / rect.width) * 100;
    const percentY = (elementY / rect.height) * 100;

    console.log(`Clicked at ${percentX}% across, ${percentY}% down`);
});
```

Listens for clicks

Gets element's position

Converts viewport coordinates to element coordinates

(Optional) Converts to percentages

For example, imagine your boss wants you to build an interactive color picker where users click on a gradient to select the page's background color, as shown in figure 13.2. The horizontal position determines the hue, while the vertical position determines the lightness.

You need to determine exactly where they clicked within the gradient to calculate the corresponding color value, as shown in Listing 13.3.

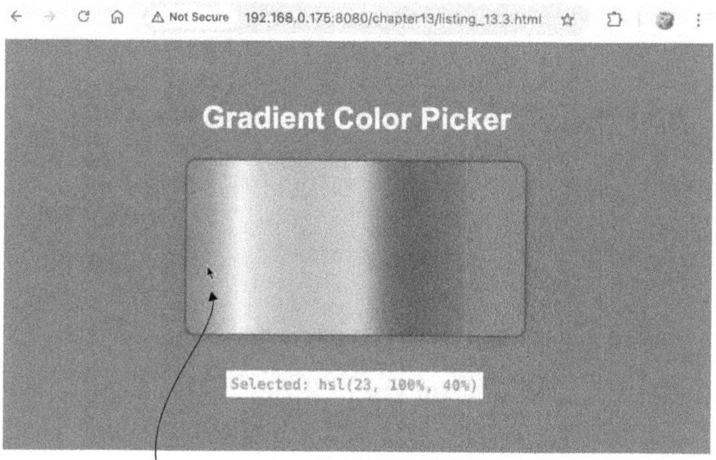


**Click inside the gradient to set the page background color.**

**Figure 13.2 An interactive color picker that sets the page background color based on where the user clicks within the element**

**Listing 13.3 Creating an interactive color picker based on element coordinates**

HTML:

```
<div id="gradient"></div>
```

CSS:

```
#gradient {
    width: 360px;
    height: 180px;
    background: linear-gradient(to right, red, yellow, lime,
        cyan, blue, magenta, red),
        linear-gradient(to top, #000 0%, transparent 100%);
    cursor: crosshair;
}
```

JavaScript:

```
const colorPicker = document.getElementById('gradient');

colorPicker.addEventListener('click', (event) => {
    const rect = colorPicker.getBoundingClientRect();

    const x = event.clientX - rect.left;
    const y = event.clientY - rect.top;


    const normalizedX = x / rect.width;
    const normalizedY = y / rect.height;
```

**Listens for clicks**

**Gets color picker's bounding rectangle**

**Calculates click position within element**

**Normalizes to 0–1 range**

```
const clampedX = Math.max(0, Math.min(1, normalizedX));     // Clamps values to
const clampedY = Math.max(0, Math.min(1, normalizedY));     // handle edge cases

const hue = Math.round(clampedX * 360);     // Calculates hue based on horizontal position (0–360 degrees)

const lightness = Math.round((1 - clampedY) * 100);     // Calculate lightness based on vertical position (0%–100%)

const hsl = `hsl(${hue}, 100%, ${lightness}%)`;     // Applies the color
document.body.style.background = hsl;
```

**EXERCISES**

**Exercise 13.1:** What is the main difference between the coordinates as given by `event.clientX` and `event.clientY` and the `left` and `top` values returned from `element.getBoundingClientRect()`?

**Exercise 13.2:** Which mathematical theorem is used to determine the distance between two fingers in a touch event?

**Exercise 13.3:** Troubleshoot the following code. The goal is to log the mouse's *x* coordinate inside the `box` div. Why is it logging the wrong value?

```
const box = document.getElementById('box');
    box.addEventListener('click', (e) => {
        const rect = box.getBoundingClientRect();
        // What's wrong here?
        const localX = e.clientX + rect.left;
        console.log(localX);
    });
```

## 13.2 Custom slider controls

While HTML's standard `<input type="range">` element for adding a slider to the page gets the job done in a pinch, its styling options are notoriously limited and inconsistent across browsers. When full creative control over the look and feel of your interface is necessary, and crucially, when full *mathematical* control is required to translate mouse movements to numeric values, crafting a custom slider is the best approach. Custom controls not only look better but can be adapted to unique interactions, such as circular dials.

Building custom sliders from scratch is a fantastic way to apply your math skills. The core of any custom slider consists of a few key mathematical operations: converting cursor positions to values, mapping coordinates to different geometries, clamping to predefined limits, normalizing angles, and ensuring smooth, predictable behavior.

### 13.2.1 Building a custom linear slider

Linear sliders are the simplest custom control, but they still require careful math to feel responsive and accurate. You need to convert pixel positions to values within a range, handle edge cases, and provide smooth interaction.

The fundamental math behind a linear slider is mapping a value from one range to another. You need to translate the pixel position of the mouse along a track into a corresponding value, such as a percentage from 0 to 100 or a brightness value from –100 to 100.

Imagine you're building a web-based photo editor. You need clean, intuitive sliders to control settings such as brightness, saturation, and contrast. You decide that custom linear sliders will give you the precise look and functionality you want. Figure 13.3 shows an implementation with three sliders—for brightness, saturation, and contrast.

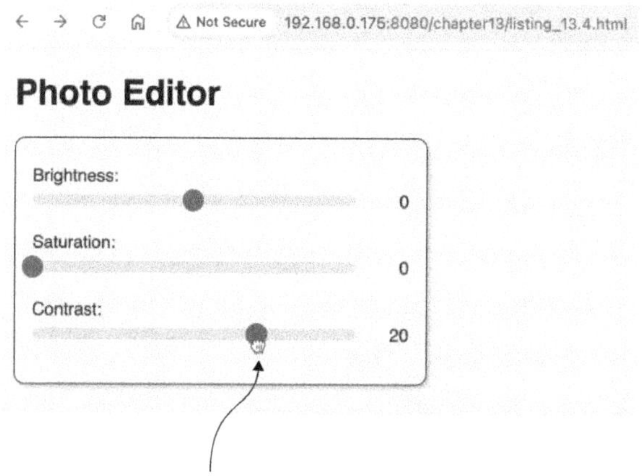


**Drag the slider handle left to decrease the contrast value, or drag it right to increase the contrast value.**

**Figure 13.3 Custom linear sliders for setting brightness, saturation, and contrast values**

Listing 13.4a shows how to implement these sliders in HTML and CSS. To keep the code simple, note that this example isn't accessible. In production use, you'd add `role` and `aria` attributes to each slider, a `focus` indicator, and a `keydown` event handler for keyboard support.

**Listing 13.4a Implementing a custom linear slider (part 1)**

HTML:

```
<h1>Photo Editor</h1>
<div class="editor">
    <p class="slider-label">Brightness:</p>
    <div class="control">
        <div id="brightness-slider"
             class="slider-track">
            <div id="brightness-handle"
                 class="slider-handle">
            </div>
        </div>
```

**Slider track** (the `brightness-slider` div)

**Slider handle** (the `brightness-handle` div)

```
        <div id="brightness-value"
             class="brightness-output">           Current slider value
            0
        </div>
    </div>
    <p class="slider-label">Saturation:</p>
    <div class="control">
        <div class="slider-track" id="saturation-slider">
            <div class="slider-handle" id="saturation-handle"></div>
        </div>
        <div id="saturation-value" class="saturation-output">0</div>
    </div>
    <p class="slider-label">Contrast:</p>
    <div class="control">
        <div class="slider-track" id="contrast-slider">
            <div class="slider-handle" id="contrast-handle"></div>
        </div>
        <div id="contrast-value" class="contrast-output">0</div>
    </div>
</div>
```

CSS (partial):

```
.control {
    display: flex;
    align-items: center;
    gap: 1rem;
}
.slider-track {
    width: 300px;
    height: 10px;
    background: #ddd;
    border-radius: 5px;
    position: relative;
    cursor: pointer;
}
.slider-handle {
    width: 20px;
    height: 20px;
    background: hsl(322 100% 31%);
    border-radius: 50%;
    position: absolute;
    top: 50%;
    transform: translate(-50%, -50%);
    cursor: grab;
}
```

The next listing shows the JavaScript that makes the magic happen.

**Listing 13.4b Implementing a custom linear slider (part 2)**

```
function setupSlider(trackId,
                     handleId,                      Function to build a slider
                     valueId, minValue, maxValue) {
```

```
    const slider = document.getElementById(trackId);
    const handle = document.getElementById(handleId);
    const valueDisplay = document.getElementById(valueId);

    let isDragging = false;
    let value = 0;
    let progress = (value - minValue) /
                   (maxValue - minValue);
    handle.style.left = `${progress * 100}%`;
    valueDisplay.textContent = value;

    handle.addEventListener('mousedown', (e) => {
        e.preventDefault();
        isDragging = true;
        handle.style.cursor = 'grabbing';
    });

    window.addEventListener('mouseup', () => {
        isDragging = false;
        handle.style.cursor = 'grab';
    });

    window.addEventListener('mousemove', (e) => {
        if (!isDragging) return;

        const rect = slider.getBoundingClientRect();
        let offsetX = e.clientX - rect.left;

        offsetX = Math.max(0, Math.min(offsetX, rect.width));

        const progress = offsetX / rect.width;

        value = Math.round(minValue + progress *
                           (maxValue - minValue));

        handle.style.left = `${progress * 100}%`;
        valueDisplay.textContent = value;
    });
}

setupSlider('brightness-slider',
            'brightness-handle',
            'brightness-value',
            -100, 100);
setupSlider('saturation-slider',
            'saturation-handle',
            'saturation-value',
            0, 100);
setupSlider('contrast-slider',
            'contrast-handle',
            'contrast-value',
            -50, 50);
```

Sets initial value to 0

Handle mouse press (start of drag)

Handle mouse release (end of drag)

Handle mouse move (dragging)

Calculates mouse position relative to track

Clamps position within track's bounds

Calculates progress ratio (0.0 to 1.0)

Maps progress to value range

Updates UI

Minimum and maximum values

The key part of this code is the `setupSlider()` function, which takes references to the `slider`, `handle`, and `value` elements, as well as minimum and maximum values. After initializing the slider to 0, the function monitors the dragging by handling the `mousedown` (start of drag), `mouseup` (end of drag), and `mousemove` (during drag) events.

Here's the general process:

1. On `mousedown`, record that the user has started dragging by setting `isDragging = true`.
2. On `mousemove`, get the mouse's horizontal position (`event.clientX`).
3. Calculate the mouse's position relative to the slider track by subtracting the track's starting left position:

```
const rect = slider.getBoundingClientRect();
let offsetX = e.clientX - rect.left;
```

4. Clamp the position to within the track's bounds:

```
offsetX = Math.max(0, Math.min(offsetX, rect.width));
```

5. Convert this pixel position into a progress ratio between 0.0 and 1.0 by dividing it by the track's total width:

```
const progress = offsetX / rect.width;
```

6. Map this ratio to your desired value range (defined by the function's arguments `minValue` and `maxValue`):

```
value = Math.round(minValue + progress * (maxValue - minValue));
```

### 13.2.2 Building a custom rotary control

Circular controls such as knobs and dials require trigonometry to convert cursor positions to angles and then to values. These controls are perfect for audio controls, color wheels, or any parameter that feels natural as a rotation.

Imagine you're building a music production app where users need precise control over synthesizer parameters, such as volume, pan, or resonance. A rotary knob provides more precision than a linear slider in less space, and it mimics real hardware interfaces. Figure 13.4 shows an implementation of a single rotary control with an indicator that can be dragged clockwise or counterclockwise to set the control value.

Listing 13.5a shows how to implement this control in HTML and CSS. Again, for production use, you'd need to add accessibility features to this code.

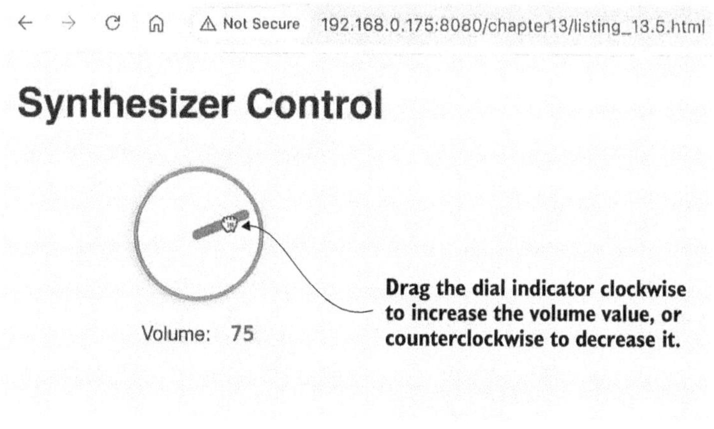


**Figure 13.4 A custom rotary control for setting volume values**

**Listing 13.5a Implementing a custom rotary control (part 1)**

HTML:

```
<div id="knob-container">
    <div id="knob">
        <div id="knob-indicator"></div>
    </div>
    <div>Volume: <span id="knob-value">50</span></div>
</div>
```

CSS (partial):

```
#knob-container {
    display: flex;
    flex-direction: column;
    align-items: center;
    gap: 1rem;
    margin-top: 2rem;
    max-width: 300px;
}
#knob {
    width: 100px;
    height: 100px;
    border: 4px solid #888;
    border-radius: 50%;
    box-shadow: 0 4px 16px rgba(0, 0, 0, 0.12);
    position: relative;
    display: flex;
    align-items: center;
    justify-content: center;
    cursor: grab;
    transition: box-shadow 0.2s;
}
#knob-indicator {
```

```
    position: absolute;
    left: 50%;
    top: 50%;
    width: 8px;
    height: 50px;
    background: #3476e6;
    border-radius: 4px;
    transform: translate(-50%, -90%);
    box-shadow: 0 1px 4px rgba(52, 118, 230, 0.18);
}
```

The JavaScript is shown in the following listing

**Listing 13.5b Implementing a custom rotary control (part 2)**

```
let knobValue = 50;
const knobMin = 0;                    // Knob configuration
const knobMax = 100;

const minAngle = -135;
const maxAngle = 135;                 // Sets angle limits (in degrees)
const angleRange = maxAngle - minAngle;

const knob = document.getElementById('knob');
const knobDisplay = document.getElementById('knob-value');

function valueToAngle(value) {
    const percentage = (value - knobMin) /
                       (knobMax - knobMin);      // Converts value to rotation angle
    return minAngle + angleRange * percentage;
}

function angleToValue(angle) {
    if (angle < minAngle) angle = minAngle;      // Clamps angle to valid range
    if (angle > maxAngle) angle = maxAngle;

    const percentage = (angle - minAngle) / angleRange;     // Converts angle to value
    return knobMin + (knobMax - knobMin) * percentage;
}

function updateKnob() {
    const angle = valueToAngle(knobValue);
    knob.style.transform = `rotate(${angle}deg)`;        // Updates knob rotation
    knobDisplay.textContent = Math.round(knobValue);
}

let isRotating = false;

knob.addEventListener('mousedown', function (e) {    // Handle mouse press (start of drag)
    isRotating = true;
    e.preventDefault();
});

document.addEventListener('mousemove', function (e) {    // Handle mouse move (dragging)
```

```
    if (!isRotating) return;

    const rect = knob.getBoundingClientRect();       // Gets knob center position
    const centerX = rect.left + rect.width / 2;
    const centerY = rect.top + rect.height / 2;

    const deltaX = e.clientX - centerX;       // Calculates angle from center to mouse
    const deltaY = e.clientY - centerY;

    let angleRadians = Math.atan2(deltaY, deltaX);       // Math.atan2 returns angle in radians

    let angleDegrees = angleRadians * (180 / Math.PI);       // Converts to degrees

    angleDegrees += 90;       // Adjusts angle

    if (angleDegrees > 180) angleDegrees -= 360;       // Normalize to −180 to 180 range

    knobValue = angleToValue(angleDegrees);       // Converts angle to value

    updateKnob();       // Updates UI
});

document.addEventListener('mouseup', function () {       // Handle mouse release (end of drag)
    isRotating = false;
});

updateKnob();       // Updates UI
```

Unlike a linear slider that only cares about one axis, a dial needs to convert the mouse's `(x, y)` position into an angle. The perfect mathematical tool for this is `Math.atan2(y, x)`. This function takes the vertical and horizontal distances from a center point and returns the angle in radians. Here's the general process:

1. Determine the center coordinates of the dial element:

   ```
   const rect = knob.getBoundingClientRect();
   const centerX = rect.left + rect.width / 2;
   const centerY = rect.top + rect.height / 2;
   ```

2. Calculate the vector from the center to the mouse pointer `(deltaX, deltaY)`:

   ```
   const deltaX = e.clientX - centerX;
   const deltaY = e.clientY - centerY;
   ```

3. Use `Math.atan2()` to get the angle:

   ```
   let angleRadians = Math.atan2(deltaY, deltaX);
   ```

4. Convert this angle from radians to degrees:

   ```
   let angleDegrees = angleRadians * (180 / Math.PI);
   ```

5 Apply the angle to the dial's `transform: rotate()` style:

```
knob.style.transform = `rotate(${angle}deg)`;
```

**EXERCISES**

**Exercise 13.4:** A linear slider track has a width of `400px`. If you want to map mouse clicks to a value range of `0` to `200`, what would be the correct value for a click that happens `300px` from the left edge of the track?

1. 75
2. 150
3. 200
4. 300

**Exercise 13.5:** In the custom rotary dial, why is it necessary to adjust the computed angle by adding 90 degrees?

## 13.3 Scroll-based animations

Scroll-based animations are a powerful way to create engaging, narrative-driven web pages. By linking an element's animation state to the user's scroll position, you can make content fade in, slide into place, or change properties as it enters the viewport. This creates a more dynamic and immersive experience than simply presenting a static page.

The math behind these effects involves tracking the user's scroll position, calculating a progress percentage, and then using that value to drive CSS properties.

### 13.3.1 Detecting scroll position

The foundation of scroll animations is understanding where the user has scrolled the page vertically, which requires basic arithmetic involving the following three properties:

- `window.scrollY`—The number of pixels the document has been scrolled down from the top
- `window.innerHeight`—The height of the viewport in pixels
- `document.documentElement.scrollHeight`—The height of the document in pixels

From these properties, you can derive a couple of key metrics. The first is the maximum scrollable distance, which is the total height of the document minus the viewport height:

```
const viewportHeight = window.innerHeight;
const documentHeight = document.documentElement.scrollHeight;
const maxScroll = documentHeight - viewportHeight;     // Maximum distance user can scroll
```

The second key metric is the user's scroll progress, which is the current scroll position divided by the maximum scrollable distance:

```
const scrollY = window.scrollY;
const scrollProgress = scrollY / maxScroll;    ← User's scroll progress
```

The scroll progress calculation gives a normalized value from 0 (the user is at the top of the page) to 1 (the user has scrolled to the bottom of the page), which is ideal for controlling animations.

Imagine you're a developer for an online publishing company. Based on user surveys and testing, the UX group has found that when users are reading long-form content, they often get frustrated because they can't easily determine how much of the content remains. The UX lead has tasked you to build a reading progress indicator that shows how far through an article the user has scrolled. The UX lead wants the progress indicator to meet the following guidelines:

- The indicator width should increase as the user scrolls, reaching the full width of the page when the user scrolls to the bottom.
- The indicator should display the percentage read, from 0% at the top to 100% at the bottom.
- The indicator background should change color as the user scrolls, from red at the top to green at the bottom.

Figure 13.5 shows the reading progress indicator.

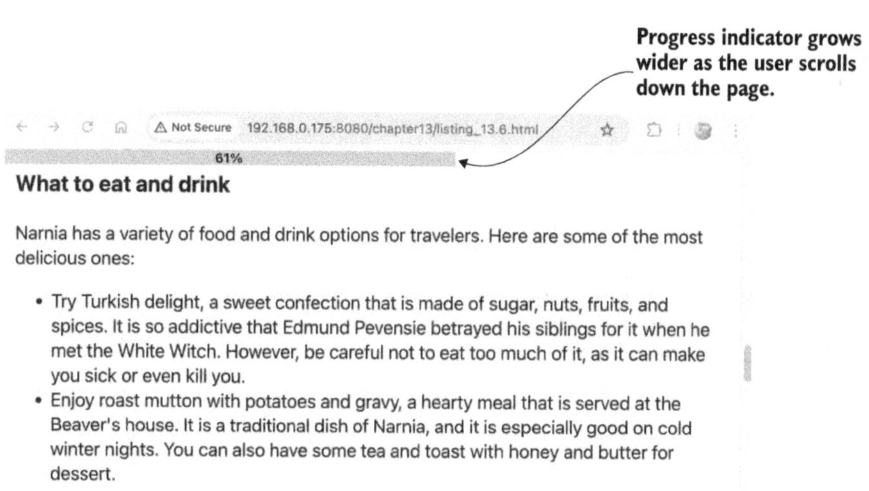


**Figure 13.5 A reading progress indicator**

The following listing shows how to implement this element.

**Listing 13.6 Implementing a reading progress indicator**

HTML:

```
<div id="progress-bar"></div>        ◄── The progress indicator
<main>
    <article>
        <!-- Article text appears here -->
    </article>
</main>
```

CSS:

```
#progress-bar {
    position: fixed;
    top: 0;                          Indicator is fixed to top-left.
    left: 0;
    height: 1rem;
    background: red;
    width: 0;
    font-size: 0.85rem;
    font-weight: bold;
    text-align: center;
    z-index: 1000;
    transition: width 0.2s cubic-bezier(.25, .8, .25, 1);
}
```

JavaScript:

```
const progressBar = document.getElementById('progress-bar');

function updateProgressBar() {
    const scrollableHeight = document.documentElement.scrollHeight -
                             window.innerHeight;
    let scrollProgress = 0;
    if (scrollableHeight > 0) {
        scrollProgress = window.scrollY / scrollableHeight;   ◄── Calculates scroll progress
    }
    progressBar.style.width = `${scrollProgress * 100}%`;     ◄── Uses progress to update indicator width

    const hue = scrollProgress * 120;                         ◄── Updates color based on progress (0=red; 120=green)
    progressBar.style.backgroundColor = `hsl(${hue}, 70%, 50%)`;

    if (scrollProgress > 0.03) {                              ◄── Displays percentage when indicator is wide enough
        progressBar.textContent = `${Math.round(scrollProgress * 100)}%`;
    } else {
        progressBar.textContent = '';
    }
```

```
}

window.addEventListener('scroll', updateProgressBar);
window.addEventListener('resize', updateProgressBar);

updateProgressBar();
```

**Updates on scroll, resize, and page load**

The `updateProgressBar()` function is called when the user scrolls (also on page load and when the window resizes). The code determines the scrollable height and the scroll progress, then it changes the indicator `width` property based on the calculated `scrollProgress` value. That value is also used to change the indicator's background color (by multiplying the `hue` value of the `hsl()` function by 120). Finally, once the indicator is wide enough, the function displays the `scrollProgress` value as a percentage.

### 13.3.2 Creating dynamic UI changes with intersection observers

Listening for the `scroll` event can be inefficient because it fires continuously while the user scrolls. A modern, more performant alternative is the `IntersectionObserver` API. This API lets you know when a target element enters or leaves the viewport (or another specified container). It doesn't rely on mathematical calculations in your code; instead, the browser handles the intersection math for you. You create an observer and tell it which elements to watch. When one of your watched elements intersects with the viewport, your callback function is triggered. This is awesome because it hands off all the intersection math to the browser, leaving you free to apply math where it counts: in your UI.

As an example, suppose you're a freelance web designer. For a client working as a book cover designer, you built a portfolio site to show off her most recent work. However, recently she pointed out that the page lacks a certain flair. As users scroll down the page, each portfolio card appears, but there's nothing to catch the user's attention. She wants you to update the page with the following effects:

- Each portfolio card should fade in as it enters the screen and fade out as it leaves.
- Each card should scale up as it enters the screen and scale down as it leaves.
- Each card should slide up as it enters the screen and sink down as it leaves.
- Each effect should increase or decrease, depending on how visible the portfolio card is.

Given these specs, you know you can use an intersection observer to modify the corresponding CSS properties directly. That is, an intersection observer on an element has an `intersectionRatio` property that tells you how much of the element is currently visible, where 0.0 is not visible at all and 1.0 is completely visible. Figure 13.6 shows the modified page with the requested effects.

Listing 13.7 shows how to implement the effects in JavaScript.

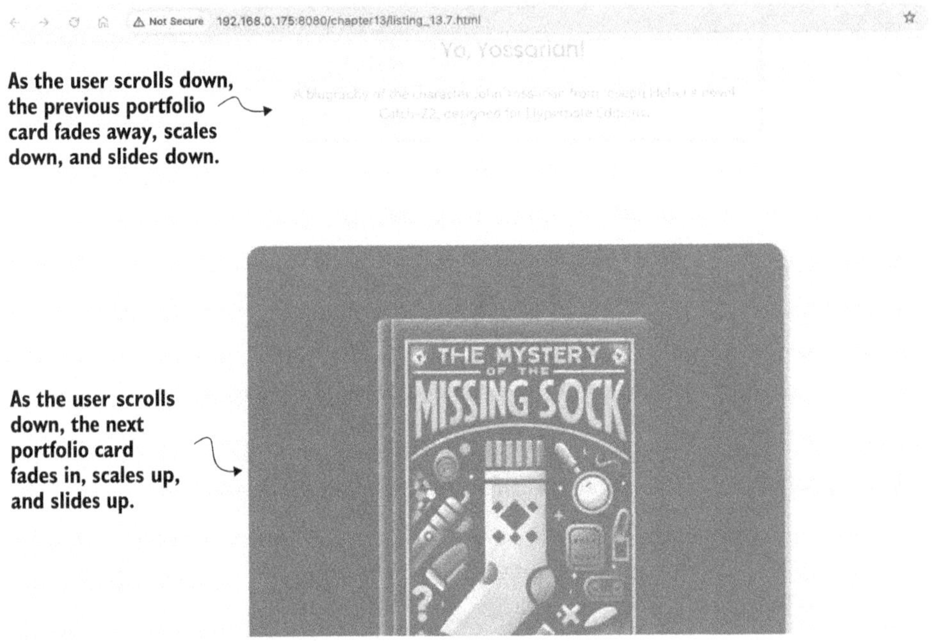


**Figure 13.6 Dynamic UI changes based on an intersection observer**

**Listing 13.7 Making UI changes with an intersection observer**

```
function setupScrollAnimations() {
    const options = {  #
        root: null,
        rootMargin: '0px',
        threshold: Array.from({ length: 101 }, (_, i) => i / 100)
    };

    const observer = new IntersectionObserver((entries) => {
        entries.forEach(entry => {
            const element = entry.target;
            const ratio = entry.intersectionRatio;

            const opacity = ratio;
            const scale = 0.8 + (ratio * 0.2);
            const translateY = (1 - ratio) * 30;

            element.style.opacity = opacity;
            element.style.transform = `
                translateY(${translateY}px)
                scale(${scale})
            `;
        });
    }, options);
```

- **Configures the intersection observer**
- **Gets entry's visibility**
- **Sets opacity to visibility**
- **Sets scale based on visibility (0.8 to 1.0)**
- **Sets translateY based on visibility (30px to 0px)**
- **Applies updated styles**

```
    document.querySelectorAll('.scroll-animate')
        .forEach(element => {
            observer.observe(element);
        });
}
setupScrollAnimations();
```

Observes all animatable elements

The `options` object configures the intersection observer as follows:

- `root`—Sets the container for intersection detection, where `null` means the browser viewport.
- `rootMargin`—Adds a margin around the root's bounding box for intersection calculations. `0px` means no margin, so elements trigger exactly when they enter or leave the viewport.
- `threshold`—Defines when the observer callback fires based on how much of the element is visible. The value is the array `[0, 0.01, 0.02, 0.03, ..., 0.99, 1.0]` (101 values from 0 to 1). The callback fires whenever the element's visibility crosses any of these thresholds.

As far as the math goes, each entry's current visibility (obtained via `entry.intersectionRatio`) is stored in the `ratio` variable and used in the code to modify the following properties:

- `opacity`—Set to `ratio`, so it's 0 when the entry is fully offscreen, and 1 when the entry is fully visible
- `scale`—Set using the formula `0.8 + (ratio * 0.2)`, which produces values from 0.8 (when `ratio=0`) to 1.0 (when `ratio=1`)
- `translateY`—Set using the formula `(1 - ratio) * 30`, which produces values from 30 (when `ratio=0`) to 0 (when `ratio=1`)

**EXERCISES**

**Exercise 13.6:** A webpage has a total height of `4000px`. The user's viewport height is `1000px`. If the user has scrolled down by `1500px` (i.e., `window.scrollY` is 1500), what's the scroll progress as a percentage?

**Exercise 13.7:** What is the main performance benefit of using `IntersectionObserver` over listening to the `scroll` event?

**Exercise 13.8:** What is the range of the `intersectionRatio` property?

## 13.4 Solutions to exercises

**Exercise 13.1:** `event.clientX` and `event.clientY` provide coordinates relative to the viewport (the visible part of the window). The `left` and `top` values from `element.getBoundingClientRect()` provide coordinates representing the position of the element's top-left corner.

**Exercise 13.2:** The answer is the Pythagorean theorem.

**Exercise 13.3:** The code is adding the element's `left` offset instead of subtracting it. Here's the current formula:

```
const localX = e.clientX - rect.left;
```

**Exercise 13.4:** The progress is `300 / 400 = 0.75`. The value is `0 + 0.75 * (200 - 0) = 150`. Therefore, the answer is 2: 150.

**Exercise 13.5:** The custom rotary dial code adds 90 degrees to the computed angle because `Math.atan2(0, 0)` returns `0°`, which points to the right (the positive *x*-axis). For a rotary knob, you usually want `0°` to point straight up (the top of the knob). By adding 90 degrees, you rotate the reference so that `0°` is at the top.

**Exercise 13.6:** Here's the calculation:

```
Maximum scrollable distance = scrollHeight - innerHeight
                            = 4000 - 1000
                            = 3000px
Progress = scrollY / scrollableHeight
         = 1500 / 3000
         = 0.5
Percentage = 0.5 * 100
           = 50%
```

**Exercise 13.7:** The `scroll` event can fire hundreds of times during a single scroll gesture, forcing your code to run constantly. `IntersectionObserver` is more efficient because its callback function only runs when a target element's visibility status changes, and not on every single pixel of scrolling.

**Exercise 13.8:** The `intersectionRatio` property tells you how much of the element is currently visible using a range from 0.0 (not visible at all) to 1.0 (completely visible).

## Summary

- The `event.clientX` and `event.clientY` properties provide a pointer's coordinates relative to the viewport's top-left corner.
- You can convert viewport coordinates to an element's local coordinates by subtracting the `left` and `top` values from `element.getBoundingClientRect()`.
- The distance between two points can be found using the Pythagorean theorem, and the direction can be found using `Math.atan2()`.
- For a slider control, you map the current drag progress to the slider value using the formula `minValue + progress * (maxValue - minValue)`.
- The user's scroll progress can be calculated as a normalized value from 0 to 1 using the formula `scrollY / (scrollHeight - innerHeight)`.
- The `IntersectionObserver` API is an efficient way to trigger actions when an element enters or leaves the viewport.
- The `intersectionRatio` property from an `IntersectionObserver` tells you what percentage of a target element is currently visible.

# 14 Canvas-based math and drawing

**This chapter covers**

- Creating canvas-based data visualizations
- Detecting hits on data elements
- Creating canvas-based particle systems
- Simulating a balloon drop, a star field, and a confetti shower

In this chapter, all the mathematical concepts you learned earlier, from geometry and trigonometry to physics and animation, come together in a uniquely creative space: the HTML `canvas` element. Unlike DOM elements, which have structure and style, a canvas is a blank slate, a grid of pixels waiting for instructions. Your primary tools for creating on this slate are JavaScript and the mathematical principles that let you control every pixel with precision.

This chapter does not cover the basics of the Canvas API itself, but it focuses instead on some core aspects of its use in modern UI development. In the pages that follow, you will learn how to translate abstract data into visual geometry, detect hits on visual elements, and create dynamic motion with physics simulations.

## 14.1 Data-driven geometry and hit detection

HTML elements provide a built-in structure for content. On a canvas, you must create this structure yourself using math. This is especially true when visualizing data, where you need to map numbers to geometric shapes. The reverse is just as important. Hit detection is the process of using the math of coordinates and shapes to determine whether a user's click or hover is interacting with something you've drawn.

### 14.1.1 Drawing a pie chart from data

Creating a pie chart on the canvas involves converting data values into angular segments of a circle. The fundamental challenge is mapping each data point to its corresponding slice angle, which requires understanding how radians relate to percentages of a whole. A full circle is $2\pi$ radians, so the task reduces to calculating what fraction of $2\pi$ each data point represents.

For example, suppose your site analytics team is creating a dashboard to display visualizations of site metrics, such as browser share. To begin the process of building the dashboard, they've provided you with some browser share numbers and tasked you with displaying them as a pie chart. This is a perfect use for the canvas, where each browser usage value can be rendered as a proportional slice of a full circle ($2\pi$ radians). Figure 14.1 shows the resulting pie chart, and Listing 14.1 shows the implementation in HTML and JavaScript.

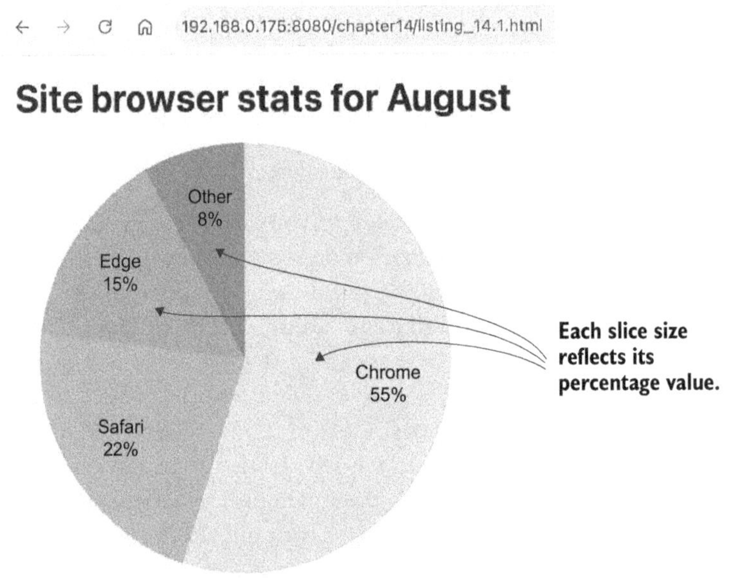


**Figure 14.1 A canvas-based pie chart of browser usage data. The relative size of each slice reflects the slice's portion of the entire pie.**

**Listing 14.1 Drawing a pie chart from data**

HTML:

```
<canvas id="pieChart" width="400" height="400"></canvas>
```

JavaScript:

```
function drawPieChart(canvas, data) {
    const ctx = canvas.getContext('2d');
    const centerX = canvas.width / 2;                    // Gets pie center
    const centerY = canvas.height / 2;                   // and radius
    const radius = Math.min(centerX, centerY) - 20;

    const total = data.reduce((sum, item) =>             // Calculates the total to
        sum + item.value, 0);                            // determine percentages

    let currentAngle = -Math.PI / 2;                     // Starting angle (12 o'clock position)

    data.forEach(item => {
        const sliceAngle = (item.value / total) *        // Calculates this slice's
                           2 * Math.PI;                  // angle in radians

        ctx.beginPath();                                 // Draws the slice
        ctx.moveTo(centerX, centerY);
        ctx.arc(centerX, centerY, radius,
        ➥     currentAngle,
        ➥     currentAngle + sliceAngle);
        ctx.closePath();
        ctx.fillStyle = item.color;
        ctx.fill();

        const labelAngle = currentAngle + sliceAngle / 2;
        const labelX = centerX +                         // Adds slice label to
            Math.cos(labelAngle) * (radius * 0.7);       // center using trig
        const labelY = centerY +
            Math.sin(labelAngle) * (radius * 0.7);

        ctx.fillStyle = '#000';
        ctx.font = '1rem system-ui';
        ctx.textAlign = 'center';
        ctx.textBaseline = 'middle';

        ctx.fillText(`${item.label}`, labelX, labelY - 8);
        ctx.fillText(`${item.value}%`, labelX, labelY + 8);

        currentAngle += sliceAngle;                      // Moves to the next slice
    });
}

const browserData = [                                    // Browser usage
    { value: 55, color: 'hsl(203 57% 85%)', label: 'Chrome' },   // data
    { value: 22, color: 'hsl(84 74% 44%)', label: 'Safari' },
```

```
    { value: 15, color: 'hsl(23 100% 60%)', label: 'Edge' },
    { value: 8, color: 'hsl(322 100% 61%)', label: 'Other' }
];

let canvas = document.getElementById('pieChart');
drawPieChart(canvas, browserData);
```

Browser usage data

There are two important mathematical operations here. The first is the formula for converting a data value to its angular representation:

```
sliceAngle = (item.value / total) * 2 * Math.PI;
```

This formula ensures that each slice's angle is proportional to its percentage of the whole dataset. Starting at `-π/2` (the 12 o'clock position) rather than `0` (the 3 o'clock position) makes the chart more intuitive to read, as pie charts traditionally start from the top.

The second math operation involves positioning the labels:

```
const labelAngle = currentAngle + sliceAngle / 2;
const labelX = centerX + Math.cos(labelAngle) * (radius * 0.7);
const labelY = centerY + Math.sin(labelAngle) * (radius * 0.7);
```

The first line calculates the middle angle of each slice. The labels are then positioned at 70% of the radius from the center of the pie using trigonometry (cos for the $x$-value and sin for the $y$- value).

### 14.1.2 *Creating an interactive bar chart*

A bar's geometry is a rectangle, so hit testing reduces to checking whether $x$ is between the left and right edges and $y$ is between the top and bottom edges. The only subtlety is mapping value to height while anchoring each bar to the chart's bottom edge.

Continuing with the site metrics dashboard, the analytics team now wants you to create a bar chart that shows the daily average unique visitors to the site. This time, the team wants the chart to be interactive so that when a user hovers their pointer over a bar, a tooltip appears showing the bar's total. Figure 14.2 shows this interaction at work, and listing 14.2a shows how to implement it.

**Listing 14.2a Creating an interactive bar chart (part 1)**

HTML:

```
<canvas id="barChart" width="400" height="400"></canvas>
JavaScript:
function createInteractiveBarChart(canvas, data) {
    const ctx = canvas.getContext('2d');
    const bars = [];
```

Store bar boundaries for hit detection

```
const tooltip = document.createElement('div');
tooltip.style.position = 'absolute';
tooltip.style.background = 'hsl(322 100% 31%)';
tooltip.style.color = '#fff';
tooltip.style.padding = '8px 12px';
tooltip.style.borderRadius = '4px';
tooltip.style.fontSize = '14px';
tooltip.style.pointerEvents = 'none';
tooltip.style.display = 'none';
tooltip.style.zIndex = '1000';
document.body.appendChild(tooltip);
```

**Creates tooltip element**

**Figure 14.2 An interactive, canvas-based bar chart of average daily unique visitors. When the user hovers their pointer over a bar, a tooltip displays the bar's value.**

The initial JavaScript code displays the first part of the `createInteractiveBarChart()` function, which takes the arguments `canvas` (the canvas element) and `data` (the data to be charted). Of particular note here is the `bars` array, which is used later (refer to part 2 of the code) to store the boundaries of each bar to enable hit detection.

The next part of the `createInteractiveBarChart()` function handles the drawing of the chart, as shown in the following listing.

**Listing 14.2b Creating an interactive bar chart (part 2)**

```
function draw() {
    ctx.clearRect(0, 0, canvas.width,
        canvas.height);
```

**Clears canvas**

```
    const padding = 40;
    const barWidth = (canvas.width - padding * 2)
                     / data.length;
    const maxValue = Math.max(...data.map(item =>
                     item.value));
    const chartHeight = canvas.height
                          - padding * 2;

    bars.length = 0;

    data.forEach((item, index) => {
        const barHeight = (item.value / maxValue)
                          * chartHeight;
        const x = padding +
                  index * barWidth +
                  barWidth * 0.1;
        const y = canvas.height - padding
                    - barHeight;
        const width = barWidth * 0.8;

        bars.push({
            x: x,
            y: y,
            width: width,
            height: barHeight,
            data: item
        });

        ctx.fillStyle = 'hsl(84 74% 44%)';
        ctx.fillRect(x, y, width, barHeight);

        ctx.fillStyle = '#333';
        ctx.font = '14px system-ui, sans-serif';
        ctx.textAlign = 'center';
        ctx.textBaseline = 'top';

        const labelX = x + width / 2;
        const labelY = canvas.height - padding + 5;
        ctx.fillText(item.label, labelX, labelY);
    });
}
```

**Initializes chart parameters**

**Clears previous boundaries**

**Iterates over the data**

**Calculates bar dimensions and location**

**Stores boundaries for hit detection**

**Draws the bar**

**Adds label at bottom of bar**

There's quite a bit of math here:

- The theoretical width of each bar (stored in the `barWidth` variable) is calculated by subtracting double the padding from the canvas width, then dividing by the number of data points:

  ```
  (canvas.width - padding * 2) / data.length
  ```

- The maximum data value (`maxValue`) is derived using `Math.max()`:

  ```
  Math.max(...data.map(item => item.value))
  ```

- The height of the chart (`chartHeight`) is calculated by subtracting double the padding from the canvas height:

```
canvas.height - padding * 2
```

- The height of each bar (`barHeight`) is derived by dividing the data point value by the maximum value, then multiplying by the chart height:

```
(item.value / maxValue) * chartHeight
```

- The left edge of each bar (`x`) is calculated by adding the left padding, the width of all the previous bars, and a small gap for spacing:

```
padding + index * barWidth + barWidth * 0.1
```

- The top edge of each bar (`y`) takes the canvas height and subtracts the top padding and the bar's height:

```
canvas.height - padding - barHeight;
```

- The actual width of each bar (`width`) is calculated by multiplying the theoretical width by `0.8` to account for the gaps between the bars:

```
barWidth * 0.8
```

With all that done, each bar's position, dimensions, and data are pushed to the `bars` array.

As shown in the following listing, the final part of the `createInteractiveBarChart()` function consists of the `pointermove` event handler for hit detection (where a "hit" means the user's pointer is over a bar).

**Listing 14.2c Creating an interactive bar chart (part 3)**

```
function handlePointerMove(event) {
    const rect = canvas
                 .getBoundingClientRect();
    const x = event.clientX - rect.left;
    const y = event.clientY - rect.top;

    let hoveredBar = null;

    for (let bar of bars) {
        if (x >= bar.x &&
            x <= bar.x + bar.width &&
            y >= bar.y &&
            y <= bar.y + bar.height) {
            hoveredBar = bar;
```

Converts pointer coordinates to canvas space

Checks each bar for a hit

```
                break;
            }                    Checks each bar for a hit
        }

        if (hoveredBar) {
            tooltip.textContent = `
                ${hoveredBar.data.label}:
                ${hoveredBar.data.value}
            `;
            tooltip.style.display = 'block';
            tooltip.style.left = `${event.clientX + 10}px`;
            tooltip.style.top = `${event.clientY - 10}px`;
            canvas.style.cursor = 'pointer';
        } else {                                       Shows tooltip
            tooltip.style.display = 'none';
            canvas.style.cursor = 'default';       Hides tooltip
        }
    }

    function handlePointerLeave() {
        tooltip.style.display = 'none';        Hides tooltip when
        canvas.style.cursor = 'default';       pointer leaves canvas
    }

    canvas.addEventListener('pointermove', handlePointerMove);
    canvas.addEventListener('pointerleave', handlePointerLeave);
    draw();

    return { draw, bars };
}
```

The `pointermove` handler first converts from viewport coordinates (`event.clientX`, `event.clientY`) to canvas coordinates (`x, y`). With that done, the hit detection math is straightforward but crucial. To be inside a bar, the point (`x, y`) must satisfy all four boundary conditions:

- x must be at or to the right of the bar's left edge (`x >= bar.x`).
- x must be at or to the left of the bar's right edge (`x <= bar.x + bar.width`).
- y must be at or below the bar's top edge (`y >= bar.y`).
- y must be at or above the bar's bottom edge (`y <= bar.y + bar.height`).

The final part of the code defines the bar chart data and calls `createInteractiveBarChart()` to create the chart, as shown in the following listing.

**Listing 14.2d Creating an interactive bar chart (part 4)**

```
const uniqueVisitorData = [
    { label: 'Mon', value: 2250 },
    { label: 'Tue', value: 3570 },
    { label: 'Wed', value: 3125 },
    { label: 'Thu', value: 4060 },
```

```
    { label: 'Fri', value: 5100 },
    { label: 'Sat', value: 6275 },
    { label: 'Sun', value: 5500 },
];

let canvas = document.getElementById('barChart');
createInteractiveBarChart(canvas, uniqueVisitorData);
```

### 14.1.3 Advanced hit detection on a donut chart

Hit detection on a donut chart is a two-step task that includes

- Calculating the distance from the pointer to the chart's center using the Pythagorean theorem to check whether the pointer is within the donut's bounds
- Calculating the angle of the pointer relative to the center using `Math.atan2()` to identify the specific slice

For example, suppose your team is creating a series of interactive visualizations for a science website. Your team lead has tasked you with creating a visualization to show the composition of seawater. The client has provided you with the necessary data and has two requirements:

- Display the data as a donut chart.
- When a user hovers over a slice of the donut chart, display a separate text element showing the element, its percentage, and a description of the element.

Figure 14.3 shows the implementation of this visualization. Refer to Listing 14.3a to learn how to implement the chart and see how the hit detection math works.

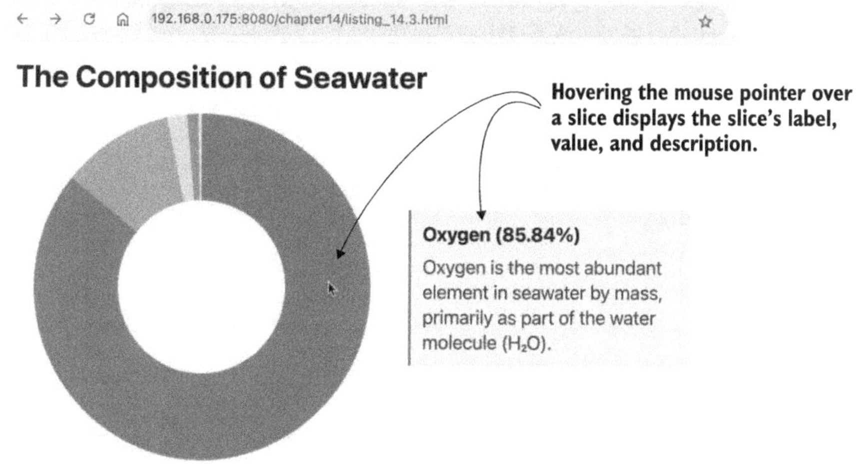


**Figure 14.3 An interactive, canvas-based donut chart of the composition of seawater. When the user hovers their pointer over a slice, a text element displays information about the data that underlies the slice.**

**Listing 14.3a Creating an interactive donut chart (part 1)**

HTML:

```
<h1>The Composition of Seawater</h1>
<div id="chart-container">
    <canvas id="seawater-chart" width="400" height="400"></canvas>
    <div id="description-box">
        <div id="description-title"></div>
        <div id="description-text">Hover over a slice for details.</div>
    </div>
</div>
```

JavaScript:

```
const canvas = document.getElementById('seawater-chart');
const ctx = canvas.getContext('2d');
const descriptionTitle = document.getElementById('description-title');
const descriptionText = document.getElementById('description-text');

const centerX = canvas.width / 2;
const centerY = canvas.height / 2;
const outerRadius = 180;
const innerRadius = 90;

const seawaterData = [
    { label: 'Oxygen', value: 85.84, color: 'hsl(203 57% 40%)',
      desc: 'Oxygen is the most abundant element in seawater by mass,
             primarily as part of the water molecule (H₂O).' },
    { label: 'Hydrogen', value: 10.82, color: 'hsl(203 57% 60%)',
      desc: 'Hydrogen is the second most abundant element,
             also a key component of water (H₂O).' },
    { label: 'Chloride', value: 1.94, color: 'hsl(203 57% 85%)',
      desc: 'Chloride is a major component of dissolved salts,
             making the ocean salty.' },
    { label: 'Sodium', value: 1.08, color: 'hsl(203 57% 50%)',
      desc: 'Sodium is the other element in table salt (sodium chloride)
             and is a major ion in seawater.' },
    { label: 'Other', value: 0.32, color: 'hsl(203 57% 90%)',
      desc: 'Includes magnesium, sulfate, calcium, potassium,
             and many other trace elements.' }
];

const totalValue = 100;
let activeSlice = null;

let currentAngle = -0.5 * Math.PI;
seawaterData.forEach(slice => {
    const sliceAngle = (slice.value / totalValue)
                       * 2 * Math.PI;
    slice.startAngle = currentAngle;
    slice.endAngle = currentAngle + sliceAngle;
    currentAngle = slice.endAngle;
});
```

Annotations:
- centerX / centerY: Center of chart
- outerRadius: px from center to outer edge of donut
- innerRadius: px from center to inner edge of donut
- seawaterData: Data for the visualization
- currentAngle: Starts at the top
- forEach: Iterates over data
- sliceAngle: Calculates slice angle
- startAngle / endAngle: Stores the start and end angle

The only significant math in this part of the code involves determining the start and end angles for each slice of the donut. Since the total circumference of the donut is 2π radians, the total angle of each slice is found by taking that slice's fraction of the whole (`slice.value / totalValue`) and multiplying it by 2π (`2 * Math.PI`). The following listing shows the function that draws the chart.

**Listing 14.3b Creating an interactive donut chart (part 2)**

```
function drawChart() {
    ctx.clearRect(0, 0, canvas.width, canvas.height);

    seawaterData.forEach((slice) => {
        ctx.beginPath();
        ctx.moveTo(centerX, centerY);
        ctx.arc(centerX, centerY, outerRadius,
                slice.startAngle, slice.endAngle);
        ctx.closePath();
        ctx.fillStyle = slice.color;
        ctx.fill();
    });

    ctx.beginPath();
    ctx.arc(centerX, centerY, innerRadius, 0, 2 * Math.PI);
    ctx.fillStyle = 'white';
    ctx.fill();
}
```

Draws all slices

Cuts out the center to make it a donut

The final part of the code handles the `pointermove` event for hit detection on the donut chart.

**Listing 14.3c Creating an interactive donut chart (part 3)**

```
canvas.addEventListener('pointermove', (e) => {
    const rect = canvas.getBoundingClientRect();
    const pointerX = e.clientX - rect.left;
    const pointerY = e.clientY - rect.top;

    const dx = pointerX - centerX;
    const dy = pointerY - centerY;
    const distance = Math.sqrt(dx * dx + dy * dy);

    let currentSliceIndex = null;
    if (distance >= innerRadius &&
            distance <= outerRadius) {
        let pointerAngle = Math.atan2(dy, dx);
        if (pointerAngle < -0.5 * Math.PI) {
            pointerAngle += 2 * Math.PI;
        }

        seawaterData.forEach((slice, index) => {
            if (pointerAngle > slice.startAngle &&
                pointerAngle < slice.endAngle) {
```

Converts pointer coordinates to canvas space

Pointer location relative to center

Distance from center

Is pointer inside donut?

Angle from center to pointer

Normalizes angle

Slice hit detection

```
                    currentSliceIndex = index;        ◄ Slice hit detection
                }
            });
        }

        if (activeSlice !== currentSliceIndex) {
            activeSlice = currentSliceIndex;
            if (activeSlice !== null) {
                const s = seawaterData[activeSlice];
                descriptionTitle.textContent =
                    `${s.label} (${s.value}%)`;               ◄ Displays slice info
                descriptionText.textContent = s.desc;
            } else {
                descriptionTitle.textContent = '';
                descriptionText.textContent = 'Hover over a slice
                                               for details.';      ◄ Clear slice info
            }
        }
    });

drawChart();       ◄ Initial draw
```

Unlike a straightforward bar chart where you can check whether a point is within a rectangle, a donut slice has curved and angled boundaries, which makes hit detection more complex. To solve this, you need to stop thinking in terms of rectangular *x*- and *y*-coordinates and start thinking in terms of polar coordinates—distance and angle from a center point:

- *Distance*—The code gets the pointer coordinates (`pointerX, pointerY`) relative to the canvas and computes the horizontal (`dx`) and vertical (`dy`) distance from the center point (`centerX, centerY`). Next, the code uses the Pythagorean theorem to get the straight line (hypotenuse) distance from the center to the pointer:

  ```
  const distance = Math.sqrt(dx * dx + dy * dy
  ```

- *Angle*—The code checks whether the calculated `distance` is between the `innerRadius` and `outerRadius` values. If so, the pointer is within the donut, so the code uses `Math.atan2()` to calculate the angle:

  ```
  let pointerAngle = Math.atan2(dy, dx);
  ```

### EXERCISES

**Exercise 14.1:** When converting a data value of 25 out of a total of 100 to an angle for a pie chart, what is the resulting angle in radians?

1. π/4
2. π/2
3. π
4. 2π

**Exercise 14.2:** Troubleshoot this code. The goal is to detect a hover on a single 50 x 50 rectangle drawn at (10, 10). Why does it fail to detect the hover correctly?

```
canvas.addEventListener('pointermove', (e) => {
    const pointerX = 20;
    const pointerY = 20;

    const rectX = 10;
    const rectY = 10;
    const rectWidth = 50;
    const rectHeight = 50;

    if (pointerX >= rectX && pointerX <= rectWidth &&
        pointerY >= rectY && pointerY <= rectHeight) {
        console.log('Hover detected!');
    }
});
```

**Exercise 14.3:** Part 3 of the donut chart code includes the following normalization of the pointer angle:

```
if (pointerAngle < -0.5 * Math.PI) {
    pointerAngle += 2 * Math.PI;
}
```

Why is this required?

## 14.2 Dynamic motion and simulation

The canvas is the ideal place for animations involving many objects because they can be drawn programmatically without the overhead of tens, hundreds, or even thousands of DOM elements. This section applies the animation and physics principles discussed earlier in the book to create dynamic, generative visuals that feel alive.

### 14.2.1 Simulating a simple particle system

A particle system is a collection of simple shapes (usually circles) managed as a group. By giving each particle properties such as velocity and by applying forces such as gravity, you can create complex, emergent behavior.

For example, the Marketing team has a big promotion coming up, and they want to make a splash by offering an eye-catching effect when the user navigates to the landing page. One member of the team has suggested a simulation of a balloon drop, where a bunch of balloons of various sizes and colors start at the top of the screen on page load, then immediately fall with gravity until they bounce off the page floor (i.e., the bottom of the viewport) and walls (i.e., the left and right edges of the viewport). The key is that both the balloon drop and the balloon bouncing must appear natural. Your product manager has given you the job of prototyping the balloon drop.

Figure 14.4 shows a simulated balloon drop in mid-animation. Listing 14.4a shows the first part of the code that implements this effect.

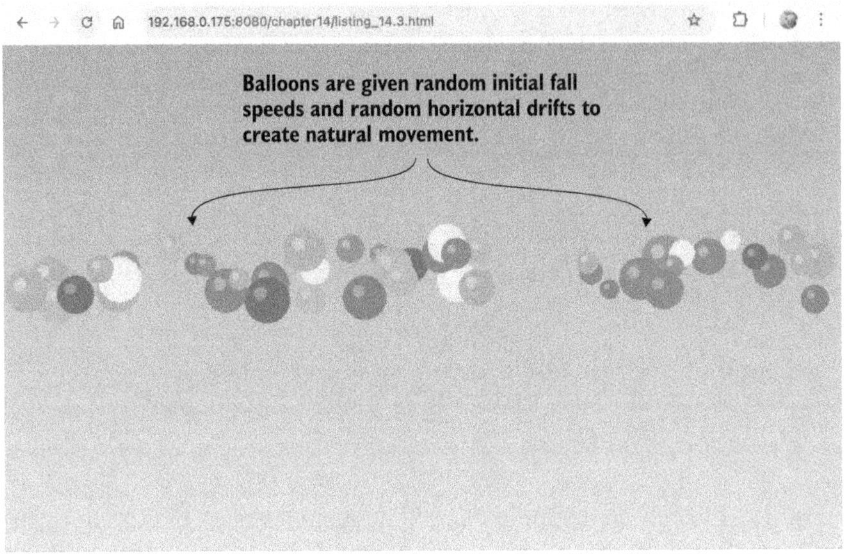


**Figure 14.4 A simulation of a simple particle system. Each balloon is given a small, random horizontal drift velocity and a random vertical fall velocity to simulate how balloons would fall naturally.**

**Listing 14.4a A simulation of a balloon drop (part 1)**

HTML:

```
<canvas id="particles"></canvas>
```

JavaScript:

```
const pCanvas = document.getElementById('particles');
const pCtx = pCanvas.getContext('2d');

pCanvas.width = window.innerWidth;
pCanvas.height = window.innerHeight;

let canvasWidth = pCanvas.width;
let canvasHeight = pCanvas.height;
const gravity = 0.08;                    // Light gravity for balloons
const balloons = [];

// Balloon colors
const balloonColors = [
    'hsl(0, 85%, 60%)',
    'hsl(30, 85%, 60%)',
    'hsl(60, 85%, 60%)',
    'hsl(120, 85%, 60%)',
    'hsl(210, 85%, 60%)',
    'hsl(270, 85%, 60%)',
```

```
    'hsl(300, 85%, 60%)',
];

// Create balloons starting at the top
for (let i = 0; i < 50; i++) {
    balloons.push({
        x: Math.random() * canvasWidth,
        y: -20,
        vx: (Math.random() - 0.5) * 1,
        vy: Math.random() * 1 + 0.5,
        radius: Math.random() * 15 + 10,
        color: balloonColors[Math.floor(Math.random() *
                                  balloonColors.length)],
    });
}
```

**Random horizontal start position**
**Starts above the canvas**
**Random, small horizontal drift**
**Random initial fall speed**
**Random size**

The key elements in this code are a light `gravity` value of `0.08` (these are balloons, after all) and the use of `Math.random()` for the initial horizontal position (`x`), the horizontal component of the velocity (`vx`), the vertical component of the velocity (`vy`), and the balloon size (`radius`). The following listing presents the code that draws each balloon.

**Listing 14.4b A simulation of a balloon drop (part 2)**

```
function drawBalloon(p) {
    pCtx.beginPath();
    pCtx.arc(p.x, p.y, p.radius, 0, Math.PI * 2);
    pCtx.fillStyle = p.color;
    pCtx.fill();

    pCtx.beginPath();
    pCtx.arc(p.x - p.radius * 0.3,
             p.y - p.radius * 0.3,
             p.radius * 0.3, 0, Math.PI * 2);
    pCtx.fillStyle = 'rgba(255, 255, 255, 0.4)';
    pCtx.fill();
}
```

**Draws balloon (circle)**
**Adds balloon highlight**

This code renders each balloon as two circles via `Math.PI`: the balloon itself and a highlight inside the balloon. As shown in the next listing, the final part of the code animates the balloons.

The final part of the code animates the balloons.

**Listing 14.4c A simulation of a balloon drop (part 3)**

```
function animateBalloons() {
    const gradient = pCtx.createLinearGradient(0, 0, 0, canvasHeight);
    gradient.addColorStop(0, 'hsl(203 57% 65%)');
    gradient.addColorStop(1, 'hsl(203 57% 85%)');
    pCtx.fillStyle = gradient;
    pCtx.fillRect(0, 0, canvasWidth, canvasHeight);
```

```
    balloons.forEach(p => {
        p.vy += gravity;                          // Applies gravity
        p.x += p.vx;                              // Applies velocity
        p.y += p.vy;

        if (p.y + p.radius > canvasHeight) {      // Checks for floor collision
            p.y = canvasHeight - p.radius;
            p.vy *= -0.6;                         // Reduces energy on bounce
        }

        if (p.x <= p.radius) {                    // Checks for left wall collision
            p.x = p.radius;
            p.vx *= -0.75;                        // Reduces energy on bounce
        }

        if (p.x >= canvasWidth - p.radius) {      // Checks for right wall collision
            p.x = canvasWidth - p.radius;
            p.vx *= -0.75;                        // Reduces energy on bounce
        }

        drawBalloon(p);
    });

    requestAnimationFrame(animateBalloons);
}

window.addEventListener('resize', () => {
    pCanvas.width = window.innerWidth;
    pCanvas.height = window.innerHeight;
    canvasWidth = pCanvas.width;
    canvasHeight = pCanvas.height;
});

animateBalloons();
```

The main part of the `animateBalloons()` function is a `forEach` loop that iterates through every balloon. The loop applies gravity and velocity to the balloon, then checks for three collisions: with the floor, the left wall, or the right wall. With each collision, the balloon's direction is reversed, and some energy is dissipated by reducing either the vertical velocity (after a floor collision) or the horizontal velocity (after a wall collision).

### 14.2.2 Creating a generative star field effect

A static background can feel lifeless. A common way to add dynamism and a sense of depth to a page, especially for landing pages or headers, is to create an animated star field. The key to making this effect look convincing is to simulate parallax instead of just moving dots around.

Imagine you're a freelance web developer and you have a client who runs a *Star Wars* fan page. Right now, the client's page for 404 (page not found) errors is very plain: a static, black background with a simple "Page Not Found" message and a link to the home page. The client would like that page to be more interesting and dynamic, with a tie-in to the site's *Star Wars* theme. Your solution is an animated star field background, with an engaging "Error 404" message that crawls up the screen, in the *Star Wars* style. Figure 14.5 shows the resulting page in mid-animation. Listing 14.5a shows the first part of the code that implements this effect.

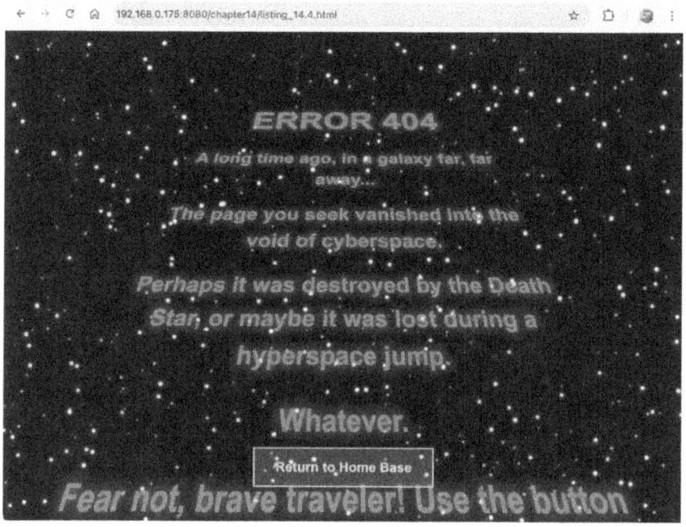


**Figure 14.5 A custom 404 page with an animated star field background. Creating stars with different velocities, sizes, and opacities provides the illusion of depth.**

**Listing 14.5a Creating a generative star field background effect (part 1)**

HTML:

```
<canvas id="starfield"></canvas>

<div class="text-overlay">
    <div class="crawl-text">
        <h1>ERROR 404</h1>
        <p>A long time ago, in a galaxy far, far away...</p>
        <p>The page you seek vanished into the void of cyberspace.</p>
        <p>Perhaps it was destroyed by the Death Star,
            or maybe it was lost during a hyperspace jump.</p>
        <p>Whatever.</p>
        <p>Fear not, brave traveler! Use the button below to
           return to safety.</p>
        <p>May the Force (and better URLs) be with you.</p>
    </div>
</div>

<button class="home-button" onclick="window.location.href='/'">
    Return to Home Base
</button>
```

JavaScript:

```
const canvas = document.getElementById('starfield');
const ctx = canvas.getContext('2d');

canvas.width = window.innerWidth;           Makes canvas
canvas.height = window.innerHeight;         full viewport

const stars = [];
const numStars = 800;
const maxDepth = 32;

for (let i = 0; i < numStars; i++) {       ◄ Creates the star objects
    const z = Math.max(0.5, Math.random()
                 * maxDepth);               ◄ Assigns random depth
    stars.push({
        x: Math.random() * canvas.width,    Assigns random
        y: Math.random() * canvas.height,   starting position
        z: z,
        speed: 0.25 / z,                    ◄ Calculates speed based on depth
        radius: (maxDepth - z) / maxDepth * 2,  ◄ Calculates size based on depth
        opacity: (maxDepth - z) / maxDepth,     ◄ Calculates opacity based on depth
    });
}
```

In the real world, objects that are closer to you appear to move faster than objects that are far away. Think of looking out the side window of a moving car: nearby trees blur past in an instant, while distant mountains seem to barely move at all. You can simulate this 3D effect on a 2D canvas by giving each star a simulated depth and linking that depth to its speed and size.

To achieve this, assign each star a random z coordinate to represent its depth:

```
const z = Math.max(0.5, Math.random() * maxDepth);
```

A small `z` means the star is close, and a large `z` means it's far away. (But you don't want a star to be unrealistically close, hence the use of `Math.max()` to set 0.5 as the minimum depth.) You then use this `z` value to calculate the star's on-screen properties to achieve the parallax effect:

- *Velocity*—A star's speed must be inversely proportional to its depth. You calculate each star's horizontal velocity (`speed`) by dividing a base speed by the star's depth:

  ```
  speed: 0.25 / z
  ```

  This makes stars that are close (small `z`) move much faster than stars that are far (large `z`). Use a larger base speed to make all the stars faster, or a lower base speed to make all the stars slower.
- *Size*—A star's apparent size will be inversely proportional to its depth. You calculate each star's on-screen radius by subtracting its assigned depth (`z`) from the

maximum depth, dividing that result by the maximum depth, and multiplying it by a base radius:

```
radius: (maxDepth - z) / maxDepth * 2
```

This makes closer stars appear larger and more prominent. Use a larger base radius to make all the stars bigger, or a lower base radius to make all the stars smaller.

- *Opacity*—A star's apparent opacity will also be inversely proportional to its depth. You calculate each star's on-screen opacity by subtracting its assigned depth (`z`) from the maximum depth, then dividing that result by the maximum depth:

```
opacity: (maxDepth - z) / maxDepth
```

All that's left now is to build the star field. The next listing shows how to do it.

**Listing 14.5b Creating a generative star field background effect (part 2)**

```
function animate() {
    ctx.clearRect(0, 0, canvas.width,
                  canvas.height);                   // Clears the canvas

    stars.forEach(star => {

        star.x -= star.speed;                       // Updates star's x position (subtract to move left)

        if (star.x < 0) {                           // If star moves off left edge, wrap it to the right.
            star.x = canvas.width;
            star.y = Math.random() * canvas.height; // Randomizes y when wrapping
        }

        ctx.beginPath();                            // Draws the star
        ctx.arc(star.x, star.y, star.radius,
                0, Math.PI * 2);
        ctx.fillStyle = `rgba(255, 255, 255,
                         ${star.opacity})`;
        ctx.fill();
    });

    requestAnimationFrame(animate);
}

window.addEventListener('resize', () => {          // Handle window resize
    canvas.width = window.innerWidth;
    canvas.height = window.innerHeight;

    stars.forEach(star => {                         // Redistributes stars for new canvas size
        if (star.x > canvas.width) star.x = Math.random() * canvas.width;
        if (star.y > canvas.height) star.y = Math.random() * canvas.height;
    });
});

canvas.style.background = 'black';
animate();
```

The `animate()` function creates the star field. A `forEach` loop iterates through the `stars` array, using the pre-calculated `speed` value to update the star's horizontal position. To create a seamless, infinite loop, the code checks when each star moves off the left edge of the canvas. Instead of destroying it, the code wraps the star's horizontal position to the opposite side of the canvas. To keep the loop looking natural, the star's vertical (`y`) position is assigned a new, random value.

### 14.2.3 Creating celebration and feedback effects

Modern web applications increasingly use celebratory animations to reward user actions and create memorable moments. Whether it's confetti falling after completing a task, fireworks exploding when a user reaches a milestone, or sparkles following a successful form submission, these effects combine physics simulation with visual design to create an emotional effect. This section explores the mathematics behind these celebration effects, focusing on particle trajectories, explosion patterns, and natural motion.

Suppose your team is building a set of pages that takes the user through a somewhat complex task. The workflow is complete, but the testing team has turned up a problem. Users are making it through the process, but they're reporting that completion feels anticlimactic. While not arduous, the task is long enough that users feel there should be something extra to mark a successful completion. The team has decided that a shower of confetti should appear when the user clicks the final button to complete the workflow. You have been tasked with creating the animation, with the requirement that it should be brief, natural-looking, and celebratory.

Figure 14.6 shows the resulting confetti shower in mid-animation. Listing 14.6a shows the first part of the code that implements the effect.

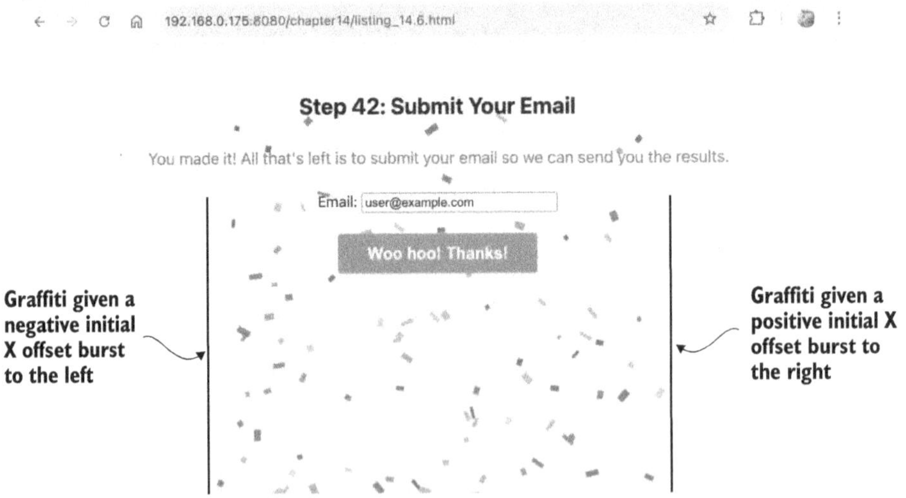


**Figure 14.6 A celebratory shower of confetti appears upon completion of the task. Each piece of confetti is a canvas rectangle given an initial random velocity, height, width, rotation, and color.**

**Listing 14.6a Creating a shower of confetti (part 1)**

HTML:

```
<canvas id="confettiCanvas"></canvas>
<div id="ui">
    <h2>Step 42: Submit Your Email</h2>
    <div class="info">You made it! All that's left is to submit
        your email so we can send you the results.</div>
    <label for="email">Email:
        <input id="email" type="email" size="30" value="user@example.com">
    </label>
    <button id="submitBtn">Complete the Task</button>
</div>
```

JavaScript:

```
function createConfettiCelebration(canvas) {        ← Generator function
    const ctx = canvas.getContext('2d');
    const confettiPieces = [];                      ← Array to hold confetti pieces
    const gravity = 0.15;                           ← Small gravity value
    const drag = 0.005;                             ← Gentle drag for drifting
    let isAnimating = false;

    function createConfetti(x, y) {                 ← Creates piece of confetti
        return {
            x: x,
            y: y,
            vx: Math.random() * 7 - 3.5,            ← Random left/right drift
            vy: Math.random() * -7 - 5,             ← Random initial upward velocity
            width: Math.random() * 10 + 5,
            height: Math.random() * 5 + 3,
            rotation: Math.random() * Math.PI * 2,  ← Random rotation and speed
            rotationSpeed: Math.random()
                ➥      * 0.2 - 0.1,
            color: `hsl(${Math.random() * 360}, 70%, 50%)`,
        };
    }

    function burst(centerX, centerY, count = 100) {  ← Generates a burst of confetti
        for (let i = 0; i < count; i++) {
            const offsetX = Math.random() * 60 - 30;  ← Random values between −30 and 30
            const offsetY = Math.random() * 60 - 30;
            confettiPieces.push(createConfetti(
                centerX + offsetX,
                centerY + offsetY
            ));
        }
    }
```

This JavaScript code shows the top part of `createConfettiCelebration()`, which is a generator function for the confetti effect. This animation keeps the physics relatively simple by using just two velocity inputs:

- `gravity`—Controls changes to the vertical component of velocity (`vy`), which starts off negative, then turns positive as the `gravity` value drags the confetti pieces down (refer to listing 14.6a)
- `drag`—Controls changes to the horizontal component of velocity (`vx`), which is given a random left (negative) or right (positive) direction that slows down over time due to the effect of the `drag` value (refer to listing 14.6a).

Tossed confetti seems to be teeming with randomness, so the `createConfetti()` function, which is used to create a single confetti piece (as a JavaScript object), mimics that by using `Math.random()` not only for the velocity components `vx` and `vy`, but also for the `width`, `height`, `rotation`, `rotationSpeed`, and `color` properties.

The `burst()` function populates the `confettiPieces` array with 100 pieces, each offset randomly from the canvas center.

The next listing shows the rest of the `createConfettiCelebration()` generator function.

**Listing 14.6b Creating a shower of confetti (part 2)**

```
function updateConfetti(confetti) {          // Applies gravity
    confetti.vy += gravity;
    confetti.vx *= (1 - drag);               // Applies drag

    confetti.x += confetti.vx;               // Adjusts speed
    confetti.y += confetti.vy;

    confetti.rotation +=
    ➥    confetti.rotationSpeed;             // Adjusts rotation

    return (                                 // Returns true if still in bounds
        confetti.y < canvas.height + 20 &&
        confetti.x > -20 &&
        confetti.x < canvas.width + 20
    );
}

function drawConfetti(confetti) {            // Draws a confetti piece
    ctx.save();
    ctx.translate(confetti.x, confetti.y);
    ctx.rotate(confetti.rotation);
    ctx.fillStyle = confetti.color;
    ctx.fillRect(
        -confetti.width / 2,
        -confetti.height / 2,
        confetti.width,
        confetti.height
    );
    ctx.restore();
}

function animate() {                         // Renders a frame
    ctx.clearRect(0, 0, canvas.width, canvas.height);
```

```
        for (let i = confettiPieces.length - 1; i >= 0; i--) {
            if (!updateConfetti(
                    confettiPieces[i])) {
                confettiPieces.splice(i, 1);
            } else {                                    Checks for out of bounds
                drawConfetti(confettiPieces[i]);
            }
        }
        if (confettiPieces.length > 0) {
            requestAnimationFrame(animate);
        } else {
            isAnimating = false;
        }
    }

    function celebrate() {                           Initiates celebration
        burst(canvas.width / 2, canvas.height / 2);

        if (!isAnimating) {
            isAnimating = true;
            animate();
        }
    }

    return { celebrate, confettiPieces };
}
```

This final part of the generator function contains the following four methods:

- `updateConfetti()`—Updates the speed, position, and rotation of a single piece of confetti:
  - The vertical component of the speed (`vy`) is adjusted by adding `gravity` value, so the initially negative (rising) value of `vy` reaches a peak when it becomes `0`. Then the confetti begins to fall as `vy` becomes increasingly positive.
  - The horizontal component of the speed (`vx`) is adjusted by multiplying `vx` by `(1 - drag)`, which gradually reduces the `vx` value to mimic the drag effects of air resistance on the confetti.
  - The `rotation` value of the confetti is adjusted by adding the `rotationSpeed` value.
- `drawConfetti()`—Draws a single piece of confetti on the canvas.
- `animate()`—Draws a single animation frame by looping through the `confettiPieces` array and calling `updateConfetti()` for each piece. If that function returns `false`, it means the confetti piece has fallen out of the canvas, so the piece is removed from the array; otherwise, the piece is drawn by calling `drawConfetti()`.
- `celebrate()`—Initiates the confetti effect by calling the `burst()` function to create the pieces, then the `animate()` function to launch the animation.

The following listing shows the final part of the code, which appears at the end of the `createConfettiCelebration()` function.

**Listing 14.6c Creating a shower of confetti (part 3)**

```
const canvas = document.getElementById('confettiCanvas');
const confetti = createConfettiCelebration(canvas);

function resizeCanvas() {
    canvas.width = window.innerWidth;
    canvas.height = window.innerHeight;
}

window.addEventListener('resize', resizeCanvas);
resizeCanvas();

document.getElementById('submitBtn').addEventListener('click', (e) => {
    confetti.celebrate();
    e.target.textContent = "Woo hoo! Thanks!";
});
```

This code gets the canvas, calls `createConfettiCelebration()`, listens for `resize` events, and listens for clicks on the button to kick off the effect by calling the `confetti` object's `celebrate()` method.

**EXERCISES**

**Exercise 14.4:** In a particle animation, if a particle has a vertical velocity `vy` of 5 and you apply a gravity value of 0.2 in one frame, what will the particle's new velocity be?

**Exercise 14.5:** Fill in the blank. To create a parallax effect for a star field, a star's on-screen size, speed, and opacity should be ________ proportional to its simulated distance (its `z` depth).

**Exercise 14.6:** In the confetti simulation, why does the vertical component (`vy`) of the confetti piece velocity start off negative?

## 14.3 Solutions to exercises

**Exercise 14.1:** The answer is $\pi/2$:

```
(25/ 100) * 2π
= 0.25 * 2π
= π/2
```

**Exercise 14.2:** The conditional check is comparing the pointer's position to the rectangle's width and height instead of its right and bottom edges. Here's the correct check:

```
if (pointerX >= rectX && pointerX <= rectX + rectWidth &&
    pointerY >= rectY && pointerY <= rectY + rectHeight) {
    console.log('Hover detected!');
}
```

**Exercise 14.3:** `Math.atan2()` returns angles in the range $-\pi$ to $\pi$, but the donut slice angles range from $-0.5\pi$ to $1.5\pi$ (refer to part 1 of the code). So, `Math.atan2()` can return negative angles in the top-left part of the donut, where the corresponding slice angles are positive. For example, you could have an `atan2` pointer angle such as $-3\pi/4$ ($-135°$), and its equivalent positive slice angle is $5\pi/4$ ($225°$). Normalizing maps the pointer angle into the same continuous range as the slice angles so the subsequent numeric comparison (whether `pointerAngle` is between `slice.startAngle` and `slice.endAngle`) works correctly.

**Exercise 14.4:** The gravity value is added to the velocity value:

```
vy = vy + gravity
   = 5 + 0.2
   = 5.2
```

**Exercise 14.5:** Inversely.

**Exercise 14.6:** In the canvas coordinate system, the point `(0, 0)` is in the upper-left corner, so `y`-values increase downward. In the simulation, the confetti is thrown upward at the start, which requires a negative initial value for `vy`.

## Summary

- The `canvas` element lets you apply your math skills directly, giving you pixel-level control over custom UI and animations.
- You can visualize data by mapping numerical values to geometric properties such as angles (for pie charts or donut charts) or dimensions (for bar charts).
- Hit detection is the process of using coordinate math to determine whether a user's pointer is interacting with a shape you've drawn on the canvas.
- Hit detection on rectangles involves a simple boundary check, while detection on circular or arc-based shapes requires trigonometry (`atan2`) and the Pythagorean theorem.
- You can create natural-looking motion by applying physics concepts such as gravity, velocity, and boundary detection to objects on the canvas.
- Frame-based physics simulations update velocity using acceleration each frame (`v += a`) and then update position using velocity (`p += v`), which produces realistic motion that follows physical laws.
- The parallax effect in particle systems is achieved by making particle depth inversely proportional to its apparent speed, size, and opacity.

# index

## A


acceleration 311
alpha blending (composing) 197
amplitude value 243
analogous colors 186
angles 16, 238, 259
animation
  Bézier curves for 277
  smooth
    using Bézier curves for 278–281
animations
  customizing with Bézier curves 292–298
    entrance animations 292
    exit animations 294
    interactive feedback animations 297
arithmetic 9
  assignment operators 24
  floating-point 35–36
  operators 23, 62
article element 91, 209
ascender, defined 207
aspect-ratio property 11
auto-fill and auto-fit algorithms 116–119
auto keyword 112


## B


bankers' rounding 45
bar charts, interactive 348
base, defined 12
base size calculation 124–127
Bézier curves 278–281
  cubic Bézier curves in CSS 281–292
  defined 278
  for animation 277
  mathematical construction of 278
  quadratic vs. cubic 279
  role of cubic Bézier curves in animations 280
BFC (block formatting context) 88
BFS (base font size) 211
BigInt data type 30, 37–39
binary representations 32
blend modes 196–203
  alpha compositing 197
  blending 197
  blending in CSS 198
  nonseparable 202
  separable 200–202
BLH (base line height) 211
Boolean values 26
bouncing effects, simulating 313–318
  bouncing ball animation 313
  pendulum-like motion 314
  simulating weight and elasticity 316
bounding boxes 253
box model 105
box-sizing 92
button elements 43


## C


canvas, dynamic motion and simulation 357
canvas-based math and drawing 345
  celebration and feedback effects 364, 368
  generative star field effect 360
  hit detection on donut charts 353
  interactive bar charts 348
  pie charts 346
canvas element 345
carousels 42

ch unit 208
circular layouts and animations 234–241
  animating circular motion in JavaScript and CSS 238–239
  circular menus with JavaScript and CSS 234–238
  creating animated spinners 240
click event handler 269
color 171
  blend modes 196–203
  complementary colors 70, 186
  converting between color models 181–185
  creating harmonious color schemes with math 185–187
  light mode and dark mode 193–196
  opacity 196–203
  specifying accessible colors with math 188–193
color-burn mode 202
color models and color spaces 172
  HSL color model 174
  LAB color space 176
  OKLCH color space 177
  RGB color model 172–174
comparison expressions 14
comparison operators 24
constant, defined 10
contrast ratio 188
control points 278, 283
controls, custom sliders 338
  building custom linear sliders 330–334
  building custom rotary controls 334–338
coordinates 252
coordinate systems 19, 96–102
  grid model 96
  negative indexing 99–100
  span notation 99
CSS (Cascading Style Sheets)
  animating circular motion 239
  arithmetic operators 62
  calc() function 63
  circular menus 236
  cubic Bézier curves in 281–292
  fluid typography with math functions 216–220
  inheritance 79–84
  layout fluidity with CSS functions 163–168
  math 6, 8, 85–90
  math basics for 55
  math functions 61, 68–76
  media queries 196
  setting limits with min(), max(), and clamp() 65
  trig functions in 233
  units 56–61
  variables 224–225
  variables in math operations 77–79
CSS Grid 93
  coordinate system 96–102
  mathematical foundations of 94–96
  track sizing algorithm 102–108
  track-sizing functions and keywords 108–119
cube root, defined 12
cubic Bézier curves 279–281
  in CSS 281–292
curves, Bézier curves
  customizing animations with 292–298
  entrance animations 292
  exit animations 294
  interactive feedback animations 297
custom sliders 338
  building custom linear sliders 330–334
  building custom rotary controls 334–338
cyclic UI 42

## D

damping, defined 320
dark mode 193–196
  CSS implementation with media queries 196
  hue and saturation adjustments for aesthetic consistency 194
  inversion 193
  inverting perceptual lightness 194
  paired light/dark palette 195
data-driven geometry 346
data type 29
declarative math 8
decrement operator 23
default values 27
degrees 16
  converting between radians and 232
dependent variable 13
descender 207
dev math
  exponents and nth roots 12
  trigonometry 17
dialog element 64
directional calculations 245–248
div element 245
dividend, defined 40
divisor, defined 40
DOM (Document Object Model)
  essential vector operations for developers 263
  geometry 253–255, 257–262
DomRect (DOM rectangle) object 254, 259
donut charts, hit detection on 353
double-hyphen prefix 77
dynamic motion 357

## E

easing functions 286–292, 306–308
EFS (element's scaled font size) 216, 226

elasticity, simulating 316
ELH (element line height) 211, 216, 226
ELL (element line length) formula 211
em units 56
Event object 246
EW (element width) formula 212, 216, 226
exponent 12, 32
exponential
  function 68
  notation 32
expressions 9–10
  building 23

## F

falsy values 27
feedback effects 364
  exercises 368
flexbox
  as responsive tool 149
  flex base size calculation 124–127
  math 127–139
  min/max constraints 140–144
flex factors 124
flex-grow values between 0 and 1 136–139
flex shorthand 135
flex-shrink calculation 131–135
floating-point arithmetic 35–36
floating-point numbers 30
font size 207
  declarations 56, 226
  property 208, 214, 218, 221
fps (frames per second) 310
fraction, defined 32
friction-based animations 318–322
  Hooke's law for spring motion 318
  simulating inertia with damping and friction 320–322
friction coefficient 320
fr units 104–105

## G

gaps, fluid 165
generative star field effect 360
geometric clipping 270–273
  clipping elements 270
  motion paths 272
geometric constraints 266–269
geometry 15
  data-driven 346
  DOM geometry 253–255, 257–262
  for UI design, mathematical foundations 252–253
gesture-based UIs, custom slider control 338
GitHub repository 179, 214
gravity, simulating 313–318
  bouncing ball animation 313
  pendulum-like motion 314
  simulating weight and elasticity 316
grayscale, converting RGB to 181
Grid (CSS Grid)
  track sizes 108–119
  track-sizing functions and keywords 108–119
grid formatting context 94
Grid layout, as responsive tool 149

## H

hard-light blend mode 202
hexadecimal representations 32
hex triplets 174
hit detection 346, 353
Hooke's law 318
HSL (hue, saturation, lightness) color model 174, 175, 186, 187, 341
  converting RGB to 181
  converting to RGB 183–185
hue and saturation adjustments 194

## I

img element 43
increment operator 23
independent variable 13
inequalities 10, 14
inertia, simulating with damping and friction 320–322
Infinity and -Infinity 33
inheritance 79–84
  cascade formula 79
  computed values versus inherited values 82
  em unit inheritance multiplier 80
  heading size 81
  percentage values and 80
  properties that inherit mathematically 79
initial containing block 157
input element 190
integer numbers 30
interactive bar charts 348
interactivity 324
  custom slider controls 338
  mouse and touch event calculations 325–330
  scroll-based animations 338–343
IntersectionObserver 341–344
inversion 193
  inverting perceptual lightness 194

## J

JavaScript 22
  animating circular motion 238
  arithmetic assignment operators 24
  arithmetic operators 23
  BigInt values 37–39
  building expressions 23
  calculating contrast ratios with 190–193
  circular menus 235
  comparison operators 24
  default values 27

easing functions 306–308
falsy values 27
logic 42
logical expressions 26
manipulating vectors in 262–269
math basics, parentheses 29
math in 7–8
modulo logic 40–43
nullish coalescing 27
number types 29–35
operator precedence 27
parentheses 29
precision issues and floating-point arithmetic 35–36
random numbers 47–51
rounding numbers 43–47
trig functions in 233
velocity and acceleration in 308–313
when to bring in 166–168
wrapping values 40–43

## L

LAB color space 176
landing pages, hero text for 219
layout fluidity 163–168
layouts, proportional 152–157
LCG (Linear Congruential Generator) 49
light mode 193–196
CSS implementation with media queries 196
hue and saturation adjustments for aesthetic consistency 194
inversion 193
inverting perceptual lightness 194
paired light/dark palette 195
linear equations 13
linear interpolation 306
linear sliders 330–334
line height 207
line-height
formulas 209
property 58, 210, 214
line length 208
lines 16, 253
line segments 16, 253
liquid layouts 154–157
logic
modulo 40–43
wrapping values 40–43
logical operators 26
loose equality 25
luminance, relative 189

## M

mantissa, defined 32
math
algebra 10
arithmetic 9
box model 85–90
canvas-based 345–346, 357, 360
CSS 77–79
flexbox 124–127, 140–144
for UI design, mathematical foundations 252–253
for web design 13, 19
frontend, benefits of learning 2
geometry 15
inequalities and comparison expressions 14
JavaScript, parentheses 29
of Flexbox 127–139
specifying accessible colors with 188–193
text and typography, exercise solutions 225
trigonometry 17
typography 207–220
web design 3–9
web design for, ratios 11
mathematical modulo operation 40
math functions 61, 68
exponential function 68
hypotenuse function 69
logarithm function 69
modulus function 70
power function 72
remainder function 73
round function 74
sqrt() function 76
media queries 149–152, 196
modular scale 221–225
choosing ratio 223
creating from scaling factor 221
implementing typographic scales with CSS variables 224–225
modulo logic 40–43
modulus function 70
motion 357
in UI design 303–308
motion paths 270
mouse and touch event calculations 325–330
MouseEvent objects 327, 328
multiplication operator 52
multiply mode 202

## N

NaN (Not a Number) 33
negative indexing 99–101
nesting percentages 153
nonseparable blend modes 202
nth roots 12
nullish coalescing 27
number coercion 34
number data type 30, 37, 39
Number object 31, 33, 36
number types 29–35
binary, octal, and hexadecimal representations 32
binary representations 32
exponential notation 32
hexadecimal representations 32
Infinity and –Infinity 33
integer and floating-point numbers 30
NaN 33
number coercion 34
octal representations 32
numeric literal 10

## O


octal representations 32
offset value 243
OKLCH color space 177
opacity 196–203, 363
  alpha compositing 197
  blending 197
  blending in CSS 198
  nonseparable blend modes 202
  separable blend modes 200–202
operands 9, 23
operation, defined 10
operator precedence 27
operators 9, 23
overlay blend mode 202


## P


paired light/dark palette 195
parallax scrolling 260–262
parentheses, importance of 29
particle systems 357
p element 84, 91
pendulum-like motion 314
percentages 58, 80
  mixing with fixed units 153
physics-based animations 302
  friction-based animations 318–322
  motion in UI design 303–308
  simulating gravity and bouncing effects 313–318
  spring-based animations 318–322
  velocity and acceleration in JavaScript 308–313
pie charts 346
pointermove event 351–355
points, defined 16, 252
polar coordinates 356
post-increment and pre-increment operator 24
procedural math 8
product card grid 109
proportional layouts 152–157
  liquid layouts 154–157
  mixing percentages with fixed units 153
  nesting percentages 153
  percentage-based layouts 152
pseudo-random number 48
Pythagorean theorem 330


## Q


quadratic Bézier curves 279


## R


radians 16
  converting between degrees and 232
random numbers 47–51
  generating random integers and floats 47
  seeding and repeatable randomness 48
  use cases in animations and UI behavior 50
range syntax 150
ratios, defined 11
rays, defined 16
readability 207
relative luminance 189, 191
responsive design 146, 147
  layout fluidity with CSS functions 163–168
  mathematical mindset 148
  media queries 149–152
  proportional layouts 152–157
  viewport-based units 157–163
  visual thought experiments 147
RGB (red, green, blue) color model 172–174
  converting to grayscale 181
  converting to HSL 181, 183–185
rotary controls 334–338
rounding numbers 43–47
  implementing bankers' rounding 45
  to specific number of decimal places 44
  to whole numbers 43
  use cases for 46


## S


scaling factor 221
scaling fonts, setting constraints on dynamic font scaling 217
scaling units 61
scroll-based animations 338–343
  creating dynamic UI changes with intersection observers 341–343
  detecting scroll position 338–341
scroll event 262, 344
section element 91
seeding 48–49
separable blend modes 200–202
size, defined 362–363
sliders 42
  custom controls 330–338
soft-light blend mode 202
source-over compositing 197
span element 243
span notation 99
split-complementary colors 187
spring-based animations 318–322
  Hooke's law for spring motion 318
  simulating inertia with damping and friction 320–322
star field effect 360
starting value, defined 13
symmetrical easing 281


## T


text
  fluid typography with CSS math functions 216–220
  modular scale 221–225

Touch object 327
track sizes 108–119
  auto keyword 112
  controlling with minmax() function 108–111
  fit-content() function 114
  repeat() function 115–119
track sizing algorithm 102–108
  algebra of grid line placement 103
  box model 105
  calculating fr unit values 105
  fr units 104
  troubleshooting 106
track-sizing keywords 108–119
triadic colors 187
trigonometry 17, 228–234
  circular layouts and animations 234–241
  converting between degrees and radians 232
  directional calculations 245–248
  inverse trig functions 233
  sine, cosine, and tangent 229–232
  trig functions in CSS and JavaScript 233
  trigonometric units 232
  wave effects 241–245
troubleshooting, track sizing algorithm 106
type coercion 25, 34
typeof operator 30
typography 206–216
  fluid typography with CSS math functions 216–220
  font size 208
  formulas 213–216
  line height 210
  line length 211
  modular scale 221–225
  readability 207

## U

UI (user interface)
  custom slider controls 330–338
  dynamic changes with intersection observers 341–343
  gesture-based 325–330
  real-world examples of math in 5
UI design 251
  DOM geometry 253–262
  geometric clipping and motion paths 270–273
  mathematical foundations 252–253
  motion in 303–308
UI math 324
unit circle 230
units 56–61
UX (user experience), real-world examples of math in 5

## V

values, wrapping 40–43
variables 77–79
vectors 16, 252–253
  animating element to mouse-click position using 264
  dragging with geometric constraints 266–269
  follow mouse 263
  manipulating in JavaScript 262–269
velocity 308–313, 362
  applying velocity equation in animations 309–311
vertices, defined 16
viewport-based units 157–163
  classic viewport units 157
  deciding which to use 162
  logical viewport units 158
  scrollbar problem 159
  sv*, lv*, and dv* families 160–162
viewport coordinate system 19
viewport units 60
visual thought experiments 147

## W

wave effects 241–245
WCAG (Web Content Accessibility Guidelines) 188
weight, simulating 316
wrapping values 40–43

## Z

z coordinate 362
zero-based indexing 98

*(continued from back cover)*

create hover and parallax effects, and constrain dragging. The book then extends this foundation into Bezier curves, CSS easing, gesture math, and scroll-based animation.

*Math for Web Design* is a masterful guided tour through the math front-end professionals actually use. Each concept appears because it solves a concrete design or implementation problem. CSS and JavaScript examples keep the explanations grounded, while exercises and solutions help you build fluency. You'll appreciate how this book builds a durable mental model layer by layer, connecting fundamentals to layout, color, typography, animation, interaction, and canvas work in a sequence you can revisit as a practical reference.

"Well structured and easy to digest."

—Majeed Siddiqui, Amazon

"A good guide for beginners to learn precise web design. An interesting reading."

—Denis Saripov, TikTok

"Offers a fresh perspective—not just as a typical frontend resource, but as a guide to understanding and applying mathematical concepts in real projects."

—Rashed Hoque, Baker Hughes Reservoir Software B.V

"Brilliant resource for any web developer looking to level up their confidence."

—Victor Jones, Lotto NZ

"Understanding these principles gives the reader a significant advantage in creative problem solving for the web."

—Seth MacPherson, Quote Factory

"Well written, well explained."

—Giorgio Vilardo, Nearform

"Covers the topic well, and teaches it well."

—Isabel Rapando, Vocanter LLC

"A detailed but approachable guide to an important subject."

—Amit Lamba, Indus Multifoods